Smoke and Mirrors

Smoke and Mirrors

*The Hidden Context of Violence
in Schools and Society*

Edited by
Stephanie Urso Spina

ROWMAN & LITTLEFIELD PUBLISHERS, INC.
Lanham • Boulder • New York • Oxford

ROWMAN & LITTLEFIELD PUBLISHERS, INC.

Published in the United States of America
by Rowman & Littlefield Publishers, Inc.
4720 Boston Way, Lanham, Maryland 20706
http://www.rowmanlittlefield.com

12 Hid's Copse Road, Cumnor Hill, Oxford OX2 9JJ, England

British Library Cataloguing in Publication Information Available

Library of Congress Cataloging-in-Publication Data

Smoke and mirrors : the hidden context of violence in schools and society /
edited by Stephanie Urso Spina.
   p. cm.
  Includes bibliographical references and index.
  ISBN 0-8476-9562-X (alk., paper)—ISBN 0-8476-9561-1 (alk. paper)
   1. Youth—Crimes against—United States. 2. Youth—Crimes against—
United States—Prevention. 3. Students—Crimes against—United States. 4.
Students—Crimes against—United States—Prevention. 5. School violence—
United States. 6. School violence—United States—Prevention. 7. Juvenile
delinquency—United States. 8. Violence—United States. I. Spina, Stephanie
Urso.

HV6250.4.Y68 S66 2000
364.36'0973—dc21

00-027143

Printed in the United States of America

♾™ The paper used in this publication meets the minimum requirements
of American National Standard for Information Sciences—Permanence of
Paper for Printed Library Materials, ANSI/NISO Z39.48-1992.

In memory of my father
Louis B. Urso
whose hard work,
appreciation of books and music,
enjoyment of the simple pleasures of everyday life,
and unconditional love for children
taught me more than all my years of schooling

It is organized violence on top which creates individual violence at the bottom. It is the accumulated indignation against organized wrong, organized crime, organized injustice, which drives the political offender to act.

—Emma Goldman, author of the words inscribed on the
Statute of Liberty

Contents

Acknowledgments

Smoke and Mirrors is written for those who seek to understand why all of the attention, interventions, condemnation, legislation, and incarceration have not worked to curb the violence in our schools and society. It is not a technical research report, although it critically summarizes and integrates relevant scholarly work. Its intended audience includes school personnel, health and social workers, parents, psychologists, sociologists, teacher educators, researchers, college students, legislators, policymakers, those in community organizations and planning, criminal justice, and anyone concerned about the future of the United States.

This book is the product of personal history, intellectual curiosity, and moral outrage. Although written for a wide audience, I did not try to water down the substance and complexity of the issues nor simplify the writers' vernacular. For my part, I have made no attempt to dilute my convictions or disguise my subjectivity, and I am solely responsible for that. *Smoke and Mirrors* is an invitation to interrogate some of our most cherished assumptions. I do not ask that you agree with the views presented here, but I do ask that you engage with them in a spirit of earnest interest and honest concern.

Any book is a collaborative effort, and this volume is no exception. To publicly acknowledge all of those who have contributed to the genesis of *Smoke and Mirrors* is no mean task. Closest to home, my gratitude and love go to my son, David, who motivates my work and brings hope to my life. Many thanks are also due to his father, Charles J. Spina, for his infinite patience schlepping books to and from the library, stoically spending hours making countless photocopies, and supplying much appreciated logistic support.

My gratitude extends to the superb staff of the Baldwin Public Library, especially to Barbara A. Hopkins, director, Frances Carey and Malvina Jacobs, inter-library loan clerks, and Helen Gittleman, assistant director and head of the reference department. They tracked down my very many requests for often obscure articles and books with alacrity, efficiency, and affability.

I am also indebted to the many professors, teachers, colleagues, and friends who have nourished my thinking over the past decade (although they may not agree with what I've written), particularly Barbara Ganzel, Clyde Yoshida, and the other denizens of Chronkhite House, Maxine Greene, Peter W. Cookson, Jr., Gary Shank, Robert H. Tai, Deborah Smith-Shank, Ricardo Stanton-Salazar, Lois Holzman, Gita Vygodskaya, Dennie Palmer Wolf, Carol Gilligan, Annie Rogers, Gil Noam, Bruce Adolphe, Robert J. Lifton, Chuck Strozier, Anita Bland, James Manno, David Chapin, Matthijs Koopmans, Devin Thornburg, Steve Freifeld, and the late Dr. Al Solomon. Al's enthusiasm for what education should and could be and his zest for living and learning continue to be a great source of inspiration to all who knew him. He is sorely missed.

Special thanks to The City University of New York Graduate Center, particularly to Gail Smith and the Office of Educational Opportunity and Diversity Programs for the opportunity to earn my doctoral degree in the midst of the intellectual excitement generated by MAGNET fellows; to Suzanne Ouellette, Michelle Fine, William E. Cross, Jr., Judith Kubran, and the faculty, students, and staff of the Social-Personality Psychology program for providing strong disciplinary roots and encouraging my further growth; and, of course, to my extraordinarily erudite colleagues at the Center for Cultural Studies for their stimulating discussion, critique, and camaraderie.

I also wish to acknowledge the significant contribution of the students I have worked with at the preschool, elementary, junior high, and high school levels, as well as in college and graduate school. Our work together continues to enlighten, excite, and embolden me to promote important educational and social issues.

To Christine Gatliffe, Janice Braunstein, and Dean Birkenkamp, my editors at Rowman & Littlefield, and to Jill Rothenberg and Jessie Klein, thank you for shepherding *Smoke and Mirrors* from a rough outline to a polished production. Your patience, advice, and support of this enterprise have been invaluable.

Finally, I want to thank the authors of this book. I have had the good fortune over the past several years to count many of the contributors to this volume as mentors, colleagues, and friends. I am indebted to them for believing in me and the importance of this endeavor. *Abrazos* to Charles "Paco" Hernandez and Jennifer Obidah for courageously sharing their personal stories; to *mi hermano por mezcla de sangre,* the perspicacious Peter McLaren, and to Zeus Leonardo and Ricky Lee Allen, whose scholarship and friendship I will always treasure; to Henry A. Giroux, whose passion for his beliefs is equaled by his acuity and his professionalism; to Donna Gaines whose listening, writing, and interpretive skills epitomize ethnography at its best; to Jessie Klein and Lynn Chancer whose boundless energy and enthusiasm for this project saw me through its more difficult phases; to the late Paulo Freire whose work has long been significant on both a personal and professional level; to Donaldo Macedo, who kept me sane during the time I spent at Harvard and continues to be a source of sense and sensibility; and especially to the truly Distinguished Professor Stanley Aronowitz, without whom this book would not have come into being.

Besides a shared belief in the necessity of critical intellectual and political community and the willingness to support those beliefs with active involvement *en la lucha sagrada,* the majority of the authors in this volume have something else in common—they have benefitted from the genius and generosity of a brilliant polymath and unflagging humanitarian— Stanley Aronowitz. Stanley's heartfelt encouragement, intellectual acumen, and rigorous standards have spawned a resurgence of critical scholarship and social consciousness which resonates throughout this book. I am honored and humbled to count myself among the members of "The Aronowitz School." It is indeed a privilege to be among such esteemed company.

Preface

Many titles for this book were proposed and rejected before the one stamped on the copy you hold in your hand was chosen. It was not easy to find just a few words to capture the intent and content of a volume that not only challenges our current notions about violence but also exposes our hidden assumptions.

Smoke and mirrors are old and respected tools of the magician's trade. Smoke obscures what is really happening on stage while mirrors both reflect and distort our perceptions and create further distractions, allowing the magician to enchant us with his incredible feats. Although thoroughly entertaining in the hands of a skilled artist whose harmless illusions are recognized as such, smoke and mirrors can be tools of deadly deception when used for more sinister purposes.

The authors of this collection, individually and collectively, decry the covert use of various "smoke machines" and "distorted mirrors" to hide important facts and divert attention from elemental issues of violence. Taking a comprehensive critical stance, each author addresses some of the fundamental societal problems underpinning the untenable situation in our schools and the communities that surround them.

We argue that school violence is not what it appears to be. It is not a localized infection that can be treated topically or even prevented by some magical "intervention." It is just one manifestation of a chronic, systemic, lethal disease both reinforced and hidden by a national ethos that romanticizes our violent past, deifies science, and celebrates aggression in business, books, sports, entertainment, domestic government, and foreign policy, while letting it shape our future. This disease is not caused by violence in media, inadequate parental control or discipline, lack of religious training, or a variety of other factors that have been the targets of much public and private fingerpointing of late. These smokescreens, as you will see in the following chapters, serve to divert attention from the real disease—its cause and prevention, its problems and solutions, its purpose and portent.

This volume is not a how-to book. There are plenty of books that suggest many ways to decrease school violence. Books on conflict resolution, stricter discipline, and other methods for "controlling" violence in school have proliferated over recent years.[1] Some work to varying degrees. Most do not.[2] They are Band-Aids used where tourniquets are needed.

Violence is a complex and multidimensional phenomenon. Traditional, incestuous disciplinary approaches to studying violence decontextualize and fragment it by focusing on only one of its levels or aspects. If we are to understand and effectively address the complicated issues of violence in our schools and society, a dialogic, inter- and cross-disciplinary approach is necessary. The chapters you are about to read represent a range of voices from disenfranchised youth to distinguished professors. The writers include psychologists, educators, sociologists, critical theorists, feminists, cultural study scholars, and journalists. They understandably do not agree on every point, but each presents a strong case for reconceptualizing the "problem" of violence and how we approach it, as well as for including voices heretofore excluded from the debate.

Our purpose in this volume is neither to negate nor disparage the efforts of social scientists, vindicate schools, attribute blame, nor relegate responsibility. It is to widen our scope and deepen our understanding of how economic, political, ideological, and discursive practices contribute to violence. Until we expand the dialogue and honestly interrogate our presuppositions, we will not be able to develop an appropriate response to violence in our cities, in our schools, and in the lives of our students.

In the introduction to this volume, "Violence in Schools: Expanding the Dialogue," Stephanie Urso Spina strips layers of varnish from the current picture of violence to reveal its true colors. Schools, socioeconomic factors, politics, religion, race, class, gendered violence, gangs, guns, crime, and law enforcement are all subject to scrutiny. Although a single book—let alone chapter—cannot possibly deal with the full range of issues, histories, and experiences of those caught in the web of violence, Spina's comprehensive overview and synthesis of the state of violence (pun intended) uncovers its multiple layers and complex dimensions, and provides a solid foundation for the chapters that follow.

Charles "Paco" Hernandez, author of the first chapter, is a K–12 educator currently teaching at a New York City correctional facility. Hernandez, a surviving gang member from the lower East side of New York, bears the scars and wisdom born of crossing those borders. His multidimensional perspective is evident as he takes us on an eye-opening tour of today's schools, gangs, and inner-city neighborhoods. Hernandez's personal and scholarly narrative captures the complex nature of gangs and the frequently discrepant literature that describes them as pathological, individualistic and defiant, and protective and familial. "Wearing the Colors" provides a reality-based antidote to the romantically glorified and gorified *West Side Story* and action/adventure film images of gang life.

Next, in "On Living (and Dying) with Violence: Entering Young Voices in the Discourse," Jennifer Obidah demonstrates the importance of including young voices in debates about violence. Sitting on both sides of the desk, she takes us into the classroom with a depth of understanding that can only be born of experience and reflection. Obidah frames her discussion of teachers' struggles with teaching under traumatic circumstances (both their own and their students') within the disparities created by the adverse situation and conditions they find themselves in. She weaves the students' narratives in and out of the contradictions of their lives, creating an informative tapestry of fear and strength, wisdom and confusion, desperation and defiance, repression and rage.

In chapter 3, "Rated 'CV' for Cool Violence," Peter McLaren, Zeus Leonardo, and Ricky Lee Allen focus on the consequences of violence that functions deceptively at the level of the sign. Using recent examples from Los Angeles, they examine the spacialization of violence through the manipulation of physical and metaphorical space by schools and communities. Their analysis vividly demonstrates that the use of interventions and programs by local law enforcement and "model" schools is really a struggle over hidden knowledge and power that "bulldozes" local spatialities and reinforces "cool violence."

In the fourth chapter, Henry A. Giroux continues the focus on youth and those who work with them. "Representations of Violence, Popular Culture, and Demonization of Youth" exposes how media, politicians, and intellectuals censure youth and how violence is used to shroud the victimization of youth. Giroux challenges teachers and social scientists to redefine the purpose of schooling; to develop counter-public spheres and transformative pedagogical conditions where strategies of interpretation, critique, and intervention address these cultural texts and how they function as public discourses; and to make learning a part of the solution.

Chapter 5, "America's Dead-end Kids," is based on Donna Gaines's 1991 book, *Teenage Wasteland*. This landmark study of the internally directed violence that is suicide is as frighteningly relevant now as when it first appeared. The rate of teenage suicide has continued to rise in the ten years since Gaines first wrote about the Bergenfield, New Jersey, "suicide pact."

Her compelling portrait of "the burnouts" and their families, school, and community draws insightful conclusions and raises important questions that defy society to persist in denying its role in the climbing statistics.

Expanding on some of the issues raised in "America's Dead-end Kids," Jessie Klein and Lynn Chancer integrate theory and case studies to counter cultural stereotypes of both violence and masculine identity. In chapter 6, "Masculinity Matters: The Omission of Gender from High-Profile School Violence Cases," they offer a provocative analysis of some of the contradictions, asymmetries, and missing data in current discussions of violence. Klein and Chancer explain how the overwhelming anguish of those who do not meet the criteria of "masculinity" models manifested itself in recent incidents of school violence. Perhaps even more importantly, they show that this is not simply a matter of "bullying" or "teasing," individual pathology, or media mimicry, but a response to a poisonous gender ideology that must be neutralized and pluralized to allow both boys and girls to experience their emotional potential.

In "Scientism and the Ideological Construction of Violence, Poverty, and Racism," Donaldo Macedo and the late Paulo Freire expose systemic global violence against children. Examining the interplay of race, ethics, and ideology, Freire and Macedo illuminate the role of science in rationalizing violence and the dehumanization of poverty, unequal opportunity, health poisoned by environmental dangers, private greed, and public squalor. They compel us to recognize the truth in Ghandi's observation that poverty is the deadliest form of violence. With vivid examples and cogent arguments, Freire and Macedo conclude by making a strong case for concretizing our memory of past atrocities to inform our present and to stop the vicious repetition of our history of cruelty.

Chapter 8, "The Psychology of Violence and the Violence of Psychology," by Stephanie Urso Spina, shows how psychology plays a crucial role in how we think and what we do about violence. Spina argues that, in its efforts to legitimate its status as a "science" and bask in the blessings of hegemony (i.e., power and money), psychology has become frighteningly anorexic. Starving theoretically and weakening methodologically, psychology suffers from the very disease it helped to create. By examining psychology's presumptuous pedigree and practice, and its interrelationship with broader social problems, Spina argues for psychology to embark on the road not taken—the road toward a critical psychology that is reflective, proactive, and socially just.

Stanley Aronowitz, in his "Essay on Violence," asks the questions the rest of us have been either too blind or too afraid to pose: Are there legitimate reasons to resort to violence? Is all violence immoral, illegal, unjustified, and evil? Is there a link between military massacres of civilians in Kosovo and classroom killings in white middle-class American towns like Littleton, Colorado? What, if any, are the alternatives? Aronowitz searches for answers in American bombings of military and civilian targets in select European countries, current teen film genres, government sanctions on private behavior, the irrelevance of schooling, and the global economic structure. Connecting macro- and microlevel ideologies and events, Aronowitz makes the political personal and shows how the personal is, indeed, political.

There is a strong consensus in the United States that something is seriously wrong with our schools and more than a suspicion that this something is related to the violence in and around them. In the last chapter, "When the Smoke Clears: Revisualizing Responses to Violence in Schools," Stephanie Spina looks at what has been done to address that "something" and why those strategies have failed. The issue she raises is: "How can we get beyond ideological prohibitions and historical models of organization, structure, and authority to imaginative possibilities?" The answer, Spina argues, is not to be found in superficial strategies and political platitudes. Change of this magnitude does not happen in the two- or four-year time span between elections, as our "representatives" would have us believe, or after one semester of a "violence prevention curriculum," as some schools have discovered. It requires reconceptualization, innovation, stamina, moral, social and financial support, communication, and cooperation. It takes the ability to weather disappointment and discouragement. It takes time, persistence, and lots of hard work. It takes honesty and responsibility. It takes guts.

Unlike domestic and foreign-policy analysts who accept violence as the answer to intra- and international problems,[3] unlike media moguls who insist that violence is the answer that keeps profit margins climbing, unlike social scientists and criminologists who compile lists of "traits" that lead to violence, we do not presume to know the answers. We have no formula, no equation, no "quick fix" to remedy the situation. But we do know we have been asking the wrong questions.

We hope only to open the debate on violence beyond a frequently misplaced focus on youth and the sadistic and voyeuristic national cultural obsession with tragedy, bloodshed, and grief; to suggest new ways to define and approach "the problem"; to expand the conceptual framework of the discourse on violence; and to contribute in some small way toward revolutionary cultural change through what will be necessarily extraordinary, collaborative efforts across sectors.

NOTES

1. See, for example, D. W. Johnson and R. T. Johnson, *Reducing School Violence through Conflict Resolution*. (Alexandria, Va.: Association for Supervision and Curriculum Development, 1995); K. Girard and S. J. Koch, *Conflict Resolution in the Schools: A Manual for Educators* (San Francisco: Jossey-Bass, 1996); James L. Lee, Charles J. Pulvino, and Philip A. Perrone, *Restoring Harmony: A Guide for Managing Conflicts in Schools*. (Upper Saddle River, N.J.: Prentice Hall, 1998); Arnold Goldstein and Jane Close Conoley, eds., *School Violence Intervention: A Practical Handbook* (New York: Guilford, 1997), 72–91.

2. See M. Posner, 1994, "Research Raises Troubling Questions about Violence Prevention Programs," *The Harvard Education Newsletter* 10, no. 3 (1994): 1–4; J. P. Comer, *Waiting for a Miracle: Why Schools Can't Solve Our Problems—and How We Can* (New York: Dutton, 1997).

3. See Noam Chomsky, *The Culture of Terrorism* (Boston: South End Press, 1988).

Introduction

Violence in Schools

Expanding the Dialogue

Stephanie Urso Spina

- A new handgun is sold every thirteen seconds in the United States.[1]
- Every half hour a child is killed or wounded by a bullet.[2]
- Every six hours in America a child between ten and nineteen-years-old commits suicide with a handgun.[3]
- Each day, almost two thousand children, or one child every thirteen seconds, is reported as abused or neglected.[4]
- Three million crimes occur on or near schools every year; sixteen thousand per school day, or one every six seconds.[5]
- For school-age youth, the chances of being a victim of a violent crime are greater than being hurt in a car accident.[6]
- Between twenty-five and thirty-five thousand murders are committed in this country each year—over ten thousand are the result of domestic violence.[7]
- Homicide is the leading cause of death for African American and Latino males under age twenty-five, and the second leading cause of death nationally for all youth under age twenty five.[8]
- In 1993, more African American children under age nine died from gun violence than police officers or American soldiers killed in the line of duty during the same twelve months.[9]
- Recent research finds that one-third of urban children interviewed had witnessed a violent death[10] and almost three-quarters knew someone who had been shot.[11]

1

- About three million violent crimes are reported in the United States each year.[12]
- Every year, 2,000 deaths, 1,412,700 serious injuries, and 18,000 serious disabilities are known to result from child abuse.[13]
- A woman is battered every fifteen seconds.[14]
- There are, at minimum, 150,000 rapes of women and children reported annually in the United States; more than 400 each day, 17 every hour, or 1 every three-and-a-half minutes. Estimates that include unreported rapes conservatively estimate the annual figure to be closer to 630,000.[15]

These statistics are not offered to sensationalize the issues, to obscure the brutality they enumerate, or to numb one into hopelessness or apathy, but rather to underscore the devastatingly high number of children, teens, parents, families, and communities who must live with the reality of what these numbers represent in human terms. Yet, while we read and hear about rampant rape, robberies, drugs, and shootings, many of us have become desensitized to their human dimensions and underlying messages. Like much of the general public, social scientists, educators, and others who work with youth often have great difficulty understanding the lives of disenfranchised students. Many of us, in part because we are professionals, have not been subject to the powerful subcultures that seduce our students with false promises and futile dreams in a world that makes their fruition improbable if not impossible. Similarly, many of us are unaware of the insidious level of violence that is poverty, of the despair and nihilism that is informed, shaped, and reproduced by the very fabric of our society—a situation that demands that we go beyond simply condemning violence and blaming schools.

CENSURING SCHOOLS

Schools have long been the scapegoat[16] for society's ills, while, at the same time, school systems in the inner city are hardest hit by the ills of society. This is not meant to absolve schools from responsibility nor to underestimate the critical value of the school's role in children's lives, but to recognize the interdependence between schooling and the sociocultural and political reality of the society within which schools exist. Americans tend to view public schools as agencies of socialization as well as education. Public schooling, as we now know it, along with imprisoning "juvenile delinquents," was a response to the rapid rise of industrialization and the first waves of mass immigration at the end of the nineteenth century.[17] At that time, the established prototype for all human service institutions was

insidious
nihilism

the asylum,[18] and the paragon of progress and productivity was the factory. Schools purposely combined the model of the factory with those institutions designed to house the sick, the indigent, and convicted criminals in order to better assimilate the diverse population[19] into their "proper" places in the hegemonic social order.[20] This "social efficiency" model lingers today in the design of school buildings and curricula as well as in the widespread assumption that it is the schools' responsibility to solve social problems.

The endurance of this model and its effects contribute to the absurdity that, while schools are supposedly part of the solution, our educational model itself fosters practices that may themselves be a form of violence.[21] Even "normalized" school practices intended to improve academic performance may actually harm overwhelmingly poor minority students.[22] These include tracking,[23] style of pedagogy, curricular and testing biases, and other "literacies of power."[24] For example, Jean Anyon's work demonstrates how textbooks are often microcosms of white, middle-class interests and situations even when minority characters are featured.[25] Yet these alienating texts are the bases for learning and evaluation. The National Curriculum Standards epitomizes the enforcement of dominant cultural values and practices that view difference as a problem to be cured, especially in vilified "disordered" or "violent" spaces like inner-city schools.[26] Inconsistent or unfair enforcement of arbitrary or oppressive rules, overcrowded classes, and the retention of uncaring or hostile teachers are other ways schools harm students.[27] Labeling, stereotyping, and similar stigmatizing wonts may also promote divisions along racial, ethnic, linguistic, and economic lines as well as precipitate school-specific violence.[28]

Division by oversimplified, oppositionally constructed taxonomies are a common strategy or means of ideological control.[29] Foucault argues that such "dividing practices" objectify the individual by labeling him in oppositional terms that reflect societal assessments of intellect, health, and criminality (e.g., dangerous/harmless, normal/abnormal, us/them, straight/gay, white/black).[30] As a nation, we "learn" to use such discursive "violence" to simultaneously discount and spectacularize violence and victims by virtue of their age, sex, color, income, or language. They are devalued by a system that manipulates public sentiment via "spin doctors" who employ euphemistic doublespeak to divert responsibility from the perpetrator to the victim. Politicians thrive on campaigns built around the imagery of juvenile and racialized crime. They drive the bandwagon that demonizes youth,[31] that makes a spectacle of students,[32] that violates basic human rights.

All of these discourses are based on surveillance techniques and practices that divide students as a group as well as individuals. The legacy of social control, not education, dominates the agenda of schools. Schools generally respond to an upsurge in violence through the use of symbols of control and authority. The omnipresence of metal detectors, guards, "security" cameras, and the like promote both a relentless awareness of possible danger and a false sense of safety. School officials claim the huge number of confiscated weapons indicates they are reducing violence when, in fact, even the $28 million expenditure to install metal detectors in New York City public schools in the 1980s has done nothing to curtail the problem[33] and has contributed to the creation of an even more insidious gendered form of violence. Jennifer McCormick describes how hand-held metal detectors pass over teenage bodies as students are required to stand with their legs apart and their hands outstretched.[34] She illustrates how this routine becomes explicitly sexual when the students are female and male security guards are present. One girl McCormick interviewed in a New York City public high school describes the experience this way:

> I hate it. I don't feel right. . . . I have to put my hands out [she places her hand on the table in front of us, fingers are stretched apart]. I have to stand straight for a few minutes, legs apart, my hands outstretched in front of me. I have to take my bracelets off, take everything out of my pockets. It's very uncomfortable, I feel embarrassed amongst everybody else. It's not good. It's not a productive way to start off school. I hate it. I don't feel right. I feel out of my element. In a way they are trying to take my shield away because with the scanning, they are looking for something I may have concealed. . . . I feel like they are trying to know my body. . . . I hear the comments or I see the looks from the guards to other girls. And through that and through the scanning, they get closer than they can ever get in a normal way. . . . I'm sure they're getting off on it. . . . I just don't like it. I don't like it. I don't like it.[35]

Yet, despite the humiliation and invasiveness of metal detectors and electronic scanners, students express the desire for security, often enduring psychic and emotional pain in exchange for what they believe to be protection from more physical and fatal forms of violence.

In truth, and contrary to what news reports and political propaganda would have us think, schools themselves are comparatively safe havens. In 1998, for example, there were approximately 20 million middle- and high-school students in the United States. Fewer than a dozen of these students killed someone at school. Nationally, youth violence comprises only 13 percent of the violent crime and 8 percent of murders reported by the FBI. This is not to downplay the tragedy of these events or to minimize the expectation that schools should be absolutely, not relatively, safe, but to underscore how disproportionate the level of fear and resources surrounding this "epidemic" of "violence in schools" is when viewed in light of the larger picture.

Consider, for example, a 1994 national survey of hospital emergency rooms which reported treating a total of 900,000 injuries resulting from violent crime. These injuries were eight times more likely (410,000) to occur in the home and five times more likely (246,000) to occur in the workplace than in schools (55,000).[36] Consider that of the two to three thousand children and youths murdered each year, 90 percent are under age twelve and 70 percent are aged twelve through seventeen.[37] Three out of every four are killed by parents or caretakers, not by other juveniles. In comparison, 42 percent of childhood deaths are caused by car crashes and other accidents.[38] We should not ignore the threat to youth from drinking, driving, and unprotected sex because it does not provoke national outrage, because it does not threaten our collective unconscious, because it does not provide emotional jolts on the six o'clock news. Yet, from the executive branch to the local level, from *The New York Times* to CNN, shootings by students are what attract attention and serve to camouflage far greater acts of violence.

The omission of such disturbing data from the discourse on violence misleadingly supports those who, like President Clinton, assert that today's grown-ups "confront a younger generation desensitized to brutality by its own 'culture' of violent media and seemingly unable or unwilling to take responsibility for their actions."[39] Legislation is another ploy used to detract attention from adult malfeasance. In 1997, for example, the U.S. House of Representatives passed a bill to "crack down" on juvenile crime by rewarding states that prosecute more underage perpetrators as adults.[40] As this volume illustrates, it is the dominant adult society, with its elected officials casting the most stones, that commits the most crimes against the most people and refuses to take responsibility for them. It is safer to blame youths who can't vote and whose voices remain unheard.

Policy makers reinforce and promote this delusional perspective. For example, the sixth National Education Goal called for every school in America to be free of drugs and violence by the year 2000.[41] The Safe Schools Act of 1994 allocated $20 million in twenty one-year grants to reinforce existing school safety programs. However, there is little if any evidence that such violence prevention programs work and some have actually worsened the very situation they were implemented to improve.[42] Rather than increasing security or technology, more fundamental issues need to be addressed—issues that lie at the very core of our society.

American schools, like American cities, are segregated racially, politically, and economically. Ethnic and racial minorities have always been disproportionately represented in the incidence and depiction of violence. It is not a coincidence that this is the case when one examines these data in the context of social and cultural factors.

SOCIOECONOMIC FACTORS

We are increasingly a nation with sharpening divisions between the "haves" and "have-nots." The top 5 percent of our citizens control over 20 percent of the country's wealth, while the 20 percent at the bottom of the economic ladder struggle to survive on less than 4 percent. The richest 1 percent of households own 48 percent of the nation's wealth.[43] As of the mid-1990s, the income of those in the top 20 percent of U. S. families was more than eleven times as much as the bottom 20 percent. During 1997, the Census Bureau reported that more than 35.5 million Americans lived in poverty, meaning they earned less than $8,183 a year if they were single, or $16,400 for a family of four. Another 12 million had annual earnings 25 percent above the poverty threshold.[44]

Even more striking is the stark inequality in the economic condition of America's children.[45] At over 20 percent and climbing, the child poverty rate in the United States is far higher than in other countries (e.g., below 4 percent in Sweden, Belgium, Denmark, and Finland)—even relatively poor ones (e.g., Ireland has about a 12 percent child poverty rate). The closest figures are from Canada and Australia, at about 14 percent, which, not insignificantly, also accompany rates of lethal violence comparatively higher than Europe, though still substantially lower than the United States.[46] In 1976, about 28 percent of American children lived in families with income *less than half* the poverty level. By 1994, 44 percent did, including well over half of poor black children.[47] On any given night, approximately 200,000 children are homeless. Children under three are consistently worse off than older children and far worse off in the United States than in any other country. (For example, the U.S. poverty rate for the youngest children is almost 50 percent higher than the next highest rates in Britain and Canada and about three times as high as Germany, four times as high as France and Sweden, and almost eleven times as high as the Netherlands.[48] Nor, despite pointed political posturing, does this represent a lack of effort on the part of the parental poor. Sixty percent of all poor children under the age of three have at least one employed parent. This includes 70 percent of poor white children, 60 percent of poor Hispanic children, and 50 percent of poor black children.[49] More than 40 percent of single mothers with a child under the age of three work full- or part-time. But these jobs do not provide a living wage and are further limited by a lack of benefits and available community support services such as child and health care. Repeated failures to pass federal initiatives that would support the needs and rights of children, while spending tax dollars on incentives to help the rich get richer or to support ludicrous and vindictive personal attacks against one's political opponents, starkly dramatizes the U.S. government's neglect of its neediest citizens.[50]

Virtually every other postindustrial nation provides some form of child care for three- to five-year-olds as well as paid leaves for parents.[51] The United States is the only postindustrial nation without a national health system to deliver accessible, high-quality preventive and prenatal health care. Infant mortality rates in the United States have been steadily increasing over the past thirty years. The United States now has the fourth highest infant mortality rate of all industrialized countries (ranking below all except Greece, Portugal, and Turkey).[52]

The situation is exacerbated by basic principles of our Darwinian market economy. Capitalist values of avarice and egocentricity undermine social cohesion by promoting individual competition and consumption over community values and productive work. In market societies, strong labor movements or truly democratic political representation are nonexistent. People who need it most are deprived of the conceptual framework, the collective consciousness, the cultural capital[53] to challenge the forces of violence.[54]

Thirty years ago, one in five city residents lived below poverty level. Ten years ago it was more than one-third and growing.[55] By 1991, the population of major U.S. cities averaged 70 percent racial ethnic minorities and over 43 percent of all American poor, including 80 percent of all African American poor.[56] Yet, adjusting for inflation, federal aid to cities was cut 60 percent between 1980 and 1992.[57] The mass exodus of businesses from cities leaves urban areas with only a minimal number of highly stratified low-wage, temporary jobs without benefits and highly technological top level professional jobs accessible only to an elite population.[58]

POLITICS, RACE, AND CLASS

The inequities noted in the previous section are not surprising when one considers their political context. Suburbanites, who include less than 10 percent minorities,[59] cast the majority of votes in local and national elections, so predominantly minority inner-city residents elect fewer state and national legislators to represent their interests. It is not that minorities do not care, or do not vote. It is a function of our electoral process. The increasingly homogeneous two-party system, geographically defined districting, and gerrymandering, are only a few ways minority voters are discouraged from participating in the political process and excluded from democracy. Although they begin as strong participants in the electoral system, minorities soon learn that their vote does not carry the same weight as a white vote in "winner-take-all majority rule."[60] Because of these and other injustices, Lani Guinier, in her book, *The Tyranny of the Ma-*

jority,[61] argues forcefully for a change to cumulative voting, which is not biased like the present system is:

> It [cumulative voting] gives each voter the same number of votes as there are seats or options to vote for, and they can distribute their votes in any combination to reflect their preferences . . . it allows voters to organize themselves on whatever basis they wish.[62]

In this way, everyone's preferences would be counted equally. Voting would focus on political interests rather than geographical location and it would become far more difficult to maintain the gross inequities of race-conscious districting.

In contrast to the 90 percent white suburban schools, over three-quarters of students in inner-city schools are African American or Latino.[63] Yet, although the need for resources is greater than in the more affluent suburbs, urban school budgets across the nation are one-tenth those of suburban schools.[64] School buildings are literally falling apart and supplies are few.[65] This is not a recent development. James B. Conant, in his 1961 book, *Slums and Suburbs: A Commentary on Schools in Metropolitan Areas*, raised similar issues.[66] Thirty years later, Jonathan Kozol's best-selling book, *Savage Inequalities*, brought national attention to even more severe economic and educational disparities.[67] Not coincidentally, urban schools continue to deteriorate as the minority population increases.

Recent research confirms that instruction in inner-city schools is frequently substandard.[68] In New York City alone, 66 percent of all students who attend high school fail to graduate. For Latino students the rate is 80 percent, for African Americans, 72 percent, for whites, 50 percent. Statistics from other cities are equally grim.[69] Teachers, "low standards," and/or lack of discipline are not to blame. (See the last chapter of this volume, for a discussion of those issues). Social class is the greatest predictor of who drops out—or gets "pushed out" of school. The failure of schools and society to recognize that this behavior is not just reactive but proactive guarantees that these problems will continue. As Willis's[70] classic study with British youth showed, delinquency is not a mechanical response to social disadvantage but active resistance to the dominant tradition by the production of alternative or oppositional practices. This resistance is rooted in the social relationships of the students' communities and is not necessarily reducible to capitalist pressures and processes.[71] Dropping out is not merely the result of alienation but is an assertive rejection of the system and what it represents.[72]

One reason rejection of the system takes forms of responses like not voting and dropping out of school instead of a more openly aggressive stand (possibly even taking steps toward a popular revolution), is because mechanisms of the class system have "always been buffered by an even more discriminatory caste system (of whites vs. blacks)."[73] Although there are more than three times as many non-African American, largely white poor than there are African American poor, poverty is generally not considered quite as damaging and demoralizing to poor whites because "blacks have always been there to occupy a position lower in the social scale than even the poorest whites."[74] There is

> a vested interest on the part of both rich and poor whites to maintain the caste system of discrimination against blacks. For the rich, it has been a cheap way (both financially and morally) to continue to possess and control a disproportionate share of the national wealth and income. And poor American whites have let themselves be distracted from paying attention to how badly they are being discriminated against by the class system, by the fact that there is always a group they can look down upon . . . that in turn buys peace for the rich, who can continue to monopolize most of the nation's wealth and income without having to be bothered by any significant threats to their privileges."[75]

Racism is the "weapon of choice" used by the ruling class to keep the working class divided.[76] The unity of the working class across color lines is "feared more than almost anything else by Corporate America which uses every form of coercion, manipulation, and violence" to keep the working class from joining forces to fight their common enemy.[77] Even Malcolm X, after a pilgrimage to Mecca near the end of his life, realized that "it isn't the American white man who is a racist, but it's the American political, economic, and social atmosphere that automatically nourishes a racist psychology in the white man."[78] It has been argued by many that racism is so deeply internalized that [most] whites are not even aware of its existence or how far they will go to keep it that way.[79] As Spina and Tai explain:

> Not seeing race is predicated on not seeing White as a race . . . Ignoring the racial construction of Whiteness reinscribes its centrality and reinforces its privileged and oppressive position as normative. Thus, Whiteness becomes a non-race, invisible to those that would seek to analyze race and racism, thereby giving it more power, more privilege, and more impunity. The non-racialization of Whiteness restricts the ability of minorities to point out racism and gives the dominant White culture more freedom from criticism in the practice of racism.[80]

Racism is so normalized in this country that in surveys,[81] newspapers, and on national television,[82] white Americans, and some (more affluent) black Americans, repeatedly express the belief that racism is no longer a problem in the United States. Why is this view, so at odds with reality, gaining support?

Perhaps one contributing factor is what Americans are not allowed to know.[83] The U.S. government has selectively repressed data which would reveal the blatantly racist "nature, location, and dimensions of violence in this country."[84] Since 1960, for example, when the U.S. Public Health Service began to calculate age-adjusted death rates separately for blacks and whites, the death rate for blacks has been consistently about 280 more deaths per 100,000 than whites.[85] In comparison, the national homicide rate is about 10 per 100,000.[86] Yet, the latter is positioned as a "national emergency, over which presidential elections are won and lost,"[87] and the former remains buried in relatively obscure government publications. If this is not "proof" enough,

> [a]ny doubt that the excess death rate among blacks is a function of the social and economic structure of our society is put to rest by epidemiological studies. Several investigations[88] have shown that high blood pressure, for example, is common among American, West Indian, South African, and other urbanized African blacks, but infrequent among rural Africans (that is, those least exposed to the social and economic structure of colonialism and white domination).[89]

Furthermore, some suggest that contemporary conservative politicians are systematically encouraging whites to blame immigrants and poor ethnic minorities for economic difficulties.[90] As Kristeva explains, such exclusionist discourse, where violence is turned against the "foreigner," the "refugee," the "immigrant," the "other," normalizes a system based on one group against all external others; i.e., a pervasive and violent form of racism.[91] Using rhetoric that blames affirmative action for the loss of "white" jobs and fosters a belief that "the deterioration of society is the fault of immigrants and people of color," conservatives both divert attention from the increasing inequality reflected in the widening gap between the upper socioeconomic groups and the rest of the populace and simultaneously divided traditional coalitions of labor, ethnic minorities, and women."[92] President Clinton has publicly blamed the victims of poverty and racism for their situation, saying that if they would "pull themselves up by the bootstraps" and "put an end to crime in their own communities," things would get better.[93] With much patriotic flourish, an ethos of callousness is legitimized under the rubric of competition, survival of the fittest, and the "American" way.

Despite invoking ideals of democracy, traditional "American" values are selectively and strategically applied by those in power, especially when defining criminality.[94] James Gilligan offers one of the most telling examples of this bias:

It is remarkable to me how seldom people recognize the extent to which many of the criminals today are contemporary versions of our own ancestors. For example . . . I vary between being amused and bemused by the moral indignation with which some politicians who happen to be Boston Brahmins denounce the scandalous behavior of young male drug dealers. These young men are, of course, classic examples of capitalist entrepreneurs, whom one would think would be extolled by these Bostonians as role models for their peers. They are, after all, making fortunes by their business activities, with tremendous returns on relatively small investments, and they often manage to save and invest their considerable earnings as conscientiously as did the Brahmins' own ancestors. The fact is that the ancestors of the latter group made the fortunes on which their descendants are now living (comfortably enough that they do not need to deal drugs) by means of the seventeenth- and eighteenth-century equivalents of drug-dealing such as slave-trafficking, opium-smuggling, rum-running, and killing.[95]

Gilligan is careful to point out that this is not meant to trivialize the devastation of illicit drug abuse but to put the construction of criminality in perspective. A Washington, D.C., high school student, reacting to the simplistic "Just Say No to Drugs" campaign, gives us an even harder dose of reality: "I make a hundred bucks an hour selling drugs. What does the President want me to do, work at McDonald's for the minimum wage?"[96]

Similarly, present-day upper-class economic crimes such as embezzlement, price fixing, fraud, professional and business malpractice, and corruption (not to mention the legalized crime of tax benefits for the wealthy at the expense of the vast majority of Americans), far outweigh the economic costs of lower-class crimes. Yet, white-collar criminals constitute only a small fraction of the prison population. Penal sanctions are primarily applied against crimes of need, not crimes of greed. This situation is sarcastically summarized by Anatole France: "The law, in its majestic equality, forbids the rich as well as the poor to sleep under bridges, to beg in the streets, and to steal bread."[97]

STREET GANGS

Another way the American aristocracy feeds off the marginalized is manifested in the paradoxes of gang culture.[98] Although gangs each have distinctive identities, they tend to be treated as a homogeneous "problem" in ways reminiscent of the stereotyping of certain racial and ethnic groups.

What images come to mind when you think of a gang? The typical picture is a group of dark-skinned male minority youths, dressed in similar clothing, swaggering together down school corridors or neighborhood streets and perceived as threatening to "outsiders." As Cummings and Monti point out:

> We would have more difficulty conceiving of gangs as young men strutting through high school corridors while dressed out in identical team jackets or a set of college students being formally initiated with secret rituals into a group dedicated to a "brotherhood," carousing, and intermittent outbursts of vandalism. Fraternities and football teams are not "gangs" in the commonly accepted sense of that term; but they do exhibit certain traits that frequently are associated with gangs.[99]

The difference is that crimes condemning gangs are considered merely "boys will be boys" antics when committed by higher-class "gangs" sporting Greek letters or football team mascots as their colors. This is not meant to excuse gang violence (of any type) or to argue that we should dismiss violent behavior as a ritual of male bonding (which we most definitely should not),[100] but to underscore the variations in our attributions of culpability both across and within these groups.

Similarly, the intolerance of personal disrespect that is part of the "street code" has been highly publicized and widely condemned. Yet the gentlemen's "code of honor" that dominated the mannered culture of the antebellum South was considered a respectable way to respond to insults. When John Dickinson, a Nashville lawyer, made offensive comments about Andrew Jackson's wife, Jackson, the future president, shot and killed the man (who also happened to be his political opponent). And every student of American history learns about the famous duel between Alexander Hamilton and Aaron Burr. When practiced by those at the top of the Southern caste system, revenge in the form of ritualized and cold-blooded killing has always been an accepted way to solve problems.

It is important to realize, despite media-manipulated perceptions, even among the most "violent" street gangs, violent behavior is relatively rare.[101] The gangs Padilla works with, for example, "participate in a violent world," but "view what they're doing as expressions of resistance, freedom, and election" and "as superior to the way of life and occupational choices of their 'conformist peers' or 'straight youth.'"[102] Gang leaders share profits with other gang members and all see their economic welfare as tied to the gang.[103] Sullivan's research also highlights gang members' awareness and positioning of crime vis-à-vis the exigencies of a market economy. He writes that the young men in these studies[104] ironically

> spoke of their criminal activities as "getting over" and "getting paid," terms that refer directly . . . to economic motivation and reflect the perception of a social structure of restricted opportunity. "Getting paid" equates crime with

work. "Getting over" means beating the system, a rigged system in which one is unlikely to succeed by competing according to the rules.[105]

Besides being blamed for increased crime, gangs also take the rap for crimes of commodification that play both sides against them. For example, on one hand, antigraffiti campaigns criminalize those who use the walls of the projects to communicate[106] while, on the other hand, downtown gallery owners get rich from the work of those few graffiti artists they charitably "rescue" to paint in lofts instead of gutters, providing trendy decor for their upscale patrons to signal their financial status and cultural savvy. The co-optation of street-gang symbols by fashion, music, and media also add a capitalist cachet to gang symbols and legends while separating them from contextual economic and social conditions. They become either superficial, disposable possessions of wealthier youth who can afford them or an attempt to gain, by association, some of the adult recognition and fear, if not respect, of one of the few groups in their age cohort that has managed to do that. The use of gang symbols by upper classes can trivialize gang culture and further marginalize gangs.[107] But it can also speak to the tenuous position of all young people in the social order.

GENDERED VIOLENCE

High levels of violence are not confined to urban schools with predominantly African American and Latino/a populations. Violence is also increasing in suburban and rural schools, especially among white male students. Although not necessarily economically disadvantaged, white male students can be marginalized in other ways. Those who do not conform to accepted roles and expectations are often alienated from the dominant culture and at the bottom of the social hierarchy of schools (nerds, geeks, fags, etc.). These "minority" students are indoctrinated with almost the same message as inner-city students: pretty girls, strong boys, thin, rich, smart kids are the ones who matter.[108] Add "white" to the list and it's the urban version.

Shooting sprees by middle-class white teenage males in small towns and suburbs in twenty-five states captured national and international headlines during the 1997–98 and 1998–99 school years.[109] In contrast, killers and victims of color and/or from the inner cities garner no such media interest. No specially trained counselors are sent to help the predominantly African American and Latino/a students in inner-city schools cope with their trauma. No emergency crews arrive with spackle and paint to remove bullet holes and other signs of violence from city schools.

In fact, after the 1999 shooting at Colorado's 98 percent white Columbine High School, newspapers featured short biographies about each of the twelve white students who had been murdered. The one African American student who had been killed was not eulogized. Instead, the papers printed a much shorter story about how angry his father was. Although all parents of these victims must have been understandably angry, only the black male parent's rage was displayed in the press, while his dead son was not memorialized like the white victims were.[110] This exploitative construction of their identities (or erasing of identity, in the case of the son) as (negatively) different from or "other" than those of the white victims and their families was not accidental, although it may not have been conscious. It was representative of the more pervasive, insidious discourses of structural racism and implies that the dominant white culture and experience is the norm.

Although racism dominates the American subconscious, sexual harassment and improprieties dominate the American consciousness. Try, as O'Toole and Schiffman urge us, to "think about the most consuming events of the last decade, those that grabbed the attention of the public through news headlines and court television and dominated daily conversation."[111] Think about the O. J. Simpson trial;[112] "ethnic cleansing" and other atrocities committed by the Serbs against Albanians in Bosnia;[113] the rape of a twelve-year-old Okinawa schoolgirl by three U.S. servicemen. All of these acts of violence share a common link: They were perpetrated by males, acting individually or in groups, "for whom violence and violation are rational solutions to perceived problems ranging from the need to inflate one's sexual self-esteem to denigrating rivals in war to boosting a country's GNP."[114] Our culture rewards men for practicing violence "in virtually any sphere of activity by money, admiration, recognition, respect, and the genuflection of others honoring their sacred and proven masculinity. In male culture, police are heroic and so are outlaws; males who enforce standards are heroic and so are those who violate them."[115]

Brutal acts by American sports heroes and foreign armies dominate the landscape of gendered violence in the media, but they represent only the smallest fraction of violent acts against women and of the dangers women face on a daily basis.[116] Even the language used to describe violence against women contributes to its perpetuity. The term "battered woman," for example, is deceptive because the harm done to her becomes an adjective, which implies it is an attribute of the woman and not something someone did to her.[117] This is particularly distressing because battering is the leading cause of injury to women in the United States. Similarly, using the term "domestic" violence to denote family violence minimizes its cruelty and masks the gender bias of what used to be known as "wife beating," or, in the words of Frances Power Cobbe, an Irish reformer and feminist of the late 1800s, "wife torture."[118] Cobbe's words, as Ann Jones notes, remind us of scenes from Charles Dickens and Thomas Hardy; from D. H. Lawrence, Dostoevsky, and Émile Zola; from Doris Lessing, Toni Morrison, Alice Munro, and Alice Walker; wife torture

> conjure(s) the scenes between beatings: the sullen husband, withdrawn and sulking, or angry and intimidating, dumping dinner on the floor, throwing the cat against the wall, screaming, twisting a child's arm, needling, nagging, manipulating, criticizing the bitch, the cunt who never does anything right, who's ugly and stupid, who should keep her mouth shut, who should spread her legs now, who should be dead, who will be if she's not careful.[119]

"Domestic violence," it may be argued, is a more comprehensive term that is not only neutral in terms of gender but also sexual preference. That assumes violence in homosexual couples is the same thing as in heterosexual relationships. It is not. Our culture clearly supports, if not encourages, wife beating. This gives it a legitimacy that differentiates it from abuse within gay and lesbian relationships. On the other hand, the marginalization of homosexuals trivializes violence in their communities and ignores its victims, despite the fact that an estimated 25 percent of all gay men and women in intimate relationships are victims of "domestic" abuse. Using gender-neutral terminology, despite the real problem of "domestic" violence committed by women against women, women against men, and men against men, the assailant in almost all cases of violence, heterosexual and homosexual, is a man.[120]

The term "domestic violence" ostensibly includes children, but they are often its forgotten victims. Aside from the increased danger of children being physically abused in violent homes, they are almost always psychologically and emotionally abused. A reported minimum of 3.3 million children a year witness violent parental abuse ranging from hitting or slapping to murder. (Because family violence is underreported, the actual figure is much higher.)[121] The problem is compounded because the combination of inadequate job opportunities and lack of outside financial and child-care support trap women (and their children) in abusive relationships. Sexual harassment, battering, rape, murder, sexual abuse of women and children, and other forms of gender violence are not random events or practices perpetrated by "other" political regimes and a few celebrities. They are intrinsic components of America's heritage and culture.

THE ROLE OF RELIGION

Although separation of church and state is a fundamental cornerstone of U.S. government, religion has always been in collusion with politics and vice versa. Martín-Baró,[122] makes a useful and appropriate distinction between vertical religiosity, which leads to alienation and oppression, and horizontal religiosity, which leads to empowering critical conscious-ness and social liberation. Both can exist individually or in combination with other religious practices, but the direction taken reflects its ideo-logical dimension.

Martín-Baró, a Jesuit priest and critical psychologist, conducted a series of studies in El Salvador which confirmed that there was a clear connec-tion between religious beliefs and sociopolitical choices. His analysis found that even though religion has individual meaning, the ideological milieu provides the context for how one interprets one's beliefs. The dom-inant western European Christian tradition is one of vertical religiosity and that, not horizontal religiosity,[123] is the "religion" discussed below.

Historically, when the shift from goddess worship to patriarchal reli-gions replaced the reciprocal relationship of nature and humanity with the superiority of man over nature (and women), the cultural sanction of violence as an expression of power and control became the norm.[124] Sex-ism, classism, and racism are replete in religious texts such as the Torah, Qur'an, and New Testament. The use of violence was both official and in-dividual. In the seventh century B.C.E., Josiah ordered the annihilation of every non-Hebrew Canaanite in order to eradicate lingering remnants of goddess worship. At "God's command," Joshua led the Hebrews to con-quer Palestine by killing every man, woman, and child they encoun-tered.[125] Catholic "holy" wars or crusades sanctioned murder, rape, and other atrocities in the name of God and church coffers. The fourteenth-century Roman Catholic Church authorized the notorious torture of the Inquisition as warnings to others who might question the authority of the Church and thereby weaken her political power.

It was also seen as a duty to colonize and Christianize the "savages" of the world. Ships were sent to the colonies with armies and missionaries and returned laden with slaves and treasures wrested from the con-quered. Churches and governments grew rich on the backs of colonialized people by destroying their cultures, their economy, their spirits, their lives. Although conquered peoples were often seen as less-than-human, religions also fostered the belief that humans are inherently bad—and women even worse. In officially sanctioned versions of Biblical texts, Eve, after all, is responsible for tempting Adam to eat the forbidden fruit and thus for their (and our) expulsion from the Garden of Eden. The stigma of Eve's sin has marked all women as less-than-man. From Augustine to Aquinas (and Aristotle before them), the female is marked as too emo-tional and impulsive and thus not "rational" enough, fickle, weak, de-ceitful, and generally morally and intellectually inferior to men.[126]

Catholicism was the first Christian religion but by no means was it the most oppressive or influential.[127] The fundamental Calvinist tenet of predestination is perhaps the strongest contender for that title. Predestination refers to the belief that people are divided into two groups—the redeemed and the damned—before they are born and there is no way to change one's fate. Because success is considered a sign of God's grace, people work hard to achieve so they (and others) can be convinced they are among the saved.[128] Those at the top of the hierarchy can then tautologically justify their position and behavior by invoking this tenet. In addition to stressing the evil of idleness and human nature, the Calvinist tradition also opposed enjoyment and personal luxuries.

The late seventeenth-century Salem, Massachusetts, witch trials were but one embodiment of this dogmatic and misogynous heritage. As Weber has shown, the Calvinist form of radical individualism that questioned the religious value of poverty and forbearance became the foundation of capitalism and an oppressive, militant, self-righteous morality. Today, it is evident in efforts limiting reproductive rights, in bemoaning the break-up of the (presumably functional) nuclear family while forcing even single mothers to abandon their children so they can work, paying men higher salaries than women who do the same work, sanctioning injustices in our law enforcement system, and opposing social justice. In short, it is the agenda of the conservative government and the "religious" right. It is the hegemonic ideology.

The heritage of vertical religiosity is not oppressive only to women and children. It harms men in ways that are sometimes even more insidious and dangerous. Since male behavior is the norm, violence and war are not only accepted as normal, but they are elevated as noble, heroic events. This only makes it more difficult to see how qualities that define "manhood," like emotional detachment, competitiveness, and toughness, can be detrimental.[129] All that matters is winning—whether it means a hostile corporate takeover that puts thousands out of work, dropping an atomic bomb on innocent men, women, and children, or shooting an "enemy" with a handgun.

GUNS AND POSES

Firearms have figured prominently in U.S. history, and their continuing presence is often attributed to the country's strong cultural sense of its frontier heritage. As Gellert points out, other countries have a similar frontier tradition (e.g., Canada and Australia) but have only a fraction of America's rates of gun ownership or gun-related homicide and violence. For example, the homicide rate among males aged fifteen to twenty-four in the United States is ten times higher than in Canada, and fifteen times higher than Australia.[130] Australia has one-seventh the proportionate private handgun ownership of the United States. Friedman and Fisher attribute this, not to a "frontier" legacy but, more accurately, to the varying historic dominance of market culture and institutions between countries such as the United States and Canada. They argue that it is not a coincidence that Canada has both more stringent controls over the sale of guns and a much more generous "welfare state" than the United States, or that Canada pioneered the kind of universal medical care system the United States has fiercely and effectively resisted in the name of a "free market."[131]

The United States has the highest rate of nonwar gun-related homicide in the world. The United States is also the only industrialized nation that does not effectively regulate private ownership of firearms,[132] even though there are currently more than 20,000 laws in the United States that deal with the sale, distribution, and use of firearms. Almost one-half of all American households have one or more firearms. Although accurate figures are not available, the American Medical Association estimates that there are approximately 210 million firearms in the United States, 60 million of which are handguns.[133]

The rhetoric that argues "if guns are criminalized only criminals will have guns" and law-abiding citizens will have no means to protect themselves is not supported by data. The majority of U.S. homicides are not committed by those with any criminal record. Most homicides are the result of a complex interaction of emotional and societal forces and are not associated with other felonies or a previous history of crime. Guns intended to protect against crime are forty-three times more likely to kill a family member, friend, or acquaintance than to kill an intruder in self-defense.[134] The risk of domestic homicide in families owning a gun doubles.[135] Adults whose parents owned a gun are twice as likely to own one themselves.[136] Data also contradict the racist-based fear exploited by George Bush in his now infamous "Willie Horton" campaign commercial. The commercial used a mug shot of an African American with a voice-over that told how he had been furloughed in Massachusetts and subsequently beat and terrorized a man and raped his wife in another state. The commercial played on the common but mistaken belief that violent crime is disproportionately committed by blacks against white victims. Although whites are more likely to own guns than blacks, blacks are three times as likely as whites to be victims of a violent crime committed with a handgun. More than 90 percent of the victims of black violence are other blacks.[137]

The "Constitutional right" argument is similarly divorced from fact. Even though the second amendment says "the right of the people to keep and bear arms shall not be infringed," all U.S. Supreme Court decisions have held that this does not protect an individual's right to private gun ownership, despite the belief to the contrary of 60 percent of Americans.[138] What about the right to *life*, liberty, and the pursuit of happiness (emphasis added)? The fact is guns are a highly profitable, major American industry in a culture where money matters most. The National Rifle Association (NRA) is a powerful, well-funded contributor to select political campaigns and advocate of the gun industry. The problem—and most important discrepancy in the data—is that when it comes to firearms, profits are measured in dollars and costs are measured in lives.

POLICE BEAT

Since July 1991 New York and other U.S. cities have been touting a downward trend in both violent and property crime. According to the FBI, national murder and robbery statistics for 1997 show a decline of 7 percent. However, as evidenced by a *Morning Edition* report on National Public Radio (NPR) on November 23, 1998, there is growing concern among the public, as well as among criminologists, that the figures merely indicate increased political pressure on police to keep crime rates low. On that program, Eric Westervelt reported that the New Orleans Office of Municipal Investigation found that dozens of crimes in the city were altered or downgraded so that tourists would not be scared away. Westervelt tells of one woman who was stabbed twelve times while resisting rape by an intruder who attacked her in her own bed. According to FBI guidelines, the crime should have been reported as attempted rape and aggravated assault and battery—a major crime. But New Orleans police classified the attack simply as an aggravated burglary, avoiding mention of anything that might appear on the violent crime reports. In another attack, Westervelt reported, "a man ended up in the emergency room with stab wounds to his back during a robbery. That, too, was written up as an aggravated burglary." This "creative crime counting" is not restricted to New Orleans or other favorite tourist destinations. Police commanders in New York, Boca Raton, Philadelphia, Atlanta, and several other cities were criticized, demoted, or transferred in 1998 for similar offenses.

Westervelt also interviewed Jim Fife, a criminologist and former New York City police officer, who said that crime statistics were the "worst official statistics in the U.S." and that current practices were not without precedent. Pressure to manipulate statistics comes not only from cities looking to boost their images, but also because promotions and pay raises are largely based on crime statistics. According to Fife, downgrading was common practice when he joined the force in the early 1960s, and continues to this day. Westervelt reported that, in 1996 and 1997, the FBI "tossed out" the Philadelphia crime reports "because they were totally unreliable." Although John Timmony, the Philadelphia police commissioner, called the majority of mistakes "stupid, careless, [or] lazy" unintentional miscodings, an investigation by the Philadelphia *Inquirer* found that statement contradicted by repeated examples of recent downgrading.

The problem is exacerbated, especially in inner cities, when citizens fail to report crimes. As Fife explained:

> The suburbanite whose car is broken into is alarmed because this is the first time this has happened and he's paying enormous taxes and he expects the police to come out with a fingerprint kit and solve the problem. The guy in the inner city to whom that happens knows it ain't gonna happen, so he doesn't bother reporting it. So almost certainly crime in the worst parts of the United States is very much underreported by citizens.

Not responding to alarms in "certain" neighborhoods represents more than dereliction of duty or a shortage of police officers. It is just one way the racial bias that pervades police departments across the country manifests itself. Other ways can be, unfortunately, far more serious.[139] Although all police officers are not racist, many police departments across the country tolerate prejudice in their ranks. Racism is the most blatantly displayed.

On Thursday, February 4, 1999, Amadou "Ahmed" Diallo, an unarmed twenty-two-year-old West African man with no criminal record, was shot to death at 12:45 A.M. in the vestibule to his apartment. He was killed by four (white) officers assigned to an elite plainclothes unit trying to solve a series of rapes and robberies in the Bronx and Manhattan. Diallo was shot forty-one times. (The four members of the New York Police Department's Street Crime Unit were subsequently indicted on second-degree murder charges and acquitted.)

The institutionalized racism and brutality of the NYPD had reached international proportions. Thousands in Guinea, including top government officials, attended Diallo's funeral. The Diallo shooting became the catalyst for a national and international debate on U.S. police practices and the racial conflict between urban officers and the communities they patrol. The president of the United African Congress, Sidique Abubakarr Wai, charged New York City officials with flagrant disregard for African lives and condemned their failure to aggressively seek the murderers of "several dozen Senegalese cabdrivers who have been killed over the past decade or so."[140] Outraged citizens of all ages, colors, and incomes gathered daily in New York, in groups ranging in size from a handful to more than 10,000, to protest police racism and brutality. Demonstrations were also held in Washington, D.C., and other major cities. On Tuesday, March 28, 1999, hundreds of police officers, nearly all of them white, marched in the Bronx in support of the four officers who shot Amadou Diallo, contending that the killing of Mr. Diallo was a tragedy but not a crime.

On February 25, 2000, a jury cleared the four police officers of murder, manslaughter, and lesser criminal charges in the slaying of Amadou Diallo. Public protests followed in Albany, the Bronx, and elsewhere. Amadou's father, Saikou Diallo called the change in trial venue from the Bronx to the state capitol "the second murder" of his son. As this book goes to press, the NAACP is demanding a federal investigation of the case and the Diallo family is planning a civil lawsuit against the city and the officers.[141]

The police do not deny that minorities are targeted as suspects. A manual used by the Public Agency Training Council in Indianapolis even suggests stopping all cars with "Jamaican paraphernalia, bumper stickers or slogans."[142] The police argue that they stop more blacks because there are more blacks in jail because blacks commit more crimes. But they fail to recognize the circularity of this reasoning. It doesn't occur to them that perhaps there are more blacks in jail because they are so targeted. They have no way of knowing how many more whites would be in jail today if they were also stopped or if criteria other than race were used.

The "profiling" controversy and the use of race and ethnicity as clues to criminality prompted state and federal investigations into police behavior across the country. However, three years earlier, in 1996, Amnesty International issued a report on "Police Brutality and Excessive Force in the New York City Police Department."[143] The human rights advocates documented the disproportionate number of people of color who were physically abused and sometimes killed, often by shots in the back, in situations that "did not warrant the use of lethal force" and were "in violation of police guidelines and international standards."[144]

Also in 1996, a New Jersey judge found state troopers engaged in the illegal practice of targeting of minority drivers, creating a "stark" disparity in which blacks were almost five times more likely to be stopped than whites. After years of denial, in April, 1999 (shortly after the Diallo murder and the massive national public demonstrations against police bias and brutality that followed), New Jersey's Governor Christine Todd Whitman, most likely with an eye on the polls, finally acknowledged that state troopers have disproportionately and improperly stopped and searched black drivers on the New Jersey Turnpike in attempts to catch drug dealers and other criminals. More than 77 percent of all drivers so targeted were members of a minority group.[145] This blatant racism is not unique to the New York area. Comparable statistics have been found in other states. In Maryland, for example, the state police agreed as part of a court settlement to track the race of drivers that troopers stopped and searched on a stretch of I-95. Only 17 percent of the drivers on that road were black, but more than

70 percent of those searched in the first 20 months were African American. The "war against crime and drugs" is clearly a race war.[146]

The police, it should be noted, are in a difficult if not impossible position. Their job is to prevent crime, yet the conditions that are responsible for high crime rates are not part of the equation. At the core of our law enforcement system is a belief that people (and especially people of color) are innately violent and need external social controls to contain them. By some convoluted form of logic, this legitimizes the use of violence to "control" violence. The job of police, by definition, is to maintain order and control, typically through coercion. The model is one of professionalized "crime fighting," reflecting its military roots in history and imagery and contributing to a "bunker mentality" that feeds suspicions of "outsiders" and fosters secrecy that minimizes accountability.[147] It applies military concepts (criminals as enemies) and terminology (war on drugs) as well as solutions (punishment) to social, political, and economic problems. It is violence used to protect even greater violence. It is violence for social control, not social good. It is violence that perpetuates a caste system reminiscent of discriminatory law interpretation, application, and enforcement in which blacks received decidedly harsher punishments, especially for crimes against whites.[148]

BEHIND BARS

The United States has a larger percentage of its population incarcerated than any other country. Between 1980 and 1994, the number of inmates in state and federal prisons and local jails increased three-fold, from 329,821 to more than 1.8 million,[149] including over 95,000 youths.[150] The overall American rate of imprisonment is now ten times as high as that of Japan. California has the largest prison system, larger than any single country in the Western industrialized world, and larger than that of France, Germany, Great Britain, Japan, Singapore, and the Netherlands combined.[151] For the past twenty years, California has imprisoned 450 out of every 100,000 juveniles—a higher percentage of its youth than any other state. Although whites are the largest racial group in the state, black and Latino youth are eight times as likely to be arrested as a white California teen. In Utah, where less than 1 percent of the state's residents are black, eight times more black youths are also held in detention. Half of the inmates in all American prisons are African American, yet blacks make up only about 10 percent of the total American population. One out of three young African American (ages eighteen to thirty-five) men in the United States are in prison or on parole. The percentage of black men in prison in this country is four times higher than in South Africa at the height of apartheid.[152] Of the 80,000 women now imprisoned, about 70 percent are nonviolent offenders and 75 percent have children. (Although women make up only a little more than 7 percent of all U.S. inmates, they are the fastest-growing segment of the prison population.)[153] More than one out of nine school-age children has one or both parents in prison. If present policies continue, this number will soon reach one out of four.[154] The National Center for Juvenile Justice reports that the number of youth age ten through seventeen who are arrested and incarcerated for violent crimes could more than double by the year 2010 if current rates continue.

The exponentially growing prison population is largely due to four interrelated factors: (1) special interests, (2) the misguided "war on drugs," (3) the equally mistaken belief that "getting tough on crime" will suppress it, and (4) the market economy.

Firstly, despite the high cost of maintenance (about $40,000 per inmate per year)[155] prison compounds have blurred the line between public and private interests. Politicians use them to scare up votes based on fear of crime. Impoverished rural areas reap financial benefits from the jobs created.[156] Private (and not so private) companies exploit the $35 billion prison budget for substantial profits. UNICOR (the acronym-like name used by Federal Prison Industries), for example, is a government corporation/ manufacturing conglomerate created in 1934 by the U.S. Department of Justice with the Federal Bureau of Prisons. In federal fiscal year 1996, UNICOR employed 17,379 inmates and had $495.4 million in sales, 61.6 percent of which went to the Department of Defense.[157] Workers are paid from $.23 to $1.15 per hour. A portion of these wages are applied to court-ordered fines, victim restitution, and other court-assessed obligations. Not a single cent of UNICOR's money goes for social security tax or any form of insurance. Nor does it help to defray the expenses of our vast prison system or the taxes we pay to support it.[158] The U.S. prison system has become a major bureaucratic, political, and economic resource, subject to all of the surreptitious dealings and injustice that go along with it.

Secondly, the percentage of inmates serving time for nonviolent drug offenses has more than doubled since the early 1980s, to 61 percent in the federal prison system and 30 percent in state systems. Some of these cases involve possession of only small amounts of marijuana or cocaine.[159] Yet, the average sentence for a first-time, nonviolent drug offender is longer than the average sentence for rape, child molestation, bank robbery, or manslaughter. Our prisons are not overcrowded because of necessity but because hegemonic self-interests find it profitable to keep them that way. To further contextualize the situation, it is also necessary to realize that, despite the $17 billion the United States is spending on the "war on drugs," the damage done by illicit drugs does not come close to that caused by legal drugs like alcohol and tobacco. In 1989 alone, tobacco killed 395,000 Americans and cocaine killed 3,618. A recent issue of the *New England Journal of Medicine* (1998) reported that properly prescribed legal drugs kill 106,000 Americans every year. That's twenty times more than are killed by illegal drugs.[160]

Thirdly, increased criminalization is simply not working. For example, a meta-analysis of systematic assessments of "tough" delinquency programs and institutionalization found that these types of programs, such as "shock incarceration" and "scared straight," produce higher, not lower, levels of recidivism.[161] California now gives youthful offenders tougher sentences than adults convicted of the same crime. According to the California Department of Corrections, juveniles convicted of murder serve an average of five years in prison, compared to adult murderers who serve an average of three-and-a-half years. Yet youth homicide rates went from 350, which was below the national average in 1970, to 1,400, or double the national average, by 1992.[162] "Get tough" policies ignore the fact that the socialization of the prison system, where violence, extortion, and rape are routine, often promotes a career in crime and little else.[163]

Fourthly, the market economy requires a high percentage of persistent poverty, which has serious consequences for children, families, and society. As Friedman and Fisher explain:

> Because a basic operating principle of market society is to keep the public sector small, individuals and families are forced to rely on individual efforts to secure some of the basics of healthy human development that less Darwinian societies, even poorer ones, provide much more reliably and accessibly. Poor but relatively generous societies, accordingly, are likely to do a better job at keeping violent crime low than wealthy but mean-spirited ones.[164]

Persistent poverty and the lack of opportunities for lucrative employment play a crucial role in crime, which is often a proactive result of complex and rational choices.[165] It is telling that Schwedinger and Schwedinger[166] report that over half of all U.S. prison inmates, in the year before their arrest, earned no income at all, and one-third had an income of less than $2,000. Underemployment and unemployment, obstacles associated with racism (such as reducing federal aid to cities and poor families), and the deteriorating position of marginalized groups in the labor market have virtually eliminated the possibility of their obtaining funds in any legitimate way. All but the very top and lowest bottom rungs on the (albeit mythical) ladder of opportunity have been removed along with the social safety net. There is no way to climb out of poverty.

CONCLUSION

The previous pages have begun to illustrate some of the paradoxes and perversions of a system that condemns violence to garner votes, punishes victims in the name of justice, scapegoats schools to camouflage its own crimes, and promotes prejudice under the guise of fairness. However, the "problem" of violence, like its "solution," runs even deeper than these. It courses through the veins of our body politic. It is inseparable from the roots of violence in American society—a cultural icon inextricably linked with history, entertainment, and economics. We admire the vigilante, glorify the gangster, idolize the gunslinger. Unless we come to grips with our past we cannot understand our present and envision the possibilities for reclaiming our future.

Our country was built on transgressive acts of violence that continue to this day.[167] It is part of the "otherist,"[168] hegemonic American ideology to counter aggression with more aggression. The narratives of our violent past and present are turned into heroic epics, romanticizing danger and negating empathy, emotion, and pain. These myths create a deceptive fraternal nostalgia (sometimes called "patriotism") that reinscribes socially sanctioned sentiments as history. From the minute Columbus set foot on Caribbean soil and the extermination of native populations began, through the savagery of slavery and its aftermath, the frequently forceful resistance to the labor movement and civil rights, and the continuing violence against immigrants and other minorities such as homosexuals, the archaic and barbaric colonial and capitalistic mindset that drives U.S. domestic and foreign policies and practices has taken us down the path of disparity, denial, and devastation.

The combination of this legacy with(in) the positivist paradigm, has led to the development of "interventions" in the "war(s) against fill-in-the-blank" (e.g., violence, guns, drugs). Although these proposed solutions may be well intentioned, violence, when viewed through the "scientific" or logical positivist paradigm and the dominant ideology (the two are intertwined), focuses on its prediction and control, which is often a thinly disguised effort to homogenize youth so they conform to hegemonic ideals.

Positivism refers to a paradigm, or belief system, that claims objectivity, truth, and certainty exist in science and that scientific knowledge is irrefutable and universal. Positivists, contrary to more critical thinkers, do not consider science a social construction that reflects a particular ideology.[169] Instead, positivism is deterministic, embracing control and prediction "[without taking] into account that human behavior is meaningful behavior that involves active agents with intentions and expectations and able to communicate with other equally active agents."[170] Positivism, by definition, rules out asking questions about domination and agency. Comte, who is often considered its founder, says the task of positivism is to maintain the status quo, to "imbue the people with the feeling that . . . no political change is of real importance."[171]

This "scientized" position, or embrace of positivistic objectivity and determinism, continues to dominate U.S. rhetoric and policy on violence, as exemplified in the popularity of "tough" deterrents (i.e., punishment) which promise solutions they cannot and do not deliver. (Positivism and the scientization of the social sciences is further discussed in chapter 8.) Furthermore, ignoring the ideological and social processes of violence by relying on an ethos of capitalist individualism and penal sanctions, in effect, punishes the true victims of violence by targeting populations labeled "high crime risks," "dangerous," and "subversive." Not surprisingly, given this country's racist propensities, the majority of these groups are young, poor, and people of color.

Alternatively, the authors of this volume maintain that onto-historical concerns are central to developing understandings of social phenomena. An onto-historical focus on violence situates it within the relationship between self and society, agency and control, power and structure. It demythologizes scientism and argues for understanding knowledge as embedded in the social, cultural, historical, and political milieu in which it is produced. It is grounded in theory, not ideology.

This position is not popular. It has been disparagingly called idealistic, unrealistic, and, with echoes of McCarthyism and all that implies, communistic. It has been discredited in public discourse and policy about violence by Wilson[172] and others[173] who argue that locating the causes of crime in conditions of social and economic disadvantage has limited value and offers almost no possibility of "practical applications" for intervention. But their practical applications, many of which are discussed in the final chapter of this book, have proven useless. Despite decades of rhetoric and a variety of (superficial) interventions, violence and crime persist. They are using a coat of paint to repair a building with a faulty foundation. It is a cosmetic attempt, a diversion, an easy way out. Yet, these superficial "practical" solutions gain increasing support while approaches grounded in theoretical (as opposed to ideological) bases are dismissed as unimportant and criticized for being neither empirical nor practical when, to the contrary, theory is both empirical and practical, as well as necessary. Theory and practice are inextricably interwoven. Practice is the basis of theory and theory is the means of changing practice.

Given this relationship, it becomes apparent why, as Stanley and Wise observe, "Most of us have been brought up to think of theory as something arcane, mysterious, and rather forbidden."[174] We think of theory as beyond our reach, unless "we" happen to be one of the elite (i.e., "intelligent," affluent, white, male). What we are not taught is that this way of thinking is a manifestation of ideology.[175] Ideology, following Marx, refers to the beliefs of the dominant class that are used to "rationalize" its vested interests and maintain the status quo.[176] Ideology has little, if any, systematic analysis of the actual socioeconomic, political, or cultural mechanisms prevalent in a society. It is a worldview that serves a normative function.

Theory, on the other hand, is thoroughly grounded in data. Without theory, data is incomprehensible. Theory explains the relationships among a set of concepts or phenomena in a meaningful way. It is defined as "explanation based on observation and reasoning" and as "principles." It can inform a more democratic, humanistic, and successful future practice instead of perpetuating present practices (based on ideology, not theory) that simply do not work.

Denial of theory allows the dominant ideology to obscure its role in practice both methodologically and in the generation of knowledge. This makes it difficult to question the status quo which keeps a majority of Americans at an unjust disadvantage. In other words, the causes of violence in our society elude many of us because those at the top do not want us to see them. They prefer to play the "blame game," making it appear that others are at fault. Opportunistic politicians have jumped on the ba[n]dwagon of perfidious sentiment, convincing many that violence is caused by (1) deterioration of the nuclear family (while they repeatedly vote down measures for child care, etc., that would help families), (2) teenage pregnancy (when evidence shows that teenage pregnancy rates have declined steadily since the 1950s[177] and that, in fact, the vast majority of fathers in "teen" pregnancies are older men, many of whom are guilty of rape and transmitting AIDS),[178] (3) welfare dependency (these politicians have led many Americans to believe that welfare is a major part of the United States budget when, in fact, basic welfare programs combined [Aid to Families with Dependent Children, Supplemental Security Income, and Food Stamps] amount to only 3.4 percent of the federal budget),[179] and (4) moral decay (have they looked at the behavior of their own group lately?). It is not an accident that they divide and scapegoat vulnerable groups. These tactics assure that the tables of power are not turned by diverting attention from the sins of the powerful and laying them on the heads of groups whose access to recourse they prohibit. This book means to expose the ideological frameworks supporting these tables of power—not so they can be turned, but so they can be replaced with tables built of more democratic wood rooted in the solid theoretical ground of a socially just society.

NOTES

1. Peter McLaren, *Life in School* (New York: Longman, 1994).

2. P. Cantor, "The Roots and Legacy of Violence," in *Suicidology,* ed. A. A. Leenaars (Northvale, N.J.: Aronson, 1993).

3. George A. Gellert, M.D., *Confronting Violence: Answers to Questions about the Epidemic Destroying America's Homes and Communities* (Boulder, Colo.: Westview Press, 1997).

4. Gellert, *Confronting Violence.*

5. U.S. Department of Justice, *National Crime Survey.* (Washington, D.C.: 1993).

6. F. M. Hechinger, *Fateful Choices: Healthy Youth for the 21st Century.* (New York: Carnegie Corporation, 1992).

7. National Coalition Against Domestic Violence, 1994.

8. R. T. Ammerman and M. Hersen, eds., *Assessment of Family Violence: A Clinical and Legal Sourcebook* (New York: Wiley, 1992); J. Garbarino, K. Kostelny, and N. Dubrow, "What Children Can Tell Us About Living in Danger," *American Psychologist* 46 (1991): 376–383.

9. Children's Defense Fund, Children's Defense Fund News Release (May 1996).

10. Cantor, "The Roots and Legacy of Violence."

11. R. L. Hampton and B. R. Young, "Violence in Communities of Color," in *Violence in America,* eds. R. L. Hampton, P. Jenkins, and T. P. Gulotta (Thousand Oaks, Calif.: Sage, 1996), 53–68.

12. U.S. Department of Justice, *Criminal Victimization in the United States, 1990* (Washington, D.C.: Government Printing Office, 1992).

13. Children's Defense Fund, 1996.

14. Susan Faludi, *Backlash: the Undeclared War Against American Women.* (New York: Crown, 1991).

15. National Coalition Against Domestic Violence, 1994.

16. See C. Allen Carter, *Kenneth Burke and the Scapegoat Process* (Norman: University of Oklahoma Press, 1996) for an illuminating exegesis of this phenomenon.

17. It is not a coincidence that "delinquency" did not become a social problem until the Industrial Revolution. The first juvenile justice institutions were created at the turn of the last century (1899–1900) to house the young criminals, who included disproportionately large numbers of immigrant children. By 1928 all but two states had a juvenile court system. See A. Platt, *The Child Savers* (Chicago: University of Chicago Press, 1969).

18. See D. Rothman, *Discovery of the Asylum* (Boston: Little Brown, 1971); D. Tyack, *The One Best System.* (Cambridge, Mass.: Harvard University Press, 1974).

19. S. D. Vestermark, Jr., "Critical Decisions, Critical Elements in an Effective School Security Program," in *Schools, Violence, and Society,* ed. A. M. Hoffman, (Westport, Conn.: Praeger, 1996), 101–121.

20. H. M. Kliebard, *The Struggle for the American Curriculum* (New York: Routledge, 1987).

21. For a thorough and accurate assessment of this situation see J. R. Epp and A. M. Watkinson, eds., *Systemic Violence in Education: Promises Broken* (New York: SUNY Press, 1997).

22. The term minority is used throughout this book. Although "minority" groups represent the majority student population of most U.S. cities, and will soon be the largest segment of the total U.S. population, these groups are still a minority in arenas of political and economic power. See Freire and Macedo, this volume.

23. Tracking is grouping students by "ability" into different curricular tracks, i.e., college preparation, vocational training, or general diplomas. Jeannie Oakes has shown the biases inherent in tracking and how it contributes to the perpetuation of social and economic inequalities. See "Keeping Track, Part 1: The Policy and Practice of Curriculum Inequality," *Phi Delta Kappan* (September 1986).

24. See Donaldo Macedo, *Literacies of Power: What Americans Are Not Allowed to Know* (Boulder, Colo.: Westview Press, 1994).

25. Jean Anyon, *Ghetto Schooling: A Political Economy of Urban Educational Reform* (New York: Teachers College Press, 1997).

26. See McLaren, Leonardo, and Allen, this volume.

27. Cantor, "The Roots and Legacy of Violence"; P. A. Noguera, "Preventing and Producing Violence: A Critical Analysis of Responses to School Violence," *Harvard Education Review* 65 (1995): 189–212; G. M. Ingersoll, *Adolescents in School and Society* (Lexington, Va.: D.C. Heath, 1982); W. B. Miller, *Crime by Youth Gangs and Groups in the U.S.* (Washington, D.C.: Office of Juvenile Justice and Delinquency Prevention, 1992).

28. Padilla's study of Chicano gang members in Chicago revealed that negative behaviors on the part of teachers, such as labeling, name-calling, belittling the child's culture, humiliating the child in class, and not expecting the child to succeed, prompted some students to participate in violent activity as "retaliation" for how they have been treated. See F. M. Padilla, *The Gang as an American Enterprise* (New Brunswick, N.J.: Rutgers University Press, 1992). See also B. Hartoonian, "School Violence and Vandalism," in *Youth Violence: Programs and Prospects*, eds. S. J. Apter and A. P. Goldstein (New York: Pergamon Press, 1986), 120–139.

29. See Pierre Bourdieu, *Distinction: A Social Critique of the Judgment of Taste*, trans. R. Nice (Cambridge, Mass.: Harvard University Press, 1987).

30. M. Foucault, *Discipline and Punish: The Birth of the Prison* (New York: Pantheon, 1977).

31. See Giroux, this volume.

32. Leslie Roman, "Spectacle in the Dark: Youth as Transgression, Display, and Repression," *Educational Theory* 46 (1996): 1–22.

33. P. A. Noguera, "The Critical State of Violence Prevention," *The School Administrator* 2 (1996).

34. J. Pastor, J. McCormick, and M. Fine, "Makin' Homes: An Urban Girl Thing," in *Urban Girls: Resisting Stereotypes, Creating Identities*, eds. D. J. R. Leadbeater and Niobe Way (New York: New York University Press, 1996), 15–34.

35. J. McCormick, "Aesthetic Safety Zones: Surveillance and Sanctuary in Poetry by Young Women," in *Construction Sites: Spaces for Urban Youth to Reimagine Social Possibility*, eds. L. Weiss and M. Fine (New York: Teachers College Press, 2000).

36. U.S. Department of Justice.

37. U.S. Advisory Board on Child Abuse and Neglect.

38. Sheryl Gay Stolberg, "Science Looks at Littleton, and Shrugs Its Shoulders," *New York Times*, May 9, 1999, sec. 4, pp. 1, 4.

39. Mike Males, *Framing Youth: Ten Myths About the New Generation* (Monroe, Me.: Common Courage Press, 1999).

40. J. Gray, "Bill to Combat Juvenile Crime Passes House," *New York Times*, May 9, 1997, pp. A1, A32.

41. "Excerpts from the National Education Goals," *Education Week* (January 31, 1990): 16–17.

42. See M. Posner, "Research Raises Troubling Questions about Violence Prevention Programs," *The Harvard Education Newsletter* 10, no. 3 (1994): 1–4 and J. P. Comer, *Waiting for a Miracle: Why Schools Can't Solve Our Problems—And How We Can* (New York: Dutton, 1997).

43. Edward N. Wolff, *Top Heavy: A Study of the Increasing Inequality of Wealth in America* (New York: Twentieth Century Fund Press, 1996).

44. Center on Budget and Policy Priorities, *Poverty and Income Trends, 1994* (Washington, D.C.: Center on Budget and Policy Priorities, 1996), 53, 64; Saul Friedman, "The Poor Still Get Poorer," *Newsday* February 12, 2000, p. B8.

45. Although this book focuses on violence and youth, it is important to realize that the elderly are also among the less visible victims of poverty and neglect. Abandonment of the elderly is already increasing. In twenty years the population over eighty-five years old will be five times what it is today. Out of this 15 million, it is estimated that 12 million will suffer from Alzheimer's disease or other forms of dementia, not to mention the other serious and chronic ailments that afflict the aged. For more on this topic see Fred C. Pampel, *Aging, Social Inequality, and Public Policy* (Newbury Park, Calif.: Pine Forge Press, 1998); Meredith Minkler and Carol L. Estes, eds., *Critical Perspectives on Aging: The Political and Moral Economy of Growing Old* (Amityville, N.Y.: Baywood Publishers, 1990); and Laura Katz Olson, ed., *The Graying of the World: Who Will Care for the Frail Elderly?* (Binghamton, N.Y.: Haworth Press, 1994).

46. Lee Rainwater and Timothy Smeeding, *Doing Poorly: The Real Income of American Children in a Comparative Perspective.* (Syracuse, N.Y.: Maxwell School of Citizenship and Public Affairs, 1995).

47. Rainwater and Smeeding, *Doing Poorly.*

48. S. B. Kamerman and A. J. Kahn, *Starting Right: How America Neglects Its Youngest Children* (New York and Oxford: Oxford University Press, 1995).

49. Kamerman and Kahn, *Starting Right*, 29.

50. For example, the Personal Responsibility and Work Opportunities Reconciliation Act of 1996 abolished earlier safety nets such as Aid to Families with Dependent Children and JOBS, a work and training program. In 1996, the financial impact of this legislation through 2002 was projected to total $23 billion cut from the food stamp program and nearly $3 billion from child nutrition programs. In addition, changes in the definition of childhood disability will deny 300,000 children Supplementary Security Income (SSI) and, according to Congressional Budget Office estimates, as many as 50,000 of these children will also lose their Medicaid benefits. Legal immigrants, including children, are no longer eligible for SSI or food stamps, and states are allowed to deny them welfare, social services, and nonemergency Medicaid, "saving" the government billions of dollars more. Work requirements were also increased by this measure, while child care assistance was decreased. However, President Clinton did manage to find $112 billion to add to

the military budget. See A. U. Rickel and E. Becker, *Keeping Children from Harm's Way: How National Policy Affects Psychological Development* (Washington, D.C.: American Psychological Association, 1997). On February 19, the Giuliani Administration in New York City announced it would implement a plan to compel the city's homeless to enroll in "workfare"—working as much as thirty-five hours a week for their welfare check and the "privilege" to stay in city shelters. This affects over 4,600 families and 7,000 single adults. There are no provisions for the children of single parents who must work, but children of families excluded from shelters would be placed in foster care.

51. See Kamerman and Kahn, *Starting Right*.

52. Kamerman and Kahn, *Starting Right*.

53. The concept of cultural capital comes from the work of Bourdieu and Passeron. They maintain that schools do not use the social and cultural resources of different groups evenly. For example, children from higher economic classes will be familiar with the language, authority, and behavior patterns of schooling while those from lower classes will not. Bourdieu argues that the cultural experiences of students from higher classes facilitate their adjustment to school and academic achievement, thereby transforming cultural resources into what he calls cultural capital. See Pierre Bourdieu and Jean-Claude Passeron, *Reproduction in Education, Society and Culture* (Newbury Park, Calif.: Sage, 1997); Pierre Bourdieu, "Cultural Reproduction and Social Reproduction" in *Power and Ideology in Education*, eds. J. Karabel and A. Halsey (New York: Oxford University Press, 1997), 487–511.

54. Although this should not be construed as downplaying the seriousness of the failures of our market economy and capitalist ideology, this is one area where recent immigrants and other marginalized groups may have an advantage over other impoverished populations. Their cultural values stressing cooperation, community, family, and the dignity of hard work may provide some protection, at least for a while, from the devastating effects of market values, a fact which does not escape them and which frequently contradicts popular perceptions of minorities. See Lawrence M. Friedman and George Fisher, *The Crime Conundrum: Essays on Criminal Justice*, (Boulder, Colo.: Westview, 1997).

55. J. D. Kasarda, "Cities as Places Where People Live and Work: Urban Change and Neighborhood Distress," in *Interwoven Destinies: Cities and the Nation*, ed. H. G. Cisneros (New York: Norton, 1993), 81–124.

56. Kasarda, "Cities as Places."

57. P. C. Brophy, "Emerging Approaches to Community Development," in *Interwoven Destinies: Cities and the Nation* (New York: Norton, 1997), 213–230.

58. Stanley Aronowitz and William DiFazio, *The Jobless Future: Sci-tech and the Dogma of Work* (Minneapolis: University of Minnesota Press, 1994); Stanley Aronowitz and Jonathan Cutler, eds., *Post-work: The Wages of Cybernation* (New York and London: Routledge, 1998); S. Sassen, *The Global City: New York, London, Tokyo* (Princeton: Princeton University Press, 1991); H. L. Gates and W. J. Wilson, "The Two Nations of Black America," PBS *Frontline* interview, February 1998.

59. D. R. Judd and T. Swanstrom, *City Politics: Private Power and Public Policy* (New York: HarperCollins, 1994).

60. Psychological research lends empirical support to the importance of outcome expectancies in choice of behavior. That is, the belief that time and energy

spent on a task will actually affect its consequences plays a significant role in persistence. (See P. Karoly, 1993, "Mechanisms of Self-Regulation: A Systems View," in *Annual Review of Psychology* 44 (1993): 23–52, eds. L. W. Porter and M. R. Rosenzweig; J. B. Rotter, *Social Learning and Clinical Psychology* (Englewood Cliffs, N.J.: Prentice-Hall, 1954).

61. Lani Guinier, *The Tyranny of the Majority: Fundamental Fairness in Representative Democracy* (New York: Free Press, 1994).

62. Guinier, *The Tyranny of the Majority*, 15.

63. U.S. Department of Education, 1996

64. Educational Testing Service, 1991

65. Jeannie Oakes, *Making the Best of Schools: A Handbook for Parents, Teachers, and Policymakers* (New Haven: Yale University Press, 1990); Jonathan Kozol, *Savage Inequalities* (New York: Crown Publishers, 1991); Stephanie Urso Spina, "Worlds Together . . . Words Apart: Bridging Cognition and Communication for Second-Language Learners through Authentic Arts-Based Curriculum." *Language, Culture, and Curriculum*, 8 (1995): 231–247.

66. James B. Conant, *Slums and Suburbs: A Commentary on Schools in Metropolitan Areas* (New York: McGraw Hill, 1961).

67. Kozol, *Savage Inequalities*.

68. Jean Anyon, "In School Reform: Toward Useful Theory," *Urban Education*, 30 (1995): 56–70; Linda Darling-Hammond, "The Right to Learn and the Advancement of Teaching: Research, Policy, and Practice for Democratic Education," *Educational Researcher* 25 (1996): 5–17; Jeannie Oakes, *Making the Best of Schools*.

69. Peter McLaren, *Life in Schools* (New York: Longman, 1994).

70. Paul Willis, *Learning to Labour* (Farnborough, Great Britain: Saxon House, 1977).

71. Michael W. Apple and Lois Weis "Ideology and Practice in Schooling: a Political and Conceptual Introduction," in *Ideology and Practice in Schooling*, eds. Michael W. Apple and Lois Weis (Philadelphia: Temple University Press, 1983).

72. Michelle Fine, *Framing Dropouts: Notes on the Politics of an Urban Public High School* (New York: SUNY Press, 1991).

73. Historically, many other minority groups, such as Jews, Irish, German, and Italian immigrants at the turn of the century, have been discriminated against and, like African Americans, stigmatized as "violent," isolated in ghettos, and so on. Yet there remains a crucial difference. These cultural groups did not have their traditions and languages intentionally and forcibly stripped away by 500 years of slavery.

74. James Gilligan, *Violence: Reflections on a National Epidemic* (New York: Vintage Books, 1997), 199.

75. Gilligan, *Violence: Reflections*, 199–200.

76. The acceptance of blacks into the middle and upper classes must also be seen within the context of white cultural oppression. The negative interpretations and denigration of less successful African Americans by the black bourgeoisie are attitudes developed in congruence with dominant racist ideology.

77. Gus Hall, "Capitalism causes violence," in *Violence: Opposing viewpoints*, eds. Scott Barbour and Karin Swisher (San Diego: Greenhaven Press, 1996), 120–127, quote on p. 123.

78. *The Autobiography of Malcolm X* (New York: Grove Press, 1966), 371.

79. See, for example, Michelle Fine, Lois Weis, Linda C. Powell, and L. Mun Wong, eds., *Off White: Readings on Race, Power, and Society* (New York: Routledge, 1997), Richard Delgado and Jean Stefanic, eds., *Critical White Studies: Looking Behind the Mirror* (Philadelphia: Temple University Press, 1997); Mike Hill, ed., *Whiteness: A Critical Reader* (New York: New York University Press, 1997); George Lipsitz, *The Possessive Investment in Whiteness: How White People Profit from Identity Politics* (Philadelphia: Temple University Press, 1998).

80. Stephanie Spina and Robert H. Tai, "The Politics of Racial Identity: A Pedagogy of Invisibility," *Educational Researcher* 27 (1998): p. 37.

81. We should be careful not lose sight of the fact that white is also a prefabricated pan-ethnicity, although structured to dominate, and that only by exposing it as such can we hope to engage with its implications. Just as the label "Hispanic" glosses over, dilutes, and suppresses the much stronger national ethnicities of Chicanos and Puerto Ricans, obscuring the historic roots of their condition as oppressed people and conflating the cultural diversity of these groups into an "amorphous mass," so too, the label "white" robs individuals of this other "amorphous mass" of their claims to diverse European cultural heritages. (From Spina and Tai, *The Politics of Racial Identity*, p. 40)

82. E.g., a week-long series on race relations on *Nightline*, May 1996.

83. See Macedo, *Literacies of Power*.

84. Gilligan, *Violence: Reflections*, 194.

85. Gilligan, *Violence: Reflections*, 194.

86. Gilligan, *Violence: Reflections*, 194.

87. Gilligan, *Violence: Reflections*, 194.

88. See Gilligan, *Violence: Reflections*, 287, for a listing of relative studies.

89. Gilligan, *Violence: Reflections*, 195.

90. T. Edsall and M. Edsall, *Chain Reaction: The Impact of Race, Rights, and Taxes on American Politics* (New York: Norton, 1991); J. Freedman, *From Cradle to Grave: The Human Face of Poverty in America* (New York: Atheneum, 1993).

91. Julia Kristeva, *Nations Without Nationalism* (New York: Columbia University Press, 1993), 3.

92. Rickel and Becker, *Keeping Children*, 156.

93. Gus Hall, "Capitalism Causes Violence," 120–127, Clinton quoted on p. 121.

94. Critical criminologists are among the minority of voices who define crime to include not only those acts deemed illegal by the state, but those acts committed by the state and other elite groups who are typically not held accountable for them. See, for example, Harold E. Pepinsky, *The Geometry of Violence and Democracy* (Bloomington, Ind.: Indiana University Press, 1991); J. Hanmer, J. Radford, and E. Stanko, *Women, Policing, and Male Violence* (New York: Routledge, 1989).

95. Gilligan, *Violence: Reflections*, 245–246.

96. Dash, quoted in Posner, "Research Raises Troubling Questions," 4.

97. Quoted in Julia Schwedinger and Herman Schwedinger, "Rape, Sexual Inequality, and Levels of Violence," in *Crime and Capitalism: Readings in Marxist Criminology*, ed. David F. Greenberg (Philadelphia: Temple University Press, 1993).

98. See Donna Gaines, "America's Dead-end Kids," this volume.

99. Scott Cummings and Daniel J. Monti, eds., *Gangs: The Origins and Impact of Contemporary Youth Gangs in the United States* (Albany: SUNY Press, 1993), viii.

100. See Klein and Chancer, "Masculinity Matters," this volume.

101. James Short, Jr., *Poverty, Ethnicity, and Violent Crime* (Boulder, Colo.: Westview Press, 1997).

102. Padilla, *The Gang as an American Enterprise*, 7.

103. Padilla, *The Gang as an American Enterprise*.

104. Although the studies cited here were done with urban male gangs, females have always been involved in gangs and gangs are becoming an increasing presence in suburbia. Suburban gangs are a relatively recent phenomenon and an important area for future study. Because few researchers have focused on female gang membership and activity, and even fewer on exclusively girl gangs, information on females in gangs has also been scant and, until recently, stereotypical and sexist. Girls in gangs have been described as serving the needs of male gang members, fronting for drug pushers, or serving other auxiliary roles. Newer studies are beginning to provide an expanded view of female roles in and contributions to gang culture, but there is still a long way to go. See, for example, G. M. Ingersoll, *Adolescents in School and Society* (Lexington: D C Heath, 1982); J. W. Williams, "A Structural Subculture: Understanding How Youth Gangs Operate," *Corrections Today* (1992): 54, 86–88; A. Campbell, *The Girls in the Gang: A Report from New York City* (New York: Basil Blackwell, 1984); A. Campbell, "Female Participation in Gangs," in *Gangs in America*, ed. R. Huff (Newbury Park, Calif.: Sage, 1990), 163–182; M. S. Jankowski, *Islands in the Street: Gangs and American Urban Society* (Berkeley: University of California Press, 1991); J. C. Oates, *Foxfire: Confessions of a Girl Gang* (New York: Dutton, 1993); Meda Chesney-Lind and John Hagedorn, eds., *Female Gangs in America : Essays on Girls, Gangs, and Gender* (Chicago: Lake View Press, 1999).

There is a similar dearth of research on violence in Native American and Asian populations. See Donna Gaines, "America's Dead-end Kids," this volume; See also Robert Hampton, Pamela Jenkins, and Thomas P. Gullotta, eds., *Preventing Violence in America* (Thousand Oaks, Calif.: Sage, 1996) for a brief review of existing studies with these populations, as well those in rural areas and more affluent neighborhoods.

105. Mercer L. Sullivan, *Getting Paid: Youth, Crime, and Work in the Inner-City* (Ithaca, N.Y.: Cornell University Press, 1989), 2.

106. See Jeff Ferrell, *Crimes of Style: Urban Graffiti and the Politics of Criminality* (Boston: Northeastern University Press, 1993) for an in-depth look at the criminalization of graffiti art and artists in one community (Denver); See Lyman G. Chafee, *Political Protest and Street Art: Popular Tools for Democratization in Hispanic Countries* (Westport, Conn.: Greenwood Press, 1993), for a broader sociocultural view.

107. Donna Gaines, *Teenage Wasteland* (Chicago: University of Chicago Press, 1991/1998).

108. The implications of this for schooling are discussed in the final chapter of this book.

109. See Klein and Chancer, "Masculinity Matters," this volume.

110. See Klein and Chancer, "Masculinity Matters," this volume.

111. Laura I. O'Toole and Jessica R. Schiffman, eds. (New York: New York University Press, 1997), xi.

112. The Simpson trial was a double feature, adding archetypical racism to gendered violence. The subtext of the trial was the portrayal of black men as categorical perpetrators of sexual and domestic violence, particularly since the victim, Nicole Simpson, was white.

113. I have followed the accepted form of reference to this war, but wanted to note that this and similar situations should not be defined in terms of bounded groups. Such reductionist and exclusionist discourse is constructed to subsume multiple subjectivities into a singular, reified entity and should be problematized. (The same holds true of our classification of people in terms of gender, income, sexual preference, and a host of other oppositional categories.)

114. Andrea Dworkin, *Pornography: Men Possessing Women*, chap. 2 (1981).

115. Andrea Dworkin, *Pornography*, chap. 2.

116. This is not to ignore crimes against men, however, during an average year, women experience 600,000 violent physical attacks by an intimate, and men experience about 50,000. (Gellert, *Confronting Violence*).

117. Ann Jones, *Next Time She'll Be Dead* (Boston: Beacon Press, 1994).

118. Jones, *Next Time*.

119. Jones, *Next Time*, 81.

120. Jones, *Next Time*.

121. Betsy McAllister Groves, Barry Zuckerman, Steven Marans, and Donald J. Cohen, "Silent Victims: Children Who Witness Violence," *Journal of the American Medical Association* 267 (January 1993): 262–264

122. Ignacio Martín-Baró, *Writings for a Liberation Psychology* (Cambridge, Mass.: Harvard University Press, 1994), 143.

123. I want to reiterate that *horizontal religiosity* can be supportive and empowering. *Horizontal religiosity* refers to an individual and collective *spirituality*. It is *not* to be confused with the crimes of politicized, power brokering *vertical religiosity* discussed here.

124. See Dennis E. Fehr, "A Revised Survey of Western Civilization," in D. E. Fehr, *Dogs Playing Cards: Powerbrokers of Prejudice in Education, Art, and Culture*, (New York: Peter Lang, 1993): 1–95; M. Stone, *When God Was a Woman* (New York: Harcourt Brace Jovanovich, 1978); M. Stone, *Ancient Mirrors of Womanhood* (Boston: Beacon Press, 1991); Ruane Eisler, *The Chalice and the Blade* (San Francisco: HarperCollins, 1987/88).

125. See Fehr, *Dogs Playing Cards*.

126. For example, in *Politics*, Aristotle describes women as by nature inferior to men. Augustine calls them "evil." Aquinas, in *Summa Theologica*, categorizes women (with children and the insane) as unable to give reliable evidence because they do not have the capacity for understanding.

127. Other religions are not exempt from male biases and violent practices. The focus here is on Christianity because that is the predominant and most influential tradition in American history.

128. Darwinian natural selection translates the same Protestant precepts into science.

129. See Klein and Chancer, "Masculinity Matters," this volume.

130. *World Health Statistics Annual* (Geneva, Switzerland: World Health Organization, 1994).

131. Friedman and Fisher, *The Crime Conundrum*, 36.

132. Gellert, *Confronting Violence*, 232.

133. American Medical Association, Council on Scientific Affairs, "Firearm Injuries and Deaths: A Critical Public Health Issue," *Public Health Report* 104 (1989): 111–117.

134. Gellert, *Confronting Violence*.

135. Gellert, *Confronting Violence*.

136. Gellert, *Confronting Violence*.

137. James Gilligan, *Violence: Reflections on a National Epidemic* (New York: Vintage Books: 1997).

138. Gellert, *Confronting Violence*.

139. Racism is far from the only bias at work here. Biases against women, sexual orientation, disability, and ethnicity are also evident. They are also underreported.

In 1990, The Hate Crimes Statistics Act was passed, requiring the FBI to prepare an annual report on bias crimes. Compliance in reporting crimes to the FBI was voluntary. In 1997, only 32 of New York's 502 law enforcement agencies submitted any hate crime reports to the agency. Of the 100 largest cities in the United States, 10 did not participate at all. Nationwide, a total of 8,049 bias-motivated crimes were reported to the FBI in 1997. Of these, 4,179 were racially biased, 1,102 were bias crimes against sexual orientation, 836 were ethnically biased, and 12 were disability biased. Alabama recorded no hate crimes. But a study by the Southern Poverty Law Center in Montgomery detailed 20 hate-related incidents that year. A recent study by Donald Green found there were six times more hate-related incidents against gays in New York City from 1994 and 1995 than were counted by the police. Bias crimes often go unreported because victims are suspicious of the police and/or afraid of being deported (in the case of illegal immigrants). When the crimes are reported by victims, the police either don't want to bother with the paperwork and energy required of bias crimes, or they don't want to give their community a reputation of bias. See Sascha Brodsky, "Reality Behind the Statistics: Many Hate Crimes Go Unreported," *Newsday*, July 8, 1999, pp. A6, A23.

140. Amy Waldman, "In a Quest for Peace and Opportunity, West Africans Find Anger," The *New York Times*, February 6, 1999, p. B6.

141. Anthony De Stefano, "Despite Verdict, Cops' Fate Unclear," *Newsday*, February 26, 2000, p. A5; Graham Rayman, Leonard Levitt, Zachary Dowdy, and Kara Blond, "Verdict: Not Guilty," *Newsday*, February 26, 2000, p. A4.

142. John Crew, the attorney who runs the ACLU's police practices unit, quoted in Jodi Wilgoren, "Police Profiling Debate: Acting on Experience, or on Bias," *New York Times*, 9 April 9 1999.

143. New York: Amnesty International, June 1996.

144. New York: Amnesty International, June 1996, 11.

145. Iver Peterson, "Whitman Says Troopers Used Racial Profiling: Minority Groups Faced Bias on the Turnpike," *New York Times*, April 21, 1999, pp. 1, B8.

146. The report on the Diallo case was compiled from a variety of news sources including television and radio news broadcasts, the *New York Times* and *Washing-*

ton Post from March through May, 1999, and personal experience and communications with involved citizens.

147. See Paul Chevigny, *The Edge of the Knife: Police Violence in the Americas* (New York, The New Press, 1995), for a history of police violence and corruption in the United States and other countries.

148. T. Sellin, *Slavery and the Penal System* (New York: Elsevier, 1976).

149. T. A. Kupers, "Trauma and Its Sequelae in Male Prisoners: Effects of Confinement, Overcrowding, and Diminished Services," *American Journal of Orthopsychiatry* 66 (1996): 189–196; Eric Schlosser "The Prison-Industrial Complex," *Atlantic Monthly* (1998): 51–79.

150. Center for the Future of Children, 1994.

151. Schlosser, "The Prison-Industrial Complex."

152. *National Household Survey on Drug Abuse: Population Estimates 1996* (Rockville, Md.: Substance Abuse and Mental Health Services Administration); *National Household Survey on Drug Abuse*, p. 19, Table 2D; Bureau of Justice Statistics, *Sourcebook of Criminal Justice Statistics 1996*, (Washington, D.C.: U.S. Government Printing Office, 1997): 382, Table 4.10, and 533, Table 6.36; Bureau of Justice Statistics, *Prisoners in 1996*, (Washington, D.C.: U.S. Government Printing Office, 1997): p. 10, Table 13.

153. Craig Lambert, "Chains of Violence: The Women of Cell Block B," *Harvard Magazine* (September–October 1999): 19.

154. Joseph Califano, *Behind Bars: Substance Abuse and America's Prison Population* (New York: The National Center on Addiction and Substance Abuse at Columbia University, 1998).

155. John J. Donahue, "Some Perspective on Crime and Criminal Justice Policy," in Friedman and Fisher, *The Crime Conundrum*, 54–55.

156. Friedman and Fisher, *The Crime Conundrum*; Schlosser, *The Prison-Industrial Complex*.

157. David Martin, "Occupational Training or Slave Labor?" *City Times*, <http://www.zolatimes.com/v2.13/FPI.html> (accessed 8/25/99).

158. Martin, "Occupational Training."

159. Testimony of Kathleen M. Hawk, director of federal prisons, subcommittee on Intellectual Property and Judicial Administration, U.S. House of Representatives, May 12, 1993.

160. Legal or illegal, no one asks why the use of substances is so prevalent. It seems that "special interests" play a major role here also, with our "leaders" once again opting for campaign contributions from corporate lobbying groups instead of the health and well-being of its citizens.

161. M. W. Lipsey, "Juvenile Delinquency Treatment: a Meta-Analytic Inquiry into the Variability of Effects," in *Meta-Analysis for Explanation: A Casebook.* (New York: Russell Sage Foundation, 1991); A. Nossiter, "As Boot Camps for Criminals Multiply, Skepticism Grows," *New York Times*, 18 December 18 1993: A1.

162. Mike Males, "Youths Are Unfairly Blamed for Violence," in *Violence: Opposing Viewpoints*: 52–59.

163. Schwedinger and Schwedinger, *Rape, Sexual Inequality, and Levels of Violence*; Friedman and Fisher, *The Crime Conundrum*; Schlosser, *The Prison-Industrial Complex*.

164. Friedman and Fisher, *The Crime Conundrum*, 30.

165. See Sullivan, *Getting Paid*.

166. Schwedinger and Schwedinger, *Living Standards*.

167. Consider, for example, this illustration of the persistence and power of the mythology and ideology of the frontier West. In 1984, Bernhard Goetz, a young white man, shot and killed four young black men in a New York subway car. In the spirit of racist self-defense and with echoes of a frontier showdown, news media admiringly labeled him the "subway vigilante." The symbolic significance of this (as well as the inherent racism of the American hegemony) contributed to the outcome of Goetz's murder trial. He was acquitted. One wonders what the verdict would have been if Goetz had been black or Latino and the victims white.

168. I use the term "otherist" to encompass all discriminatory "ists," like racist, sexist, classist, as well as additional biases against those considered "others" according to the dominant ideology. These include homophobia, bias against sexual preference, the handicapped, the overweight, etc.

169. See Bruno Latour and Steve Woolgar, *Laboratory Life: The Construction of Scientific Facts* (Princeton: Princeton University Press Reprint Edition, 1986). See also Stanley Aronowitz, *Science as Power: Discourse and Ideology in Modern Society* (Minneapolis: University of Minnesota Press, 1988).

170. Jonathan Smith, Rom Harre, and Luk Van Lagenhove, *Rethinking Psychology* (Newbury Park, Calif.: Sage, 1995), 15.

171. Cited in H. Marcuse, *Reason and Revolution* (Boston: Beacon Press, 1960), 346.

172. James Q. Wilson, *Thinking about Crime* (New York: Basic Books, 1975).

173. E.g., Sen. Joseph R. Biden, Jr. argued for tougher laws and sentences in "Combating Violence in America," an address given to the Wilmington, Delaware, Rotary Club, 16 Dec. 1993; Patrick F. Fagan, in "The Real Root Cause of Violent Crime," published by the Heritage Foundation in *Backgrounder*, 17 March 1995, blames the break up of the American family (independent of context) for increased violence.

174. Liz Stanley and Sue Wise, *Breaking Out Again: Feminist Ontology and Epistemology*. Rev. ed. (New York and London: Routledge, 1993), 45.

175. What we are defining as ideology here has been called "Grand theory" by Stanley and Wise. I have used "ideology" because it is less confusing than "grand theory" when compared to "theory." Both terms refer to virtually the same phenomenon.

176. Karl Mannheim, *Ideology* and *Utopia* (New York: Harcourt, Brace & World, 1929/36).

177. Pat Burdell, "Teen Mothers in High School: Tracking Their Curriculum," in *Review of Research in Education* 21 (1996): 163–208, ed. Michael W. Apple.

178. For example, over half of the fathers of babies born to girls under age fifteen are at least five or six years older than the mothers. In only 8 percent of all teenage births (which is 1 percent of all U.S. births) are both parents under eighteen years of age. As reported by public health epidemiologist Jim Kent, nearly all heterosexually transmitted HIV among teens of both sexes are contracted from adult men. Many of those cases are the result of rape. When both heterosexual partners are teenagers, risk of AIDS infection is almost nonexistent. See D. L.

Landry and J. D. Forrest, "How Old Are U.S. Fathers?" *Family Planning Perspectives* 27 (1995): 159–161; J. Greene, "Sex Between Teens, Adults Growing Factor in AIDS Spread," *Oakland Michigan Press*, March 7, 1994, p. A8; K. A. Moore, C. W. Nord, and J. Peterson, "Nonvoluntary Sexual Activity Among Adolescents," *Family Planning Perspectives* 21 (1989): 110–114; Alan Guttmacher Institute, *Sex and America's Teenagers*. (New York: Alan Guttmacher Institute, 1994).

179. Comer, *Waiting for a Miracle*.

1

Wearing the Colors

A Personal Narrative from a "Die-hard" Educator

Charles "Paco" Hernandez

For some, gangs may provide, and for some, gangs may destroy. Contrary to popular stereotypes, gangs are not all the same. Each is different. When I first joined, gangs in my neighborhood showed class unity and ethnic diversity. They were made up of a group of people in a similar situation who wanted to stick together and have fun too. They protected the neighborhood and fighting was a question of honor. They respected each other's territories. They looked out for their own. They never ratted on each other. They had a strong code of ethics. In many places they still do.

Isabel Nunez writes about a West Coast gang in the community where she teaches and where "the gang provides protection, financial support and general services, and; the community provides safe haven and non-cooperation with law enforcement." She is worth quoting at length:

> The dominant ideology asserts that gangs "prey on their terrorized communities." However, this idea was called into question just this past Wednesday while I waited with my students for their parents after school. I observed a gang father picking up his kindergarten child, and clearly visible under his tank top were the large numbers "90650" tattooed across his chest. 90650 is our zip code in Norwalk, and certainly reflective of dedication to community as permanent body art. . . . [Another] afternoon at about 3:30 P.M., a teacher's car was broken into and vandalized in the staff parking lot. Several homes face the parking lot from directly across the street, but none of the residents could describe the perpetrator. At a staff meeting the following morning, the teacher [said]: "I can't believe these people care so little about keeping the ex-

41

cellent teachers that are here at Edmondson. You know, people get the neighborhoods they deserve." I am certain any teacher who expects people to, in her mind, jeopardize their families' safety for the integrity of her car radio, which will go home along with her to spend the night in a nice, clean, safe, white suburb, is a destructive element in the community. Happily, she left our school less than six months later.[1]

Similarly, Dwight Conquergood, who lived in a Chicago housing project for five years, lists the five sacred virtues of the People nation as "love, honor, obedience, sacrifice and righteousness," and the six sacred virtues of the Folks nation as "love, wisdom, strength, sincerity, knowledge and understanding."[2] Padilla notes as well that *The Latin Kings Manifesto* proclaims that the gang is "entrusted with a divine mission, one that transcends personal gains and recognition" and directs "all our powers and all our desires into the mission of human service."[3]

In my old neighborhood, however, now most gangs know only violence, enforced ignorance, and selfishness. Much so-called gang violence is the individual violence endemic to conditions of poverty[4] which, despite reports of a growing economy, have gotten worse for the poor, especially poor children. The American society they experience is more implicitly and therefore more dangerously discriminatory than that of their parents. Many have seen their parents struggle for little or no reward. They don't have to read Fine's study of a New York City Comprehensive High School to learn that dropping out, one of the supposedly destructive consequences of gang involvement, can actually serve as protection against the psychological damage inflicted by the high school as an ideological institution,[5] or to find out that schooling serves to maintain the large, psychically broken economic underclass required to support a capitalist society. They live it. I have lived it. This is my story.

LIFE IN THE PROJECTS (LESSONS IN CLASS LEARNED OUT OF SCHOOL)

My name is Charles "Paco" Hernandez. I am the oldest of three children born to deaf Puerto Rican parents in the projects of New York in the sixties. As a child, I was abused and treated like crap by an alcoholic, drug-addicted father at home and by my classmates at school. I couldn't take it anymore. I understood my parents' deafness and accepted it as a way of life. What I wouldn't accept—what I couldn't accept—was the ridicule and poverty they faced.

My first hard-core fight was when another kid signed to my parents in a dirty gesture: "Fuck you this! Fuck you that!" I saw my father ignore him and walk away. My mother told the kid, in sign language, to go away.

He laughed at her. We went upstairs and I cried. I grew older and wiser over the next few months, but the pain inside me also grew.

One day, I went to the Spanish grocery store in our neighborhood. There was this notorious gang that hung out there. They all lived in the same projects I lived in. All of the gang members wore cut-off denim jackets with the lettering "Smith Bros." I stared at those "colors" with the skeleton in the middle of it. They were mean—very mean guys. They chased anybody out of the projects who didn't live there. People in the projects talked about them all the time. It was safe and if you did not go in the hood looking for trouble, you were okay. That same kid who cursed at my parents was there, wearing those colors. I was wearing my badly worn-out jeans and P. F. Flyers. The kid spat at me and I turned to him. He stood there with his friends laughing. I was just twelve years old. I hated this kid. He pushed me and pushed hard. My hands felt his face and the screaming started. My fists were on every part of his body. Then I realized that I was the one screaming and the kid was on the ground, bleeding from his mouth and nose. The gang members glared at me with flared nostrils. They gathered around me and fists began coming at me from all angles. I did not go down. I did not cry. I continued to fight to the very end. My reward was my opponent's colors.

The gang members were my new family and if it meant going to the end for them, so be it. That was our law. They would have done the same for me. My parents did not know I had joined the gang. The gang had hurt them deeply, but I was beyond my parents' control. My father and I were having some serious fights. I remember breaking his nose once. One night I pulled a gun on him and told him that me and my mother were not going to be hit anymore. The night before, I had walked into his room and placed a double-barreled shotgun to his head. I was going to pull the trigger for all the things he did to me. I am glad that I did not shoot him that night. A few days later, he came home drunk, swinging and cursing at everyone and everything. I was not going to put up with this. I fought back. We went outside and had it out. He left with some serious bruises and a broken nose. Two days later he came back. Knowing he couldn't get away with this behavior anymore, he no longer took his frustration out on his family. Over time, the drinking became controlled and the drug use lessened. He became aware of what he was doing and today he is a good, sober, straight man, and I thank God I did not kill him. To tell you the truth, I would have missed him.

As the oldest son, I felt responsible for everyone in the house. If there was no food, I would get it somehow. My first experience with incarceration was the sixty hours I spent in the bullpen of Manhattan Criminal Court in New York. I was fourteen years old. What choice did I have other than stealing food to feed my family? I couldn't make enough money to pay for the week's groceries. As Nunez argues, "entrepreneurship on the part of gangs should be immune to criticism by virtue of its necessity—it often constitutes the sole source of income for entire families [who] . . . don't have the luxury of advocating revolution from within ivy-covered walls."[6] I was arrested for extortion, racketeering, and six counts of first-degree assault. The charges were dropped.

Times were getting rough and the gang was getting into heavy things—breaking into stores, robbing, stealing, beating members of other gangs for their colors. We were even extorting protection money from local businesses. Then came my introduction to Smith and Wesson. That piece of iron gave me such a rush that nobody could have messed with me. The shooting became a Fourth of July party every night for the next few years. The white man's high became the minorities' nightmare. Drugs were popular and easy to get. Things changed quickly for me. I lost many of my friends. My attitude changed. When I fought, I no longer cared about the other person. Every Friday at the bar and after-hours club, I was in a fight. One night I was attacked by another gang. They slammed an "ax" on my head, fracturing my skull. I was furious and wanted revenge. My whole gang went after this guy and they got him.

Family Court. Criminal Court. Supreme Court. All for gang activities. I was arrested on adult charges of first-degree assault shortly before my seventeenth birthday. A family member suggested that I be placed in the military instead of serving time. Five to fifteen years in prison or a stint in the military. The prosecutor turned to the judge. "Your call," he said. I was terrified. The judge lectured me: "With this crime you are punishable for five to fifteen years in a state facility. Yet, your parents are deaf and depend on you. I recommend that you enlist in the armed services as your sentence, for a term of no more than four years, in a unit that will make a man out of you." I found myself praying and thanking God. I became a soldier. Sure enough, it made me a better man and a professional killer. I now knew how to kill.

After taking part in the invasion of Grenada and finishing my tour of duty, I returned home. The gang was still there. I could not get a job. The military never provided me with job skills. The only job I knew how to do was being the muscle and hurting people. So, I joined my friends in the gang. I could trust them and feel safe with them, and they had always had money while I had none. I was arrested a year later, practically right out of the service, for using the survival skills the Army taught me. A week later, I punched a State Correction officer into a coma. I waited eighteen months to be sentenced before the charges against me were dropped once again. In the meantime, the gang I grew up with changed their name to "Die-hard." The entire Lower East Side feared this gang that took over four housing projects and the whole of alphabet city. (Alphabet city refers to the streets in lower Manhattan that have letter names instead of words or numbers.) I reached out to the crew and became the middle man for the Die-hards.

I was soon involved in several firefights and, in return, I was caught in an ambush in which I was hit on the right side of my face and the right side of my thigh. I survived after thirteen hours of surgery including extensive facial reconstruction with 230 stitches in my mouth, which was wired for six months. I was fearless. I stayed in the gang. One night, a rival gang put a hit on all the guys who were involved in a power struggle to distribute a new drug called "Crack." This changed the entire face of the crew and I knew it was time to slow down. Getting high on everything that passed by me day by day seemed to bore me and now I had to watch my back. These guys were killers and the body counts were pretty high. I saw myself carrying my own coffin. It was time for a change.

CROSSING BORDERS

I left the gang (which is another story) and applied for the New York City Police Department. I went through a series of investigations and they told me that, with my history and former life style, it would be impossible for me to become a police officer. I finally got a job as a bodyguard for the editor-in-chief of a publishing company. The man wrote and spoke with great eloquence and was highly regarded by everyone who knew him. I had never known anyone who commanded such respect—and he did it just by reading and writing. This, I saw, was real power. I wanted to go back and help the help the kids in my neighborhood realize this too. I wanted to teach them about alternatives to drugs, guns, and violence; alternatives to living on the streets; alternatives I had never even dreamed existed. After a few years with the publisher, without missing a single day's work, I enrolled in college and earned a bachelor's degree in elementary education.

I had hoped to have earned my master's in education by now, but there have been many obstacles. I have been stopped by discrimination and prejudice only four courses (twelve credits) shy of completing the degree requirements. The first courses I took went well and the professors were supportive and encouraging. One, a school principal, asked me to teach in his school. Another invited me back to show a film about my experiences and speak to her other classes. She continues to support my efforts to reach the wider academic community.

Then one night I happened to be in the park when the Latin Kings were trying to recruit members. The kids they solicited did not want to be part of a gang. They were seriously threatened. In order to protect the kids, I intervened in the situation. The gang members left the kids alone but came after me with their guns drawn. As I ran, I fell and broke my hand. Early the next day, while waiting to see a doctor, I phoned the university and told them I would be unable to come to class that morning. In the meantime, I filed a report with the police, hoping to provide additional support for the kids. They asked how they could reach me if they needed more information and I told them where I'd be each day—either at home, at work, or in class. The following week I went to class and apologized to the instructor for my absence, explaining what happened. He reprimanded me in front of the entire class, shouting at me, among other things, "You people will amount to nothing." As it happens, later that same morning the police came to the campus and had a security officer ask me to meet them in the lobby. I left class and went to speak to the officers. On my return to class I was met with a loud barrage of insults, curses, and ethnic slurs (I was the only male Latino in the class) from the instructor. He continued to bad mouth me to everyone he knew in the school. In one class, where I had received an A on a paper I wrote about how deaf children communicate, the professor now insisted I never came to class and gave me an F for the course. Ultimately the disparaging instructor succeeded in having me suspended and the university has not allowed me to finish work on my degree. I was told I could not write and needed remedial work. My phone calls have not been returned. My letters remain unanswered. Follow-up calls and letters as well as requests by supportive faculty members have not been responded to. Since my coursework is so near to completion, it is not feasible to transfer to another university.[7]

However, counter to that instructor's stereotypical image of "my kind," I have been far from idle. I have worked for the New York City Board of Education as an elementary school teacher and at a SIE (Specialized Instructional Environment) VII Special Education Program, a day treatment program for severely emotionally disturbed children from ages eleven to fifteen. As crisis coordinator for the latter, I tried to break down the silent wall between the teachers and the kids. We were there to educate these kids. But we also had to educate teachers about these kids lives. Much of my responsibility was to break up the fights and mediate between gang rivals and other conflicts and to teach teachers about the code of ethics of the street and understanding a gang's language and culture. Budget cuts then left me unemployed, doing odd jobs in film, serving as a bodyguard, and taking part-time jobs until I became a teacher again.

I now work as a teacher for the New York City Department of Juvenile Justice. The students in my self-contained classroom are ten to sixteen years old, the majority of whom are neglected, abused, and addicted to drugs since early childhood. They include murderers and rapists, facing sentences of nine years to life. Most never went to school and all have poor reading skills. Students generally remain in my five-and-a-half-hour class from three to five months while waiting for trial, a court appearance, or probation. Instruction is somewhat traditional but highly individualized. This is the only facility under the jurisdiction of the New York State Education Department that is allowed to teach multicultural curricula. Most of these students know nothing about their own heritage. They are used to being told by society that they are worthless scum and worse because they are Puerto Rican, because they are poor. Knowing nothing else, they believe it and internalize it. Once they learn something about Puerto Rican history they realize how wrong this is. Their self-esteem improves considerably. In addition to "basic" skills, I also teach what I call "quality of life." I do not tolerate crap. I play jazz and classical music during classes and talk to them frankly and honestly. We talk (in Spanish and English) about life and life skills—like how to read (and read between the lines of) a newspaper. The changes are dramatic. In academic terms, for example, the reading level of the class went from first to fourth grade in just eight weeks. In psychological terms, attitudes and behavior have changed remarkably. Others want to get into the class. It has become something to look forward to in a world where that has never existed before.

However, no one can work miracles. Over 75 percent of these boys will be back because they have no other recourse. They are desperate. Many have asked to come home and live with me. It is heartbreaking. Teachers can make a difference, but we cannot do it alone. It is unfair to expect us to. Schools are understaffed, undersupplied, and under increasing pressures on many fronts. Teachers may be the only ones who can reach these kids before its too late. Teachers may be their last hope—their only hope. But hope alone is not enough. These kids need to learn more than how to survive. They need to learn that there is more to life than the way of the streets and that there is a way out. And for there to be a way out takes, as the African adage borrowed by Hillary Rodham Clinton says, an entire village.

This is different from the "paternalistic effort toward salvation" that is, in Nunez's words, "yet another form of colonization." She describes how we are all "at risk for coercion into complicity with the hegemonic functions designed to be performed by 'liberal,' or 'progressive' subjectivities."[8] Nunez uses Sofia Villenas's personal account of her experience as a Chicana ethnographer in a Latino community to illustrate this. She tells how Villenas, intoxicated by the experience of inclusion, became complicit in the hegemonic agenda of problematizing the community she was studying. She soon recognizes her co-optation, however, and realizes that any gain in institutional power is paid for by a corresponding surrender of cultural identity. Villenas realigns herself with her community. Nunez concludes: "The 'miracle' of breaking free from gang life serves to protect present power and ideology by ensuring that any socioeconomic progress is accompanied by a step toward the cultural norm."[9]

The point is, there is a price to pay for everything you do. One has to go to "the other side" to get the skills, but we don't all sell out. The sell-outs are those who, seduced by illusions of power, forget who they are and don't return to the community or who, for example, join the police force, come back to the community, and become drug dealers because they think that now, with their blue uniform, they can get away with it. That's selling out. Those who come back to the neighborhood as part of the neighborhood are the real "miracles." We can teach, write, and speak to different groups. We can be effective role models because there is a spiritual kinship with these kids. There is a common ground, a common experiential base. And an uncommon opportunity to make a difference in their lives.

NOTES

1. I. Nunez, "A Call for Solidarity: Decolonizing Resistance Culture Beyond the Academy." (Paper presented at the first National Conference on Ethnographic Inquiry and Qualitative Research in a Postmodern Age. Los Angeles, Calif., June 1997), 6.

2. D. Conquergood, "Homeboys and Hoods: Gang Communication and Cultural Space," in *Group Communication in Context: Studies of Natural Groups*, ed. L. R. Frey (Hillsdale, N.J.: Lawrence Erlbaum, 1994), 23–56.

3. F. M. Padilla, *The Gang as an American Enterprise.* (New Brunswick, N.J.: Rutgers University Press, 1992), 85.

4. Nunez, "A Call for Solidarity."

5. M. Fine, *Framing Dropouts: Notes on the Politics of an Urban Public High School.* (Albany, N.Y.: SUNY Press, 1991).

6. Nunez, "A Call for Solidarity," 5.

7. However, since that appears to be the only option, I am exploring the possibility of completing my degree elsewhere without having to repeat courses already taken. I am fortunate to have the help of supportive professors, employers, and officials in this matter.

8. Nunez, "A Call for Solidarity," 8.

9. Nunez, "A Call for Solidarity," 9.

2

On Living (and Dying) with Violence

ENTERING YOUNG VOICES IN THE DISCOURSE

Jennifer Obidah

> What's up, y'all? This is LeAlan Jones and I just feel like talking tonight. . . . I'm five foot seven and 147 pounds. I live in the ghetto. I'm supposed to be a loser. I'm supposed to be on the six o'clock news shooting people's heads off. I'm supposed to be the one that you grab for your purse when you walk by. I'm the person that doesn't vote. I'm the person that is supposed to drink. I'm the person that supposed to smoke weed. I'm the motherfucker that is supposed to fill your jails. I'm the person that you make examples to your kid of what not to be like. I'm supposed to be a basketball player. I'm supposed to make it only because of affirmative action. I'm not supposed to be positive. I'm not supposed to be educated. I'm not supposed to know what I know. But I do.
>
> —L. Jones and L. Newman with D. Isay in *Our America*

In the preface of the book *Our America*, Cornell West tells about being invited to the White House to discuss a possible speech by President Clinton on urban youth.[1] He relates that Clinton's staff wanted a list of "the nation's top scholars and experts" with whom they could consult about the deplorable circumstances—"immoral maldistribution of wealth, high levels of unemployment, dilapidated housing, decrepit schools, inadequate health care, unavailable child care, and shattered familial and communal bonds"[2]—of some Americans' lives. West informed Clinton's staff that it would be better for the President to "*sit and talk with ten young people from the 'hood' for two hours*" [emphasis added] after which he would have more than enough for such a speech.[3] Neither Clinton nor his staff ever convened such a meeting, and their reactions to his suggestion caused West to wonder whether or not the democratic process in America was one that "highlights engaging, listening, and responding to the very people who are affected by public policies enacted by the powerful." West heralds *Our America* as an opportunity for all of us, including the president and his staff, to listen and to learn.

The narratives featured in this chapter helped two teachers to learn about violence from young people. This chapter presents the words of eighth-grade students from two public schools, one a kindergarten through eighth-grade school located in New Jersey and the other a middle school in Northern California. I was the teacher at the school in Northern California, and Anita Bland is the teacher in New Jersey. Both Anita and I saw the need to hear and know our students' perceptions of the effects of violence in their lives and incorporate these perspectives into educating them. In this way we engaged in more effective teaching and enhanced the learning that occurred in our classrooms.

My work on death and violence among youth and its effects on public schooling began five years ago. As a teacher at the middle school, I became aware that my students were frequently exposed to violent deaths, and consequently, this aspect of their realities had an effect on the educative process taking place in my classroom. One particularly significant lesson for me was realizing that children who live with violence as an everyday reality are important sources of knowledge about the challenges of violence and death on today's youth. As their teacher I incorporated students' knowledge about death into classroom learning activities, and one result of this was the creation of a newspaper that was written by the students for the school community.

Anita Bland is one of the teachers at an inner-city school in New Jersey who is involved in an educational project, *Creating Original Opera,* sponsored by the Metropolitan Opera Guild in New York City. This program engages students in the creation of an opera company and the writing and performance of an original musical work based on their own experiences. Anita has been involved in this endeavor since 1986. Shortly before this chapter was written, one group of Anita's students decided to focus their opera on the role of violence in their lives. The narratives from the New Jersey students are taken from data collected by Stephanie Spina, consisting of interviews and discussions with students and essays they wrote during and after their engagement in creating and performing that opera.[4]

In this chapter I argue that listening to these children can assist educators in knowing how to be more effective, both in the policy-making and educative process, when addressing the issue of violence among the youth. Youth can impart knowledge that both educators and policy makers would find useful in the development of more effective solutions to the problem of violence—if they would only listen. I begin with an overview of the rise in juvenile crime arrest rates followed by a look at research on the social and psychological effects of children's frequent exposure to violence. Interwoven in this overview are the eighth graders' statements about why and how violence occurs in their communities. I then question why, despite the intimate knowledge of violence derived from the lived experiences of these youth, their narratives are frequently omitted from the violence discourse. This question leads into an analysis of the generally held negative perceptions of youth and violence in today's society with the narratives. Students' narratives demonstrate their awareness of and reactions to such perceptions. These narratives also offer a critique of schools' and teachers' effectiveness in assisting the youth with the challenges and consequences of living with violence as an everyday reality. The students' voices presented here are not many and are thus not generalizable to the population of the schools that these students attend, much less the entire population of youth living in the inner cities of America. However, these perspectives resonate with voices of other young people in similar circumstances that are reported elsewhere.[5] As such, narratives in this chapter are presented without references to individual students; first, to ensure the anonymity of the students, and second, to maintain a collective resonance of voices seldom noted in the discourses on violence. It is hoped that the narratives presented here highlight this need, particularly as it becomes clear that disparities exist between the needs and concerns of the general public about violence among youth, and the needs and concerns of the youth themselves—needs and concerns that become apparent only when we listen to what young people have to say. I believe that effective solutions can only come when these disparities are resolved.

VIOLENCE AMONG YOUTH

Beginning in the late 1980s after more than a decade of relative stability, the juvenile violent crime arrest rates soared. A 1995 report from the Office of Juvenile Justice and Delinquency Prevention on juvenile offenders and victims states that "from 1976 to 1991, 23,000 persons under age 18 were known perpetrators of homicide in the U.S., an average of more than 1,400 per year."[6] The report also notes that "between 1984 and 1991 the rate at which juveniles ages 14 to 17 committed murder increased 160 percent."[7] Many of the students from both schools indicated that homicide and other forms of violence were normal occurrences in their lives. One of the eighth graders from New Jersey described violence as "the use of force in a way that harms a person or property." Another noted that "violence is not only being physically hurt but also mentally hurt." This student continues that "when a child has to see his or her siblings getting a whipping they all get hurt. I'm not saying that people or parents shouldn't teach their kid(s) right from wrong but you don't have to beat them to death. Violence is also mental, like telling a kid that people don't like them or telling them that they are ugly or stupid. Sometimes kids use violence to impress themselves or someone else." Below are the voices of other students giving firsthand accounts of the violence they witness and why they think it occurs:

> People act violent sometimes because of something that they need and they want to steal it or kill someone for it. There is a lot of violence in my neighborhood because of the people and poverty and all of the drugs being sold.

> Violence is generated by anger and misery. When a person is furious they can strike anything or anyone without cause. This fury is caused when a person loses their job and must face a series of obstacles. He or she can take no more and they explode in violence. This explosion hurts loved ones both physically and mentally. They destroy others emotionally and sometimes even kill them at night. But the main victims are [the perpetrators] themselves for they are trapped in a cage of fear because their minds are confused when they are so frustrated. They don't know what they are doing. These people aren't responsible for their action—especially kids.

> I see violence everyday in my neighborhood and it is not a good sight. Seeing somebody die is like seeing yourself die.

> There is a lot of violence in this state. You see it everywhere you go. There is violence in the school and outside on the streets. People are killing one another or beating up on one another. A day doesn't go by that you don't see violence.

> The thing that bother me is everybody say you gotta be somewhere or you gotta do something to somebody to get shot. A bullet ain't got nobody name on it. You could be standing around minding your own business and somebody start shooting. You never know.

What Is Violence to Me
Violence to me is my neighborhood.
Full of madness, fighting, and killing in the hood.
Stolen cars riding through the night. Crashing and
getting chased by the police and thinking its nice and fun.
Violence comes from your mind and your surroundings,
meaning your friends who just got to do mischief all
day, everyday, selling drugs for money, no job, no education.
A never ending vicious cycle.

The cause of this rise in juvenile crime and violence is reported as resulting from the development of the crack cocaine drug industry in poor and working-class inner-city communities across the country.[8] Importantly, with this boom in the drug industry, access to and use of handguns dramatically increased. It comes as no surprise then that children, such as the eighth graders above, born in the mid- to late-1980s and living in communities where drugs and guns proliferate, would grow up with gun violence and homicide as "normal" in their environment. Nonetheless, though they may live with violence as a part of everyday life, these children still suffer adverse consequences.

In Los Angeles County in 1982, 10 to 20 percent of the homicides in the city were witnessed by children, and, in Chicago, virtually all the children in one public housing development had a first-hand encounter with a shooting by age five.[9] In a similar study, Martinez and Richters [10] examined exposure to violence for 165 children ages six to ten years from a low-income, moderately violent area of Washington, D.C. More than half of these students had witnessed a violent act, and a significant number of them had been victimized by some form of violence. Martinez and Richters found that "both self-reported victimization and exposure to violence in the community were related to distress symptoms."[11] Distress symptoms include depression and other subdued, mute, and avoidant behavior linked to traumatic specific behaviors.

Another study was conducted by Fitzpatrick and Boldizar[12] with 221 low-income, predominantly (99 percent) African American youth living in eight central-city housing communities. These youth were between the ages of seven and fourteen years The results of this study indicate that 43.3% of the respondents had witnessed a murder. These researchers note that "as the number of purposeful and random shootings in neighborhoods and schools increase, the likelihood of younger persons witnessing such violence will also increase."[13] Regarding the reports of post-traumatic stress disorder (PTSD) among these youth, the results in this study were similar to the earlier mentioned study conducted by Martinez and Richters, with a significant correlation between frequent exposure to violence and increased reporting of PTSD symptoms. Other studies conducted in urban inner cities concluded that, in addition to PTSD, exposure to community violence was also significantly associated with other signs of acute trauma among children.[14] Clearly, thousands of children across America are affected by violence, as victims, witnesses, and even as offenders. Jean Anyon noted in the Children's Defense Fund *State of America's Children Yearbook 1994* that "more American children died from firearms on the killing fields of America than American soldiers died on the killing fields of Vietnam."[15]

One result of living in circumstances of frequent exposure to violence and suffering from effects such as depression and PTSD is that many young people worry about premature death. In my conversations with the young people at the middle school in Northern California, I asked how many of them worried about dying young. Some students frankly admitted their fear of dying at a young age as a result of a random shooting. One student notes the reason why she worried about dying young was that she "stay[ed] outside all the time and there's so much going on in the city. You can't hide from it so if it's your time to go, it's your time to go. I always be outside and I don't know when somebody's gon' try to come kill me." Another student was eloquent in her fear of the suffering that could accompany getting shot and realizing that you were about to die. She stated,

> I'm scared to die. I'm plain scared to die. I know a lot of people say they not scared to die. But I'm scared to die. If you get shot and you don't die instantly than what you gon' do? You gon' say "oh well, I'm just gon' die?!" I'm ducking every bullet I can.

The students above expressed fears that are not often attributed to teenagers. These feelings stand in opposition to the views of scholars and others who argue that adolescents have a tendency to engage in reckless behavior, in part, because of a lack of fear of the consequences. While this may be the case for some teenagers, it is certainly not the case for all teenagers. Fear was very present in these young people's narratives since they knew first-hand the *real* threat of death.

However, an alternate consequence of their frequent exposure to violence was that other students from both schools had distanced themselves from it to the point where some expressed that they no longer worried about dying young:

> I don't get scared anymore. I'm so used to it. Two of my brothers dead, about 50 a my cousins . . . I mean, what's to be scared of now? I just been around it for so long. I ain't even scared. I don't care. I mean, that's just the way I feel.

> It doesn't bother me. Four of my cousins got shot. We all used to be together. Three of them lived, and one of them died. One got shot in the leg, one shot in the stomach, one got shot in the back and one got shot in the head. He died. And I used to be with them, going places and whatever. It don't worry me.

> People get used to it [people getting killed] cause you see it all around you. The way the violence surrounds us, you see it on television, somebody you know dies, when you say 'somebody die' its not unusual anymore. We don't even think twice about it.

> Ain't nothing you can do about it. I mean, how can you avoid somebody shooting you? What can you do? You can't do nothing.

> You might have your plans set up. You got too much to live for.

> When it's your time to go, you gon' go.

In this stage of desensitization, young people may be very hard to reach, and it may, in fact, be a result of this coping mechanism of distancing themselves—rather than a lack of fear—that may cause young people to engage in dangerous behaviors. However, from these narratives a pattern of experience seems to emerge: Young people become aware of the violence, and this awareness is followed first by fear, and finally, perhaps as a way to cope, distance and desensitization. Though this is surely not the only path that young people travel as they struggle to cope with violence, knowing that such paths exist can assist adults in helping youth. It may be easier, for example, to reach a student who feels afraid than one who feels that their situation is hopeless and inevitable.

In summary, violence among youth increased at such an alarming rate that by 1991 medical and public health officials declared a national health emergency. Yet, despite the devastating effects of violence on children and the intimate knowledge with which some of them have come to know and experience violence as part of their everyday lives, for the most part their voices and perceptions either are never sought, or are ignored. In the following section, I will examine why young people's opinions about an issue they know so well through lived experience are rarely sought. I will also discuss some of the myths and generally held beliefs about violence by and among youth.

PUBLIC PERCEPTIONS OF YOUTH AND VIOLENCE

Despite the present media attention proclaiming youth violence as a new trend in American society, violence among youth has always been a part of the social fabric of America. In a historical perspective of youth violence, Croddy begins with synopses of three news reports.[16] One described a murder of a young man that resulted from a drunken brawl. Another described the death of an innocent young girl that resulted from a "drive-by" shooting between rival gang members. The third was based on a news report of the Leopold and Loeb murder, which was the kidnapping and brutal murder of a fourteen-year-old by two young college men from upper-middle-class backgrounds. These incidents took place not in the 1990s, but in 1837, 1930, and 1924 respectively, and they exemplify the fact that youth violence has been around for a lot longer than people today realize or are willing to admit.

Concern over crime and violence started to rise in the mid-1990s when, fueled in part by the media's focus on violence, it appeared to many that the issue seemed to be moving beyond the boundaries of so-called ghetto neighborhoods. In fact, the vast majority of the reports of violent crime among youth, then and more recently, focused primarily on youth in impoverished neighborhoods known as "ghettos."

Ghettos are pockets of communities located in resource poor environments, where high rates of poverty and related stressors create a difficult life for members of that community. Historically, in the United States, the term *ghetto* referred to parts of cities largely inhabited by immigrant Jews from central and eastern Europe who came to America in the early part of the century. Today's ghetto communities are seen exclusively as communities of economically disadvantaged minorities, particularly African Americans and Latinos. However, despite the change in the racial make-up of the ghetto communities, there are common threads between the early ghettos and the communities referred to as such today. Some of the primary threads are concentrated poverty, economic destabilization, and isolation from mainstream America.[17]

Additionally, in the early part of the century, as is the case today, trafficking in illegal substances exacerbated the rates of violence in these neighborhoods, though the profits from outlawed alcohol have been replaced by the profits from illicit drugs. Although the question about whether or not violence is worse today has yet to be answered, what is clear is that violence among youth is not new. What is also not new is the view of ghetto communities as hotbeds that nurture perpetrators of violence. One consequence of this view is that people living in these neighborhoods are the primary focus of violence discourse and policy actions (many of them punitive) that are established to combat violence.

In his discussion of the history of the juvenile justice system in this country, Ayers[18] highlights the contributions of Jane Addams, with help of other "child-saving" patrons, to the establishment of the first children's court on July 1, 1899, in Chicago. Though Ayers observes that Addams and the others acted primarily out of concern for the welfare of children, he also discusses their conceptions of "other people's children," the children whom they were focused on "saving." These were the children who lived in poverty, in homes described as "destitute" with parents deemed "unfit"; children of the "have-nots," whose lives could only be saved by the intervention of the "haves." Resonant with the earlier discussion of ghetto communities, Ayers cites Jane Addams' comment that "four-fifths of the children brought into the Juvenile Court in Chicago are the children of foreigners. The Germans are the greatest offenders, Polish next."[19] This comment distinguished the children who were in need of the help of people like Jane Addams and at the same time pinpointed those who were juvenile delinquents. In turn, this perception fostered action based on what Ayers refers to as "a single, severe assumption":

> We—the respectable, the prosperous, the superior, and (especially in modern times) the professional—know what is best for *Them*—the masses, the poor, the outcast, the wretched of the earth. . . . Other people are made into the objects of our interest and experimentation. They are rendered voiceless and faceless.[20]

Despite the good intentions of Jane Addams and others, the tendency to conceptualize the poor as having the ability to specially produce delinquents has been operant from the inception of a juvenile justice system. Ayers summarizes that "the notion of 'juvenile delinquency,' then and now, focused on children of the urban poor—from Charles Dickens's 'street urchins' to today's 'superpredators.' "[21]

In contemporary times, with the changing faces of poor Americans and present day immigrants from so-called whites to so-called people of color, this conception of the juvenile delinquent has intensified, as referenced above in Ayers's description of today's youth as "superpredators." Dohrn expands on this conception in her discussion of the "false fears and hard truths" about youth violence. She writes that

> much of America is convinced that young people—particularly African American youth and children of color—are a menace; that these children, violent and without remorse, must be contained and feared. Many adults seem convinced that most adolescents are different from the teens we once were, that they are no longer children, that they are *bad*.[22]

These statements represent public indictment of all youth, and African American and other minority youth in particular, even though as Dohrn goes on to note, "less than one-half of 1 percent of all juveniles in the United States were arrested for violent offenses." Additionally, the author writes that

- of the relatively small number of juveniles arrested, only 5 percent of them were arrested for a violent crime;
- if all the youth violence were eliminated, 86 percent of the violent crimes would still exist;
- the majority of children in detention and correctional facilities are there for nonviolent offenses; and, as argued earlier,
- youth violence in this society is not new.[23]

Nonetheless, the conception of youth as delinquent provides as least one explanation of why the voices of these youth are deemed irrelevant in discussions about an issue that so affects their lives. It is as if to say that the voices of youth cannot be relevant because they are the cause of the problem. Thus, those youth who are poor, who find themselves faced with concentrated, society-induced adversities such as poverty, community estrangement from mainstream society, drug and alcohol abuse, and violence, are also forced to battle the historical, generally accepted perception that they are the primary cause for the dire circumstances in which they find themselves. Within this notion is the idea that, in fact, *all* poor and minority youth have the proclivity to become delinquent. Moreover, these youth are also blamed for the drain their supposedly self-perpetuated circumstances place on the "productive" citizens of this society. The prevalence of these misrepresentations results in the popular, albeit erroneous, perception that such individuals are not capable of *knowing* what's best for their own lives.

An unfortunate result of the public perception of youth as responsible for the problem of violence leaves no room for the voices of their resistance to be listened to. I posit schools as the place where students should be allowed to express their views and perspectives about this and related issues. However, teachers and school administrators, as members of this society, may also be influenced by misperceptions about the youth in schools in their classrooms. It is inevitable that these misconceptions affect the interactions between teachers and students, especially in urban inner-city schools.

TEACHERS WHO SERVE YOUTH COPING WITH VIOLENCE

The omnipresent threat of violence in the lives of thousands of America's youth severely detracts from the quality of life in their families and communities and affects the schools and teachers serving them. Unfortunately, in many schools in poor communities, teachers inhabit a landscape shaped by a tidal wave of violence coupled with public anger and frustration against young people. In writing about her experiences as a teacher at Medgar Evers High School in the Watts community of Southern California, Diver-Stamnes notes how she and her colleagues "often felt we were on the front lines in a war without having been given the weapons to fight the battle."[24] She explains that having little or no specialized training for teaching in the inner city and using inferior textbooks and equipment in a filthy, dilapidated school building added to the stress the teachers felt. Diver-Stamnes' experiences highlight how violence affects the teaching and learning that occurs in schools similar to the one in which she taught. Approaching violence in the schools from this perspective exposes teachers' struggles in educating students in these environments. On the one hand, they are called upon to impart knowledge and skills to increase the opportunities for their students' futures, yet, with limited resources and support, teachers often experience a sense of futility in their efforts to educate their students for a future that is questionable in literal terms of students' survival. Importantly and correctly, Diver-Stamnes contextualizes students' literal death in the symbolic death of neglect and hopelessness conveyed in the disregard of the school by the district. She uses the neglect exemplified in the lack of resources and building maintenance, among other things, to expose the myths of meritocracy and equality promised by an education which obviously was not being offered to the students at Medgar Evers High School, despite the good intentions and best efforts of teachers like Diver-Stamnes.

Additionally, perceived or actual violence among the youth may deter teachers' involvement with students because of fear for their own personal safety. Given the traumatic circumstances under which they are forced to teach, and perhaps buying into popular opinion that *all* of the young people in these environments are prone to violence, some teachers choose not to become involved with their students. Dohrn comments that "teachers on the front lines have reason to both champion the needs of children *and* to be genuinely afraid."[25] Often teachers, parents, and those who work with youth are both frightened and besieged, and, as a result, may decide to distance themselves as much as possible from realities of their students' lives, such as violence. Then there are others, Anita Bland and myself, who acknowledge that, because our lives are indeed very different from the lives of our students, there is a need to know about their lives in order to more effectively teach them. We allowed our classrooms to be forums where we could learn more about the everyday struggles of the young people we teach.

I believe that schools offer us the best hope of reaching millions of children, in particular children who are frequently exposed to violence and who still manage to get to school everyday. As I will show in the narratives detailed later in this paper, these children offer unique insights about the challenges they face as a result of their experiences, insights which can be utilized in the development of more effective ways for adults to help these young people deal with the violence and loss. In the remaining pages, I present the voices and perspectives of youth. These youth offered commentary regarding the effectiveness of schools and teachers in combating the problem and offered viable solutions to the problems of violence in their lives.

LISTEN TO THE CHILDREN

In the students' narratives are themes of desensitization and their fears and concern about their own mortality and future described earlier. In the following pages, the students discuss peer pressure to be involved with gangs, distrust of the police, and frustration with the paramedics. Students comment on the stereotypical representations of African Americans in the media as a contributing factor to the unreliability of the paramedics in saving children's lives. The students also address the ineffectiveness of schools and teachers in assisting them to cope with the violence in their lives. As their narratives will show, the above issues are presented in an interrelated complexity, not as separate, compartmentalized issues, which is the way policy makers usually present the issues to the public. For example, students examine the issue of gangs in relation to parental involvement and police harassment.

In a discussion, one young African American male said, "I think the people who join gangs, their parents don't teach them better." There were very loud protests following this statement. Some responses were:

> Its not about that though.

> Everybody says it starts at home. Maybe you do get your good training at home but it don't matter about your good training at home. You gotta get out on the street and show people that you are different. Its about not being left out.

> It ain't about starting at home because my brother is dead today. My momma did everything for me and my brother. I mean he had a good home. She gave us a place to stay, gave us everything we wanted, so it ain't about what happened at home. And look where he at, he dead right now. So it don't come from home.

Similar narratives were recorded in the predominantly Latino/a classroom of the New Jersey middle school:

> If I had to put this violence to an end I would get a lot of these parents together and teach them how to control their kids.

> It's not the parents' fault that their kids are violent because you never know if they are teaching their kids not to do violence. Some of them [the kids] could get it from the streets.

In the above statements, the young people juxtaposed the parental efforts to dissuade their children from becoming involved with the wrong crowd with peer pressure faced by young people to do otherwise, and as one of the students noted, "it's about not being left out." These young people crystallized the real challenge of negative peer pressure despite the "good training" they may receive at home. Their understanding that people live in these neighborhoods because of their family's economic circumstances contrasts with the usually proffered perspective that young people involved in gangs are all from dysfunctional families or families where the children are neglected.[26]

Students' awareness that some parents were trying, though often unsuccessfully, to prevent their children from participating in destructive behavior also contributed to the students' critique of how African Americans in low-income neighborhoods are portrayed in the media's reporting of violence:

> If you're a teenager and you get killed, automatically, they say you were in a gang. Everytime a teenager gets killed, they just say its gang related, au-

tomatically. No questions asked. If a Mexican person or a Black person get killed in a bad neighborhood, everyone assume they a drug dealer. You can't just assume because somebody get killed they a drug dealer. That's just not right.

I'm not racist or nothing. But most of the time when a White person get killed, he or she was an innocent bystander. But if he was Black or Mexican, it was gang related. Like that Chinese guy that got killed, they say it was gang related.

I remember, I was little when this happened, my cousin he worked for the mayor over in [a nearby city]. He got shot and killed and the media and everyone was talking about how he was gang related, but he was all trying to help the mayor. Everytime I talk to my dad about it he says it's prejudice."

Its a lotta youngsters, Black youngsters dying and they don't solve who kill who, but now if its a White person, its on the news, its on everything. Black people die everyday and you don't hear about it. It don't be on the news.

In the above quotes, the students invoke the racial disparities pertaining to the reported death of a young person of color versus that of a young white person, and the tendency of the media to blur the lines of distinction between the victim and the perpetrator in reporting the violent deaths of minority youth and establishing the possibility of innocent victims only in violent deaths of white youth. The students were very aware of a public perception of the youth in their neighborhood as "bad" and, as such, involved in misconduct, namely, gang activity, which unfortunately for them resulted in their death. This rationalization thus implicates the victims in their own demise and, conversely, absolves society's responsibility to address the problem beyond asking teenagers to make better choices for their lives. However, the voices of the students disrupt such rationalizations and invoke the likelihood of the dead teenager as possibly an innocent bystander. The students' narratives broaden the discourse of violence beyond a rhetoric of wrongdoing to include the loss of young innocent African American teenagers and other teenagers of color.

Students' awareness of negative public perceptions of youth also has an impact on their perceptions of the role of the police in their neighborhood. As was discussed earlier, these students were wary and distrustful of the police after some of the experiences they have had with law enforcement officers:

The world is so bad and everything [bad] look like its the Black people. We cannot be afraid of gangs, because there is a legal gang called the po-leece [students' phonetic expression of the word "police"]. They walk the town with guns. They can do a drive-by anytime they like. They can beat anybody they like as we seen [reference to the Rodney King beating] and get away with it. That's the gang we can be afraid of.

I saw some people trying to rob this guy. I was across the street when it happened and so they [the police] came to me, trying to arrest me cause I was across the street. They said I helped them [the robbers] and I was across the street when it happened. My dad said if I go to court they probably gon' convict me cause I'm Black. I don't like that. That's not right.

I was once talking to a police officer who said that when they get the reports that people getting shot, when they [the police] hear the neighborhood, they say they take their time on purpose. The police just say, we're not going to go. We'll just let them kill themselves. So the police will take their time on purpose if someone get shot in a bad neighborhood.

My auntie, she live in a bad neighborhood. She called the police one night cause a boy over there bothering my cousin, and they was out there and they was about to fight and she called the police cause they had a gun or a knife or something. She called the police and the police would not come cause they didn't want to come in the neighborhood.

When my cousin got killed, the police took a really long time. This lady had called the police before my cousin had even got killed. This boy came up on him and he tried to rob him and my cousin said "You ain't robbing me." And then the lady, it was in front of this lady's house and she called the police and you know the police ain't come till like, till about an hour after my cousin was dead. My cousin was laying on the sidewalk he and this other boy cause he shot him at the same time [as he was shot] . They [the police] didn't come till about an hour later. Now two damn bodies laying out there on the sidewalk, laying there , and they didn't come till about an hour later. I think my cousin woulda made it if the police had came.

Students expressed a lot of anger because of law enforcement officers' seeming disregard for the lives of young people. Students' mistreatment by the police, and in some instances conversations with members of the force, confirmed their perceptions that the role of the police in their communities was not one of protection and service, but rather, punishment and surveillance.[27]

Geoffrey Canada's report of his childhood encounters with the police buttresses the above statements. He wrote that "most police officers who work in the inner cities are not from these neighborhoods. They have no appreciation of the culture or the makeup of the community. They find themselves in a strange environment where the people are often hostile. They don't recognize any sense of community—they see chaos instead— and so often they can't discriminate between one element of the community and another. They end up treating everyone as if they were guilty until proven otherwise."[28] Ironically, in a comparison of the mortality rates of police and children, the Children's Defense Fund reported that "a child dies from gunshot wounds every two hours while a police officer is killed by guns every five days and nine hours."[29]

Too frequently we hear of incidents of police brutality with citizens of poor neighborhoods. In her analysis of the many factors contributing to violence among the youth, Prothrow-Stith comments on the inhumane treatment of young males—and those of African American racial identity in particular—by the police in cities such as Long Beach and Los Angeles in California, Boston, New York, and Philadelphia. She cites a belief held by police that

> even the most innocent-looking youth may be armed with deadly force, and willing, even eager, to use that force. To protect themselves, the police feel that they must treat every kid in every inner city neighborhood as a potential killer. This belief has caused relations between police and communities of color, never good to begin with, to deteriorate.[30]

While Prothrow-Stith frames her argument within the present-day crisis of increased access and use of handguns by youth in the inner cities, Canada[31] discusses perspectives about African Americans that were held by police in 1959. While Prothrow-Stith frames the police's beliefs as a response to the frequency of deadly force used by the youth—although she does note that relations between the two groups was "never good to begin with"—both Canada's and her examples are threaded with a disregard and lack of respect held by the police for members of inner-city communities. One student offered an example from her own life of how the perceptions of the community and the attitudes of the police combined to adversely affect the timely medical treatment of victims of violence:

> When you call them [the police] like 3 or 4 in the morning they don't come at all. But the reason most of the Black kids is dying though is because of the paramedics. Its like when my brother got killed, they [the paramedics] don't come before the police. They wait for the police to come, to come rescue . . . , because they be so scared to come into the Black community. I guess they think they gon' get beat up or something if they don't take care of them [the victims] right, so they wait for the police to come, in order for them to come. I guess they were scared to come into the neighborhood.
>
> They building a new [medical center in the neighborhood]. They should make a trauma center in there. They gotta fly all the way to [a trauma center several miles away]. They be killing them here, but they [the victim] gotta wait for the helicopter to come, pick 'em up, they gotta fly all the way to [the hospital] All the kids are dying in [the city] so they should just make a hospital [here] to treat the kids.

Overwhelmingly, these students were acknowledging society's indictment and consequent marginalization of entire communities under siege by both sides of the law, where all police behavior was justifiable, where paramedics were afraid to come, and where hospitals could not be built despite the incredible need. Attention to the voices of the youth might lead one to wonder how far the implementation of new policy regarding timely arrival of paramedics in high-crime neighborhoods would go toward changing students' perceptions of adults' ability to help them cope with violence.

Finally, the students were eloquent in their appraisal of what schools can do:

> School's the place where all these different kids from all these different environments come together, so what you'd expect is the same feelings they would have at home or on the streets, they bring it to school. I feel like there's such a generation gap between the kids and the teachers, and when the kids come to school, they already have the feeling that they can't talk to them. So the teachers who really want to reach the kids are completely blocked out. They give up and they're just the same as all the teachers who don't care.

> They [the teachers] expect too much from us [given what we have to deal with].

> Its kinda hard to talk to your teachers because you kinda feel like that they don't know what's going on cause they're older and they wouldn't understand. They just don't understand how we feel about our community; how we feel about people dying. They just don't take the time out to talk to us about that.

As far as these students were concerned, schools as they have experienced them were incapable of doing anything about violence among the youth.

Nonetheless, the need for more caring adults in the lives of children dealing with violence is imperative. Through their essays and conversations in these classrooms, for these moments of time in their school experiences, students were able to talk about an issue that had a significant impact on their lives and one which they live with daily. The students' narratives presented in this paper highlight how important the voices of the youth are in understanding and addressing the complexities of youth violence. Violence and poverty do not only affect these youth and their families. They affect our schools, our society, and, inevitably, our future.

CONCLUSION

History indicates that violence among the youth is not a new phenomenon. It is a multicausal problem affecting all segments of the population, although it has reached epidemic proportions in the inner cities of America. Numerous studies have detailed not only the chilling correlation between the accessibility of handguns and the death toll among the youth in America's inner cities, but the adverse consequences on children's mental and physical health that have resulted from frequent exposure to violence.

However, public perceptions of youth as menaces—minority youth and African American males in particular—result in the stigmatization of all youth in these inner-city neighborhoods.[32] This stigmatization further obscures the voices of youth who are not part of the problem but who are, most definitely, part of the solution. It is at this juncture that the role of schools and teachers in the lives of these young people can be useful. However, the values and beliefs of society and our government, not just schools and teachers, need to come to terms with the disparities that hinder the creation of viable alternatives for these young people. Current discourses and consequent policies on youth violence obviate the narratives of the youth living in the midst yet not a part of the violence. To legislate effective policy addressing youth violence it is necessary to hear—to listen to—the voices of those most affected by the issues: the youth themselves.

NOTES

1. Cornell West, preface to *Our America: Life and Death on the South Side of Chicago,* eds. L. Jones & L. Newman, with D. Isay (New York: Scribner, 1997), 177.

2. West, *Our America,* 11.

3. West, *Our America,* 12.

4. *Creating Original Opera* is a national educational outreach program of the Metropolitan Opera Guild in New York City sponsored in part by the GE Fund and the Geraldine R. Dodge Foundation. Stephanie Spina, the editor of this volume, served as a consultant for part of a multiyear collaborative evaluation of the opera program, conducted by PACE (Projects in Active Cultural Engagement) at the Harvard Graduate School of Education. The narratives used here, although based on essays and interviews that were not part of the opera project or its evaluation, owe much to the context that program provided. (For additional information about the opera program, see *Evaluations of Creating Original Opera* (Cambridge, Mass.: PACE, 1995–96 and 1996–97).

5. See W. Ayers, "I Walk with Delinquents," *Educational Leadership* 55 (1977): 48–51; Geoffrey Canada, *Fist, Stick, Knife, Gun: A Personal History of Violence in America* (Boston: Beacon Press, 1995); and P. Orenstein, *School Girls: Young Women Self-Esteem and the Confidence Gap* (New York: Doubleday, 1994).

6. U.S. Department of Justice Office of Juvenile Justice and Delinquency Prevention, *Juvenile Offenders and Victims: A National Report.* (Washington, D.C., August 1995): 56.

7. *Juvenile Offenders,* 56

8. Canada, *Fist, Stick;* A. Diver-Stamnes, *Lives in the Balance: Youth, Poverty and Education in Watts.* (New York: SUNY Press, 1995); D. Prothrow-Stith, *Deadly Consequences: How Violence is Destroying Our Teenage Population and a Plan to Begin Solving the Problem* (New York: HarperCollins, 1991).

9. C. C. Bell and E. J. Jenkins, "Community Violence and Children on the Southside of Chicago." *Psychiatry* 56 (1993): 46–54.

10. P. Martinez and J. E. Richters, "The NIMH Community Violence Project II. Children's Distress Symptoms Associated with Violence Exposure." *Psychiatry* 56:(1993) 22–35.

11. Martinez and Richters, "The NIMH Community," 22–35.

12. K. M. Fitzpatrick and J. P. Boldizar, "The Prevalence and Consequences of Exposure to Violence Among African American Youth." *Journal of the American Academy of Child and Adolescent Psychiatry* 32(1993): 424–430.

13. Fitzpatrick and Boldizar, "The Prevalence and Consequences of Exposure to Violence," 427.

14. S. Eth and R. Pynoos, *Developmental Perspectives on Psychic Trauma in Childhood: In Trauma and Its Wake.* (New York: Brunner and Mazel, 1984); L. Fingerhut, J. Kleinman, E. Godfrey, and H. Rosenberg, "Firearm Mortality Among Children, Youth and Young Adults 1–34 Years of Age, Trends and Current Status: United States, 1979–1988," *Monthly Vital Statistics Report* 39 (1991): 424–430; L. Freeman, H. Mokros, and E. Poznanski, "Violent Events Reported by Normal Urban School-aged Children: Characteristics and Depression Correlates." *Journal of the American Academy of Child and Adolescent Psychiatry* 32 (1993): 419–423; B. Shakoor and D. Chalmers, "Co-victimization of African American Children Who Witness Violence and the Theoretical Implications of its Effect on Their Cognitive, Emotional, and Behavioral Development," *Journal of the National Medical Association* 81 (1989): 93–98.

15. Children's Defense Fund, *State of America's Children Yearbook 1994.* (Washington, D.C.: The Children's Defense Fund, 1994), vii.

16. M. Croddy, "Violence Redux: A Brief Legal and Historical Perspective on Youth Violence," *Social Education* 61 (Sept., 1997): 258–264.

17. K. Auletta, *The Underclass* (New York: Vintage Books, 1983); W. J. Wilson, *The Truly Disadvantaged* (Chicago: University of Chicago Press, 1987).

18. W. Ayers, "I Walk with Delinquents," 48–51.

19. Ayers, "I Walk with Delinquents," 41.

20. Ayers, "I Walk with Delinquents," 41.

21. Ayers, "I Walk with Delinquents," 42.

22. B. Dohrn, "Youth Violence: False Fears and Hard Truths," *Educational Leadership* 55 (Oct., 1997): 45–47.

23. Dohrn, "Youth Violence," 46.

24. Diver-Stamnes, *Lives in the Balance, 108.*

25. Dohrn, "Youth Violence," 47.

26. See also A. Abner, "Gangsta Girls," *Essence Magazine* 66 (July 1994): 64–66, 116–118; and Charles "Paco" Hernandez, "Wearing the Colors: A Personal Narrative from a 'Die-hard' Educator," this volume.

27. See Peter McLaren, Zeus Leonardo, and Ricky Lee Allen, "Rated 'CV' for Cool Violence," this volume.

28. Canada, *Stick, Fist,* 128.

29. Quoted in Canada, *Stick, Fist,* 147.

30. Prothrow-Stith, *Deadly consequences,* 122.

31. Canada, *Stick, Fist.*

32. See Henry Giroux, "Representations of Violence, Popular Culture, and Demonization of Youth," this volume.

3

Rated "CV" for Cool Violence

Peter McLaren, Zeus Leonardo,
and Ricky Lee Allen

Hay que hacer la opresión real todavía más opresiva añadiendo a aquella la con-
ciencia de la opresión haciendo lu infamia todavía, mas infamente, al prego-
narla. [Real oppression is made still more oppressive by adding to it the
consciousness of that oppression, making infamy even more infamous
while proclaiming it.]

—Marx and Engels[1]

This is how one pictures the angel of history. His face is turned toward
the past. Where we perceive a chain of events, he sees one single catastrophe which keeps on piling wreckage upon wreckage and hurls it in
front of his feet.
  The angel would like to stay, awake and dead, and make whole what
has been smashed. But a storm is blowing from Paradise, it has got
caught in his wings with such violence that the angel can no longer
close them. This storm irresistibly propels him into the future to which
his back is turned, while the pile of debris before him grows skyward.
  The storm is what we call progress.

—Walter Benjamin[2]

In recent years, violence in U.S. schools has taken on increasing importance as parents, educators, and students experience unparalleled structures, if not the physical threat, of daily assaults. Gun control in schools
has inspired a bunker mentality as urban campuses throughout the country institute weapon checkpoints when students enter their site of learning. Real, physical violence has become a possibility in the daily lives of

many students, especially those whose schools represent a symptom of structural inequalities at the local level. However, and without downplaying the painful reality of physical violence, we want to focus on the invidious and infectious consequences of discursive violence, to construct a language of critique that unseams the representation of violence and the violence of representation. That is, we want to explore the ways in which schools propagate violence at the level of the sign and at spaces of struggle over meaning.

VIOLENCE AS A "GIFT"

Discursive violations often escape critical scrutiny due to their often less-than-immediate effects and the ways they symbolically inscribe student subjectivities. We are arguing that because of its commonsense association with communication, discourse becomes normalized as a natural exchange. Yet, according to Foucault, this represents the power of discourse.[3] Discourses normalize the codes of knowing and render them legitimate as part of an overall rationalization process. What Foucault's resistance postmodernism lacks in terms of a strategy to subvert the power of violence (since power begets power) can perhaps be found in Jean Baudrillard's theory of the gift.[4] Originally the gift was an anthropological import developed by Marcel Mauss to explain aspects of Melanesian and Polynesian symbolic cultures. He explains their rituals this way:

> Many ideas and principles are to be noted in systems of this type. The most important of these spiritual mechanisms is clearly the one which obliges us to make a return gift for a "gift received." Refusing to give is like a "declaration of war" . . . No one was free to refuse a present offered to him. Each man and woman tried to outdo the others in generosity. There was a sort of amiable rivalry as to who could give away the greatest number of most valuable presents. . . . The objects are never completely separated from the men who exchange them. . . . Failure to give or receive, like failure to make return gifts, means a loss of dignity.[5]

Mauss's observations of gift rituals inspired Baudrillard's theory of the gift as a "symbolic exchange." Baudrillard prefers the indeterminacy or ambiguity of symbolic exchange to the economic determinism of political economy. On some level, material violence has become an alibi for our general lack of attentiveness of discursive violence. Baudrillard's rearticulation of the gift should not be taken as a literal offering. It represents a fundamental *challenge*. As Pierre Bourdieu puts it: "If it is not to constitute an insult, the counter-gift must be *deferred* and *different*, because the immediate return of an exactly identical object clearly amounts to a refusal (i.e., the return of the same object)." (Italics in original.)[6] Failing to appropriately receive or return a "gift" institutes power in favor of the giver. For as Bourdieu reminds us, giving is a form of possessing.[7] The intent behind the gift is very important; the gift is meant to honor those with noble motivations and to relegate others to an ignominious status. In order to preserve equilibrium in symbolic exchange, one must reciprocate a gift with a counter-gift.

By using Baudrillard's theory of symbolic exchange (and to a lesser extent Bourdieu's), we understand discursive violence to be a form of "gift." In schools, subaltern discourses and their carriers are given the "gift" of silence. This is manifest in various ways. For example, in order to become full participants in classroom discourse, students of color must forfeit their cultural capital in exchange for a white, patriarchal, and heterosexual perspective. This produces an identity crisis in students who find themselves having to choose between academic "success" and cultural integrity.[8] This gift of silence is sometimes returned by marginalized students in the form of nonparticipation. That is, silence begets silence as these objectified subjects relatively penetrate the ideology behind success and disqualify themselves.[9] In fact, this form of censored voice leads to other forms of violence because it denies subjects their right to name the world.[10]

In his study of the "mass," Baudrillard salvages silence as a strategy which engenders violence in its own right. He theorizes the silence of the mass as such:

[T]heir strength is *actual*, in the present, and sufficient unto itself. It consists in their silence, in their capacity to absorb and neutralise, already superior to any power acting upon them. . . . The mass absorbs all the social energy, but no longer reflects them. For every question put to it, it sends back a tautological and circular response. It never participates. (Italics in original.)[11]

In addition to the more conventional interpretation of silence as a sign of alienation from the total process of labor or due political process, we must consider seriously Baudrillard's suggestion that transgression is to be found in silence. One only has to recall the aggressiveness engendered by a person who refuses to participate in an argument by enacting the "silent treatment." The non-verbal, yet semiotically aggressive, message from such a response is unequivocal in its attempt to subvert the power of speech. The overbearingness of argumentative perspectives is canceled out and thrown back to itself with the apathy of the object(ified). Thus, the violence instituted by a curriculum that dismisses the Other's perspective is compromised (at times canceled) by the power of those who do not wish to participate in its language games. The challenge for transformative educators is to redirect this return gift of silence toward the desire for collective transgression, an organic hush over the administrative gaze.

Discursive violence is often the subtle maintenance of more overt forms of violence. Theorizing the mechanics of covert violence, Bourdieu has activated a concept of "symbolic violence."[12] According to Bourdieu, symbolic violence is veiled in rituals and symbolic interactions. He writes,

> [W]hen domination can only be exercised in its *elementary form*, i.e., directly, between one person and another, it cannot take place overtly and must be disguised under the veil of enchanted relationships, the official model of which is presented by relations between kinsmen; in order to be socially recognized it must get itself misrecognized.[13] [Italics in original.]

We arrive at the "legitimate" use of authority at the level of the symbolic and *soft* violence. In other words, symbolic violence is the *cool* and "euphemized" version of material, economic violence. In contrast to the hot violence of material exploitation, cool violence functions under the pretenses of guiles and ruses, of which the gift (e.g., obligations) is only one of many. The object of violence falls victim to its machinations, not so much through coercion, but through *complicity* and by embodying the objective structures of violence vis-à-vis the *habitus*. (Italics in original.)[14] The power behind sanctioned violence is administered more efficiently when it can cloak itself as other than itself; that is, as an objective structure. Symbolic violence works best in the absence of outright oppressive consequences, but through disciplinary mechanisms that make it the precondition for participating in symbolic interactions. According to Bourdieu, power, like symbolic violence, is often misrecognized for what it is. Of power, Foucault writes,

> Power is tolerable only on condition that it mask a substantial part of itself. Its success is proportional to its ability to hide its own mechanisms. . . . New methods of power whose operation is not ensured by right but by technique, not by law but by normalization, not by punishment but by control, methods that are employed on all levels and in forms that go beyond the state and its apparatus.[15]

Symbolic violence and symbolic power work side by side. They inscribe our actions without at the same time producing them. The legitimation of power is generated as a symbolic surplus value which is secured by reifying differences into distinctions through equally reified rituals and customs.[16]

Thus, we arrive at the relative importance of discourse in liberating students from violent regimes of signification supporting and supported by material social relations of capitalist exploitation. Critical educators must recognize the important role that discourse plays in inscribing the subjective choices of students. Discursive violence occurs when the historical *work of meaning* is obscured and meaning is fetishized as natural and not recognized as being produced in historical struggle. Or as John Thompson suggests, discursive violence is the power to make certain meanings or significations *stick*.[17] Violence here is a product of the struggle over the signified. Although we are arguing for the relative importance of ideas at the level of discourse, we are not suggesting that ideas themselves are real, but that they produce real consequences.

Discourses in themselves do not produce material realities, as if utterance by itself gives rise to the existence of its contents. However, this does not negate the historical effects of reification whereby narratives told over and over again (and supported by institutional structures) become reified material realities, as in the case of educational tracking. Oakes has found that despite negligible *academic* differences at a young age between children from different races, narratives regarding who is intelligent, for example, and who is not (and supported by tracking practices) produce real, material consequences such that children from different races exhibit disparities in test scores as they advance in age.[18] In turn, this form of narrative violence manifests itself in social and economic outcomes, limiting the life chances of many students of color. However, we have seen the pitfalls of the position that there is "no outside" to discourse, as if "monsters are as real as material things."[19]

Certain discursive repertoires are a direct result of material forces and realities. We tell narratives because we have experienced something and desire to communicate its meaning. In this manner, discourse is based on a slice of material reality. Students create discourses about school life and the myriad interests which inscribe them as they make sense of experience through language. We want to make it clear that experiences never speak for themselves, as if language captures their essential, transcendental meaning. Meanings are concomitant with the limited constellation of discourses to which subjects have access (e.g., their concepts, epistemic rules, and ideological interests). Educators can provide students with the gift of critical discourse, a condition where meanings are neither arrived at through semiotic closure in order to leave signifieds in historical abeyance nor are they indeterminate to the point where students fail to find the agency to act. Hence, though language alone cannot negate violence, a change in discursive structures produces change *effects* that become available for counter-hegemonic purposes. We hope to make this line of reasoning clearer as we proceed.

At the very least, radical discourses allow students to "see" social life in more critical ways so that they can ask questions which may, in turn, lead to an increased desire for social justice. The violence of dominant discourses buries underneath their interests a mound of meanings associated with marginalized voices. Yet, these subaltern voices subvert hegemony when recovered for revolutionary purposes. Students need to critically interrogate those memories, voices, and perspectives in history that the current episteme has repressed in order to recognize that the history of U.S. education has been built upon the backs of the oppressed.

If the act of seeing is a de facto act of violence because there is much that is veiled from our view, then critical educators must forge a new discourse around what it means to "see" the world. Upon our *perception* of them, ideas are said to be registered by the body. That is, they are grasped by the experiential senses as these are inscribed by discourse. At their *inception*, ideas are signified through language; they are given shape through linguistic imprints and terms. This is the moment when an idea becomes a linguistic sign. At their *conception*, ideas become part of mental schema in the Kantian sense of fitting them into *a priori* categories. Through *deception*, ideas produce forms of false consciousness which, according to Marx, obscure the objective basis of social life in commodity production, that social existence produces human consciousness, not vice versa.[20] Inception, perception, conception, and deception are all ways of (mis)viewing an idea. Moreover, they are all part and parcel to the process of hegemony at the level of the sign.

If the act of seeing is, on some level, a recapitulation of hegemony—and therefore, a form of violence—then a transformation of our construction of world views is necessary. Critical educators must forge a new discourse around *contra-ception*, or those sensibilities and strategies which are counter-hegemonic, in order to assist students in a radical critique of the ways they currently "see" the social order. Contra-ception enables us to understand, as structured social beings, that *subjects do not only read signs but that signs also read them*. Through contra-ception, progressive teachers can proceed to deconstruct the "political economy of the sign," or how commodities are produced as sign and the sign as commodity.[21]

Contra-ception builds a language of critique around the ways violence is perpetrated on the Other and simultaneously commodified for profit. Take the event of Mike Tyson's biting Evander Holyfield's ear. There has been much discussion in the media around the violence manifested in this single act at the expense of critical reflection over the *general* violence in the sport itself. In Baudrillardean terms, the ear biting becomes an *alibi* for boxing's violent political economy. At the infamous fight, a spectator picked up a piece of cartilage which had fallen onto the mat from Holyfield's ear. It is estimated that the piece of flesh has a market value of $30,000. Mainstream discussions of the event have failed to critique the commodification of the spectacular image found in men of color pummeling each other, almost to the point of physical discordance, for a living. Contra-ception would work toward a critical re-view of these and other violent relations.

However, contra-ception also guards against essentialist readings of social life. Any reading is at best partial. Social life is not an unmediated relation, or a simple correspondence between the real and the experience. Rather, subjects live daily life as an imagined relation to the real relations of production.[22] That is, world view (or Althusserian ideology) comes to subjects in the form of representations of the real. Contra-ception partakes of a discursive function that disaggregates and disarms violent representations from potentially transformative ones. It constitutes a way of seeing the social that provides students with the basis for a critical pedagogy of everyday life—a life never fully present to itself, but one that is represented through particular interests and specific ends.

THE SOCIO-SPATIAL CONSTRUCTION
OF COOL VIOLENCE REGIMES

Within what Foucault calls modernistic *govern/mentalities*, an institutionalized scenario privileges a view where violence is quantified and historicized, individuals and their communities are vilified, places (such as inner-city schools) are demonized, bureaucratic plans are rationalized and legalized, and seemingly violent "Others" are marginalized. From this perspective, violent "Others" become objects of panoptic space where the disciplinary gaze of govern/mentalities cellularizes their bodies into "private" places: e.g., prison cells and detention rooms in schools. For instance, consider the new program of territorial surveillance instituted by the Los Angeles Police Department (LAPD). In a low-income Latino section of Los Angeles' San Fernando Valley, bright red banners on the light poles of Parthenia Street signal to passing motorists that they are entering an "LAPD Video Zone, Buy Drugs, Go To Jail." There are two images at the bottom of the LAPD Video Zone banners: one is the outline of a camcorder and the other is a person behind prison bars. Commenting critically on the way police officers of the LAPD manipulate the spatial significance of sending people to prison, Steve Herbert states:

> Jailing is the most satisfying way in which the police can cleanse a dirty area; it is a surgical dislodging of the cancerous agents that pollute the lives of the good people. It is in this sense, a satisfying moral act, a clear victory of good over evil, an active removal of the problem and a restoration of peace and tranquillity. . . . Space is thereby purified of its moral pollution.[23]

Meanwhile, across the street from the Latino community is the upscale commercial center of the city of Northridge with its signs of invitation that welcome wealthy and desiring consumers. There are no state-produced signs warning of the oppressive dangers of capitalism and whiteness, at least not "obvious" ones.

Curiously, violence is a signifier conflated in an identification and location that is too settled. Typically, the subjectivity of violence is narrowly defined around psychosocial consequences of violence, rather than an engagement of differing understandings of violence. For example, the recent debate over the television ratings system has resulted in TV programs being labeled with a "V" for "violent content." The arguments in mainstream media focus exclusively on the rationalized psychological effects that these supposedly violent images have on children rather than on what constitutes violence in the dialogue and electronic images of TV programming. The symbolic violence in the *criteria* used to justify the ratings themselves are hidden from view. A contra-ceptive discourse moves the recognition of violence from the occasional act of physical harm or property damage towards a critical awareness of the pervasive and "violent" conditions of oppression operating at the level of everyday life. Moreover, an examination of subjectivity might shed conceptual light on the fixed and natural state of objective violence in public discourses.

The exploration of subjectivity has been dominated by questions of meaning such as "What is violence?" This type of reflection is often imbued with the political belief that governmental action can only succeed if the nature of a problem is definitively understood. However, this line of inquiry is problematic if the vision guiding the search seeks a singular subjectivity that has analytically concocted a transcendental truth as to the ultimate presence and meaning of violence. Postmodern, poststructural, postcolonial, and feminist theorists have struggled to deconstruct universal knowledge claims for their mythical and monolithic tendencies. These contestations have also problematized relationships between knowledge and identity such that assumptions of essentialized subjects are giving way to notions of decentered subjectivities that represent partial knowledges within situated totalities.[24] Since knowledges of violence have been constructed in this same modernistic milieu of definitive meanings, essentialized subjects, and techno-rational bureaucratic responses, this milieu must be deconstructed as well for its relationship to hegemonic constructions of both subjectivity and objectivity. Or as Althusser puts it, it is not people's thoughts that are necessarily alienated, but the social formation itself that produces an alienated subject.[25] Alienation is the violent separation of objective reality from subjective experience which results from the contradictions between labor and capital. Although material violence is certainly important, the objective realities of violence are related to differentially positioned conceptualizations, or "imaginaries," that are socially represented in discourses which allow people within particular communities to discuss violence. In other words, there are communities whose occupants share a sense of a common reality relative to their experiences with violence which they signify to each other. However, powerful communities are able to institutionalize their discursive renditions of violence, thus dominating marginalized people at multiple geopolitical levels, such as in the establishment of the LAPD Video Zone.

Moreover, these power differentials in the discourses of violence are not simply naturally occurring events. Relationships of domination are social constructions with histories and geographies that are often reified (which maintains the same power relationships between communities over time and space even as meanings and language may change or "slip") in part by the ideological processes found within discourses. As Derrida and Saussure have argued, language is governed by rules that are not so much about "positively" defining what something is as they are about "negatively" defining what something is not.[26] Saussure recognizes that identity is never merely an issue of positive presence but one of relation with the other terms in its environment.[27] To Derrida, identities are negatively defined by their Other which completes their supplementarity.[28] This undeniable absence which supplements the metaphysics of presence both gives form to identity while subverting its certainty. For example, one cannot make sense of the center without its margins, white without black, or master without slave. Although the first terms in the binary are privileged signifiers or are parasitic on the second terms, they are internally divided identities and achieve their register interdependent with their repressed Other. Human thought and experiences are so complex and varied that every attempt to "understand" the world through language necessarily and simultaneously involves "misunderstanding" the "worlds" of others.[29] Since all that is human cannot be synthesized into linguistic representations, language is a social process that is product and producer of both presences, which are spatial and temporal realities, and absences, which are spatial and temporal occlusions. Violent absences must be contra-ceptively recovered as they are continually produced and reproduced by hegemonic discourses. A contra-ceptive discourse recognizes the "not yet discoursable" and works to excavate these "private" perspectives into public spheres of political discourse, all the while trying to avoid what Ryan calls "semiotic positivism," or the over-reliance on signs.[30]

A contra-ceptive discourse recognizes that the public spheres of political discourse are surveilled and bordered by logocentrisms and structurations that inscribe and delimit subjectivity and legitimate particular expressions of reason. The logocentrism of violence communicated through hegemonic discourses hide or mask representations of violence that exist outside of conceptual and perceptual borders, yet are given presence by those same borders. As a transgression of representational borders, resistance to discursive violence occurs when the object of violence begins to *own* the violence produced by the process through which she has been signified and engages in an act of *resignification*. Judith Butler describes this form of resistance as a "mobilization against subjection."[31] She writes, following Foucault, that signs can be used for purposes counter to those for which it was designed:

> Even the most noxious terms could be owned, that the most injurious interpellations could also be the site of radical reoccupation and resignification. But what lets us occupy the discursive site of injury? How are we animated and mobilized by that discursive site and its injury, such that our very attachment to it becomes the condition for our resignification of it? Called by an injurious name, I come into social being, and because I have an inevitable attachment to my existence, because a narcissism takes hold of any term that confers existence, I am led to embrace the terms that injure me because they constitute me socially. The self-colonizing trajectory of certain forms of identity politics are symptomatic of this paradoxical embrace of the injurious term. As a further paradox, then only by occupying—being occupied by— that injurious term can I resist and oppose it, recasting the power that constitutes me as the power I oppose. . . . any mobilization against subjection will take subjection as its resource, and that attachment to an injurious interpellation will, by way of a necessarily alienated narcissism, become the condition under which resignifying that interpellation becomes possible. This will not be an unconscious outside of power, but rather something like the unconscious of power itself, in its traumatic and productive iterability.[32]

Subject formation involves reworking injury and subjection through resignification, which can challenge the subject's attachment to subjection in order to re-form subjectivity.

What our poststructural critique of violence and language suggests is that the question of "What is violence?" is itself hiding the more spatially overt question of "Where is violence?"[33] Regimes of power are also constitutive of and constituted by space. Subjects come to occupy places and spaces by the workings of power and discourse. Space, in other words, scripts subjectivity. As Sibley explains:

> The processes of social segregation observable in the modern city, for example, are mirrored in the segregation of knowledge producers. The defense of social space has its counterpart in the defense of regions of knowledge. This means that what constitutes knowledge, that is, those ideas which gain currency through books and periodicals, is conditioned by power relations which determine the boundaries of "knowledge" and exclude dangerous or threatening ideas and authors.[34]

Through a spatially conscious contra-ceptive discourse, a critical spatial theory of violence seeks to bring into view representations from the margins that question and transform the cool, distanced, and dominant centers of violent spatial logics. We argue that violence should be examined spatially because it is typically sensed as an act that not only needs a space in which to occur but also is a disruption, or "violation," of the rules and order of that space. Sibley contends that the rules which order space follow a hegemonic desire for "purity" and "defilement" in the social construction of self and community, leading to the exclusion of deviant others. Speaking on the relationship between alienation and physical space, he states that

> thus, the built environment assumes symbolic importance, reinforcing a desire for order and conformity if the environment itself is ordered and purified; in this way, space is implicated in the construction of deviancy. Pure spaces expose difference and facilitate the policing of boundaries. The problem is not solely one of control from above whereby agents of an oppressive state set up socio-spatial control systems in order to remove those perceived to be deviant and to induce conformity. . . . [E]xclusionary tendencies develop in the individual and . . . exclusionary practices of the institutions of the capitalist state are supported by individual preferences for purity and order. . . . A rejection of difference is embedded in the social system.[35]

The consequences of violating pure and ordered spaces of a particular spatial territory, whether it be a school district, city, or nation-state, usually result in being socially "assigned" to repressive or oppressive "residual" spaces such as prisons, housing projects, or "low-track" educational programs.

Furthermore, the power to control the purification and ordering of spatial territories is related to notions of "community" that both exclude and occlude. This is especially salient and problematic when powerful communities experience a "moral panic" caused by a perceived disjuncture of and threat to their pure and ordered spaces. Such moral panics are expressed spatially by casting out offending "Others" from valued territory or by reappropriating violent "residual" spaces of the Others in order to reform it.[36] For example, the San Francisco Unified School District has implemented a program of "reconstitution" whereby schools scoring low on district evaluations have had most of their faculties and administrations transferred to other school sites in an effort to spatially "cleanse" school cultures. Of course, the reconstituted schools are typically located in neighborhoods where poor students of color reside. When exclusionary and occluding communities achieve state, media, and institutional power, the consequences of their representations of Others can be devastating.

A critical spatial language opens possibilities for contra-ceptively transgressing the borderations imposed by privileged communities that exclude and occlude. For example, the spatial term "region," as opposed to local, nation, or global, is a flexible way of contextualizing examinations of sociospatial relations that wish to consider the productive relationships between community, territory, and power. Region and regionalization are especially important concepts for a critical understanding of the spatialness of violence. A region is not simply a natural topographical area associated with a river valley, desert, or mountain range. Derived from the Latin root *regis*, which means "of the king," a *region* is a space, such as land, body, or mind, that is territorialized through the rationalization and enforcement of *regulations*. Regionalization is maintained through the *regimentation* of a state of governance and logocentrism known as a *regime* which produces subjectivities that make the spaces of everyday life appear to be *regular*. In modernistic regimes of liberalism, for example, regions and their regulations have been structured into, among other things, laws that are normative and normalizing forces in the maintenance of govern/mental territories such as nations and cities.[37] The existence of "criminality" demonstrates that constructions of spatial violence have been institutionalized as part of legal systems and territorial rule. For instance, in 1993 conservatives in the British government proposed a bill which sought to restrict the presence of Gypsies in the English countryside because they are seen as "nomadic spatial deviants" and "filthy." Invoking nostalgic images of a bucolic English utopia with redcoated huntsmen and quaint cottages that is now being violated by the presence of Gypsies, Sir Cranley Onslow, a supporter of the measure, decried that:

> [This section of the bill strengthens] the position of those people who want law and order to prevail in the countryside. The creation of a new offense of aggravated trespass is a significant step forward that will be widely welcomed in all parts of the country *where people have become all too used to disorder, intimidation and violence prevailing and interrupting the lawful pursuits of those who live in the country, value it and want to continue with their countryside sports.* (italics in original)[38]

As this quote illustrates, the primary problem of the normalization and naturalization of regional rules is that they structure an impression that there are both times and places that are free or detached from violence, that is, that exhibit the banality of "everyday life," whereas violence occurs only in traumatic, extraordinary instances. Moreover, in the world of Onslow's English countryside, Gypsies are the ones who endure conditions of violence simply by being present in a region where they are not welcome. Yet Onslow has the audacity to claim that it is the Gypsies who violate his space by supposedly disrupting his fox hunts. Unfortunately, Onslow is in a position of power to promote a law to regulate his violent spatial imaginary by criminalizing Gypsies.

Through its partnership with the production of blinding regionalizations, violence is rarely perceived as an ongoing presence or condition perpetuated by acts of representational injury. A violent condition is only acknowledged when it is imagined as a natural association with isolated, irregular, and demonized subregional space, such as a "barrio" or "inner-city school." Children who grow up in these denigrated subregional spaces are said to be "living in violence" whereas other spaces, such as white suburbs, are read as being nonviolent and "safe." This Manichean dichotomy of good versus bad spaces is itself symptomatic of a society that is violent at its roots. A contra-ceptive discourse on the spaces of violence must interrogate dominant conceptualizations of space itself, particularly those that disconnect different spaces and spatialities from their inter-related, inter-reactive, and interdependent social constructions. Conceptualizations of space, or conceived space, dictate perceptions of spatial reality and sociospatial relations such as govern/mental policies on violence through the legitimation and institutionalization of appropriate spatial knowledge. Conceived space has the potential to be both product and producer of spatial violence. It can also be a colonizer of subjectivity as it is inscribed and implemented in spaces such as the explicit and hidden curriculum of schools. The interplay between knowledge/space/power at microgeopolitical levels, such as the classroom, serves to reify blinding regionalizations and territories of surveillance.

Like violent discourses, space and spatial knowledge should be scrutinized for their modernist tendencies to produce and occlude violence. A contra-ceptive discourse on violence must correspondingly name and deconstruct the dominant ways in which spatial knowledge is conceived and practiced. Western (educational) institutions are closely associated with views of space that are trapped in binary opposition between objective and subjective space. Objective space, or the spaces of everyday life that are often identified as "reality," have been overemphasized, especially by those who are almost exclusively structural and scientific, such that the names and meanings of objective spaces are assumed to be naturally occurring and obviously understood. This rigid view of space is affiliated with a scientific, modernist project of quantifying or describing objective space so that "evidence" can be gathered to create a convincing argument in the public spheres. This desire for evidence collecting constructs epistemologies which seek information that will influence an audience of the powerful, that is, policy makers and bureaucrats. For example, racial and ethnic identities of body spaces are frozen into categories on census forms in an effort to produce disciplined "demographics" while many completing these forms must struggle to decide which box to check for their own identity. Special education and bilingual education students must be officially categorized and identified by state agencies in order to receive funds for their programs. These same categories also act to normalize the mainstream curriculum and perpetuate their own existence in what are often marginalized programs. In modernist forms of objective space, violence is also quantified as crime statistics, reinforcing the notion that violence is limited to "known" typologies such as murder rates or percentages of students in gangs, thereby masking a critical consideration of the oppressive conditions and acts of representational violence targeted at exploited people. The fixed views of objective space can be particularly violent because they are discursively enacted by those with institutional power in ways that deny and structure the alternative realities of marginalized people.

On the other side of the modernist epistemological binary, the discourse of subjective space is often used to counter rigid views of objective space by offering different meanings and interpretations. Soja describes subjective space, or, as he calls it, "imagined space," as the site of the mental contemplation of space, or the conceptual and subjective spatial plans of the mind.[39] For instance, before the LAPD implemented its Video Zone program, first it had to perceive a problem in particular spaces and then it had to devise a plan to "solve" the problem. This process was mediated through the imaginings of space held by those in the LAPD. Jill Leovy of *The Los Angeles Times* describes how the spatial imaginations of the police have even been accommodated in plans to developed disciplined spaces in "unruly" neighborhoods:

> Burbank police were losing the turf war with gang members over West Elmwood Avenue. So the city rolled out a weapon against which gangs couldn't compete: Money. Lots of it. . . . Using the millions of dollars at its disposal, the city staged a wholesale takeover of one of its worst areas, the notorious 100 block of Elmwood, buying 11 buildings and performing drastic surgery on a cul-de-sac that was once a magnet for trouble. . . . "We took away their homeland," one police officer said. . . . The new street design has a distinctive law enforcement stamp. Officers reviewed blueprints at every step. Police recommended a 14-foot-high wrought-iron fence be erected just behind the buildings, blocking the normal escape routes used by gang members when police cruised down the block. The city built curbs too high to drive over, but not so high they become inviting places to sit. The new decorative plants are covered with spines and thorns to discourage the hiding of guns or contraband.[40]

Educators and educational planners also use manipulations of space to discipline "unruly" students and students from "unruly" places, whether through a "basic skills" curriculum, seating arrangements, expulsions and transfers, or busing programs. In fact, many public schools in Los Angeles have prison-like fences such as those recommended by the Burbank Police for Elmwood.

Discursively structured systems of spatial metaphors that stand in place of the real are closely tied to abstract representations of space or "imagined space."[41] For example, "school" is a spatial metaphor in the way it represents a place where formalized acts of education take place. However, the meaning and purpose of places called "school" is far from settled because schools are implicated in sociospatial struggles over knowledge and power. When Paul Willis describes how the curriculum of a school reproduces class stratification,[42] he is conveying a very different political image and understanding of what a school is than someone who imagines the school to be an appropriate "sorter" of human capital into their rightful social locations. Imagined space is representationally violent when it is idealized as a utopian space of agency, such as when education is discussed as a space that opens the benefits of society to everyone. There is a tendency in modernist subjective space to solidify or fix spatial metaphors such as "school," "nation," and "inner cities," and to veil their sociospatial production from our view. After all, nations, schools, and inner cities have not always existed, particularly as they are in their current forms.[43]

The irony of the spatialities of modernist epistemologies is that an emphasis on objective space cannot be elaborated without invoking a subjective spatiality, and an emphasis on subjective space cannot be realized without experiencing objective spaces. As Soja argues, spatial thinking is not a question of being *either* real *or* imagined because it is always *both* real *and* imagined.[44] In other words, the perceptual is always interreactive and interdependent with the conceptual. The focus of critical spatial analysis should then be more concerned with *social space*, which is the realm where the differential and *ideological* production of real-and-imagined spatialities are socially constructed such that some spatialities are legitimated and regionalized in ways that both produce and mask subaltern spatialities.[45] Critical spatial analysis seeks the representational violences in social space that are hidden in the hot margins of the cool, abstract, and idealized modernist spaces of violence. Social space is where we should question the constructed spatial regimes that both allow and limit our perception of violence. Since social space is structured primarily through language, a critical semiotics of violence needs to articulate a theory of semiotics that embraces critical spatial theory.

Working towards a description of a critical semiotics of violence, we begin with a brief description of "semiotics." Saussure's theory of signs (or semiotics) held that language could be broken down into two fundamental elements, the signifier and signified; the first a linguistic form (e.g., a written or spoken word—*parole*), the second its intended meaning.[46] Together, the signifier and signified create the sign. Signifiers are not necessarily articulated forms, but invocations of "the psychological imprint of the sound," as in a sound-image or thought. Signifieds are "mental representations of the meaning" attached to signifiers.[47] As such, Saussurian linguistics opposes the Naturalists' claim that there exists an essential relation between things and words.

A critical semiotics of violence releases the sign "violence" from its symbolic functioning and disrupts its unitary meaning. It reveals the textuality of violence and the unnamed logocentric practices that are its conditions of possibility. It displaces the sanctioned and often sanctimonious ways in which violence as a realm of meaning delimits itself. It problematizes the status of violence as self-evident and natural. A critical semiotics of violence problematizes various sites of violence as marked by space/power/knowledge production systems. It recognizes that the symbolic structuring of dominant spatialities of violence necessarily produces counterspatialities of violence that should be represented, although they will never be fully present for discussion. Conversely, violence should not be isolated solely to a critique of discourse on the topic of violence because the discursive act and condition of masking subaltern representations is violent regardless of the topic in question. The logic that produces subaltern spaces is related to their denigrated state of "readiness" or "preconditioning" for capitalistic exploitation.

So, *cool violence*, in contradistinction to the detached and detaching views of space as seen from within modernist epistemologies of violence, is an ever-present condition of representational acts and disjunctured spaces that are significant in that they relate to material consequences of oppression. Cool violence is an institutionalized regime in that it ideologically regulates blinding regionalizations of violence associated with modernist, capitalist, masculine, and white supremacist ways of seeing space. In cool violence regimes, violence is itself a spatial metaphor that signifies harm perpetrated on a given space by the violation of the commonsense rules of that space. Acts of violence are located in spaces that have been socially constructed as mostly existing in a state of nonviolence.

For instance, residential suburbs are rarely considered violent as opposed to the often demonized "barrio." Spatial nonviolence is partially perpetuated by "violent memories" of past places that are dictated by a nostalgia which obliterates any sense of the production of difference through cool violence. By omitting past relationships in the racialization, genderization, and capitalization of spaces, violent memories act normatively to delegitimate knowledges that emphasize the interconnectedness of spatial differentiation and power, thereby reifying the conditions of cool violence. In the discourse of cool violence, normative conditions of nonviolence in a protected space may be referred to and maintained by allegedly "neutral" evaluative signifiers such as "safe," "healthy," "sound," "clean," or "well managed." Cool violence also masks constructed notions of "privacy" or spatial "ownership."

Through the construction of privacy, the act of violence is not just to the space but also to the owner(s) "in charge" of that space. In the capitalist regime of cool violence, groups or individuals are allowed to maintain private spaces as long as they remain within the "commonsense rules" of ownership. Violence is then said to occur when nature or other people commit an act (not a produced condition) that breaks the socially constructed rules of safety and privacy for that space. Conditions of violence are identified when certain places become symbolically attached to "Others" who are seen as breaking the rules of ownership. LAPD Video Zones, school reconstitution reforms, and urban renewal projects are just a few examples of the spatial logic and practice of cool violence. Through the detached and detaching spatialities of modernistic epistemologies, these situations of supposedly "improper" or "dirty" ownership are blamed on those who inhabit "violent places."

Embodied space is one of the specific sites located in cool violence regimes. The body is a contested site of the blinding regionalizations of cool violence and modernist spatial epistemologies that must be contraceptively recovered through a space-conscious critical semiotics. Constructed in relation to the metaphors of industrial and techno-capitalism, the body is a machine for the production of value, thus making it the atomistic unit of social agency in a field of free-market competition. The capitalist body as value-production machine has been simultaneously regionalized by medical and biological discourses that regulate the normalized, "systems" view of the body. These discursively structured, scientific logics of normalized bodily "functions," "safety," and "health" cloak the capitalist body in an illusion of mechanistic form and purpose that validates the belief in and the desire for an optimum state of nonviolent bodily conditions. Additionally, a common sense of self-ownership regulates a region of seemingly natural bodily privacy. However, the mere fact that society does not allow you to do what you want with your own body should suggest that this privatization of the body is socially constructed (e.g., prostitution, suicide, abortion, and sodomy are often subject to legislation). From this perspective, bodily violence is the result of an act that disrupts the regulated functions, safety, and health of the body in a way that threatens the value of the body. Through cool violence, the body is regimented such that it reflects the current regime of capitalism; the form of the body closely follows the function of capitalism.

This capitalist and modernist construction of the body disguises the general condition of cool violence. The body as commodity is constantly being produced and consumed through capitalist regionalizations of differential value. Systems of capitalist enfleshment commodify bodies through multiple social constructions such as race, class, gender, sexuality, and citizenship. The body is real in that it inhabits material space, but it is also imagined as a sign constructed in disjunctured ways that are interrelated to sociospatial struggles over power and reason. The body serves as an image machine of sorts that is continually read, consumed, and reproduced through the regional discourses inscribed by regulatory logocentrisms. For example, modernist governmentalities that produce a "nation" also enflesh all human bodies as either "citizen" or "alien" such that aliens within the traditional national boundaries are more likely to be marginalized, especially in core capitalist nations like the United States. Enfleshment is an ongoing state of cool violence in modernism because problematic logocentrisms precondition and essentialize social gazes that correspond to the reification of marginalization for denigrated "Other" bodies, thereby reproducing them as regions of capitalist exploitation that are implicit in nation-state formations. This symbolic and material cool violence also has representational significance in that the lived spatialities of marginalized bodies are made to appear irrational and non-sensical to the oppressors, thus violating the real-and-imagined spatial knowledges of the disenfranchised.

Another region of cool violence is property. Within capitalist regimes of exploitation, property consists of a regionalization of the ownership of objects, which in various times and places has included human beings, land, ideas, buildings, consumer goods, and signs. Sensibilities of privacy have been constructed around commonsense rules on the procurement of property and its sound, safe, and organized maintenance and management. The metanarrative of property ownership in capitalism suggests that property is obtained through a meritocratic system of individual ability and perseverance in a free-market economy. When property continues to be read as functioning within the logic of capitalism, a state of cool violence goes unrecognized. In other words, property becomes a condition of nonviolence. However, when the property regulations of capitalism are violated to the extent that property has been significantly devalued, the term "violence" is often used to describe this occurrence.

For example, news media often follow perceived "outbreaks of violence," such as that associated with storms or rioting, with estimates of property "loss" or "damage" quantified through the capitalist objectification and regionalization of space. In the United States, Hurricane Andrew, which passed over Miami in 1992, is described as the "most costly disaster" in U.S. history. Certainly the enslavement of blacks and the genocide of native peoples are "greater" U.S. disasters. Even so-called public spaces are still considered as property in that they are owned by the same state that regulates and is regulated by modernist notions of privacy and cool violence. The quick and blatant sacrifice of Koreatown by the police during the 1992 Los Angeles uprisings shows the selective engagement of capitalist state protection with public spaces.[48] Considered unprofitable by the local state apparatuses, the police left Koreatown to burn and Korean merchants were forced to protect themselves.

Of course, what the regime of cool violence masks is the ever-present condition of violence associated with the differential production of "property" in both its real and imagined connotations. Capitalism relies on the possibility of locating and owning spaces of exploitation that provide surplus value. However, spaces for production do not exist naturally and are socially constructed.[49] "Ownership" of production spaces is subject to sociospatial power differences in the struggle to define and regulate property "rights." This struggle cannot be separated from previous historical and geographical conditions and regulations. In the case of property, violence exists in the logocentrism of ownership and the reproduction of differential abilities to own in a regime of a reified meritocracy. Since capitalism is also related to the logics of whiteness and masculinity, spaces also become differentially commodified and valued as they simultaneously become associated with particular racialized and gendered bodies.[50] When these differences become hegemonically rationalized as separate and natural, conditions of violence persist. The marginalization of certain people's lived spatialities in this system of property demonstrates cool violence because their representations of property are absent from the discourses of social institutions.

Consider the discursive violence involved in media treatment of gang violence. Wayne Mellinger has analyzed the manner in which the *Los Angeles Times* covered street-gang murders between 1994 and 1995.[51] We wish to extend some of Mellinger's insights into our own analysis of a recent four-part series the *Times* ran from Sunday, May 25, 1997, to Wednesday, May 28, 1997. Working his way through a montage of journalist reporting on gangs, Mellinger argues that we read these stories as postmodern "channel surfer," as "decentered and distracted" spectators, as "textual flaneurs whose eyes stroll through this spectacular pagescape rapidly scanning for juicy stories, shocking images, and useful information."[52]

He further argues that these stories comprise little more than "emotion-rousing stories," and "public spectacles of private troubles,"[53] and that few of these murders are reported in any sociological detail in the *Times*. They are mostly "brief, detail-depleted one paragraph stories banished to the second page of the Metro section."[54] The saturated "moral panics" that are *not* suppressed in the *Times* include stories on "welfare queens," serial murderers, and acts of terrorism. Mellinger speculates that whereas sensational gang stories were once needed in order to "whip up fear and build consensus concerning the need for police intervention," the police and the media no longer consider gang murders to be as newsworthy as in earlier years, perhaps out of fear that crime will be amplified or the image of the city worsened. In an era of "post-Fordism in which the boundaries between reality and simulation are blurred,"[55] what we see more and more in the *Times* is the implosion of information into entertainment. The *Times* risks substantially hurting tourism if too many gang homicide stories are run. Furthermore, the necrophiliac logic which teaches that death can come from anywhere, anytime, ruptures the postmodern sensibilities of Angelino valley dwellers who prefer Los Angeles to be associated with majestic palm tress, placid swimming pools, and endless shopping spaces. When stories of gang members can be found sandwiched between advertisements for the Broadway, Robinson's, Von's, and Ralph's, few of them deal with the structured and sociogeographical aspects of gang violence. Mellinger writes:

> In demonizing gang members, media representations fail to understand the real problem and its political economic origins. To understand this epidemic of youth violence we must acknowledge and condemn the political economy and lived reality of poor youth in the inner city. The cause of much juvenile crime can be found in the rampant youth poverty that exists in many parts of Los Angeles.[56]

The *Times* series on gang life focused on life at a thirty-six-unit building at 8960 Orion Avenue, one block east of the San Diego Freeway in North Hills, at the center of the San Fernando Valley. Once a working-class community that housed California State Northridge students, the area surrounding the Orion Avenue complex was now home to the Langdon and Columbus street gangs. The housing complex has become both a refuge and a prison to immigrants from Mexico, Guatemala, El Salvador, and Puerto Rico. In order to cover the stories, two of the three *Los Angeles Times* journalists lived in an apartment at the complex that, we are told, was enclosed by iron gates and barbed wire. During their three-month investigation, they managed to meet the building's many residents including gang members, factory workers, welfare recipients, "scavengers who collected cans and bottles," and even one "bounty hunter" who worked for a medical clinic and got eight dollars for each customer she delivered. But the most detailed descriptions were of gang members. We learn for instance:

> There was Woody, stabbed by a drunk. Crazy killed himself, as he predicted, playing Russian roulette. Blanca was shot in the mouth by a San Fernando gang. Chatto was gunned down on his way to church. There were Leon, Gordo, Downer, Joker and finally, Pee Nut, a mischievous artist who climbed onto the roof of Langdon Ave Elementary School one Yule season and wrote, "Have a Pee Nutty Christmas."[57]

On August 7, 1997, Matea Gold reported in the *Times* that "classroom drop-and-cover routines" which were used during the cold war in preparation for a nuclear attack were now being used in area schools to "teach children to sprawl flat at the sound of shots." They are called "drop drills," "crisis drills," or "bullet drills." Usually, school lockdowns are initiated during the drills as well. One nearby school in Lennox has monthly "drop exercises" and an "annual outdoor sniper drill." Principal Anna McLinn of Marvin Avenue Elementary School is quoted as saying:

> If students heard a loud noise, they were trained to drop to the ground and crawl as if they were in the service, keeping their bodies flat. . . . If you stand up, the bullet could hit you. . . . This was an area where Uzis would go off next door. . . . It's nothing for my youngsters to see a shooting a couple of blocks from school. When you're looking at a community where this is almost normal, you have to be prepared.[58]

"Drop drills" are credited with saving the life of students at Figueroa Street Elementary School in February 1996 when Alfredo Perez was seriously injured by a stray bullet. Of course, "drop drills" are approaches that react to the symptoms of a violent society and do little to make the streets a safer place. When capitalist social relations accord certain people the status of deviants, it is not surprising that little is done to provide the necessary social and economic conditions for young people to acquire dignity and hope in their lives.

Although many residents were described as hard-working but down on their luck, the journalists noted that, in general, "we found people . . . living lives of paralyzing deprivation."[59] While the journalists described efforts by local residents to build a sense of community, attempts by police to fight drug-dealing, and actions by the local church to provide spiritual and social services, they conceded that little could be done outside of small incremental successes. Not one of the four parts in this series seriously linked life on Orion Avenue to larger economic relations in the wider society or attempted to situate crime in the context of the way in which Los Angeles has been ravaged by capitalism. Wayne Mellinger offers the following statistics:

> 16 percent of the city's 3.6 million people live below the poverty level, 333,000 are officially unemployed. . . . Massive reductions in social services in the city have left parts of the city with shattered school systems with dropout rates over 50 percent, the poor with virtually no emergency care, the streets packed with thousands of homeless, and infant mortality rates approaching third world levels.[60]

While the series often offered sensitive and heartfelt accounts of family life at the apartment complex on Orion Avenue and chronicled both the despair and the hope for a better future of many of the people who live there, it failed to connect the lives of individuals to worldwide economic conditions and the internationalized profit-making conditions under global capitalism. For the journalists, personal attributes determine whether or not a gang member escapes Orion Avenue and is able to rebuild his or her life outside of the neighborhood. Failure to do so is also individualized or psychologized, as it is connected to pathological family life, lack of work skills, or the habitual lure of gang solidarity and quick profits. The lives of inner-city poor are seemingly unconnected to the fact that half a million employees have been laid off each year for the last six years, while on a worldwide scale direct investment (mostly by United States) in creating foreign plants and operations has soared to $325 billion. The distribution of incomes between capital and labor is unsettling, especially in the United States. While workers' wages in terms of real hourly wages and family incomes have taken a downward turn between 1983 and 1992, the net worth of the top 1 percent of the nation has increased by 28 percent. Such greed, avarice, and indifference to human misery has created a "Judas economy" of betrayal and destruction.[61]

Discursive violence is about the density of discourses and multiple economic interests they serve, and the emancipatory knowledges that are displaced or submerged. Here the *Los Angeles Times* partakes of cool, discursive violence in its attempt to portray the reality of gang violence. Here the neighborhood is primarily seen visually as a space of decay. The journalists write from a position of logocentric occularcentrism in which the mark of the social disappears under a claim of access to the unmediated presence of the neighborhood. There is a latent system of signification at work here that stresses only that which can be seen. They remain blind to the social codes that legitimate their particular acts of seeing and nonseeing. Exploitation is more than an epistemological phenomenon; it is an economic, social, and cultural set of relationships. The systems of intelligibility that inform the analysis of the Orion Avenue neighborhood remain insensitive to their own historical conditions of production. The inhabitants of Orion Avenue are assumed to be responsible for their own condition. They live in crowded facilities behind a barbed wire fence. Outside the fence is the "street," a space of drug corruption, violence, and death. It is a tangible space that is out of control, even with regular police monitoring, surveillance, and periodic arrests. The description of this "material space" is really a negative image of the garrison of the colonial mind that sees itself in the middle of conquered territory that it has to suppress forcefully in order to defend civilization. The fact that the journalists remark that Beverly Hills residents would never tolerate the time it takes for police to respond to complaints on Orion Avenue locates the residents on Orion Avenue as lacking the necessary symbolic capital as well as property value to warrant the same kind of protection under the law as residents who occupy spaces of ruling-class interests. This double standard with respect to law enforcement illustrates the alarming disjuncture between neighborhoods produced within an episteme of community that is regulated by binary oppositions such as innocent/criminal, sane/pathological, worthy/unworthy. These opposed, yet interdependent pairings become the dichotomous codifications of difference or grid upon which oppression and domination are coordinated in a regime of truth.

There is a false assumption at work which suggests that empirical data in the form of selected interviews combined with a physical description of people and surroundings is sufficient to explain the psychodrama of their lives, why these people are poor, and why they seemingly will remain so. Such forms of cool violence journalism, while making well-intentioned efforts at "thick description" are unable to locate urban dwellers within the social totality and ensemble of social structures in which they are produced, and within the abstract space (local, regional, and national) in which their subjectivities are formed. A critical semiotics of space, we are arguing, will be able to foreground the imperial imaginary in which space is produced and enable new "mappings" of urban space that will intervene in the subject formation of individuals such that they will be able to reconquer the "spaces" of their lives through the development of a new spatial imagination, a new cartography of subjectivity. In this sense, spatial practice becomes a form of political intervention,[62] an instance of counter-hegemonic praxis.

So, where is violence? It exists not just in the regular forms of the occasional act or isolated condition, but in the cool violence perpetrated by the conceptual space of modernist epistemologies and their associated logics of whiteness, masculinity, and capitalism. Cool violence is slippery and cannot be easily regulated by bureaucratic solutions without committing more violence. In terms of schooling, educators, educational researchers, and educational technocrats must conceptualize and counter the cool violence that differentiates educational spaces into systems of power. Imagine that a so-called model school in Beverly Hills, California—one of the most affluent municipalities in the world—is perceived as violent because it serves to rationalize a view that sees it as an "exemplary, ordered educational condition." Do you imagine this school as racialized? The "model-ness" of this school would most likely be studied through modernist spatial epistemologies and fashioned into "visions" for "educational reform" through the fixed, naturalized, and essentialized spatial metaphors associated with cool violence.

Meanwhile, cool violence is reinforced as a demonized school somewhere in Los Angeles is given "*the* model" to follow, hoping this will curb the violence in a "barrio" or "inner-city" school. Powered by the force of spatial legitimation, the model bulldozes over local spatialities. Unfortunately, local spatialities of the disenfranchised are often themselves caught in colonized conceptions of violence that lead to hopelessness and self-hate. Although our bodies and possessions are marked with it, cool violence remains out of sight, and out of mind. Cool violence is a form of discursive domination, one which diffuses itself at the level of the political economy of signs. It is a gift which can only be canceled through a critique of the work of educational texts. As the oxygen of state repression, cool violence is invisible yet life-sustaining in a social order dependent upon capitalist exploitation.

NOTES

This chapter was previously published in *Discourse* (Spring 1999). It is reprinted here with permission.

1. Karl Marx and Fredrich Engels, *The Sacred Family and Other Texts* (Mexico: Editorial Grijalbo, 1962), 6.

2. Walter Benjamin "Theses on the Philosophy of History" in *Illuminations* (New York, Schocken Books, 1979).

3. Michel Foucault, *Discipline and Punish: The Birth of the Prison* (New York: Vintage Books, 1979).

4. Jean Baudrillard, *The Mirror of Production* (St. Louis: Telos Press, 1975); *Seduction* (New York: St. Martin's Press, 1979); *Symbolic Exchange and Death* (Thousand Oaks, Calif.: Sage Publications, 1993).

5. Marcel Mauss, *The Gift* (New York: Norton, 1967), 5–40; See also P. McLaren and Z. Leonardo, "Jean Baudrillard's Chamber of Horrors: From Marxism to Terrorist Pedagogy," in *Revolutionary Multiculturalism: Pedagogies of Dissent for a New Millennium*, ed. P. McLaren (Boulder, Colo.: Westview Press, 1997), 114–149.

6. Pierre Bourdieu, *Outline of a Theory of Practice* (Cambridge: Cambridge University Press, 1977), 5.

7. Bourdieu, *Outline*, 195.

8. Signithia Fordham, "Racelessness as a Factor in Black Students' School Success: Pragmatic Strategy or Pyrrhic Victory?" *Harvard Educational Review* 58, no. 1 (1988): 54–84.

9. Peter McLaren, *Schooling as a Ritual Performance: Towards a Political Economy of Educational Symbols and Gestures* (New York: Routledge, 1993); P. Willis, *Learning to Labor* (New York: Columbia University Press, 1977); J. MacLeod, *Ain't No Makin' It* (Boulder, Colo.: Westview Press, 1987).

10. Paulo Freire, *Pedagogy of the Oppressed* (New York: Continuum, 1993).

11. Jean Baudrillard, *In the Shadow of the Silent Majorities* (New York: Semiotext, 1983), 3, 28.

12. P. Bourdieu, *Outline*; P. Bourdieu, and L. Wacquant, *An Invitation to Reflexive Sociology* (Chicago: The University of Chicago Press, 1992).

13. Bourdieu, *Outline*, 191.

14. Bourdieu and Wacquant, *An Invitation*, 167.

15. M. Foucault, *The History of Sexuality*, Vol. 1 (New York: Vintage Books, 1978), 86, 89.

16. Bourdieu, *Outline*, 195.

17. Cited in T. Eagleton, *Ideology* (London: Routledge, 1991), 195.

18. Jeannie Oakes, *Keeping Track* (New Haven: Yale University Press, 1985).

19. D. Macdonell, *Theories of Discourse* (Oxford: Basil Blackwell, 1986), 73.

20. K. Marx, "Selected Texts," in *Ideology*, ed. T. Eagleton (London and New York: Longman, 1994), 23–30.

21. J. Baudrillard, *For a Critique of the Political Economy of the Sign* (St. Louis: Telos Press, 1981).

22. L. Althusser, *Lenin and Philosophy* (New York: Monthly Review Press, 1971).

23. S. Herbert, *Policing Space: Territoriality and the Los Angeles Police Department* (Minneapolis and London: University of Minnesota Press, 1997.), 155.

24. Donna Haraway, *Simians, Cyborgs and Women* (London: Routledge, 1991).

25. Althusser, *Lenin and Philosophy*.

26. G. Biesta, "Deconstruction, Justice and the Question of Education." *Zeitschrift fuer Erziehungswissenschaft* 1, no. 3 (1989): 395–411.

27. Jacques Derrida, *Of Grammatology*, trans. G. Spivak (Baltimore: Johns Hopkins University Press, 1976)

28. Ferdinand de Saussure, *Course in General Linguistics*. (Chicago: Open Court Classics, 1983).

29. Biesta, *Deconstruction*.

30. M. Ryan, "Foucault's Fallacy," *Strategies: A Journal of Theory, Culture and Politics* 7 (1993): 132–154.

31. Judith Butler, *The Psychic Life of Power: Theories in Subjection* (Stanford: Stanford University Press, 1997).

32. Butler, *The Psychic Life of Power*, 104.

33. See also G. Biesta, *Where Are You? Where am I? Identity, Intersubjectivity, and the Question of Location*. Paper presented at the University of California, Irvine, 1997.

34. D. Sibley, *Geographies of Exclusion* (London and New York: Routledge, 1995), xvi.

35. Sibley, *Geographies*, 86-87.

36. Sibley, *Geographies*.

37. N. Blomley, *Law, Space and the Geographies of Power* (New York: Guilford Press, 1994).

38. Cited by Sibley in *Geographies*, 107.

39. E. Soja, *Thirdspace* (Cambridge, Mass.: Blackwell Publishers, 1996).

40. J. Leovy, J. "Burbank Buys Turf to Clean Out Gang," *Los Angeles Times*, 31 August, 1997, A1, A30.

41. Soja, *Thirdspace*.

42. Willis, *Learning to Labor*.

43. S. N. Haymes, *Race, Culture, and the City: A Pedagogy for Black Urban Struggles* (Albany: SUNY Press, 1995).

44. Soja, *Thirdspace*.

45. E. Soja and B. Hooper, "The Spaces that Difference Makes: Some Notes on the Geographical Margins of the New Cultural Politics." in *Place and the Politics of Identity*, eds. M. Keith and S. Pile (London: Routledge, 1993): 183–205.

46. Saussure, *Course in General Linguistics*.

47. F. Gadet, *Saussure and Contemporary Culture*. (Great Britain: Hutchinson Radius, 1986), 32.

48. P. Ong, K. Park, and Y. Tong, "The Korean-Black Conflict and the State." In *New Asian Immigration in Los Angeles and Global Restructuring*, eds. P. Ong, E. Bonacich, and L. Cheng (Philadelphia: Temple University Press, 1994), 264–292; S. Cho, "Korean Americans vs. African Americans: Conflict and Construction." In *Reading Rodney King: Reading Urban Uprising*, ed. R. Gooding-Williams (New York: Routledge, 1991), 196–211; E. Kim, "Home Is Where the Han Is: A Korean-American Perspective on the Los Angeles Upheavals." In *Reading Rodney King*, 215–235.

49. J. Urry, *Consuming Places* (London: Routledge, 1995).

50. Haymes, *Race, Culture, and the City*; D. Massey, *Spatial Divisions of Labor*, 2nd ed. (New York: Routledge, 1995).

51. W. Mellinger, "Reading the News in the Age of Postmodern Mass Media: Gang Murders in the Los Angeles Times," *Cultural Studies* 2 (1997): 217–236.

52. Mellinger, "Reading the News," 222.

53. Mellinger, "Reading the News," 222.

54. Mellinger, "Reading the News," 223.

55. Mellinger, "Reading the News," 225.

56. Mellinger, "Reading the News," 233.

57. J. Johnson and C. Cole, "Gang Life's Grip Proves Hard to Escape," *Los Angeles Times*, 27 May 1997, A22.

58. M. Gold, "Urban School Drill: Duck and Cover for Gunfire," *Los Angeles Times*, 2 Aug. 1997, A20.

59. J. Johnson, "Surviving on a Block Ruled by a Gang," *Los Angeles Times*, 25 May 1997, A30.

60. Mellinger, "Reading the News," 233.

61. W. Wolman and A. Colamosca, *The Judas Economy: The Triumph of Capital and Betrayal of Work* (New York: Addison-Wesley, 1997).

62. S. Pile, *The Body and the City: Psychoanalysis, Space and Subjectivity* (London and New York: Routledge, 1996).

4

Representations of Violence, Popular Culture, and Demonization of Youth

Henry A. Giroux

DEMONIZING YOUTH

Blamed for drug abuse, exploding crime rates, teenage pregnancy, spiraling cigarette addiction, and a host of other social and economic problems, youth are repeatedly scapegoated by politicians, the dominant media, and numerous liberal and conservative intellectuals. Examples of such scapegoating have become so commonplace in the media that they suggest the emergence of a new literary idiom. For example, commenting on contemporary youth in *Wired*, right-wing sensation Camilia Paglia bashes young people for their inability to think critically about any serious political issue:

> I think [young people] become hysterical. They become very susceptible to someone's ideology. The longing for something structured, something that gives them a worldview, is so intense that whatever comes along, whether it's fascism or feminist ideology (which to me are inseparable), they'll glom onto it and they can't critique it. You see the inability of the young ... to think through issues like date rape.[1]

Not to be outdone, the liberal magazine *George* recently ran a series of stories under the headline "Why Kids Are Ruining America." Spearheading the assault, novelist Bret Easton Ellis claims that the budget crisis, collapsing middle class, and rising crime do not represent the biggest threat to America. On the contrary, he claims "Kids Are ruining all of our lives." Smugly invoking his own elite experience of youth as a model of nostalgic yearning, Ellis's resentment of working-class urban youth is utterly unrestrained. Ellis's co-contributors reinforce his stereotypes with stories about why kids kill, blow money, control the entertainment industry, and are in need of more laws and regulations.[2] Echoing the ideological sentiments of the Bob Dole/Ralph Reed crowd, the contributors to *George* are indifferent to the social, political, and economic realities that most poor, black kids[3] have to face in an age marked by the dismantling of public services and a rabid commitment by Washington policy makers to a market logic that defines citizenship as an act of consuming rather than as a compassionate practice of social and political responsibility. Rather than work to expose and break the cycle of poverty, despair, and hopelessness that many young people face in America, Ellis and his co-contributors shamelessly mobilize adult fears and hysteria by constructing youth as an invading army of killers and drug fiends against which society is going to have to defend itself.

Such commentaries reinforce and legitimate what has become a standard perception of young people in American culture, one that is echoed in Hollywood films such as *Dumb and Dumber* (1994), *Clueless* (1995), and *Kids* (1996). These films and others portray kids either as vulgar, disengaged pleasure seekers or as over-the-edge violent sociopaths. Similarly, television sitcoms such as *Friends* portray young people as shallow, unmotivated navel-gazers without the slightest interest in a larger social and political world. While many of the characters frequently experience unemployment, low-wage jobs, and high-credit debts, such experiences become at best fodder for comic relief and at worst completely nullified by their hundred-dollar haircuts, expensive makeup, and slick apartments. These white middle-class youth are defined largely through their role as conspicuous consumers, their political indifference, and their intense lack of motivation to engage a world beyond their own self-indulgent interests.

One of the most incessant and insidious attacks waged by the media has been on poor urban, black youth in the United States. Represented through a celluloid haze of drugs, crime, and sex, black youth—as in a slew of recent Hollywood films including *Boyz N the Hood* (1991), *Sugar Hill* (1993), *Menace II Society* (1993), and *Clockers* (1995)—are viewed as menacing and dangerous. In addition, popular representations of youth in the music press take on a decidedly racial register as they move between celebrating the politics of cynicism and rage of white singers such as Alanis Morrisette and Courtney Love and, on the other hand, giving high visibility to the violent-laden lyrics and exploits of black rappers such as Snoop Doggy Dogg and the recently deceased Tupac Shakur and Notorious B.I.G.

Caught between representations that view them as either slackers, gangsters, or sell-outs, youth are increasingly defined through the lens of contempt or criminality. If not demonized, youth are either commodified or constructed as consuming subjects. For instance, in the world of advertising, prurient images of youth are paraded across high-gloss magazines, pushing ethical boundaries by appropriating the seedy world of drug abuse to produce an aesthetic that might be termed "heroin chic." Capitalizing on the popularity of heroin use in films such as *Trainspotting* (1996), fashion designers such as Calvin Klein portray barely dressed, emaciated young models with dark circles under their eyes as part of an advertising campaign that combines the lure of fashion and addiction with an image of danger and chic bohemianism.

Yet, the corporate exploitation of youth does not account for the insurgent racism that breeds a different register of violence against young people. Racism feeds the attack on teens by targeting black youths as criminals while convincing working-class white youths that blacks and immigrants are responsible for the poverty, despair, and violence that have become a growing part of everyday life in American society. As the gap between rich and poor widens and racism intensifies, conservatives and liberals alike enact legislation and embrace policy recommendations that undermine the traditional safety nets provided for the poor, the young, and the aged.[4] As the reality of high unemployment, dire poverty, inadequate housing, poor-quality education, and dwindling social services are banished from public discourse, white and black youth inherit a future in which they will be earning less, working longer, and straining to secure the most rudimentary social services. The promise of economic security and the house in the suburbs provide an increasingly irrelevant set of referents for gauging one's relationship to the so-called American dream. As evidence of the nation's diminishing commitment to equality of opportunity, working-class youths and youths of color are increasingly warehoused in educational institutions where rigid discipline and defunct knowledge are coupled with a cultural addiction to excessive individualism, competitiveness, and Victorian moralism.

One measure of the despair and alienation youths experience can be seen in the streets of our urban centers. The murder rate among young adults eighteen to twenty-four years old increased 65 percent from 1985 to 1993. Even more disturbing, as James Alan Fox, the Dean of the College of Criminal Justice at Northeastern University, pointed out recently, is that "murder is now reaching down to a much younger age group—children as young as 14 to 17. Since the mid-1980s, the rate of killing committed by teenagers 14 to 17 has more than doubled, increasing 165 percent from 1985 to 1993. Presently about 4,000 juveniles commit murder annually."[5] With soaring indices of poverty among children, a changing world economy characterized by subcontracting, an explosion in domestic sweatshops, and the proliferation of low-wage factory jobs, the most notable feature about the crisis of democratic public life appears to be the expendability of youth.

In a society gripped by the desire to lose itself in a rendering of a mythic past and an equally strong desire to relinquish responsibility for the future, youths become the main casualties. As a case in point, the assault on youth is happening without the benefit of adequate rights, fair representation, or even public outcry. Children can't vote, but they can be deprived of basic rights, spoon-fed an ethos of excessive materialism, and assaulted by a glut of commodified violence in the media. Contrary to the logic of a conservative-dominated Congress, building more prisons will not solve the problem; neither will reducing student loans or privatizing public schools. What can teachers, cultural workers, and other public intellectuals do in light of such an onslaught against children's culture? What pedagogical and political possibilities exist within and outside of schools for progressives to address the economic, political, and racial problems destroying the hopes of a decent future for the next generation of youth? The effects of such an assault on both young people and the fabric of democratic life poses an urgent challenge for teachers and social scientists to redefine the connection between their roles as public intellectuals and their responsibility to address the major problems facing young people today. Such a task means, in part, addressing how strategies of interpretation, critique, and intervention might be fashioned within those institutional and pedagogical spaces that provide representations for how youth define themselves and how they are defined by adult society.

YOUTH AND THE POLITICS OF CULTURE

If schools represent crucial sites to educate young people to address the central problems of unemployment, racism, violence, and the major political dilemmas faced by a generation of poor white and black youth, educators will have to address the nature of the current assault on education and its relationship to a broader attack on the basic foundations of democracy. The threat posed by the increasing vocationalization of education and the ongoing attempts by liberals and conservatives to remove all obstacles to the regulation of corporate practices and eliminate the language of equity and social justice from broader discussions about public life suggests that public intellectuals must join together to create a national movement for the defense of public education and other public goods.

Rather than exclusively serving the stripped-down needs of the multinationals, educators, and other cultural workers need to develop counterpublic spheres and transformative pedagogical conditions in a variety of sites. Such a task would aim at enabling students to critically engage diverse forms of literacy, writing, and knowledge production through the broader lens of public problem solving in order to better understand and transform the political, economic, and ideological interests that shapes the postindustrial world they will inhabit.[6]

Central to such an effort would be developing a new discourse for making visible those historical narratives that recount the important struggles for democracy that have unfolded in social movements extending from the civil rights struggles of the 1950s to the oppositional politics waged by organizations such as Act Up in the 1990s. Such movements need to be studied for the pedagogies and politics at work in the struggles against injustice and engaged as transformative forms of knowledge to be incorporated into strategies of understanding and intervention.

Teachers, administrators, and cultural workers must also redefine the purpose of schooling, not as a servant of the state nor to meet the demands of commerce and the marketplace, but as a repository for educating students and others in the democratic discourse of freedom, social responsibility, and public leadership. At the heart of such a task is the need for teachers and other cultural workers outside of educational sites to join together and oppose the transformation of the public schools into commercial spheres largely responsible for "the training and credentializing of the growing technical-professional managerial work force."[7] This means not only waging battles against the new professionalism with its rather gutless refusal to challenge the forces of privatization and economic and social decay that threaten public education, but also vigorously opposing those institutional and pedagogical instances of power, discourse, and social practice that silence education for citizenship, abstract learning from public life, and remove politics from questions regarding ownership over means for the production of knowledge. Schools need to provide students with conditions for learning acts of citizenship and a sense of democratic community. As Robert Hass, the Poet Laureate of the United States, elegantly reminds us: "The market doesn't make communities. Markets make networks of self-interested individuals. Schools have a more noble political and pedagogical role which is to 'refresh the idea of justice, which is going dead in us all the time.'"[8] Clearly such challenges should not be limited to schools. Counter-public spheres can be developed in neighborhoods, through social-service agencies, and in other sites that would combine the task of raising consciousness about the violence being waged on children and what it would mean to translate such consciousness into direct political and policy-making legislation.

CULTURAL PEDAGOGY

Progressives must also revive critical attention to conflicts within the terrain of culture and representation that lie at the heart of struggles over

meaning, identity, and power, particularly as they address issues regarding how youth are constructed and demonized within a broader
public discourse. Many progressives have viewed the struggle over culture as less significant than what is often referred to as the "concrete"
world of material suffering, hunger, poverty, and physical abuse. While
such a distinction suggests that representations of physical abuse and its
actual experience cannot be confused, it is also imperative to understand
how material reality and discourse interact. The struggle over naming
and constructing meaning also concerns how we constitute moral arguments and judge whether institutions, social relations, and concrete experiences open up or close down the possibilities for democratic public
life. Struggles over popular culture, for instance, represent a different
but no less important site of politics. For it is precisely on the terrain of
culture that identities are produced, values learned, histories legitimated, and knowledge appropriated.

Culture is the medium of public discourse and social practice through
which children fashion their individual and collective identities and
learn, in part, how to narrate themselves in relation to others.[9] Culture is
also the shifting ground where new and old ways of understanding the
world are produced and legitimated in the service of national identity,
public life, and civic responsibility. As a site of learning and struggle, culture becomes the primary referent for understanding the multiple
spheres in which pedagogy works, power operates, and authority is secured or contested.

At stake here is a rejection of the increasingly fashionable notion that
such struggles are merely viewed as a stand-in for some "real" politics
that are at worse inevitably replaced or at best delayed. Instead such
struggles should be viewed as "a different, but no less important, site in
the contemporary technological and postindustrial society where political
struggles take place."[10] This should not suggest that academics or other
cultural workers engage cultural texts as the privileged site of social and
political struggle while ignoring either the historical contexts in which
such texts are produced or the underlying economic and institutional
forces at work in producing, legitimating, and distributing such texts.
Clearly cultural texts must be addressed and located within the institutional and material contexts of everyday life without reducing the issue of
politics, pedagogy, and democracy to simply questions of meaning and
identity.[11] At the risk of overstating the issue, I want to emphasize that I
am not suggesting public intellectuals reduce the politics of culture to the
politics of meaning, but recognize that any progressive notion of cultural
politics and pedagogy must be concerned with "relations between culture
and power because . . . culture is a crucial site and weapon of power in the
modern world."[12]

If educators and others are to develop a cultural politics that links theoretical rigor and social relevance, they also must further the implications of such a politics by acknowledging the importance of those diverse educational sites through which a generation of youth are being shaped within a postmodern culture where information and its channels of circulation demand new forms of understanding, literacy, and pedagogical practice. This suggests addressing how and where politics are being constructed and used in a global world steeped in visual and electronically mediated technologies that are refashioning the control and production of new information-based knowledge systems. Kids no longer view schools as the primary source of education, and rightfully so. Media texts—videos, films, music, television, radio, computers—and the new public spheres they inhabit have far more influence on shaping the memories, language, values, and identities of young people. The new technologies that influence and shape youth are important to register not merely because they produce new forms of knowledge, new identities, new social relations, or point to new forces actively engaged in new forms of cultural pedagogy, but also because they point to public spheres in which youths are writing and creating their histories and narratives within social formations that are largely ignored or only superficially acknowledged in trendy postmodern symposiums on music, youth, and performance.

Popular culture represents more than a weak version of politics or a facile notion of innocent entertainment. In its various registers, from cinema to fanzine magazines, popular culture constitutes a powerful pedagogical site where children and adults are being offered specific lessons in how to view themselves, others, and the world they inhabit. In this sense, the cultural texts that operate within such spheres must be addressed as serious objects of social analysis by anyone who takes education seriously. But recognizing that Hollywood films, for instance, function as teaching machines demands more than including them in the school curricula as a matter of relevance; it also demands that educators interrogate such texts for the connections they propose between epistemology and ethics. For instance, as Geoffrey Hartman has argued there is a pedagogical connection between "how we get to know what we know (through various, including electronic, media) and the moral life we aspire to lead."[13]

Raising ethical questions about cultural texts is not meant to deny that such texts register different readings for youth. On the contrary, I am proposing that popular culture texts have important pedagogical consequences. Difficult as it may be to gauge precisely what is learned from reading, listening, or engaging such texts, educators need to analyze how popular texts function as public discourses. By focusing on representations of popular culture as public discourses, it becomes possible to shift our attention away from an exclusive focus on narrow, formalistic readings in order to explore the ways in which such texts bear witness to the ethical dilemmas that animate broader debates within the dominant culture. Such pedagogical inquiries become particularly important when raising questions about the political limits of representation—particularly when they portray children in degrading terms, legitimate the culture of violence, and define agency and desire outside of the discourse of compassion and moral responsibility. Expanding the political importance of the pedagogical also raises the crucial issue of what role academics and other cultural workers might play as critical agents; that is, as public intellectuals willing, as Raymond Williams argues, "to make learning part of the process of social change itself."[14]

As the right wing wages war against sex education, condom distribution in schools, free speech on the Internet, and school libraries that carry allegedly "pornographic" books, there is a curious silence from progressives and other cultural workers about the ways in which children are portrayed in films, advertising, and media culture in general. Little is said about how the media floods popular culture with representations of senseless violence, misogynist images of women, and lazy, drug-crazed, and dangerous black men. While it is important for progressives to continue to argue for freedom of expression in the defense of films or other cultural forms that might be deemed offensive, they also need to provide ethical referents within such discourses in order to criticize those images and representations that might be destructive to the psychological health of children or serve to undermine the normative foundations of a viable democracy.

Appeals to the First Amendment, the right of artistic expression, and the dignity of consent are crucial elements in expanding cultural democracy, but they are insufficient for promoting an ethical discourse that cultivates a politics of nonviolence, self-responsibility, and social compassion. Progressives must begin to demonstrate a strong commitment to exposing and transforming structures of domination that operate through the media and particularly through those spheres that shape public memory and children's culture. That children derive meaning from the media suggests a broader concern for making those who control media culture accountable for the pedagogies they produce. Larger-than-life violence, sensationalism, and high-tech special effects in the media can promote a "psychic numbing" and moral indifference in children.

Zygmunt Bauman is correct in arguing that "there is more than a casual connection between the ability to commit cruel deeds and moral insensitivity. To make massive participation in cruel deeds possible, the link between moral guilt and the act which the participation entails must be severed."[15] All too often this is precisely what happens when culture is completely commodified, when popular culture is viewed as morally neutral or irrelevant, and when subordinate groups are excluded as moral subjects within dominant regimes of representation. But rather than being addressed by educators and others, such issues are often re-articulated by right-wing fundamentalists whose basic aim is to close down rather than expand the imperatives of a social and cultural democracy. Educators need to build upon a significant body of theoretical work in which popular culture is not exempt from the discourse of political analyses and moral evaluation. At the very least, popular culture as an important site of contestation and struggle should not be handed over to conservatives such as Bob Dole and William Bennett, who find it a convenient scapegoat for reasserting a Victorian-inspired morality and a nostalgic rendering of the past in which young rappers would have been turned over to the "cold war" police and teen mothers would have been forced to put their offspring in state-sponsored orphanages. In opposition to such a discourse, progressives must neither romanticize nor dismiss popular cultural texts. They must use such texts, along with other forms of traditional knowledge, as serious objects of critical analyses both within and outside of schools.

EDUCATION AND DEMOCRACY

At the risk of overstating the issue, young people inhabit a society that is not only indifferent to their needs but scapegoats them for many of the problems caused by the forces of globalization, downsizing, economic restructuring, and the collapse of the welfare state. Those youth who have come of age during the culture of Reaganism that began in the 1980s are increasingly used as either bait for conservative politics—blamed for crime, poverty, welfare, and every other conceivable social problem—or "defined in relation to the processes and practices of commodification."[16] The attack on youth coupled with an insurgent racism have transformed the electronic media culture that shapes today's youth into a battleground. Targeted as trouble and troubling, dangerous and irresponsible, youths face a future devoid of adult support, maps of meaning, or the dream of a qualitatively better life for their own families.

The growing demonization of youth and the spreading racism in this country indicate how fragile democratic life can become when the state is hallowed out and the most compassionate spheres of public life serving children—public schools, health care, social services—are increasingly attacked and abandoned.[17] Part of the attempt to undermine those public spheres that provide a safety net for the poor, children, and others can be recognized in the ongoing efforts of the right to "reinstall a wholly privatized, intimate notion of citizenship."[18] Such a constrained notion of citizenship reinforces and legitimates conservatives' attempts to shift policy initiatives at the local, state, and federal levels away from investments in social services to policies that support widespread efforts aimed at surveillance and containment. Such policies have resulted in the proliferation of laws passed in nearly a thousand cities to either inaugurate or strengthen curfews designed to keep youths off the streets and to police and criminalize their presence within urban space.

In the new world order, citizenship has little to do with social responsibility and everything to do with creating consuming subjects. This notion of citizenship finds a home in an equally narrow definition of pedagogy and the racial coding of the public sphere. In the first instance, conservatives define pedagogy so as to abstract equity from excellence in order to substitute and legitimate a hyperindividualism for a concerted respect for the collective good. In the second instance, both the media and the representations that flood daily life presume that the public sphere is almost exclusively white. Blacks are rarely represented as a defining element of national identity or as an integral presence in American life. Reduced to the spheres of entertainment and sports, blacks occupy a marginal existence in white America's representation of public life, largely excluded from those public spheres in which power and politics are negotiated and implemented. While the immediate effects of this assault on public life bear down on those most powerless to fight back—the poor, children, and the elderly, especially those groups that are urban and black—in the long run the greatest danger will be to democracy itself, and the consequences will affect everyone.

Ignoring the attack on a generation of young people who appear to have become utterly dispensable to the dominant governing and cultural institutions of society does not bode well for the future of democracy. Demonizing youth not only absolves adults of their civic responsibilities as critical citizens, it also weakens the conditions for carrying on pedagogical and political struggles crucial for a healthy democracy. Addressing the problems of youth suggests reclaiming the space of political and pedagogical work to find ways to inspire students to address the pressing problems of joblessness, segregated schools, overcrowded classrooms, inadequate child care, and health coverage as well as the economic, gender, and racial basis of injustice and inequity that permeate contemporary society.

CONCLUSION

Educators and other progressives need to "take a stand" while simultaneously refusing either cynical relativism or doctrinaire politics. Educators who are concerned about young people in this country must begin to find new ways to connect knowledge to power, and authority to moral responsibility as part of a broader effort to improve the health, education, quality of life, and possibilities for youth at a time in history when youth are the first to be abandoned as the social welfare system is dismantled by a Republican-led Congress and a centrist president who has ratified one of the most Draconian welfare-reform policies this country has ever implemented. Those who work with youth need to establish the priority of ethics and social justice over the logic of the market and the language of excessive individualism. As the notion of the public cracks under the assault of reactionary budget-cutting ideologues, it appears all the more imperative for cultural workers in a variety of educational sites and public spheres to focus their work on the importance of youth as part of a broader concern with the construction of critical citizens and democracy itself. In part, this demands that teachers take their own politics seriously and enter the public arena to engage pressing social issues; equally important is the need for teachers to address learning and persuasion as essential pedagogical elements in opening up spaces for authority to be questioned, for youths to narrate themselves and be listened to by those in power, and to create pedagogical practices that enable youths to learn how to be the subject of history rather than reduced to a cog in its unfolding.

As democracy recedes in the United States, the obligations of responsible adults to educate youth to take up the challenges they will face must be reclaimed as a crucial public responsibility. If democracy is to be viewed not simply as a voting procedure but as an ongoing struggle to link power and justice, equality and freedom, and individual rights and social obligations, it is essential that youths participate in such a process. Youth signifies, in all of its diversity, the possibilities and fears adults must face when they reimagine the future while shaping the present. To the degree that large segments of youth are excluded from the language, rights, and obligations of democracy indicates the degree to which many adults have abandoned the language, practice, and responsibilities of critical citizenship and civic responsibility. As I maintained at the beginning of this chapter, there can be little doubt that American society is failing its children. The crisis of youth represents the crisis of democracy writ large. We need to focus attention on this crisis and work to address the complex issues that define it and the resources and strategies needed to address it. Defining themselves less as marginal figures or as professionals acting alone, educators must recover their role as critical citizens and organize collectively in order to address those economic, political, and social problems that must be overcome if young people are going to take seriously a future that opens up rather than closes down the promises of a viable and humane democracy. In short, we need to make despair unconvincing and hope practical.

NOTES

1. C. Paglia and S. Brand "Hollywood: America's Greatest Achievement." Reprinted in *Utne Reader* (November/December, 1994), 79.

2. B. E. Ellis, "Why Kids Are Ruining America," *George* (June/July, 1996), 96–103.

3. While this paper uses the terminology "black" and "white," this is in no way meant to suggest that people of color can be subsumed under the category "black." Clearly, questions of racial identity are multifaceted and complex and involve diverse ethnicities and social groups including Asians, Latinos, and others. Moreover, the specificity of race relations take on a different register when dealing with groups other than African Americans. My focus here is on black/white relations because of the historically contingent urgency of such relations and the use of such discourse in the popular press.

4. On the politics and economics of wealth, welfare, and race, see M. L. Oliver and T. M. Shapiro, *Black Wealth/White Wealth* (New York: Routledge, 1995).

5. For an excellent analysis of these issues, see H. C. Boyt, "Citizenship Education and the Public World," *The Civic Arts Review* (Fall 1992): 4–9.

6. J. A. Fox, "A Disturbing Trend in Youth Crime." *The Boston Globe*, 1 June 1995, 19.

7. R. Strickland, "Curriculum Mortis: A Manifesto for Structural Change." *College Literature* 21 no. 1 (1994): 282

8. In S. Pollock, "Robert Hass," *Mother Jones* (March/April 1997): 19–21.

9. It is hard to believe that any serious scholar of contemporary youth can ignore the political importance of the cultural terrain in shaping the identities of young people. For one such instance, see M. Males, *The Scapegoat Generation: America's war on Adolescents,* (Monroe, Me.: Common Courage Press, 1996). Males believes that how young people learn to imagine themselves, others, and their place in the world is determined almost exclusively by generational forces and economic considerations. The political and pedagogical force of cultural institutions simply drops out of his account of young people.

10. H. Gray, *Watching Race: Television and the Struggle for "Blackness."* (Minneapolis: University of Minnesota Press, 1996), 6.

11. See L. Grossberg, "Toward a Genealogy of the State of Cultural Studies," in *Disciplinarity and Dissent in Cultural Studies*, eds. C. Nelson and D. P. Gaonkar (New York: Routledge, 1996), 131–148.

12. Grossberg, "Toward a Genealogy."

13. G. Hartman, "Public Memory and its Discontents," *Raritan,* 8 no. 4 (spring 1994): 28.

14. R. Williams, "Adult Education and Social Change," in *What I Came to Say,* ed. R. Williams (London: Hutchinson-Radus, 1989), 158.

15. Z. Bauman, *Life in Fragments* (Oxford: Basil Blackwell, 1995), 148.

16. L. Grossberg, "Adolescents and Their Music," in *Disciplinarity and Dissent in Cultural Studies*, eds. C. Nelson and D. P. Gaonkar (New York: Routledge, 1996), 27.

17. S. Aronowitz, *The Death and Rebirth of American Radicalism*. (New York: Routledge, 1996).

18. C. Nelson and D. P. Gaonkar, "Cultural Studies and the Politics of Disciplinarity: An Introduction," in *Disciplinarity and Dissent in Cultural Studies*, eds. C. Nelson and D. P. Gaonkar, (New York: Routledge, 1996), 7.

5

America's Dead-end Kids

Donna Gaines

In the suburban town of Bergenfield, New Jersey, on the morning of March 11, 1987, the bodies of four teenagers were discovered inside a 1977 rust-colored Chevrolet Camaro. Two sisters, Lisa and Cheryl Burress, and their friends, Thomas Rizzo and Thomas Olton, had died of carbon monoxide poisoning. Lisa was sixteen, Cheryl was seventeen, and the boys were nineteen.

"Teenage suicide" was a virtually nonexistent category prior to 1960. At the time of the Bergenfield suicides it was described as the second leading cause of death among America's young people; "accidents" were the first. More than 400,000 adolescents attempt suicide each year. The rate of teenage suicide (ages fifteen to twenty-four is the statistical category for teenage suicide) has tripled in the past thirty years. The suicide rate for younger children (ages ten through fourteen) has more than doubled over the last fifteen. The actual suicide rate among teens is estimated to be even higher, underreported because of social stigma. Then there are the murky numbers derived from drug overdoses and car crashes, recorded as accidents. To date, teen suicides account for 14 percent of youth mortalities.

Authors, experts, and scholars compiled the lists of kids' names, ages, dates, and possible motives. They generated predictive models: Rural and suburban white kids do it more often. Black kids in America's urban teenage wastelands are more likely to kill each other. Increasingly, alcohol and drugs are involved. In some cases adults have tried to identify the instigating factor as a lyric or a song. In 1987 it was Judas Priest and Ozzy

Osbourne. Today it is Marilyn Manson, or a popular film about the subject—the suicide of a celebrity, too much media attention, or not enough.

Some kids do it violently: drowning, hanging, slashing, jumping, or crashing. Firearms are still the most popular. Others prefer to go out more peacefully, by gas or drug overdose. Boys do it five times as often as girls, though girls try it more often than boys. Gay and lesbian youth are at least three times more likely than heterosexual youth to attempt suicide. It does not seem to matter if kids are rich or poor.

The Bergenfield suicide pact was alternately termed a "multiple death pact," a "quadruple suicide," or simply a "pact," depending on where you read about it. Some people actually called it a *mass* suicide because it reminded them of Jonestown, Guyana, in 1978, where more than nine hundred followers of Jim Jones poisoned themselves, fearing their community would be destroyed.

I wondered, did the "burnouts" see themselves as a community under siege? Like Jim Jones's people, or the 960 Jews at Masada who jumped to their deaths rather than face defeat at the hands of the Romans? Were the "burnouts" of Bergenfield choosing death over surrender? Surrender to what? Were they martyrs? If so, what was their common cause?

For a long time now, the discourse of teenage suicide has been dominated by atomizing psychological and medical models. And so the larger picture of American youth as members of a distinctive generation with a unique collective biography, emerging at a particular moment in history has been lost.

"Greasers," "beats," "freaks," "hippies," "punks," "thugs," "slackers," "goths." From the 1950s onward, these groups have signified young people's refusal to cooperate. In the social order of the American high school, teens are expected to do what they are told—make the grade, win the prize, play the game. Kids who refuse have always found something else to do. Sometimes it kills them. Sometimes it sets them free.

In the 1990s, as before, high school kids at the top are the "jocks," "preps," "brains," depending on the region. In the late 1980s, in white suburban high schools in towns like Bergenfield, the "burnouts" are often kids near the bottom—academically, economically, and socially.

How did kids *become* "burnouts"? I wondered. At what point were they identified as outcasts? Was this a labeling process or one of self-selection? What kinds of lives did they have? What resources were available for them? What choices did they have? What ties did these kids have to the world outside Bergenfield? Where did their particular subculture come from? Why now? Why here?

What were their hopes and fears? What did heavy metal, Satan, and suicide mean to them? Who were their heroes, their gods? What saved them and what betrayed them in the long, cold night? Was the suicide pact an act of cowardice by four "losers," or the final refuge of kids helplessly and hopelessly trapped? Could kids be labeled to death? How much power did these labels have?

I wanted to meet other kids in Bergenfield who were identified as "burnouts" to find out what it felt like to carry these labels. I wanted to understand the existential situation they operated in—not simply as hapless losers, helpless victims, or tragic martyrs, but also as *historical actors*, determined in their choices, resistant, defiant.

Because the suicide pact in Bergenfield seemed to be a symptom of something larger, a metaphor for something more universal, I moved on from there to other towns. For almost two years I spent my time reading thrash magazines, seeing shows, and hanging out with "burnouts" and "dirtbags" as well as kids who slip through such labels.

On most nights they just hung around the Circle at the end of Georgian Court, in the Foster Village garden apartment complex behind the shopping center. They did that for years. For a special occasion, they'd head out to the Palisades, to the cliffs overlooking the Hudson River. The park closes after dark but if you come here at night, and you're cool about it, you can have some privacy.

On the night of September 2, 1986, a group of close friends arranged to have a going-away party for a friend who was moving. Lisa Burress's boyfriend, Joe Major, dropped by the house to ask her to drive out to the cliffs with him. They had been seeing each other about six months. From all reports, Joe was a guy with personality and substance. People adored him. He was someone they could talk to, confide in about anything. His friendship was something people cherished. He was a leader, a good person.

Joe was also a little reckless; he was a drinker, and that sometimes worried his parents. School wasn't his thing either. He got in trouble, cut classes, and eventually just dropped out. But he had gotten his equivalency and he was working in his father's welding business. Joe loved fishing and he was full of life. He was the center of Lisa's world. But that night Lisa's mother and stepfather insisted she stay home. It was her sixteenth birthday and they had other plans for her.

Joe left and headed out to the cliffs with a couple of cases of beer. Everybody was having a good time. Tommy Olton had to miss the party; he was away at an alcohol rehab program at Fair Oaks.

Something horrible happened on the cliffs that night. Joe Major was joking around, he was high, he walked out on a ledge. He was much too close to the edge. Joe's best friend, Tommy Rizzo, cautioned him to get back. A moment later Joe slipped and fell two hundred feet to his death as Rizzo looked on. After that, Tommy Rizzo had trouble sleeping at night.

Lisa said she would never enjoy her birthday again because that was the day Joe died. She didn't talk about it much but she and her sister, Cheryl, kept Joe alive. They visited his grave in Paramus regularly, telling friends they were "going to see Joe." They left little presents for him, flowers, notes.

Lisa and Cheryl prayed to Joe. He was included in their prayers to God and to their late father. Dennis Burress was a truck driver who had died of an apparent drug overdose ten years earlier, at the age of twenty-eight. The sisters were six and seven at the time. Their mother remarried and they did not get along with their stepfather at all. It was well known to friends and clergy that the family had "problems."

Cheryl had dropped out of high school but was working on her equivalency. Cheryl was outgoing and full of energy. Lisa, the quiet one, was still in school. But both girls had many friends; they were popular girls, responsible babysitters. The neighbors liked them—especially how the sisters spent their free time teaching the younger girls dancing and cheerleading.

In the months after Joe's death, the sisters seemed to be doing okay. Like Tommy Olton and Tommy Rizzo, the sisters were "known" to authorities. They had "histories" of substance abuse. But Cheryl also had plans for the future. She told people she was happy about her life. Lisa kept things inside more. She and her sister were very close; they were almost never apart. Around three weeks before the suicide pact, Lisa had started seeing Tommy Olton and one of her girlfriends started seeing Tommy Rizzo.

Tommy Rizzo worked periodically as a roofer for his dad's construction company. Sometimes he did landscaping too. He had dropped out of school in 1985 and had been trying to get into the service, but he wasn't really sure it was what he wanted.

After Joe Major's death, Tommy Rizzo started having nightmares; he changed—he just wasn't himself. At one point he was arrested for drunk driving and entered a rehab program. He dried out, and then he tried getting his life in order. Things started to look up for him.

After Joe's death, Rizzo and Olton became best friends. They were regular Bergenfield guys who liked to have fun, drive around, and look for girls. Early in the friendship they tried to support each other in their newfound sobriety. They went to AA meetings and worked hard at their jobs. But that didn't last. Eventually, they started drinking again.

If Tommy Rizzo was sweet, Tommy Olton was rowdy. His parents had divorced when he was young, and he had gone to live with his father in Washington. He didn't get along with his stepmother, so eventually he returned to Bergenfield to live with his mother.

Tommy Olton's father had committed suicide a few years back. Some people said Tommy was in the house and saw his father blow his brains out with a gun. But that was just a bad rumor. Tommy was in a drug rehab program in Pennsylvania when that happened. He was fourteen.

To people who didn't know him, Tommy Olton seemed seriously burnt. But to his friends he was a great guy, the life of the party. He was lots of fun. They understood he had some problems; they loved him.

Over the six months that followed the death of Joe Major, the four friends seemed to gravitate closer to each other. Bonded together by their common loss, they kept Joe alive. In death, Joe was deified, the way any lost loved one will be. They turned to each other to fill the void. Some of their friends thought this wasn't such a good thing.

People close to the situation said the two boys talked about suicide on and off for a few weeks before they died. But then other people had the opposite impression. They didn't think there was anything unusual, anything to signal a suicide pact. They were convinced that their friends were happy. But the weekend just before the suicide pact, things did begin to turn.

On March 6, a Friday night, a bunch of people were hanging out at the Rizzo home. At one point, Tommy Olton fell down the stairs and cut his head. His friends called for an ambulance, but when it arrived, Olton wouldn't go. According to a friend, Olton started talking about suicide. The friend told him to stop thinking that way.

Later, the group went over to a friend's apartment to watch a fight on television. They had been drinking for a while when Tommy Olton complained of dizziness. They called an ambulance again. When it arrived Tommy Rizzo tried to ride with his friend, but his request was denied. Angry, Rizzo slammed a door of the ambulance, accidentally injuring an attendant. Police arrested him and charged him with disorderly conduct.

Meanwhile, the ambulance attendants noticed three superficial cuts on Olton's right wrist. He admitted to a member of the Ambulance Corps that he had slashed his wrists earlier, that he had been drinking heavily and that he wanted to kill himself. This was reported to an unidentified nurse at Englewood Hospital, where Olton subsequently refused medical treatment. A friend picked him up at the hospital, and they went to pick up Tommy Rizzo at the police station.

That weekend, friends rallied around Olton to offer him their support. But by Sunday, he had had a fight with his mother and was staying at the Rizzos' home. Mrs. Rizzo had no idea he was suicidal.

The next day, Cheryl called one of her friends, crying because of a bad fight with her mother. She told him that she had hit her mother and that she really hated her stepfather—things were worse than ever. She asked if she could stay at his place for the night. Fearful of aggravating her friend's girlfriend, Cheryl left the apartment early the next day. Later that day, Lisa was suspended from school.

By evening, the sisters were getting ready to go out. Cheryl broke a date she had, telling her friend she was "going to see Joe." He assumed she meant visiting his grave in Paramus. A little later the sisters called the Rizzo house, inviting Rizzo and Olton to hang out.

Much of that night seems to have been spent just riding around Bergenfield. Around 3:00 A.M. Tommy Olton's Camaro pulled into the Amoco station across from Foster Village. They bought three dollars worth of gas and tried to pull a ten-foot hose from a car vacuum cleaner at the station. The manager, Terry DeRosa, said no, they couldn't take the hose. He said later that he never asked what it was for. Since they were his friends, he wouldn't have questioned their motives. The four kids didn't push it; they appeared to be in good spirits, so he didn't think anything of it.

They left the gas station and drove across the street to the Foster Village apartments. Pulling into the complex, they made their way to a vacant garage, recently appropriated for hanging out. Their bodies were discovered by a tenant at around 6:30 A.M. They had died in garage 74 sometime between 4:00 and 5:30 A.M.

When the police found their bodies, Tommy Olton was in the driver's seat. Tommy Rizzo was in the back with Lisa and Cheryl. A pack of razor blades was on the right front floor. A single blade was found in the back, next to Rizzo. But very little blood was found in the car. In the trunk were a purse and knapsacks filled mostly with clothing.

Autopsies of the four kids revealed alcohol and average street doses of cocaine. Authorities speculated that they were on a downside, coming down around the time they died. And they found razor slash wounds on the wrists of both boys. Fresh wounds covered the scar tissue from the old ones.

No one close to them understood why they did it. Their parents couldn't understand it. Tommy Rizzo had just signed up with the Marine Reserve; Cheryl had seemed her usual cheery self. Mrs. Olton was so sure her son Thomas had been in a positive frame of mind. She was especially proud of him because he had recently volunteered to help kids in a children's rehab program.

Some friends believed it just happened spontaneously. They probably started talking about Joe and their recent misfortunes. They had gotten high and now they were crashing. Maybe they started talking about how life was just a piece of shit. Maybe they agreed it always had been and always would be. So they just decided fuck it, let's just do it. Let's just *go see Joe*.

On a brown paper bag found next to their bodies, the four kids had tried to explain. In a lengthy suicide note signed by each of them, they criticized their families, and indicated that they felt unloved. They asked to be buried together. This request was denied. There were three wakes, one for the sisters and one for each of the boys. The crowds in attendance at their wakes proved that indeed they were loved.

Then, before people could even catch their breath, there was a second suicide pact. A copycat. Exactly one week after the first, same place, same way. This time it was a couple — he was seventeen, she was twenty. They were also described as dropouts and friends of the four youths. Boyfriend and girlfriend, both working in restaurants. Two more burnouts huffing octane in garage 74. Also in a Chevy Camaro.

The door of the garage had been locked following the deaths on March 11, but apparently the lock had been recently broken. According to people close to them, the couple had been extremely upset over the recent loss of their friends—Tommy Rizzo had been buried the day before.

But the suicide pact of March 18 was aborted. Police found the couple dazed by the fumes, but alive. According to reports, the couple were taken to police headquarters, where they signed a statement admitting they had attempted suicide. Then they were signed into the psychiatric unit of Bergen County Hospital by court order.

In between the first and second suicide pact, in an isolated incident not far from Bergenfield, John Staudt, twenty, of Clifton, died in his family's garage of carbon monoxide poisoning. North Jersey was now experiencing what suicide experts call a "cluster effect."

Bergenfield Police Captain Daniel McNulty told reporters, "Every kid who has suicidal tendencies is coming out of the woodwork." Some of the town's "street" officers were badly shaken by the deaths. According to Bergenfield Administrator Louis Goetting, a few police were "pretty emotionally involved dealing with [these individuals] over a long period of time and I've got some cops looking themselves in the eye and saying, 'Is there something I didn't do?' "

The deaths of four teenagers who were beloved by friends but alienated from family, school, and community loomed over the town. After the second suicide pact, people in Bergenfield began to get the chilling feeling that maybe it didn't all just start the night Joe Major fell from the cliffs.

Within the previous twelve months, in addition to Joe Major, three other local youths had died suddenly and violently. They were all high school dropouts, three were in trouble with the law, alcohol was involved each time, and suicide had not been conclusively ruled out. Following the suicide pact of March 11, and the "copycat" that followed, experts reexamined the previous deaths.

In August 1986, in a death listed as alcohol-related, Paul Brummer, twenty, was found floating in Cooper's Pond. In May, Brummer had been indicted on an armed robbery charge.

On June 14, Christopher Curley, twenty-one, died after being hit by a Conrail train on the border between north Bergenfield and Dumont. According to prosecutor Larry McClure, Curley had been charged, with Steven Kesling, in a theft. Curley's older brother Martin told reporters that Christopher felt he had been "set up" by police. He told Martin they had planted stolen items on him.

Then, on September 27, nineteen-year-old Steve Kesling died under a Conrail train not far from where Curley died, on the tracks just north of Dumont. Kesling had been scheduled to appear in court on the theft charge two days before his death. Steve Kesling and Chris Curley were best friends.

The four individual deaths in the year prior to the suicide pact of March 11 were also among "burnouts." All eight youths were described as friends or acquaintances—ten including the "copycat" couple who survived.

After her son's death, Thomas Rizzo's mother told reporters, "They have a pact going here in Bergenfield, and they are dying one after another." Kids in adjacent towns agreed. Long before Bergenfield, there had been a wave of teenage suicides in north Jersey. In less than one year, by January 1980, in isolated incidents, six West Milford youths had taken their own lives. In 1984, in nearby Passaic County, eight persons between the ages of fifteen and twenty-four killed themselves. Kids from nearby towns laughed nervously, speculating, "By the year 2000 the entire youth population of New Jersey could wipe itself out!" Nobody really knew what to think.

People elsewhere speculated about the suicides, clucking their tongues. "There's something wrong with New Jersey. All that radon gas. Too much toxic waste, too many malls." In Bergenfield the adults spoke of "something evil in the air," like this was *The Village of the Damned*.

The high visibility of rock-and-roll kids in Bergenfield gave adults the impression that there were heavy-metal-instigated suicide cults in the town. There was talk of Satan and black magic, because some kids listen to Ozzy Osbourne, Iron Maiden, and Motley Crüe and because of some scary song titles on a cassette tape cover of AC/DC's *If You Want Blood, You've Got It* found on the floor of the garage where the four kids died.

While the four previous deaths had been ruled accidental, the suicide pact on March 11 left no doubts. Their deaths meant that the four kids got to call the last shot. They abandoned the people who were close to them without warning. They threw the ball in someone else's court once and for all.

"Why did they do it?" Nobody had a clue. The four kids never said a word. Friends wondered why they didn't see it coming. Across America, parents figured it was the drugs, kids figured it was the parents, but most people admitted they just didn't know. As people in Bergenfield tried to understand how this most recent suicide pact was possible, blame passed from the kids' allegedly "fucked-up families" to their presumable "authoritarian school" to their ominous pleasure in "heavy metal music" to "the wrong friends," and most predictably, to "drugs." Finally, "the media" were held responsible for the "contagion effect" often associated with teenage suicide. In the best of times, parents are confused by teenage activity. Now they were panicked.

By now, enough towns across America had experienced the unthinkable that leading Bergenfield officials rightly understood that the "problem of hopelessness" among youth was national, not local. Still, nobody had been prepared for the suicide pact and the contagion effect that it triggered in Bergenfield and elsewhere.

The day after the Bergenfield suicide pact, news had come of a copycat suicide 700 miles away, in Alsip, Illinois. Nancy Grannan, nineteen, and Karen Logan, seventeen, were best friends, high school dropouts, both waitresses. The two died of asphyxiation in Grannan's car, inside the garage of the Logans' home. Bergenfield officials feared all the media attention might have set them off. This, the aborted copycat in Bergenfield, and the suicide in Clifton, exacerbated the feeling that it would never end.

Then, the four kids' story was buried with them. The police would not release their suicide note, claiming it was too personal. Bergen County prosecutor Larry McClure believed that releasing the note would be destructive. He feared it would "romanticize" the situation. Adults agreed.

Like most young people watching events in Bergenfield unfold, my teenage cousins thought this was the worst insult. Even in death, the parents won out. The dicks wouldn't even let them get their last word in. Denied to the bitter end.

Then, friends of the victims asked to have the American flag at Bergenfield High School flown at half-mast. Their request was denied. After all, they were told, their friends weren't heroes or anything. Some of the neighbors did lower theirs, and then the town held a community prayer service. Not a memorial, but a gathering together, a healing, a statement of community.

The people of Bergenfield turned to the clergy, to the "mental health people," their mayor, the superintendent of schools, the chief of police— the spiritual and political leaders of the community. Neighbors comforted each other. What did this mean? What did it say about their town? What had they done wrong? "Why us?" Friends of the deceased reached out to the siblings of the suicides. Parents could not fathom that this had actually happened. Friends cried openly in the streets.

Bergenfield was hard-pressed to come up with answers, to curtail the possibility of *more* copycat attempts, to comfort its residents and pull itself together. The weekend after the suicide was ominous: Friday the 13th *and* a full moon. Because Bergenfield claims the largest Irish American population in Bergen County, the annual St. Patrick's Day parade had been scheduled there. Such a celebration could be uplifting, but there was concern about alcohol consumption. Mayor O'Dowd was anxious to restore normalcy and the sense that life goes on. On the advice of mental health professionals, the town went ahead with the parade. Over 12,000 people showed up.

From the beginning, from the day the four bodies were discovered, television cameras were rolling.

"Are you burnouts?"

"Are you gonna commit suicide?"

Kids threw eggs at the reporters. They yelled and cursed from the smoke line outside their school. That first day, as the news of their friends' deaths broke, the kids just wanted to be left alone. Bergenfield High School officials had to ban reporters from school property. Students were visibly upset by them, crying.

The kids were tight lipped and wary of reporters. They warned one another, "Don't tell them anything." When they could, the kids tried to convince the world watching them through the lens, "We're not druggies . . . it's not drug-related." Then they'd beg the reporters to leave. "Can't you see you're hurting people?"

The privacy of a town in mourning versus the public's right to know. A town proud of the many resources it has to offer its youth. A community where eight kids had died, and two more had tried. Privacy to heal and to constitute the truth as it must be told to the rest of the world. Privacy and the need to make peace with the unthinkable.

After a few days, the reporters were driving everybody nuts, badgering kids for details, forcing conclusions from people before they had a chance to sort things out, putting everyone involved on the defensive. But the people fought back, tried to protect themselves. There were boasting and tales of local heroism—retaliatory gestures against the media. One rumor had Tommy Rizzo's father waving a baseball bat at reporters. Nobody confirmed that this actually happened, but nobody blamed him either. They figured it was his right to defend his family's honor and the memory of his son against outsiders.

People were confused. They wanted to mourn but also to avoid giving it too much attention, glorifying suicide. They wanted to talk about it but feared setting off more incidents. They wanted to figure out what had happened but resented how "everything had gotten blown out of proportion" by the media.

But Bergenfield was not the first or last "typical American town" to suffer a media assault in the aftermath of a collective tragedy, to complain that a local event had been "blown out of proportion," that reality had been warped by the leering and gaping of the electronic eye. News reporters, particularly television crews, had surfaced as malevolent intruders in communities across America wherever teenage suicides had occurred.

At first, such towns were on the defensive; after a while they got mediawise, learned how to appropriate the technology for their own purposes. The "truth" would be told on their terms or not at all. After a while the school simply refused to talk to anyone. The kids became streetside performance artists; parents and loved ones prepared themselves, becoming practiced at regulating the flow of information.

Then they began laying blame. Under attack, close friends of the victims tried to defend themselves against the more bizarre rumors. They denied repeatedly that they were part of a cult: "We watch each other's backs;" "We're like a second family." They described their clique: "We're not a pack like they say. We're just a bunch of guys who love each other."

But parents and officials saw things differently. For them, this bond was disturbing. School superintendent John Habeeb said, "That kind of support system often has a destructive agenda." Tommy Rizzo's mother said she was touched by the loyalty her son's friends showed to her younger son and to the younger brother of Tommy Olton. They offered to spend time with the kids, to play with them, to help them mourn. But Mrs. Rizzo also confided that at one point, she and her husband had considered moving out of Bergenfield to separate Thomas, Jr., from his friends.

The school also came under attack. The day after the suicide pact, an estimated four hundred Bergenfield residents packed the high school auditorium to express their anger at the school for its "lack of compassion in dealing with troubled students." Marian Henderson, a youth counselor from Parsippany, charged that Bergenfield High School's students have a "sense of hopelessness and powerlessness" which she attributed to an "oppressive disciplinary policy that includes no warnings or second chances." Students applauded, and when John Habeeb tried to interrupt her, a man from the audience shouted him down. "Baloney. Let her speak."

Superintendent Habeeb was "visibly shaken by the allegations," and defended the school's suspension policy. He denied that Bergenfield High School "encourages" students to drop out. And he cited the 1.9 percent dropout rate. The school reported an enrollment of 1,150, so that's approximately 22 kids in a town of about 25,000. That's comparable to the dropout rate in Bergen County. It's not that bad

But parental anger persisted. One Bergenfield father railed, "I don't see us working to keep [troubled students] in school. . . . I find it reprehensible that this has happened. A look at your suspension policy might be in order." The day after the suicide pact, Bergenfield High School students told reporters that they were still being suspended and "encouraged to drop out."

Yet the school refused to discuss its expulsion policy. Instead, officials stood behind the "terse" six-paragraph statement they had issued defending the school's services, claiming, "The needs of the student body [were] identified and addressed by Bergenfield faculty and staff."

Parents and kids complained that school authorities had been slow to respond to widespread drug use and alcoholism; they had hired the drug counselor only one week before the suicides. The school, in turn, charged that parents were dumping their child-rearing responsibilities on educators.

Around the time of the big meeting at the school, a few Bergenfield High School dropouts spoke to reporters. They likened life at Bergenfield High School to prison. There were charges that "the school is all too eager to push out troubled kids for minor infractions." One eighteen-year-old dropout told reporters, "I was a problem so they asked me to leave. I felt worthless."

After the meeting at the school there was a flurry of activity. To some, the activity seemed exemplary. To others, it was people just trying to cover their asses. All sorts of mental support services were installed, energized, or trotted out.

There had been a break in the order of things in Bergenfield. And for a day or two competing truths had come to the surface. But the old patterns soon fell back into place. "Mainstream" kids evinced a desire to remain separate from the kids they called "the burnouts." It emerged soon after the suicides, and was articulated anytime representative "Bergenfield youth" were given an opportunity to speak publicly.

The confrontation between angry Bergenfield parents and the school and the news media's subsequent airing of the town's dirty laundry brought about a vigorous backlash; first, against the "burnouts" for putting the town on the map and for giving the school a bad name, and then the community rallied against the "irresponsibility" of the reporters.

Parents openly expressed the fear that people would associate all children from Bergenfield—their children—with *those* kids. College-bound students worried that their school would get a bad name. School officials worried about budget cuts, liability, and accountability. Everybody was afraid the town would be marked forever. It was obvious nobody wanted to be identified with what the papers described as "the fringe students at Bergenfield High who self-mockingly call themselves burnouts." Yet officials, experts, parents, and Bergenfield High's top students publicly espoused a new ethic of caring about their alienated youth.

Police Chief Warren Burkart described the four members of the suicide pact as "pain-in-the-ass kids." Not really bad kids but obviously "going nowhere fast." According to local authorities, they were a minority among the town's young people, "members of an insular teenage subculture known as the 'burnouts' . . . many of whom come from troubled or broken homes, drop out of school, and have trouble holding jobs." News reports portrayed them as teens who "hung out with a scruffily disgruntled group put down as the burnouts, sharing a fondness for punk fashion and heavy metal music."

Reporters covering the story after the suicides noted that Bergenfield's "burnouts" wore leather and looked tough standing around together; alone, engaged in conversation, the reporters found the youths to be polite, even shy. The youths' identification as "burnouts" would be mentioned repeatedly though never explored in any detail. Yes, "the burnouts" were dropouts from the mainstream, but not all of them were high school dropouts.

The burnouts' bond was cultural—not ethnic, racial, or religious—although it seemed almost as strong. As I would later learn, some kids who were labeled as burnouts were actually good students. Yet by virtue of their friends, their clothing, and their interest in a certain type of music, they could be identified and categorized as burnouts. The unabashedness with which kids in Bergenfield were identified as belonging to an outcast youth subculture was unique to any reported teenage suicide. But nobody noticed.

On the first anniversary of the suicide pact, a number of special follow-up news reports aired on local and national television. We saw many of the same faces—officials, loyal students, mental health administrators. Over the year the town had gained a certain moral authority—it had survived the suicide pact as well as the media invasion. The community had learned something and had grown. By now, Bergenfield's representatives also knew how to work media.

On ABC's *Nightline*, we would learn of Bergenfield's "new awareness," its comprehensive battery of preventive services. There was a hot line, and Bergenfield police were getting special training for suicide calls. Bergenfield High School would implement a "peer leadership" program. Parents would get involved. Officials would seek out federal and state funding so that these programs could continue to help Bergenfield's youth. The town had been successful with its rational responses to serious social problems. This is how Bergenfield would present itself to the television world.

On the local news, there was a brief clip of a follow-up visit to Bergenfield High, on the anniversary of the suicide pact. Wholesome and alert students selected to represent the school sat around a table with their principal, Lance Rosza, and reiterated what had become *the* story about the Bergenfield suicide pact. The four kids "had nothing to do with the school." They had "chosen" to drop out. They committed suicide because they had "personal problems."

Police Lieutenant Donald Stumpf, who had also served as school board president, admitted that Bergenfield was "weak on dropouts." A juvenile officer, Stumpf noted that once the kids drop out, "they go to never-neverland." Maybe that's where they came from, since the school took every opportunity to point out that it had nothing to do with its students' dropping out. Suddenly the "burnouts" appeared in this state of social dislocation, as if by magic. They had no involvement with the school or the town. By choice they turned their backs on all the available support, concern, and care. They were self-made outcasts, disengaged atoms floating in space somewhere over Bergenfield. There was no discussion of the process, only the product.

Once we all agreed that the four kids had banded together in a suicide pact because they had *personal problems*, we no longer needed to ask what "the burnouts" were alienating themselves from. Or what role their identification as "burnouts" played in the way they felt about themselves, their families, their school, or their town.

If we understood the Bergenfield suicide pact as the result of *personal problems*, we would then have to remove the event from its social context. And once we did that, the story according to "the burnouts" would never be known. It would be buried with the four kids.

There were other reasons why "the burnouts" themselves weren't being heard. First, they had little access to the media. They weren't likely to be on hand when Bergenfield High School authorities needed bright, articulate youth to represent the school or town to reporters. "Alienated youth" don't hang around teachers or shrinks any longer than they have to.

Second, to the chagrin of their caretakers, "burnouts" aren't particularly "verbal." The basic life-world shared by teenage suburban metalheads is action oriented: best understood in context, through signs and symbols in motion. It would be hard to convey one's thoughts and feelings to reporters in the succinct lines that make up the news.

In the beginning "the burnouts" did talk to reporters, but things got twisted around— "the papers got the story all fucked up"—and besides, they really hated hearing their friends and their town maligned by strangers. So they clammed right up.

The kids everybody called burnouts understood this: Once you open the door, they've got you. You're playing their language game. Whatever you say can be held against you. Better to keep it to yourself. So programs existed in Bergenfield but "the burnouts" didn't dare use them. They may have been outcasts, but they weren't stupid. They knew how to avoid trouble.

Kids who realize they are marginal fear reprisals. Over and over again I was asked not to mention names. And no pictures. As a rule, teenagers love performing for the media. It's a game that lets adults think they understand "kids today," and it's fun. But "the burnouts" were now media-wise. They knew better. They wanted complete control or they weren't saying shit.

So by design and by default, nobody really got to hear what "the burnouts" had to say. Like any other alienated youth since the conceptu-alization of "youth" as a social category, they don't like to talk to adults. About anything. After the suicide pact a few "burnouts" told reporters they were reluctant to confide in school guidance counselors because the counselors might tell their parents and "they'd be punished or even sent to a psychiatric hospital."

The idea of troubled youth doing themselves in was especially dis-turbing to a town that boasted more than thirty active programs for its youth prior to the suicide pact of March 11. Yet Lieutenant Stumpf noted that the Bergenfield kids who most needed the services would not make use of them.

Authorities had acknowledged that the more "alienated" or "high-risk" youth of Bergenfield would not voluntarily involve themselves with the town's services. But the kids weren't talking about what it was that held them back, why they weren't looking to confide in the adults.

In the local papers, experts called in to comment on the tragedy referred to this as "the conspiracy of silence"—the bond of secrecy between teenage friends. While there was some acknowledgment that this reflected the kids' terror of "getting in trouble," nobody questioned whether or not this fear might be rational.

Yet it was becoming clear that for Bergenfield's marginally involved youth, the idea of going to see a school guidance counselor or really "opening up" to parents, shrinks, and even clergy was inconceivable. It was apparent that even if they had done nothing wrong, they felt guilty.

By now it was also apparent that the "burnouts," as a clique, as carriers of a highly visible "peer-regulated" subculture posed a threat to the hege-mony of parents, teachers, and other mandated "agents of socialization" in Bergenfield. The initial blaming of the suicide victims' friends for what-ever had gone wrong did take some of the pressure off the parents and the school. This was predictable—after all, "Where'd you learn that from, your friends?" is a well-traveled technique adults use to challenge and suppress a kid's dissenting view.

Readings of youth, from the *Rebel Without a Cause* 1950s to *The River's Edge* 1980's to the *Kids* 1990s, have explored the young person's long-standing critique of the adult world: Nobody talks about what is really going on. Especially not parents, and never at school. The "burnouts" un-derstood that very well. Yet the "insularity" of this group of outcasts frus-trated adults everywhere. It annoyed them as much as "explosive inside views" might have titillated them.

These kids were actively guarding their psychic space because the adults controlled everything else. Yet the experts on the scene continued to urge the "burnouts" to purge. Forget about it. It's no secret: You give them an inch and they'll take a self. Bergenfield's alienated youth population already had a different way of seeing things. How *could* they reach out and speak up when every day up until the suicide pact, and shortly thereafter, they were encouraged to suppress what *they* perceived to be reality? When living means having to deny what you feel, disassociating yourself to survive, you'd better stay close to your friends or you could start to believe the bullshit. Yes, the "burnouts" carried the news, they knew the truth. They all understood what that "something evil in the air" was. Alone, it made them *crazy*. Together, it made them *bad*.

Historically, we have been ambivalent about suicide; sometimes it was expected as an expression of loyalty. In India and Japan such "altruistic" suicides were deeply embedded in the cultural assumptions about the roles of the widow and the warrior, respectively. Under Jewish law, suicide is forbidden. Yet in the history of the persecution of the Jews, there is a reverence for suicide as preferable to slavery, rape, or forced conversion. The mass suicide at Masada in A.D. 73 has always been viewed as heroic —the will to freedom in the face of inevitable Roman enslavement. The image of martyr-as-hero is deeply embedded in our culture, from religion to pop, from Jesus Christ to John Lennon.

The Roman Catholic Church once refused burial rites to suicides. Suicide was seen as a profound renunciation of spiritual belief. In modern times the church has come to view the person who commits suicide as not in his or her "right mind." The suicide victim cannot be held accountable for the act.

In the scientific imagination, suicide is viewed as a disease —like drug addiction or depression.

But when people talk about teenage suicide, the word "romance" is often invoked. Supposedly, suicide is not real to young people. They are anesthetized to life and desensitized to death. They don't understand that it is final, irreversible. The poetics of suicide appeal to those most vulnerable to influences, and the young lack the resources needed to buffer the violence of an emergent self.

It is also believed that young people kill themselves to get attention or revenge. Suicide is now hip, dangerous, the final resistance to adult authority, a last stand against conformity. To some kids, suicide is death before dishonor, heroism over defeat. Because attempts so greatly outnumber actual suicides, suicide is as much a statement of the desire to control life as it is to end it.

Death has taken on new meaning in the last twenty years. To the postmodern imagination, suicide is titillating. It is the last great taboo. Having exhausted sex, death—by suicide or homicide—becomes the final frontier of sensate experience; new pleasures. People disagree on whether the taboo on suicide should be strengthened or deconstructed. Are we better able to suppress the urge by making it unthinkable or by thinking it through?

Sometimes our fascination with these forms of final obliteration appears to reflect a collective death wish. Esoteric knowledge is invoked to help explain these things. Astrologers point to Pluto in Scorpio or its position relative to Uranus, the final death gasp of the Piscean age. We talk to God, we read the scriptures, the prophecy of Armageddon, the predictions of Nostradamus.

Rates of recklessness among young people have increased in the last twenty years. Not only are there more suicides, but more homicides and fatal car crashes too. To understand this, we may give up God and metaphysics and turn to Marx. We ponder the final stages of capitalism. We blame it on bureaucracy, on the problems of waste and surplus absorption, social inequality, bourgeois decadence, the welfare state, the religious right, political repression. Or else the decline of the patriarchal family, peer group pressure, designer drugs, violence in films, television, and music.

We condemn ourselves for our capitalist economy predicated on consumption and waste, our desire for spectacle and pleasure. Yet now, the international electronic eye of TV broadcasts disaffected post-Glasnost Soviet youth into our living rooms—cynical, alienated, dressed in Iron Maiden and Ozzy Osbourne T-shirts, hanging out, partying in vacant lots, alcoholic. They too fear they have "no future." Restless, wasted youth now appear as an international malaise among industrialized nations. These kids, too, want the truth. They want adults to deep their promises, or else 'fess up to the false ones. Until then, they too will refuse the game.

For young people, suicide promises comfort. It is a violent seductive release, a means to an end, a soothing and delicious deep sleep. In the context of young lives lived like rapid fire, but focused nowhere, suicide seems thrilling, intoxication, contagious. Death and suicide become eroticized, as terror and rapture, self-loathing and self-gratification.

Transhistorically, cross-culturally, humans have placed enormous burdens on their young. Sometimes these burdens have been primarily economic: the child contributes to the economy of the family or the tribe. Sometimes the burden has been social—the child is a contribution to the immortality of our creed. Be fruitful and multiply.

But the spiritual burden we pass on to the child may be the most difficult to bear. We expect them to fulfill an incompleteness in ourselves, in our world. Our children are our vehicle for the realization of unfulfilled dreams, our class aspirations, our visions of social justice and world peace, of a better life on earth. Without this hope in the future *through the child* we could not endure slavery, torture, war, genocide, or even the ordinary everyday grind of a "bad life."

In a now famous footnote in *Suicide*, written almost a hundred years ago, the French sociologist Émile Durkheim described fatalistic suicide as "the suicide deriving from excessive regulation, that of persons with futures pitilessly blocked and passions violently choked by oppressive discipline." Where there is overregulation, explains Durkheim, "rule against which there is no appeal, we might call it fatalistic suicide."

But as far as young people are concerned, fatalistic suicide is not the whole story. True, young people are among the most regulated in our society. With the exception of people in total institutions, only the lives of animals are more controlled. Yet most experts attribute youth suicide to anomie—the opposite of fatalistic suicide in Durkheim's thinking. To be anomic is to feel disengaged, adrift, alienated. Like you don't fit in anywhere.

Where fatalistic suicide may result from overregulation, anomic suicide is attributed to nonintegration. Young people are in the peculiar position of being overregulated by adults, yet alienated from them. Many are integrated only into the world shared with their peers—some may be overly integrated into that world, as in gangs or subcults. Young people are always somewhere on a continuum between overregulation and nonintegration. In the 1980s, both ends of this continuum grew to extremes.

By the beginning of the 1990s, young people began to demand some recognition as a social category, to present themselves as a self-identified collectivity, aware of their many differences but bound together by one thing: age. Like every other minority, kids are now fighting back. They try to control media misrepresentation and adult misinterpretation of their activities and goals. Many are engaged as activists—as fascists, anarchists, separatists, nationalists, feminists, and Greens. Some now struggle for their civil rights as homosexuals or petition for their reproductive rights and also for the rights of the unborn. Other American kids work to protect the environment or on behalf of the homeless.

Young people continue to seek recognition, hoping to become visible and viable in the social landscape. In the 1980s, adults noticed youths as their suicide rates began to alarm us. By the 1990s, homicide rates, juvenile crime, and gang activity upstaged suicide as the focus of adult concern. In the early 1980s, 50 percent of the forty-four largest U.S. cities reported gang problems. By 1992, the figure had grown to 91 percent, and the next thirty-five largest cities also reported gang problems.

Gangs are also spreading to nonurban youth populations, appearing in suburbs and small towns, even on Indian lands—remote, rural, impoverished. Nationwide, the number of Native American gangs has more than doubled since 1994. The Bureau of Indian Affairs estimates there are 375 gangs with 4,650 members, up from 181 gangs in 1994. The overall homicide rate on Indian lands has soared 87 percent in the past five years. Life on the reservation can be brutally isolating; some families are destitute, without hope. The alcoholism death rate for Native American youths aged fifteen to twenty-four is 5.2 per 100,000 population, compared to 0.3 for non-Native Americans. The accident rate, too, is higher for Native American youths. Their suicide rate is 2.3 times the corresponding rate for white populations, and their homicide rate, while about 9 percent lower than for all races combined, is almost two times the rate for white kids.

The Navajos are the largest Indian nation in North America, with 110,000 members living on 26,000 square miles extending into Arizona, Utah, and New Mexico. The Navajo Nation has 55 gangs with 900 members, who outnumber and outgun the police. Navajo youth identify with and idolize Latino gangs. Not only are the Latinos defiant pop culture icons, they are an Hispanicized Indian people with visibility and street authority. Navajo kids are proud to be "down with the brown." Gang membership offers recognition, community, economic opportunity, and relief from the relentlessly remote geography of reservation life. Gang membership may temporarily lower suicide rates by focusing inward rage outward, but gangs may be seen as a suicide pact of another sort, a collective death wish, a peer-regulated willingness to die for the greater glory of colors and turf.

During the 1990s the media have continued to wallow in the social pornography of the day, generating images of young people committing heartless, heinous crimes. "A new generation of callous criminals?" asks *People* magazine. There's "Prom Mom," the eighteen-year-old who delivered her son in the ladies' room on prom night, dumped him in the trash, then went back to dance. Even younger and more ruthless, privileged fifteen-year-old wiggers Christopher Vasquez and Daphne Abdela are accused of stabbing their forty-four-year-old drinking buddy to death in Central Park —thirty times—before dumping the body into the lake. Then there's the tragic twelve-year-old Malcolm Shabazz, troubled grandson of Malcolm X, who torched grandmother Betty Shabazz to death.

By 1998 we began to see a new breed of angry American child. Two dead in Pearl, Mississippi, two in Springfield, Oregon, three in West Paducah, Kentucky, five at Jonesboro, Arkansas. After all the suicide pacts and gang-related killings, these mass shootings herald a new nonurban white boy's disease, part gangster, part militia, part serial killer. There's a logical line from Bergenfield to Littleton. Yet most of America remains in denial. In 1987, Satan, AC/DC, and the dreaded peer group were blamed for the Bergenfield suicides. Now it's Marilyn Manson, the National Rifle Association, and Doom, a video game. This is dead wrong. It takes a village to destroy a child.

America has plans for its unruly youngsters. Uncooperative children of privilege are the new growth market for psychiatric drugs and hospitals, while out-of-control poor kids suffer a different fate. Since the late 1970s a majority of states have changed their laws to make it easier to try juveniles as young as thirteen years old as adults. We now legislate kids into poverty, then legislate them into prison. Youth advocates report children in adult institutions are 500 percent more likely to be sexually assaulted and 200 percent more likely to be beaten by staff than kids placed in juvenile centers. They are also more likely to be attacked with a weapon.

While we adults hold young people responsible as if they were fully empowered, emancipated adults, when it comes to civil liberties we conveniently view young people as "children" needing our protection, guidance, and support. In recent years we have seen the rise of constitutionally shaky legislation affecting young people that would seek to impose curfews, force drug testings, enable search and seizure, block access to shopping malls, limit the right to assemble, limit access to abortions and birth control, and deny welfare benefits. At the same time, public schools are overcrowded, safety nets are fraying, and the resources to nurture young people and protect them from homelessness, hunger, parental abuse, and poor health are getting slashed and burned.

The 1990s brought a psychic blow to the baby bust—the deaths of respected rock heroes. Kurt Cobain died of white boy disease (suicide), and Tupac Shakur of black boy disease (homicide). Yet the resilience and goodness of young people prevail. Most labor on in faith, holding fast to some remnant of the American Dream. They love and support their parents even as the labor force pulls families apart and the nation fails to support family life in any meaningful way. In terms of intergenerational politics, adults have no time or money for kids. The logical outcome of this disregard and disrespect should be violent rage against the machine. Instead, kids blame themselves, suffer sadness privately, show signs of widespread clinical depression. They act out the emptiness we have given them, hoping to fill the moral and spiritual vacuum with sex, drugs, booze, and commodity fetishes. Of course some American kids appear morally bankrupt—look who their role models are.

In the years after the Bergenfield suicide pact, great thrash metal bands got dropped from labels, and the popcult zeitgeist changed. Clothing styles, values, and scenes were transformed as the flannel hordes emerged from Seattle and grunge inherited the earth. Kurt Cobain was an alienated stoner kid who grew up in a trailer park in a small town outside Aberdeen, Washington. The product of a broken home, this lumpenprole hero not only made it out of teenage wasteland alive, he soared to the highest ground. Cobain was the Great White Hope for kids trapped in bad lives across America's nonurban wastelands. His triumph gave them hope, faith that you could be yourself, be human, and not get totally destroyed. In *Nirvana*, Cobain transformed a kid's private hell into a generation's collective howl. He wasn't supposed to blow his brains out at twenty-seven. But his inner agony won out over his band, his wife, and his child. Cobain's suicide anointed him as the baby bust's first celebrity martyr.

Young people fought back with style and grace. The 1990s brought exhilarating subcultural innovation, particularly among middle-class youth. Girls made forays into male-dominated genres of hip hop, hardcore, and metal. College-based "alternative" youth culture came above ground with grunge music. Slackers and bohemians congregated at coffeehouses and online at Internet cafes. Despite adults' dismissing them as apathetic and self-centered, young people actively supported social causes, entered politics, and donated to freedom struggles across the world. Myths about their generation were exploded as young people showed themselves to be pioneering, industrious, and bold in the marketplace. After blaming underemployed, underutilized youths for their lack of motivation, adults saw that given some real opportunity, young people were eager to learn and earn.

In the 1990s, bands such as Hole, L7, and Bikini Kill brought new life to feminism, as journalists and scholars pondered "Women in Rock." Riot Grrl fanzines and activities brought girls a new cultural authority. With an agenda that let it bleed from the inside out, they articulated every female torment from anorexia to incest. Post-punk queercore music scenes set the stage for lesbian and gay kids to come out loud and strong. They found heroes in Ru Paul, Sleater-Kinney, Melissa Ethridge, Tribe 8, Pansy Division, Wayne/Jayne County, k.d. lang, and Ellen DeGeneres.

Like lesbian and gay kids, Native American youths suffer suicide rates two to three times higher than other kids. Blackfire is a Navajo punk band that walks in two worlds. Their music mixes traces of ska and hardcore with more traditional Indian sounds. A sibling trio, their father is a medicine man. As the Jones Benally Family, Blackfire and their father tour the world performing twenty-seven intertribal Native American dances in the hope of linking people back to their culture. The family dances in traditional hand-sewn garb, with eagle feathers passed down over generations. Born in the heart of "Big Mountain" Arizona, on the reservation, Blackfire rarely plays in bars; the group opposes the alcohol abuse that has devastated reservation life, land depletion from strip-mining of coal, and oppression and relocation of Natives. Concerned over suicide rates, gang-related violence, and alcoholism, Blackfire hopes to steer kids away from death culture and towards proud Native traditions.

Blackfire's lead guitarist Klee Benally says, "Our generation has a whole lot of anger. We can try to turn negative into positive, be productive. We can make the world a better place. It's all about respect. Respect is a big word in all disputes—you dissin' me? We all come from an indigenous culture, we all have spirituality. Who you are is passed down. All cultures have a basis in respect. We have to think for our children's world, how we want them to grow. Maybe we can teach our children." He believes schools today fail because they want to teach kids "what" they are, not "who" they are. "What they are in American society is consumers."

Young people hunger for meaning and connection as well as material things. The baby bust generation has been described as "the most socially pluralistic ever," multicultural, diverse, flexibly. Actually, you can see this in America's 1990s version of rave culture where lines of gender, race, and class wash out to a sea of body-modified (bomo) androgynous celebrants. In a do-it-yourself scene that flourishes underground, peer orchestrated, here today and gone tomorrow, the fragmentation of postmodernity becomes creative expression. Dancing alone, together, on the grimy warehouse floor, to the pulsating bass-drum beat, on drugs that simulate ecstatic, holy communion, individuality within collectivity is realized. The connectivity and technological omniscience promised in the Aquarian age has arrived, not in us, as we suspected in the 1960s, but in them, now.

Walk tall, hang loose, stay free.

NOTE

This chapter was adapted from Donna Gaines, *Teenage Wasteland* (Chicago: University of Chicago Press, 1998).

6

Masculinity Matters

THE OMISSION OF GENDER FROM
HIGH-PROFILE SCHOOL VIOLENCE CASES

Jessie Klein and Lynn S. Chancer

Seven boys, ages eleven through eighteen, killed a total of twenty-three children and five adults, and wounded sixty-seven in a recent spate of school shootings. Popular media explanations blame violence in the media, lax gun-control laws, working parents, and pure chance. We argue that these responses predominantly address symptoms, while underlying causes are revealed instead in an unexplored culture of violence embedded in everyday relations of gender and sexuality. Three sanctioned "male" behaviors help explain the boys' motivations: misogyny, gay-bashing, and violence.

April 20, 1999, Littleton, Colorado: Eric Harris, age eighteen, and Dylan Klebold, age seventeen, were not the first boys to wage war on the "preps and jocks" in their high school. From their point of view they were retaliating against years of abuse. When they opened fire in their school cafeteria, they killed eight boys, four girls, and one male teacher and wounded twenty-three students before committing suicide.[1]

Disturbing similarities exist between the victims at Columbine High and the targets in four other high-profile school massacres. In all of these school shootings the perpetrators were young boys who aimed their bullets at girls who rejected them and/or at other boys who attacked their masculinity by implying they were homosexual. On May 21, 1998, in Springfield, Oregon, Kipland Kinkel, age fifteen, augured the Colorado motives, killing two "jocks" who tormented him for being "small." He shot four people dead (two boys and his parents) and wounded twenty-two others.[2]

The eleven people killed in the first three cases were female. On December 1, 1997, Michael Carneal, age fourteen, killed a girl who didn't return his affections. Then he killed two other girls, and wounded five of his schoolmates in West Paducah, Kentucky. He said he was tired of being called a "faggot."[3] In March, 1998, fourteen-year-old Mitchell Johnson of Jonesboro, Arkansas, proudly publicized his "vow to kill all the girls who had broken up with him." Johnson and his accomplice, Andrew Golden, age eleven, shot Johnson's ex-girlfriend, killed four girls and a pregnant teacher, and wounded nine girls and one boy. Of their fifteen victims, fourteen were female.[4] In October 1997, in Pearl, Mississippi, sixteen-year-old Luke Woodham stabbed his mother to death, picked up his brother's hunting rifle, and drove to school where he killed his ex-girlfriend and her best friend and wounded seven others. "I am not insane," Woodham wrote in a letter before his shooting spree. "I am angry. I killed because people like me are mistreated every day."[5] Woodham also reported he was tired of being called "gay."[6] Eric Harris' diary revealed a similar rage at ridicule by "preps and jocks" who called him "homosexual." He also wrote, "I am not crazy."[7]

Because the boys in all five cases considered it normal to defend their "manhood" against a form of "gay-bashing" and/or from rejection by girls, the incidents obviously implicated gender. However, the social construction of masculinity was not among the problems the media cited to explain the killings.

The first of the ensuing sections reviews popular explanations of school violence offered in media accounts soon after the crimes. Second, we return to the specific circumstances surrounding the crimes to show how gender, and specifically expectations of masculinity, were germane to these cases and therefore startling for being omitted from media and public scrutiny. Third, we look at the ramifications of omitting gender. Finally, we offer some directions for change in both the short and the long term. This analysis is based on the perusal of more than 200 articles about the five cases written in the *New York Times*, the *Los Angeles Times*, local newspapers, and online sources. Our argument is that analyzing "ordinary" masculinity is essential for understanding and reducing high levels of violence in U.S. society.

POPULAR EXPLANATIONS IN THE MEDIA

Given the shock and loss experienced within each community, it is not surprising that people grasped at the most visible explanations that come to mind. As debates in the media raged, four social problems gained the greatest momentum in accounting for the eruption of school-based violence. The most popular explanation was lack of gun-control laws in the United States. The second was excessive violence in American media. A third diagnosis blamed the young killers' parents. A fourth interpretation was much more resigned: random violence emerged as an explanation (or non-explanation) in and of itself. The violent events were considered unrelated, unlikely to happen in the first place, and certainly not part of a disturbing trend.

First, the National Rifle Association was accused. Stricter gun-control laws were hailed as the primary means to prevent massive school shootings. Kristen Rand, the Violence Policy Center's director of federal policy, blamed the NRA for marketing guns to children.[8] She referred to advertisements directed at male teenagers, like this ad in *Gun Press* magazine regarding an assault weapon for sale:

It is one mean looking dude . . . considered cool and Rambo-ish by the teenage crowd; to a man they love the AP9 at first sight. Stuffed to the brim with Nyclad hollow points, the pistol is about as wicked a piece as you can keep by your pillow. . . . Take a look at one, And let your *teenage son* tag along. Ask him what he thinks.[9] [emphasis added]

Indeed, some parents of the homicide victims became activists against gun accessibility. Believing lax gun control was responsible for the death of her daughter in Arkansas, one mother campaigned heavily for Chuck Schumer against Al D'Amato on this issue in the 1998 New York State Senate campaign. "What Al D'Amato doesn't seem to understand is that guns are killing our children. . . . We need a Congress that cares about families like mine," she proclaimed.[10] President Clinton leapt to the task after the fourth school shooting, calling for a team of experts to write a guidebook to help school officials see warning signs and to adopt a "zero tolerance" policy toward guns.[11] Fire Chief Dennis Murphy, in Springfield, Oregon, agreed. "We can end mass school violence via guns. What we need to do is create airport-like security for schools . . . so stop saying we can't do it."[12]

Access to guns dramatically increases the capacity to kill and indeed multiplies the death toll. Ronald Stephens, the executive director of the National School Safety Center, said astutely, "In the old days kids would walk away from a fight with a few bruises. Now it's a body count."[13] But blaming guns and focusing exclusively on policy ultimately deflects attention from the underlying causes motivating these boys to use guns in the first place. It implies that as long as the violence does not cause multiple deaths, such fights are "normal and acceptable." We argue that these expanded numbers are part of a growing cultural problem: the normalization of violence in masculinity. But, instead of examining social relations more closely, other targets of blame are created. Each of these scapegoats defends itself by directing the culpability elsewhere.

Buttressed by evidence that several of the boys enjoyed violent video games, music, and movies, the NRA reinforced accusations directed at media violence. After Jonesboro, responding to Senator Diane Feinstein's efforts to ban the sale of high-capacity ammunition magazines,[14] Wayne LaPierre, Executive Vice President of the NRA, ridiculed the bill with a ludicrous commentary:

> She might as well ban sheet metal and springs because that's all a magazine is made of. What would make a bigger impact on problems like what happened in Jonesboro is for Senator Feinstein to talk to the entertainment industry in her backyard about stopping the showing of gratuitous violence without consequence. . . . That's what people in stores, gas stations, and shopping malls all over the country are saying about Jonesboro. No one has said, "Gee we need another magazine ban."[15]

Helping the NRA to avoid the spotlight, experts were quoted to strengthen this interpretation. For example, according to Alvin Poussaint, Professor of Psychiatry at Harvard Medical School,

> In America, violence is considered fun to kids. They play video games where they chop people's heads off and blood gushes and it's fun, it's entertainment. It's like a game. And I think this is the psychology of these kids—this "Let's go out there and kill like on television."[16]

This perspective ignores the possibility that part of what is encouraged in the media is a hyper-masculinity only realized when violence is enacted. It fails to ask "Is violence so influential, or is it the repeated models of male killers winning female adoration and male admiration only when they viciously destroy their enemies?"

In addition to contradictory research about whether violent imagery causes real violence,[17] this argument also detracts from the deeper problem. Just as in 1968 when Frederic Wertham blamed Vietnam representations on TV for hardening citizens to war,[18] epithets directed at movies today ignore the effects of actual violence, faulting instead the media's reflections. It assumes a simple behaviorist approach towards life, as if people are only "blank slates" without critical or resistant capacities. Instead we should look at the larger context: these crimes take place in a country which, compared to other industrialized nations, has the highest rates of homicide and rape, the greatest proportion of people jailed, and the only legalized death penalty.[19]

Finally, shouldn't more attention be paid to the words the young killers spoke on their own behalf? When asked if a film he had seen recently, *The Basketball Diaries*, motivated his shooting, Michael Carneal, the child killer in Kentucky, responded, "I don't know why it happened, but I know it wasn't a movie."[20]

A third interpretation blamed the parents of the young perpetrators. Cal Thomas, author of *Uncommon Sense*, insists that "violence in the media" and "lax gun-control laws" are mere excuses that miss the real culprits: "working parents." After Jonesboro, he writes, "some say it's violence on television and in films . . . that alone seems an incomplete excuse. . . . Others say it's guns. But the boys accused in the killings stole guns from relatives who bought them legally for hunting." Instead, Thomas argues, youth violence develops when "too many children are dumped into day care so that busy, career-oriented parents can pursue lifestyles they believe will bring them happiness."[21] Thomas commends women who give up these pursuits to go back to the family. "Two professional friends of mine have had enough. They're quitting high-paying, broadcast media jobs to go home to their husbands and children."[22] Oliver North also supported this position, insisting it was "unconscionable" to blame guns or make it the federal or local government's responsibility, when it was entirely the fault of bad parenting.[23] Such an accusation indicts mothers who do not or cannot stay home to care for their children. Blaming single and working women, this diagnosis ignores the multifaceted and complex dynamics taking place within families.[24] Moreover, at least four of the boys who killed lived in two-parent traditional families.[25]

The fourth explanation was a lack of explanation, declaring the child shooting sprees "random" acts of violence. Vincent Schiraldi, Director of the Justice Policy Institute, issued a statement responding to the shootings and emphasizing that statistically violence in schools in down: "My answer is always the same: I cannot explain it because no such trend exists."[26]

This lack of response also came after the Colorado shooting. Dismissing all possible causes, Sheryl Stolberg wrote in the *New York Times*:

> The sheriffs missed the Web site ravings. The psychiatrist missed the hidden rage. The parents missed the pipe bombs. If only somebody had spotted the warning signs, a terrible tragedy might have been averted. . . .
> That is a comforting thought for a nation scarred and grieving. But viewed through the prism of science, it isn't necessarily true. . . .
> Indeed if there is anything left to be said about the recent tragedy in Littleton Colorado it may be this: the cold, hard reality of the deadliest school

massacre in American history is that it was the statistical equivalent of a needle in a haystack. Because such events are so rare, and because it is impossible to eliminate risk from life, there may be no larger lessons to draw, and no way to prevent another one.[27]

Using "science" to lend authority to her analysis, Stolberg joins a national denial and further confounds the consequential issues.[28] Statistics may reflect an overall decrease in crime and violence.[29] But when five school shootings are committed by boys, directed predominantly at girls and at boys who called the perpetrators "gay," and then followed by numerous copycat efforts, further explanation is required.[30]

Out of inadequate explanations came deficient and sometimes destructive responses. Lisa Snell from the Reason Public Policy Institute writes that since 1986 the federal government deployed increasing numbers of metal detectors and security guards throughout the nation's schools. Far from preventing school violence, she argues, some researchers state that these interventions may cause violence to proliferate. Students, teachers, and parents resign themselves to "violence as a normal state of affairs," instead of trying to transform the school culture proactively.[31] But after the 1997–1999 tragedies, the same provisional measures were installed. Some schools banned school lockers where weapons could be hidden. Other districts only allowed transparent bookbags. In West Paducah, Kentucky, bookbags and backpacks were entirely forbidden. In Denver, and then in cities across the nation, even wearing black trench coats to school was prohibited.[32] In Mississippi, it became a capital crime to kill on school property. The law was dubbed "Christy's Law" after Christina Menefee, Luke Woodham's ex-girlfriend and first victim.[33] Proposals that children as young as eleven be tried as adults and receive the death penalty were widely demanded.[34] But the earlier interventions did not prevent the 1997–1999 school shootings from occurring, and the recent increase in defense systems and harsh penalties are unlikely to do better. Already misused as a means of containment, the use of prison technology in schools can be disconcerting and ultimately ineffective, even if understandably perceived as a preventive measure.[35]

And, after the unimaginable horror in Colorado, even more unexpected conclusions were drawn in desperate efforts to explain the events and prevent the trend from continuing. Many who tried to deny responsibility previously began submitting to the accusations. For instance, the NRA scaled down its Denver conference out of unprecedented respect for the possibility that lax gun-control laws contributed to the Colorado massacre.[36] Similarly Marilyn Manson, attacked for inspiring the young killers in Kentucky, Oregon, and Colorado, temporarily accepted these charges and canceled his concert tour.[37] The Clinton administration even asked Hollywood, a huge supporter of the Democratic party, to be aware of the implications of violence in films.[38]

Even so, it is our contention that effective change cannot occur without looking closely at the emerging patterns among the shootings, and the role "normalizing violence in masculinity" plays. First, each boy specifically targeted culprits accused of threatening his masculinity: the girls who rejected him and/or "popular boys" who called him feminizing names. Second, each boy was part of an outsider group and complained of being made marginal within his community. Third, teasing boys on the lower rungs of the social ladder at school was tolerated, if not encouraged, by other students as well as by many faculty. Fourth, rage at girls and homosexuals was similarly sanctioned. Finally, the boys' violent threats and involvement with guns was equated with normal masculine behavior and thus caused no prior alarm.

WHY GENDER MATTERS

Critiques of masculinity are a fairly recent development in the field of Cultural Studies and Gender Analysis. Historically, feminist scholars stressed obstacles women face when venturing outside the strict confines of "femininity." More recently, gender theorists have started to address destructive masculinity expectations.

In *Masculinities*, Connell explains that relations of domination operate between men and women, as well as among men themselves. He argues that teasing is one of the deadliest blows to a boy's self-image, devastating to his sense of himself as a "man." To describe the complexity of masculinity, Connell identifies four types: hegemonic, subordinate, marginalized, and complicit. Hegemonic refers to the form of masculinity most legitimized in a given society; in contemporary contexts, military heroes, successful businessmen, or powerful politicians may represent this type. Men who have this power embody stereotypical masculine traits such as being unemotional, tough, authoritative, and controlling. Boys who are most clearly differentiated from women and homosexuals are classified here, at the top of the masculinities' hierarchy. On the other hand, gays and men perceived as gay are relegated to the bottom of the ladder. Their masculinity is subordinated. Finally, in a culture where white, heterosexual, wealthy men hold the greatest power, marginalized masculinity refers to men within stigmatized groups relating to race or class. Complicit masculinity comprises the majority of men who also do not meet the omnipotent expectations of manhood, but who subsequently benefit from the subordination of women and gays. Even though they are not hegemonic, they still receive a "patriarchal dividend" in that they reap status-power benefits just by virtue of being men.[39]

HEGEMONIC MASCULINITY

Within their school hierarchies, the boys who killed were considered nerds, geeks, and/or gay. It was the more privileged "preps and jocks" who were given stature in the school, received attention from girls and admiration from other boys and were treated with respect by their coaches and teachers. The boys who killed were persecuted by these youth, rejected by girls, and dismissed by authorities. Connell argues that inequalities "between masculinities" often breed violence. This violence may be aimed against females and/or against males perceived as gay or feminine. In Connell's words,

> Many members of the privileged group use violence to sustain their dominance. Intimidation of women ranges across the spectrum from wolf-whistling in the street . . . to murder by a woman's patriarchal owner. Most men do not attack or harass women; but those who do are unlikely to think themselves deviant. On the contrary they usually feel they are entirely justified, that they are exercising a right. They are authorized by an ideology of supremacy.[40]

Thus, subordinating women is a ritual asserting masculinity, and an opportunity for men to demonstrate that they are "not women." Bernard Lefkowitz describes this poignantly in *Our Guys*. He writes about the 1989 Glen Ridge, New Jersey, trial which convicted local "jocks" for committing gang rape. For Lefkowitz, "the ordinary nature of misogyny" contributed to the genesis of the assault. He documents how the town leapt to the defense of the young men, who were "hegemonic" by Connell's definition, with a "boys will be boys" defense. As happens far too commonly, the young girl was blamed for her victimization; she was labeled "promiscuous, a tease, a flirt."[41] Lefkowitz exposes a taken-for-granted masculinity, which allows this misogyny to reign unchallenged. The boys were known to disturb classes with dirty jokes, and to treat women in the school contemptuously.[42] "They didn't know girls as equals, as true friends, as people you cared about . . . these young jocks had a callous, abusive manner with girls," writes Lefkowitz.[43] Even so, boys are encouraged to aspire to this model of manhood, idealizing competition, domination, and, sometimes violence.

SUBORDINATED MASCULINITY

Just as masculinity hierarchies characterize the Glen Ridge school culture, status distinctions among males persist within the communities where these school shootings occurred. Connell's second category of masculinity explains how heterosexual boys perceived as feminine can experience "gay bashing" in the same way as hegemonic men often persecute women and gays. Connell explains:

> Gay masculinity is the most conspicuous, but it is not the only subordinated masculinity. Some heterosexual men as well as boys are expelled from the circle of legitimacy. The process is marked by a rich vocabulary of abuse, including wimp, nerd, sissy, mama's boy, dweeb, geek. . . . Here too, the symbolic blurring with femininity is obvious.[44]

Michael Carneal, Luke Woodham, Eric Harris and Dylan Klebold complained they were called homosexual (a theme present in other school shootings not discussed here).[45] All the boys said they were tired of the teasing, and each referenced perceived challenges to their manhood.

Specifically, Woodham reported that he was ridiculed about his physical appearance and called "gay."[46] He said he was responding to a lifetime of abuse. Stephanie Walker, a senior at Pearl High School, confirmed his reports: "Other boys knocked books from his hands and he took it without so much as a cuss word. He never fought back when other boys called him names."[47] Walker continued, "he was picked on for as long as I can remember. Most people who aren't popular get picked on."[48]

In the Kentucky incident, Carneal reported to a psychiatrist that he felt tormented by whispers at school that he was gay[49] and when other kids called him a "faggot."[50] In a school journal, he wrote, "after a cruel day at H.M.S. (Heath Middle School) when someone put in the school newspaper that I was gay, I went home and cried, yes I admit it, I cried."[51] Michael struggled with how "unacceptable" it is for boys to cry, admitting this reluctantly even in his own private thoughts. He cried again when asked why he committed the shootings. "I guess I just got mad 'cause everybody kept making fun of me." When asked what names he was called, the boy added (à la Connell), "nerd, and they were always calling me crack baby, and freak, 'cause I'm different, I guess."[52] In middle school, someone pulled down Carneal's pants in front of his other classmates, part of a series of humiliations he suffered.[53] He wrote obsessively about harming the "popular, 'preppie' students" whom he blamed for his mistreatment.[54]

Time Special Report recorded in Jonesboro that "Mitchell seemed to yearn for male approval." "Mitchell always wanted to prove to me that he was a tough guy," his father Scott Johnson told *Time*.[55] Trying to compensate, by "talking tough," Mitchell was often beaten up by other boys.

In Littleton, Colorado, Dylan Klebold and Eric Harris's motivation was also related to anger over masculinity expectations and hierarchies. They wanted to kill the "jocks" who called them "gay." The "jocks" corroborated these claims. Ben Oakley from the soccer team said, "nobody really liked them . . . the majority of them were gay. So everyone would make fun of them." Jon Vandermark, a sophomore said, "they were called freaks, homos and everything in between."[56] The animosity between the jocks and these boys was palpable in the school. When Klebold and Harris began shooting, many of the jocks clearly understood why. Senior Dustin Thurmon, from the wrestling team admitted, "the ones they shot first were the ones who made fun of them. They could have got me, 'cause yeah, I made fun of them, sadly I did," and then "they should have been able to take it."[57] But, clearly they didn't want to "take it." It was these experiences that the boys said drove them toward their "mission." Marching into the cafeteria at Columbine High School, Harris and Klebold shouted, "All jocks stand up. We're going to kill everyone of you."[58]

Relentless attacks on these adolescents' masculinity seemed to inspire a fierce assertion of rebellion through violence. In *Slow Motion: Changing Masculinities, Changing Men*, Lynne Segal writes that homophobia is a means to keep all men in line by oppressing gay men and expressing contempt for men when they express emotional qualities associated with femininity.[59] For instance, "jocks" attacked boys they perceived as "feminine" to prove to themselves and to others that they themselves were not gay. Consequently, the attacks by the hegemonic boys were motivated by homophobic impulses not unlike the defensive terror and rage engendered in the victims-turned-killers. Segal says boys are taught to despise the "feminine enemy within themselves" and to try to destroy any person that draws attention to these rejected aspects of their experience and personality.[60]

Many of the boys who killed blamed their parents and teachers for not trying to stop the abusive and demeaning remarks and actions directed at them. Two shot their own parents, and Harris left a note in his room:

> If you are reading this, my mission is complete. . . . Your children who have ridiculed me, who have chosen not to accept me, who have treated me like I am not worth their time are dead. . . . I may have taken their lives and my own—but it was your doing. Teachers, parents, LET THIS MASSACRE BE ON YOUR SHOULDERS UNTIL THE DAY YOU DIE. [emphasis in original][61]

Irrespective of the specific social conditions at Columbine High, it is unfortunate that some teachers, parents, and other authoritative voices are also known to participate in teasing and otherwise denigrating boys who appear "feminine." Where protection is desperately needed many children report instead that some adults actually collude with their oppressors.

MARGINALIZED MASCULINITIES

Connell called a third relationship to masculinity "marginalized." Again, this refers to males isolated from the white, well-to-do, heterosexual hegemonic males. Following Connell's argument about these categories being dynamic rather than static, one can envision both "subordinated" and "marginalized" males as sometimes engaging in violent rebellion against socialized masculinity and those who represent it.

Alan Wolfe wrote a *New York Times* editorial depicting these divisions between "jocks" and "outsiders" as a historical reflection of upper class prejudice. As Wolfe put it,

> If Littleton had its cliques that is because upper-middle class suburbia is one big clique. Racism, homophobia and anti-Semitism, all of which were reported at Columbine became examples of the kids doing to each other what their parents did to the "out" groups they left behind for a better life.[62]

The Reason Public Policy Institute in Los Angeles reports that violence is evenly divided between rural, suburban, and urban schools.[63] Given this, it is less surprising that retaliatory violence against "jocks" takes place in affluent areas. Instead, bewildered reactions suggest that violent prejudice in these communities is so tolerated as to be considered normal or barely visible. Another example of this is manifested in fraternity hazing. This form of normalized violence in masculinity was recently exposed in wealthy communities as "a largely hidden phenomenon in which high school and college athletes" report that they "let themselves be physically abused or humiliated as a rite of passage" for entry into exclusive sports teams, fraternities, or other groups. In the last twenty years over eighty people were killed in these rituals,[64] but awareness of this tacitly accepted violence is only now beginning to surface.

Thus the boys in the school violence cases retaliated from a different social position than the "marginalized boys" whom Connell usually contextualizes as relating to class or race. In the school shootings, marginalization involves social isolation occurring predominantly among upper-class and white people themselves. Indeed the "jocks" in Colorado were the ones who named the outsider boys "The Trenchcoat Mafia."[65] In this respect, mostly white cliques persecuted other white "outsider" kids for being different. From here the boys' resistance to being both subordinated and marginalized in their masculinities materialized in organized and violent revenge.

All the boys who killed were part of specific "outsider groups" and most of them had concrete ideologies they used to try to justify their actions, namely Friedrich Nietzsche, Adolf Hitler, and Satan. Some of them apparently idealized Nietzsche's "Superman," perhaps as an antidote to the attacks on their manhood. Indeed, in 1924, it was Nietzsche that

Nathan Leopold, age eighteen, and Richard Loeb, age nineteen, credited when they killed fourteen-year old Robert Franks, and then, in 1997, was cited by Luke Woodham and the boys who helped him plan his attack.[66] In Woodham's group, initially called the Third Reich and later called the Kroth as a reference to Satan, these boys said they read Hitler's *Mein Kampf*, Nietzsche's *Gay Science*, and various Satanic literature together.[67] In a culture increasingly stressing immediate gratification, for these boys picking up guns was like a "fast-food Nietzsche"— a short cut to a powerful masculinity.

Harris and Klebold were obsessed with Nazi history, shouting "Heil Hitler" periodically, and wearing clothes decorated with swastikas. Their massacre was purposely executed on April 20, Hitler's birthday.[68] The combination of Hitler's diabolical call for power and this common misunderstanding of Nietzsche, as well as their fascination with the increasingly popular Satan icon as a path towards individual power, can be seen as a distorted, but still consistent effort towards "self-empowerment" and rationalization for their retaliation.

Related but differently, Mitchell Johnson claimed to be a member of a well-known gang, "The Bloods." He wore red colors to school and used "secret hand signals" he said he learned from other members.[69] Investigators said there was no evidence that Johnson actually belonged to this group, but his insistence indicated at least that this was his fantasy: to be part of a powerful, violent group in opposition to what he saw as a less forgiving environment at his high school.[70] Michael Carneal was part of a Gothic group referred to as "the Black Group" or the "The Zoo Crew." Carneal, Harris, Klebold, and Kinkel were all said to dress Gothic-style in long black trench coats. (Johnson and Golden wore camouflage.) The Gothic culture often included playing violent video games like Doom and Quake, referencing Satan, and listening to the music of Marilyn Manson.[71] Ali Onta, director of publicity for Cleopatra Records, the nation's largest Goth label in Los Angeles, describes Goth as "very depressing kill-yourself music,"[72] perhaps an indication of how bad these boys were feeling. The boys taking refuge in these groups seemed to long for acceptance by these alternative cliques since they felt rejected by the mainstream. Together, they could try to defend their self-esteem and their sense that they were "different."

Harris and Klebold manifested another form of Connell's marginalized masculinity when they targeted one of their only black classmates, Isaiah Shoels. Connell explains that marginalized men are likely to turn their anger at other men they believe can be dominated. Here an intricate dynamic within Connell's categories occurred, as Shoels was both a star football player (and therefore in one respect hegemonic), as well as African American (and therefore in another respect, himself marginalized). The naked wrath directed at Isaiah as they hurled racial epithets and shot him three times in the head can be seen as a manifestation of both forms of deadly masculinity: exercising an imagined right to domination, and simultaneously reacting against a perceived hegemonic oppressor.[73]

Indeed, it was not only hegemonic male youth who were targeted for compensatory violence. Females, too, were marked. In each of the first three shootings as well as the more recent ones in Atlanta, Georgia, and Flint, Michigan, the boys said they had difficulties with a girl. They then vented their rage at the girl(s) they believed made them feel powerless. While they were not the most "powerful" in the school, even these subjugated boys could still feel dominant over girls, whom they simultaneously experienced as both their victims and their oppressors. The Michigan boy wrestled with other issues including crack-addicted, incarcerated parents and abject poverty. But it is still significant that the incident he said motivated his shooting was the fight he had with the young girl just before he shot her dead. That both children were only six-years old lends even more urgency to these matters.[74]

Let us look more closely at where, and how, boys in these cases often turned their rage toward females. When asked why Woodham stabbed his mother to death and then killed his ex-girlfriend and her best friend, he answered that he was distraught over his breakup with his girlfriend, Christina Menefee. "I wasn't aiming at anyone else," he said.[75] Greg Eklund, lead investigator of the Rankin County Sheriff's Department, said it was the leader of Luke's group, Grant Boyette, who encouraged Woodham. Boyette allegedly told Luke to stop whining about Christina and "just kill the bitch" so that he wouldn't have to see her everyday in school.[76]

In Kentucky, Michael Carneal's first shot killed Nicole Hadley, a girl who sat next to him in band practice and with whom he sometimes studied at her home after school. Although it was not mentioned at the time, Jonah Blank reported that she was the object of Michael's unrequited love. Her mother Gwen Hadley confirmed this: "He was in love with my daughter Nicole, and Nicole had no interest in him," she said. Michael had telephoned Nicole nightly in the weeks before the shooting.[77] His classmates testified that not having a girlfriend was a source of frustration and social embarrassment for him. The next two girls Michael killed also played beside him in the band.[78]

Just four months later in Joncsboro, Arkansas, Mitchell Johnson "vowed to kill all the girls who had broken up with him." The *New York Times* reported the word around school was that "Mitchell was mad because 11-year-old Candace Porter 'dumped him.'" Some said she teased him and called him names that implied she found him unattractive.[79] Porter was among the people targeted. Drew Golden, age eleven, was also recently rejected by his girlfriend, Jennifer Jacobs, before he joined

Mitchell Johnson in the Jonesboro shooting.[80] All five people Johnson and Golden killed were female: four girls and a pregnant teacher; of the wounded students, nine out of ten were girls.[81]

Finally, on May 20, 1999, exactly one month after the Columbine shootings, Thomas Solomon, age fifteen, wounded six students at his high school in Atlanta, Georgia. He also stated that he was suicidal, and angry that his girlfriend had broken up with him.[82]

ANOTHER TWIST IN MARGINALIZED MASCULINITY

Many of the boys who killed were considered "excessively" involved with computers and the Internet. Some were known as "hackers."[83] Perhaps they were trying to escape to a technological world where their perceived "weakness" might be less visible. Compensating for the lack of intimacy in their "real" lives and their inability to assert themselves against relentless abuse, these boys looked for an alternative life. They may have thought it was only in this virtual community that they could make any impact at all. Their sense of inadequacy could be temporarily relieved with seemingly conventional masculine rewards in a dynamic game of Doom or Quake where if victors, they could feel master of their universe. But it turns out that the Colorado boys, for instance, failed even in the cyberworld. Their friend Kristen Thiebault played these games with them "all the time," she said. "Eric and Dylan always lost."[84] They were particularly upset when they were beaten by girls, she added, an indignity that certainly didn't help their efforts to develop a stalwart manhood endowed with increasingly high expectations.

And the boys' interest in computers also set them further apart from the "popular" kids in their more sports-focused communities. This comprises yet another historical division among the more wealthy. In 1978, Pierre Bourdieu describes "fractions of the middle class" as engaged in a war between powerful groups who have "symbolic capital" or prestige in the community, and the dominated who have "cultural capital," a form of intelligence or scholastic achievement.[85] Like the value placed on "hegemonic preps and jocks," Bourdieu contends, a bourgeois education values sports over culture. He explains that the dominant class perceives their relation "to the dominated fraction" (including intellectuals, artists, and professors) "in terms of the opposition between the male and the female, the virile and the effeminate."[86] Today computer "geeks" might be added to Bourdieu's list of people who potentially gain "cultural capital" as a result of their specialized intelligence. The boys who killed were generally considered bright with exceptional computer savvy. But, their talents were devalued in these athletic-centered communities and, instead, the young boys were "feminized" à la Bourdieu, and referred to as gay.

GUN POWER

Guns have a particularly clear-cut relationship to masculinity, both literally and figuratively. In these cases, they helped transform the boys' subordinated and marginalized masculinity into a feeling of strength; through guns, compensatory power could be exerted.[87] Guns became a means for the boys who killed to take control rather than be controlled, subordinating "popular boys" with the power of their ammunition, and, similarly, vanquishing girls who "dumped them."

Connell suggests that the adult gun lobby in America asserts a specifically masculine power through rifles. He writes that when politicians try to control guns, their actions are seen by gun owners as "emasculating;" "while hegemonic masculinity is typically invisible as a fixed component of most daily institutions, the gun lobby exists as the visible exposure of these power relations."[88]

For instance, Eric Harris was denied entry to the Marines one week before he committed his crimes. With his father already a proud retired Air Force Major, Harris may have felt this last rejection, coupled with years of abuse by "jocks," was the last and most glaring blow his masculinity could endure.

These murders occurred because boys believe they are supposed to be strong and powerful, especially in the face of emasculating remarks. All the surviving perpetrators said they felt more important after they committed their crimes. "Murder is gutsy and daring,"[89] announced Woodham. Michael Carneal said he brought the guns to school because he "was trying to get people to like him. I showed them to them, and they were still ignoring me. I just wanted the guys to think I was cool."[90] After the incident, Carneal said: "I was feeling proud, strong, good, and more respected. I didn't think I would get in trouble, I thought it would make me popular."[91] For these boys, firing guns was immediate "masculine" gratification, an easy way to even the score in one lethal swoop. "One second I was some kind of heartbroken idiot," explains Woodham, "and the next second I had the power over many things."[92]

In another high-profile case three boys ages fifteen, sixteen, and seventeen, were accused of molesting and killing three eight-year old boys in West Memphis, Arkansas. Damion Echols, one of the accused, expressed sentiments similar to Woodham's on the courtroom stand. When asked how he thought the killers might have felt after the deed, he said, "It probably made them feel good, made them feel power, made them happy." He said it was common sense that a person who would commit this kind of act would feel good, a remark that gave the prosecuting attorney pause. "It's common sense that killing three eight-year-olds would make you feel good?" he asked suspiciously. Irrespective of Echols's actual guilt, it is important to understand what makes so many boys from "outsider groups" empathize with this perspective.[93]

INTEGRATING OTHER THEORIES OF MASCULINITY

The above section focuses on how young men in five highly publicized school violence cases turned to guns and used shooting to express masculinity. But, in analyzing "gender matters," it is also necessary to examine why masculinity anxieties characterize some young boys' personalities. The ideas of four gender theorists, integrated with the five case studies, show why "masculinity" develops in social opposition to "femininity."

Pollack offers a social–psychological explanation, writing that sometimes "as young as five or six, and then again in adolescence, boys are forced to separate prematurely from their parents, and expected to be independent."[94] This was a particularly salient difficulty for Woodham who said that when his father abandoned them he felt forced to be the "man" of the family. "I was seven years old, trying to hold the family together," he said.[95] By acting "appropriately" tough and autonomous, young boys disguise their feelings of vulnerability and loss by creating what Pollack calls a "mask of masculinity." Instead of the range of emotions available to women, boys are permitted only anger, and the means to control their other feelings with "calm and cool" fronts.[96] Lack of intimate relationships and connection, combined with intense pressure to suppress their emotions, can boil into an uncontrollable and lethal rage ultimately erupting in violence. Pollack added more recently that this "mask of masculinity" played a role in all the school shooting cases.[97] Boys tired of being perceived as weak and "feminine" demanded "male" authority.

In *Theorizing Masculinities*, Michael Kaufman also writes that developing masculinities often means suppressing needs and emotions. These feelings do not disappear: "they are simply held in check or not allowed to play as full a role in our lives as would be healthy for ourselves and those around us."[98] It is not surprising, then, that boys both involved and uninvolved with the killings make efforts to maintain such hard, unemotional "masculine" personae. For example, one eight-year-old boy who escaped the shooting in Jonesboro was asked if he was scared. He responded proudly, "Everybody in my class started crying. But, me, I thought my lord, why're they all crying?"[99] Obviously this eight-year-old child felt forced to be a "man" when his friends were literally shot and killed before his eyes. Michael Carneal, in Kentucky, also struggled with these conflicts. One of his classmates commented that Michael "wouldn't show his emotions to people very often except for occasions when he would break down and cry or something."[100] Like the other victims-turned-killers, Carneal seemed compelled to take the abuse "like a man," though in truth the pain had become too much. Luke Woodham made a point of tallying the specific abuses he had endured before the massacre, believing the murderous act would redeem him. He demanded that people perceive him as powerful and manly. "I am not spoiled or lazy, for murder is not weak and slow-witted,"[101] he said. Woodham denies his needs in favor of the omnipotence he believes "manhood" entails.

In *The Reproduction of Mothering*, Nancy Chodorow writes that when boys separate from their mothers, they must differentiate themselves as "not female" or "not the qualities embodied by their mother." Since their mothers are often the person to whom they are most connected, they feel compelled to repress their needs for love and relationships during this separation process. This becomes a burgeoning conflict as males as well as females crave intimacy, and yet men feel they must demand "from women what men are at the same time afraid of receiving."[102] Woodham demonstrated this difficulty most visibly. In a conflicted crisis on the courtroom stand, he said his mother deserved it, and then, "I loved my mother, I know she forgives me." A similar conflict was expressed about his ex-girlfriend, Christina: "I actually had someone in my life to love," he said. But he had sought her out and shot her at point blank range that fateful day.[103] And Kinkel helped his mother carry in the groceries, said "I love you" to her, and then shot her dead.[104]

Clearly, Woodham struggled with issues relating to his mother, accusing her of smothering him, not letting him "grow or learn," and accompanying him and Christina on dates for entire evenings.[105] He may have experienced this lack of space as an obstacle to separating from her and developing relationships with new love objects.

In sum, these writers diagnose why masculine identity develops as an extreme opposition to the mother's relational qualities, causing instead alienation and rage. Psychologically, Chodorow recommends the active presence of a nurturing male parent to help boys understand they can be male and yet enjoy intimacy even though it is currently associated with "femininity." Sociologically, transformation needs to take place in myriad institutions including school, family, community centers, and media representations. But now, when boys behave violently, make threats, turn to guns, hate girls, and fight aggressively for higher positions in the complex social hierarchy of "masculinities," they are acting at an extreme end of a "normal" male continuum.

OVERLOOKING HOW "MASCULINITY MATTERS"

With the disturbing thought that violent shootings might presently exist at the extreme end of "normal" male behavior, it should not be surprising that masculinity was overlooked in dominant explanations of school violence. For the most part, masculinity demands are not seen as a social problem. Rather hyper-male expectations tend to be made "normal" in three specific ways: accepting a "boys will be boys" ideology, tolerating violence, and condoning misogynist and homophobic attitudes and acts. Given these three forms of day-to-day normalization, one might almost expect to find gender all but omitted from public discourse, despite its on-going relevance.

THE "BOYS WILL BE BOYS" IDEOLOGY

The "boys will be boys" ideology is characterized by Thomas L. Friedman in the *New York Times*. He summarizes a common response to the massacres:

> The shootings in Littleton were not by deprived youths, and they were not carried out by an obviously depraved single gunman, who could be written off as a psycho. Rather they happened in a "Leave It to Beaver" neighborhood, and the gunmen were Wally and Eddy Haskell.[106]

Friends and acquaintances considered Eric Harris and Dylan Klebold to be typical boys. The *New York Daily News* reported the town's perceptions that the "horrifying slaughter hardly squares with the eerily normal lives of the teens blamed for one of the worst crimes in United States history."[107] Though it was well known that the boys idolized Hitler, spoke of blowing up the school, and had homemade bombs visible in their bedrooms, a "boys will be boys" ideology seemed capable of rationalizing even these extreme fantasies of violence.

Luke Woodham spoke of guns, torturing animals, and his own rage. But again, no one was alarmed by his comments. "Kids talk. That's all I can say. Kids talk a lot," said one resident in Mississippi. Another added, "Just talking, just threats, just trying to be big and bad."[108] After Jonesboro, Richard Rodriguez, an editor of Pacific News Service, wrote an opinion piece for the *Los Angeles Times* reminding readers that boys doing cruel things to other children has always been considered normal. Rodriguez argues,

> In truth, nothing is surprising about the cruelty of children. It is as routine as a boring summer day when kids torture insects or animals. All of us remember from our own childhood, bullies and midget tyrants. One child puts a razor blade in a bar of soap in the school bathroom; another places broken glass in the playground sand. . . . All week long, one had the sense that not one of the experts had read William Golding's *Lord of the Flies* or been to a summer camp.[109]

Rodriguez confirms popular perceptions that acting cruel and aggressively hostile is perfectly "normal" for boys. He uses a work of fiction to proclaim that the nature of men has always been vicious, further implying that boys are not capable of being self-reflective and responsible for their behaviors.

ACCEPTING VIOLENCE

Because guns are an accepted part of life in all of these suburban and rural communities, the boys' fascination with them did not cause much concern. For instance, while Carneal was expressly not considered a "gun enthusiast,"[110] his former girlfriend had seen him with a gun. She said, "He was trying to sell it, not use it, that's why no one told a teacher." Later on, she elaborated, "It's not like he hadn't brought a gun to school before, OK?"[111] Michael was not seen as obsessed with guns because it was expected that boys would be fascinated with guns and bring them to school.

Like most of the other boys convicted for school shootings, Kinkel also made his obsession with violence, guns, and bombs evident. He demonstrated how to build a bomb with a timing device in one class and, during English, announced his plans to "shoot everybody." No one took him seriously.[112] Kinkel's tendency towards violence and bombing was also considered normal. Jamon Kent, the Springfield Superintendent said Kinkel was "an average, everyday kind of kid." For a boy his age, Kent continued, Kinkel's temper and gun obsession were "a typical kid response."[113]

When Eric Harris wrote an essay portraying himself as a shotgun shell, his English teacher became alarmed and informed his father, Wayne Harris. However, according to Marilyn Saltzman, spokesperson for the Jefferson County Public Schools, the teacher decided that the essay reflected a normal interest "consistent with his future career aspirations" once she learned that Mr. Harris was a retired Air Force officer and that Eric was trying to join the military. One can only imagine what else is considered typical in this context.

Mark E. Manes, accused of providing the two gunmen with one of the semiautomatic pistols in the Colorado case, provided a similar defense. His lawyer, Robert I. Ransome, insisted that when Manes accompanied the boys on three shooting expeditions, it did not mean he knew the boys were capable of this kind of behavior. "When you're up shooting in the woods with a bunch of kids who love to shoot at things, the obvious assumption is, 'Hey, they like guns and they like to shoot.' " Ransome continued indignantly, "He never got to the point of thinking what they might do with it. It never crossed his mind."[114] But now we need to ask: Why is it a foregone conclusion that boys "love to shoot?"

In all five cases, people claimed the boys were "conventionally" violent. As Mrs. Bowles, a mother of five in the Colorado community put it, the trench coat owners were "just like any other young men, interested in bamboo sword fights, *Star Wars*, and computer games."[115]

TOLERATING MISOGYNY

In the end, that the press ignored, failed to pursue, and/or belittled the gender themes in these crimes ought to be shocking for a factual reason alone: The primary targets of murder in the first three incidents were the female objects of the boys' unrequited love. But in more than two hundred articles perused for this essay, only a few referenced violence against women as influencing these events. One place gender was mentioned came in a letter to *The New York Times*. Douglas T. Shapiro reflects on the Arkansas incident in a way applicable to three of the five shootings. Shapiro asks:

> Is it a coincidence that all five victims killed by a "random" spraying of bullets were female? It is chilling to think that the threats that preceded these murders were ignored because we believe it is perfectly normal for adolescent boys to hate girls and want to kill them. When will we learn that "boys being boys" is a pathetic excuse for ignoring deeply misogynist tendencies?[116]

In *The American Jurist*, Kyle Velte agreed, maintaining that it was as if violence against women was an acceptable fact calling for resignation rather than transformation. She mentions a judge in Baltimore, Maryland, who excused a man who shot his wife in Washington, D.C. when he caught her with another man. The judge said, "I seriously wonder how many married men would have the strength to walk away . . . without inflicting some corporal punishment." Another man who stabbed and killed his wife during a marital break-up in January 1995 was released from custody when the judge decided he posed no threat to society.[117] Connell's argument that men use violence "to sustain their dominance over women," sometimes rationalizing "murder by a woman's patriarchal owner," emerges visibly here.[118] Not surprisingly, the FBI calls violent attacks by men the number one threat to the health of American women.[119]

Yet, contemporary responses continue to accept and expect this behavior. Alvin Poussaint, another of the few people to address the fact that the boys' victims were girls, exemplifies what Shapiro most feared—that such hatred and murderous feelings towards females are "normal." When asked if he considered the violence in Jonesboro a misogynist crime, Poussaint said, "It is not unusual for boys in this age group to have antagonistic relations with girls. The older boy felt rejected by a girl. So his anger was personal, but then generalized to all girls. He saw girls, more than boys, as the villain."[120] While Poussaint may or may not deplore this condition, the expectation contributes to the misguided belief that boys' hostility towards girls is "normal."

BEYOND MASCULINITY

While focusing on the omission of why gender matters, this analysis is not meant to discard public concerns about gun accessibility, violence in the media, or the impact of parents. Instead, our aim has been to place these concerns in a wider social context without mistaking symptoms for causes. If guns are more controlled, and killings decline, this will be a positive development. To be sure, the children who killed had access to a huge arsenal of guns and ammunition, tempting these insecure boys to use them for immediate gratification of "masculine" power. However, gun-control measures, although necessary, are insufficient. Similarly, if violence in the media is also a symptom, reflecting rather than causing violent tendencies, cultural changes in masculinity expectations would subsequently decrease interest in such violent imagery, and violence in media would decline due to diminishing demand. Last, blaming and criminalizing parents is also misdirected. Families need to be viewed within a complex matrix of social dynamics which reinforce destructive gender stereotypes. Taken together and understood in relationship to "masculinity," each of these explanations contributes to decreasing the symptoms of school violence. But identifying and addressing the causes will effect real change.

WHY THE PROBLEM OF MASCULINITIES AND SCHOOL VIOLENCE NOW?

At the turn of the twenty-first century we benefit from a huge literature which documents the oppression of women by analyzing forced splits between masculine and feminine aspects of the self. This division has historically made it more difficult for women to take powerful positions in society and to act assertively. It has also discouraged men from being sensitive and emotional. While many women have made strides against these prescriptions, men have generally had more conflicted responses. In *Changing Men*, Michael Kimmel writes that, for many men, "these critiques have prompted a terrified retreat to traditional constructions; to others it has inspired a serious reevaluation of traditional world views, and offers of support for the social, political, and economic struggle of women and gays."[121] Males who "retreat to traditional constructions" may feel even more extreme manifestations of "masculinity" are necessary to compensate for their perceived inability to meet new masculinity expectations that include respect for gays and women as well as for "feminine" parts of their personality.

Part of this retreat to more extreme masculine norms is particularly self-destructive. Men report feeling pressured to look "bigger and stronger" than was necessary in past generations. This has led some to develop eating disorders previously limited predominantly to women. With increasing proportions, more men also take dangerous supplements to increase their muscular physique.[122] The escalating and destructive socialization for men to look "ever more masculine" is documented by Dr. Harrison G. Pope, a psychiatrist from Harvard, who says this training begins when boys are very young. For instance, the G.I. Joe dolls marketed to boys are now at least as unrealistic in body shape as the Barbie dolls which target girls. Pope points out that, during the Vietnam War in the 1960s, G.I. Joe had the equivalent of twelve-inch biceps; in 1999, the doll's biceps were the equivalent of twenty-seven inches on an adult male,[123] as much an anatomical impossibility as Barbie's proportions.

Furthermore, the "G.I. Joe Extreme" doll wears "an expression of rage"[124] which, according to Pope, suggests this emotion is particularly important for young boys. Thus, while women develop more strength, men have increasingly "hyper-male" expectations with which they need to contend, and masculine identity becomes more problematic for the "normal" boy.

In addition, revisions in male identity vary in relation to female progress. Writing about the United States at the turn of the last century, Michael Kimmel describes men reacting regressively to women's achievements: Fear of the women's suffrage movement created the "cult of the outdoor man." Kimmel also contends that men who retreat from being caring and nurturing may also fail to question traditional male excesses including rape, violence, spouse abuse, gay-bashing, high-risk sexual behavior and drunk driving.[125] In a European context, Klaus Theweleit in his book, *Male Fantasies*, describes the sexual politics of fascism as a response to men feeling weak at this historical moment. He believes these politics developed in part from a fear of the women's suffrage movement and from the German defeat in World War I.[126] More recently, Connell argued that women's liberation and the difficult experiences with Vietnam "stirred new cults of true masculinity in the United States," idealizing violent adventure movies, expanding the gun cult, and developing what he refers to as a paramilitary culture.[127]

Having difficulty maintaining the traditional superiority demanded of a more complex masculinity that can also embrace femininity, and helpless to differentiate themselves from an ever-growing and versatile female identity, these gender theorists acknowledge that some men are abdicating their relationships with strong women. They look instead for dynamics that are more compatible with historically learned patterns.

This phenomenon is causing some women to rethink their recent achievements. Against the history of feminism struggling for equality between the sexes and for an expanded emotional continuum for both genders, some women are beginning to reinforce old male and female norms by demanding a return to their own subordination.[128] Books like *The Rules* received national attention trying to restructure contemporary dating relationships in a way reminiscent of the 1950s. Contributing to this disturbing trend, Wendy Shalit's *Returning to Modesty* recommends that women return not just to the 1950s, but the "1850s"[129] and start by withholding sex before marriage.[130] In *The Lipstick Proviso*, Karen Lehrman encourages successful women to try to wait for a man to call. She writes:

> Waiting for a man can be frustrating and infantalizing, especially for women who are used to asserting and fulfilling their needs in every other area of their lives, but this voluntary restraint has to last only until a 'relationship' develops, which for better or for worse is typically quite soon.[131]

Grappling with the problem of retreat that Kimmel, Connell, and Theweleit describe, Lehrman laments that there are few men who are not threatened by independent women. "Men who are both strong and successful themselves seem to be far less intimidated by strong and successful women. . . . Unfortunately these men are still relatively rare," she says.[132] "While most of them (men) were quite flattered to receive a call from a woman, many had this funny little habit of running when pursued."[133] Instead of expecting men to develop a new masculine identity that embraces strength and sensitivity simultaneously, this theory expects both women and men to capitulate to historically constructed gender expectations, limiting both men and women's full expression.

Pollack sees these views as part of the social attack on boys' self-esteem. He rejects the notion that boys are "sexual aggressors, driven by their frantic biological urge for sex."[134] Instead, this perspective, itself enforced by the "boy code," causes boys to demonstrate the bravado expected from them. Inside, he says, they are "not self-sufficient loners," but "yearners for connection."[135] Many boys in Pollack's study reject the dictum to play sports and to be domineering with girls, expressing instead more diverse wants and needs. Pollack also notes that boys can display an "intellectual bravado,"[136] even though they are now more likely than girls to dropout of high school, less likely to go to college, and less likely to pursue graduate programs.[137] Boys' "intellectual bravado" is no more an indicator of a "natural" proclivity than their "sexual bravado," but rather the outcome of hurtful and powerful social influences.

To show something of this phenomenon statistically, Pollack's analysis contributes important insights to the National Institute of Mental Health (NIMH) research on depression. According to the NIMH, 12 percent of women and 7 percent of men experience a major depressive illness each year.[138] Disturbing yes, but Pollack's findings provide even more staggering information. He writes that because of the "boy code," boys feel compelled to appear tough and independent even when they are truly depressed. As a result of these socially imposed and finally internalized pressures, they are less likely to report their genuine pain on psychological studies or surveys. Pollack says advanced research tells us that boys are just as depressed as girls, but they don't necessarily "look" depressed to others. He also notes a recent epidemic in suicides for young men.[139] The NIMH officially recognizes that while women report attempting suicide about twice as often as men, males are more likely than females to die by suicide.[140] Girls may talk about their feelings more, but if boys were allowed the same socially sanctioned vehicles of self-expression, we might hear more about their pain; instead boys are more likely to act on their despair.

All told, social expectations now demand that men be physically ripped—with twenty-seven inch biceps—and some women demand that men become more aggressive in intimate relationships than has been expected for 40 or even 140 years. Needless to say, becoming a "man" is a goal increasingly difficult to attain. Boys contend with at least six conditions undermining their human potential: (1) homophobic harassment challenging masculinity, (2) access to few emotions besides anger, (3) a socialized inability to resolve the Catch-22 where men feel they "need from women what they feel they cannot have," (4) a burgeoning rage at women for representing these needs, (5) expectations to separate too early, and (6) access to guns that offer the possibility for instant male power. These factors conspire to create a gender crisis erupting in the phenomenon of school shootings which the United States now must address. What is to be done? The following sections suggest needed directions for the long, as well as the short run.

CONCLUSION

Redefining Normal

Recent school shootings are only extreme ramifications of the stark divisions between what is considered "feminine" and what is considered "masculine." Alternative emotional expressions have been virtually inaccessible to many young boys. One of the authors, Jessie Klein, the supervising counselor at a small, progressive New York City public high school, talked with students about their reactions to the shooting in Colorado. The responses were all too familiar. While many students certainly condemned the actions of the young killers, they also understood the rage Eric Harris and Dylan Klebold felt after being teased. A number of students who felt persecuted relayed their own fantasies about shooting huge numbers of other students.[141]

Ironically, New York City students do not have easy access to guns and other ammunition as do boys in the rural and suburban communities where these crimes occurred. In Manhattan, few children hunt animals with their parents. In Mississippi, Kentucky, Arkansas, Oregon, and Colorado, using guns is a way of life for young boys. A Kentucky paper reports, "All of these states promote the use of guns for hunting and 'protection,' and foster what social psychologist Richard Nisbett calls a 'culture of honor' that teaches males to avenge perceived slights and insults."[142] It is this "culture of honor" that needs to be redefined.

At the school where Klein works students were recently asked to discuss the controversy concerning whether the Ku Klux Klan should be able to march in New York City without wearing their hoods. The students raised a different concern. They wanted to know why they shouldn't be able to "beat up" the Klan for their racist views. The teenagers insisted that their parents and friends encouraged them to fight to defend their honor, and the "talking heads" on television news shows often argue derisively and support wars to settle disputes. It is only the teachers at the school who discourage fighting, they complained.[143] In such urban schools, girls often display a bravado not unlike their male classmates. This suggests they too feel compelled to defend themselves violently against perceived slights to their "honor." Contemporary masculinity expectations may reject "femininity" itself, enforcing the "boy code" for girls as well as boys. Stanley Aronowitz refers to this cultural phenomenon in this volume when he argues that school mediation programs fail because violence is so deeply embedded in the fabric of American culture. Instead, it is necessary to get to the root of such disturbing notions of "common sense" that may be far too common, even though they do not make sense at all.

Redefining Masculinity

Why are violent impulses so acceptable in young men? When Eric Harris threatened three times to kill Mr. Brown's son, Brooks, why did the police fail to act? Was this another casualty of the "boys will be boys" ideology?[144] The same oblivious response occurred on four previous occasions when Woodham, Carneal, Johnson, and Kinkel publicly announced their plans to decimate their schools before they consummated their mission. After each incident, community members who knew them best insisted they were "average" and "typical" boys. Here again, lies the problem—and the solution. Greater sensitivity to the destructive demands of historical and contemporary gender expectations may lead to an earlier detection of such unbridled rage. Ultimately transforming cultural consciousness so that, for instance, boys have access to a wider range of emotions than anger would go a long way towards decreasing male violence. When boys feel weak, sad, scared, anxious, lonely, or depressed, the negative experience is unnecessarily magnified when they feel this also indicates a lapse in the "tough disposition" manhood demands. Needs for love, support and self-expression are just as salient for boys as for girls. A first step is making these many feelings acceptable and "normal" for men as well as women. For when men can also express a wide range of emotions, they have more access to the full continuum of their own personalities. Additionally, if men are less frightened by feelings traditionally associated with "femininity," their disdain towards homosexuals and their need to distinguish themselves so starkly from women will decline.

Create Community

Another important step towards change is creating communities where both boys and girls feel connected and supported. The cruel social hierarchies in the boys' high schools reflect an aggressively competitive culture at large which values a "Nietzschean" "hyper-male" individualism over a "feminine" emphasis on relationships necessary for building community. Teasing, name calling, and other types of harassment should be discussed on a regular basis at faculty meetings and in classes. Faculty can also improve this problem by role modeling collegial and cooperative relationships for their students. When teachers form cliques and consolidate power unequally, students subtly learn this behavior is normal and acceptable. Instead, cooperation and respect need to be hallmarks of any school community.

A strong school community also encourages students to speak out against hurtful prejudice and to support one another in building an environment that won't tolerate abuse. The resurgence of "high standards" exemplified by single-minded knowledge-assessing multiple choice tests devalues the equally important skills pertaining to living in a respectful and democratic community. This is a priority overlooked at our peril. Students need individual attention to help them develop their perspectives and to express themselves regularly. This will go a long way toward preventing alienation and rage and promoting self-acceptance, self-esteem and positive social dynamics.

After these five school shootings, everyone attested to the normality of both the boys and their families. Even their hatred toward their ex-girlfriends was "understood." The young killers themselves insisted that they were "angry, not crazy" and that they committed their crimes consciously on behalf of all people who are mistreated.

The horrors of these crimes will never be forgotten, especially in the unremitting grief of the parents, friends, and relatives of the victims. But we need to listen to the cries of the perpetrators as well and address the destructive hierarchies, overpowering needs, homophobic abuse, and unattainable masculine expectations the boys at one level set out to destroy. Though they did so wrongfully and criminally, the boys vented their rage and demanded a change in the social structures that oppressed them. They made their anguish painfully clear. Ignoring their words and deeds jeopardizes the future of all our children.

NOTES

1. Bill Hutchinson, "A Bomb Found: Teen Gunmen Aimed to Blow-up School," *New York Daily News*, April 23, 1999, 3.

2. Timothy Egan, "Oregon Freshman Goes to Court as Number of Deaths Rises to 4," *New York Times*, May 23, 1998, via Proquest, May 10, 1999; Maxine Bernstein, "Kinkel's Boyhood Troubles Explode in Rage, Destruction," *The Portland Oregonian*, May 30, 1999; PBS Video *Frontline: The Killer at Thurston High*, WGBH Educational Foundation, PBS, 1999.

3. Jonah Blank, "The Kid No One Noticed, Guns Would Get His Classmates' Attention," *U.S. News*, <http://www.usnews.com/usnews/issue/981012/12padu.htm> October 12, 1998 (last accessed October 31, 1999).

4. Rick Bragg, "5 Are Killed at School: Boys 11 and 13 Are Held," *New York Times*, May 25, 1998, via Proquest, March 6, 1999.

5. Lisa Popyk, "I Knew It Wouldn't Be Right," *Cincinnati Post*, <http://www.cincypost.com> November 9, 1998 (last accessed June 12, 1999).

6. John Cloud "Of Arms and the Boy: All Kids Battle Demons. Why Did These Five Lose?" *Time.com* <http://cgi.pathfinder.com/time/magazine/1998/dom/980706/box4.html> July 6, 1998; vol. 152, no.1 (last accessed May 30, 1999).

7. James Barron, "Warnings from a Student Turned Killer," *New York Times*, May 1, 1999, A12; Dave Cullen, "The Rumor That Won't Go Away," *Salon News* <http://www.salon.com/news/feature/1999/04/24/rumors/index.html> April 25, 1999 (last accessed 16 May 1999).

8. The Policy News Information Service, "News and Events: Daily Briefing/Young Guns: How the Gun Lobby Nurtures Youth Gun Culture,"

<http://www.policy.com/news/dbrief/dbriefarc12.htm> August 4, 1998 (last accessed April 24, 1999).

9. David C. Anderson, "What the Gun Control Movement Can Learn from the Anti-Tobacco Campaign," *American Prospect* 46 (Sept./Oct. 1999), 28.

10. James Dob, "D'Amato Cites Storm Aid and Schumer Gun Control," *New York Times*, October 16, 1998, p. B5, via Proquest, March 6, 1999.

11. White House Press Secretary Michael McCurry, "School Shooting Address," <http://www.UnitedStatesGovernment/Information/Resource> 9 April 1999, (accessed 27 April 1999).

12. C. Ray Hall, "Solving the Dilemma of School Violence: 4 Schools, 5 Shooters, 59 Victims, A Special Report," *The Louisville Courier-Journal* <http://www.courier-journal.com/cjextra/schoolshoot/SCHsolvingdilemma.html> 6–9 Dec. 1998, (accessed 9 April 1999).

13. Terrence Monmaney and Gre Krikorkian, "Violent Culture, Media Share Blame, Experts Say," *Los Angeles Times*, 26 March 1998, A16, via Proquest, 23 April 1999.

14. Bullet delivery systems.

15. Steve Berry and Jeff Brazil, "California and the West," *Los Angeles Times*, 3 March 1998, A3, via Proquest, 23 April 1999.

16. Lori Leibovich, "Making Sense of Jonesboro," *Salon Magazine: Mother's Who Think* <http://www.salonivorytower.com/mwt/hot/1998/03/30hot.html> 30 March 1998 (accessed 31 October 1999).

17. For example: James Q. Wilson, "Violence, Pornography, and Social Science," and R. M. Liebert, E. S. Davidson, and J. M. Neale, "Aggression in Childhood: the Impact of Television," both in *Where Do You Draw the Line*, ed. Victor B. Cline, (Provo, Ut.; Brigham Young University Press, 1974).

18. Frederic Wertham, "Is TV Hardening Us to the War in Vietnam?" in *Violence and the Mass Media*, ed. Otto N. Larsen, (New York: Harper and Row, 1968).

19. Elliott Currie, *Crime and Punishment in America*, (New York: Henry Holt and Company, 1998).

20. Blank, "The Kid No One Noticed."

21. Cal Thomas, "Revenge of the Children in Denver," *Denver Post* (1 April 1998), B9.

22. Thomas, "Revenge of the Children," B9.

23. Peter Applebome, "Round and Round in the Search for Meaning," *New York Times*, 29 March 1998, Sec. 4, 1, via Proquest, 6 March 1999.

24. Professor of Family Studies Stephanie Coontz believes this concern is misplaced. She responds to a comment that chastises mothers who choose to have a baby without a father. Coontz says there is a litany of things that parents do consciously or unconsciously that pose risks to kids, including having a kid to save a marriage, neglect, parent conflict, a mother or father's depression, decaying neighborhoods, and overwork. But she says, "whatever the disadvantages of the choice, women who make a thoughtful choice to plan for a wanted baby come rather low on my action needed list." (National Public Radio, Talk of the Nation, Washington, D.C., 27 July 1999.)

25. Cloud, "Of Arms and Boy"; Pam Belluck and Jodi Wilgoren, "Caring Parents, No Answers in Columbine Killers' Pasts," *New York Times*, 29 June 1999, A1, via Proquest, 7 July 1999.

26. Vincent Schraldi, "Media Misleading on School Shootings," *The Progressive*, Madison, Wisconsin, 26 May 1998.

27. Sheryl Gay Stolberg, "Science Looks at Littleton and Shrugs," *New York Times*, 9 May 1999, Week in Review, 1. Against the evidence presented in this chapter, other experts were also quoted by the *New York Times* to claim there were no patterns in these cases. When the United States Secret Service was asked to turn its attention to finding indicators that might help deter school violence, the agency rejected three major themes clearly visible in these five crimes. The Secret Service says perpetrators are not necessarily made into outcasts, socially isolated, or generally male; the assassins will not necessarily make a public threat prior to committing the act; and finally, the killers may not express hatred for their victims but can easily shift from one victim to another. (Bill Dedman, "Secret Service is Seeking Pattern for School Killers," *New York Times*, 21 June 1999, A10). But each boy we are discussing exactly fit all these categories.

28. Ellen Willis, *Don't Think: Smile: Notes on a Decade of Denial*, (Boston: Beacon Press, 1999).

29. See Stephanie Urso Spina, "Violence in Schools: Expanding the Dialogue," this volume.

30. John T. McQuiston, "Wave of Copycat Threats Leads to Swift Responses Across U.S.," *New York Times*, 24 April 1999, A15; Paul Hoversten, "Copycat Behavior Emerges, Kids Mimicking Acts of Violence." *USA. Today*, 27 April 1999, 4A.

31. Lisa Snell, "School Violence Defies Solution," *The Times-Picayune*, 27 March 1998.

32. James Brooke, "Attack at School Planned a Year, Authorities Say," *New York Times*, 25 April 1999, via Proquest, 12 July 1999, A1.

33. Martin Kasindorf, "Survivors Attack Violence: Some Parents of Slain Students Shun Lawsuits and Instead Campaign for Political Remedies," *USA Today*, A8, 30 May 1999.

34. Sam Howe Verhovek, "Texas Legislator Proposes the Death Penalty for Murderers as Young as Eleven," *New York Times*, 18 April 1998, via Proquest, 6 March 1999.

In 1924, Defense Attorney Clarence Darrow won the case against the death penalty for Nathan Leopold, Jr., and Richard Loeb (who kidnapped and murdered Bobby Franks, age fourteen) on the basis of their youth at age nineteen. From his closing speech:

> Is youth a mitigating circumstance? Well, we have all been young, and we know that fantasies and vagaries haunt the daily life of a child. We know the dream world we live in. We know that nothing is real. We know the lack of appreciation. We know the condition of the mind of a child. Here are two boys who are minors. The law would forbid them making contracts, forbid them marrying without the consent of their parents, would not permit them to vote. Why? Because they haven't that judgment which only comes with years, because they are not fully responsible.

Quoted in Hal Higden, Crime of the Century (New York: G.P. Putnam's Sons, 1975), 191. Darrow (famous for defending John T. Scopes who was arrested for teaching Darwin's theory of evolution in a small school in Tennessee) took the case because it was a "rare chance to strike a blow against capital punishment." He thought he was articulating the perspective that would "dominate the future" (Higden, Crime,

124). Instead in similar situations today politicians demand the death penalty for children as young as eleven. (And, in some states teaching theories of evolution in public schools is still no more legitimate than teaching creationism.)

35. See Spina, "Violence in Schools," this volume.

36. Eric Slater and Lianne Hart, "NRA Event Draws 800 Protesters," *Los Angeles Times*, 2 May 1999, A12, via Proquest, (accessed 10 July 1999).

37. James Sterngold, "Terror in Littleton: The Culture: Rock Concerts Are Canceled," *New York Times*, 29 April 1999, National Desk Archives; Eric Slater and Lianne Hart, "NRA Event Draws 800 Protesters," *Los Angeles Times*, 2 May 1999, A12, via Proquest, 10 July 1999.

38. Katharine Q. Seeyle, "Clinton Holds Youth Violence Summit," New York Times, 11 May 1999, A14.

39. Robert W. Connell, *Masculinities* (Los Angeles: University of California Press, 1995), 79.

40. Connell, *Masculinities*, 83.

41. Bernard Lefkowitz, *Our Guys* (New York: Vintage Books, 1997).

42. Lefkowitz, *Our Guys*, 84.

43. Lefkowitz, *Our Guys*, 91.

44. Connell, *Masculinities*, 79.

45. For instance, Barry Loukaitis, age fourteen, was the young killer in Moses Lake, Washington, in October, 1997. He also said he killed a "popular" boy because the boy had called him a "fag." Lisa Popyk, "Violence Is Seductive to New Breed of Killers," *Cincinnati Post*, <http://www.cincypost.com/news/2kill110998.html> 9 Nov. 1998 (accessed 31 Oct. 1999).

46. Cloud, "Of Arms and the Boy," 5.

47. Gina Holland, " 'I am not insane, I am angry:' Suspect in Pearl handed classmate a chilling note," Biloxi, Mississippi *Sun Herald* <http://www.newslibrary.com/deliver.com/deliverccdoc.asp?SMH=133002> 3 Oct. 1997 (accessed 31 Oct. 1999).

48. Holland, " 'I am not insane.' "

49. Jim Adams, C. Ray Hall, James Malone, and Rochelle Riley, "In Search of Why: Warning Signs," *Louisville Courier-Journal*, 9 Dec. 1998 <http://www.courier-journal.com/cjextra/schoolshoot/schwarningsigns.html> (accessed 7 April 1999).

50. Blank, "The Kid No One Noticed."

51. Jim Adams, "Carneal Bared His Alienation," *Louisville Courier-Journal* <http://www.courier-journal.com/localnews/1998/9812/18/981218.html> 18 Dec. 1998 (accessed 20 June 1999).

52. Jim Adams and James Malone, "Outsider's Destructive Behavior Spiraled into Violence," *Louisville Courier-Journal* <http://www.courier-journal.com/localnews/1999/9903/18/990318carn.html> 18 March 1999 (accessed 24 April 1999).

53. Blank, "The Kid No One Noticed."

54. Adams, Hall, Malone, and Riley, "In Search of Why," 4.

55. Cloud, "Of Arms and the Boy."

56. Dave Cullen. "The Rumor That Won't Go Away."

57. Patrice O'Shaughnessy, "Time of Teen Joy Ends in Sorrow," *New York Times*, 23 April 1999, 34-35.

58. Bill Huchinson and Paul Schwartzman, "The Anatomy of a Rampage," *New York Daily News*, 23 April 1999, 37.

59. Lynne Segal, *Slow Motion: Changing Masculinities, Changing Men*, (New Brunswick, New Jersey; Rutgers University Press, 1990), 158.

60. Segal, *Slow Motion*.

61. MSNBC Staff and Wire Reports, "Note from Gunman Warns of More Violence to Come," MSNBC Home <http://www.msnbc.com/news/261055.asp> 24 April 1999 (accessed 24 April 1999).

62. Alan Wolfe, "Littleton Takes the Blame," *New York Times*.com, 2 May 1999, Editorial Desk.

63. Rick Bragg, "5 Are Killed at School: Boys 11 and 13 are Held," *New York Times*, 25 May 1998, A1, via Proquest, 6 March 1999.

64. Robert D. McFadden, "Eight Wrestlers at High School Are Accused in Hazing," *The New York Times*, 25 Feb. 2000.

65. Jodi Wilgoren, "Caring Parents," A1.

66. Lisa Popyk, "I Knew It Wouldn't Be Right;" Dorothy Rabinowitz, "A Leopold and Loeb for the Television Age," *Wall Street Journal*, 17 May 1999, A26, via Proquest, 10 July 1999; Higden, Crime of the Century, 210.

67. Cloud, "Of Arms and the Boy;" Lisa Popyk, "I Knew It Wouldn't Be Right."

68. Dirk Johnson and Jodi Wilgoren, "A Portrait of Two Killers at War with Themselves," *New York Times*, 26 Apr. 1999, A1; Hutchinson, and Schwartzman, "The Anatomy of A Rampage."

69. "Alleged Shooters Known As Troublemakers," Albany, New York *Times Union*, 26 March 1998, A6, via Proquest, 10 July 1999.

70. Jon Jeter, "Arkansas Boys Talked Big but Weren't Seen as Menace," *Washington Post*, 30 March 1998, A01.

71. Jim Adams and James Malone, "When Outsiders Destructive Behavior Spirals into Violence."

72. Todd S. Purdam, "Goth Genres, Fringe Rock and Germany," *New York Times*, 22 April 1999, 28. Manson himself declared that this was a misinterpretation of his music. "The somewhat positive messages of these songs are usually the ones that sensationalists misinterpret as promoting the very things I am decrying," he writes. Marilyn Manson, "Columbine, Whose Fault Is It?" *Rolling Stone*, June 24, 1999.

73. Fifteen of the two thousand students at Columbine High School were African American. (Cullen, "Outsiders, Even Among the Outsiders.")

74. David Barboza, "A Life of Guns, Drugs, and Now, Killing, All at 6," The *New York Times*.com, <http://nytimes.com/library/national/030200mich-shoot-edu.html> 2 March 2000 (accessed 2 March 2000).

75. Timothy Egan, "From Adolescent Angst," 6.

76. Popyk, "I Knew It Wouldn't Be Right."

77. Blank, "The Kid No One Noticed."

78. Blank, "The Kid No One Noticed."

79. "News Summary," *New York Times*, 29, March 1998, A2, via Proquest, 6 March 1999.

80. Cloud, "Of Arms and the Boy."

81. Rick Bragg, "Five are Killed At School."

82. The Associated Press, "Profile of Georgia School Gunman," <http://www.aol.com/mynews/news/story.adp/cat=010712&id=1999052105151653> 21 May 1999 (accessed 23 May 1999).

83. PBS *Frontline;* Blank, "Guns, he concluded would get his classmates attention;" Adams, Hall, and Malone, "In Search of Why;" Hutchinson, and Schwartzman, "The Anatomy of a Rampage."

84. Jodi Wilgoren, "Society of Outcasts Began with a $99 Black Coat," *New York Times,* 25 April 1999, 30.

85. Pierre Bourdieu, "How Can One Be a Sports Fan?" in *The Cultural Studies Reader,* ed. Simon During (New York: Routledge, 1994) 339.

86. Bourdieu, "How Can One Be a Sports Fan?" 344.

87. Leopold and Loeb also articulated fantasies of killing men who tried to overpower them (Higden, Crime of the Century, 204). They selected a small boy to kidnap and murder mainly because it would be "easy to overpower him." (Higden, 256).

88. Connell, *Masculinities,* 212.

89. Popyk, "I Knew It Wouldn't Be Right."

90. Blank, "The Kid No One Noticed."

91. Blank, "The Kid No One Noticed."

92. Popyk, "I Knew It Wouldn't Be Right."

93. Echols pleaded not guilty, but was found guilty by the court and sentenced to death by lethal injection; the case is on appeal. (*Paradise Lost: The Child Murders at Robinhood Hills*, Film Documentary, West Memphis, Arkansas: Cabinfever Entertainment Inc., 16 May 1993).

94. Pollack, *Real Boys,* 11.

95. Diane Sawyer, "A Voice From Jail, Interview with Teen Who Went on Shooting Spree," *ABC News.com: On Air,* <http://more.abcnews.go.com/onair/ptl/html_files/transcripts/ptl112a.html>(12 Nov. 1997), (accessed 19 April 1999).

96. Pollack, *Real Boys,* 13, 14. Emotional expression is then divided somewhat arbitrarily along gender lines. Women who comfortably feel sad and scared often report difficulties experiencing anger. Boys taught to feel shame about fear and unhappiness, on the other hand, are consistently encouraged to express their rage.

97. Dayna Harpster, "Angry Young Men Depression, Anger and Shame Are Fueling the School Shootings, Say Experts on Boyhood," *Times-Picayune,* 26 April 1999, E1.

98. Michael Kaufman, "Men, Feminism, and Men's Contradictory Experiences of Power," in *Theorizing Masculinities,* eds. Michael Kaufman and Henry Brod (Los Angeles: University of California Press, 1995) 148.

99. S. Braun and J. R. Moehringer, "5 Shot Dead at School in Arkansas: 2 boys held," *Los Angeles Times,* 25 March 1998.

100. Adams and Malone, "When Outsiders Destructive Behavior Spirals into Violence."

101. Moehringer and Montgomery, "Kroth."

102. Nancy Chodorow, *The Reproduction of Mothering: Psychoanalysis and the Sociology of Gender* (California: California University Press, 1978), 199.

103. Popyk, "I Knew It Wouldn't Be Right."

104. Bernstein and Egan, "Oregon Freshman."

105. Popyk, "I Knew It Wouldn't Be Right."

106. Thomas L. Friedman, "Kosovo and Columbine," *New York Times*, 4 May 1999, Op-Ed, 31.

107. Bill Hutchinson and Kevin McCoy, "Slay Scenario on Video Tape," *New York Daily News*, 23 April 1999: 35.

108. Brian Cabell, "Small Town Rocked by Bizarre Murder Case," CNN Interactive: U.S. News (21 Oct. 1997) (accessed 12 June 1999).

109. Richard Rodriguez, "The Jonesboro Tragedy; Consequences Teach A Chilling Truth," *Los Angeles Times*, 29 March 1998: Opinion Desk, via Proquest, 23 April 1999.

110. Blank, "The Kid No One Noticed."

111. Adams and Malone, "When Outsiders Destructive Behavior Spirals into Violence."

112. Timothy Egan, "Oregon Student Held in 3 Killings; One Dead, 23 Hurt," *New York Times*, 22 May 1998: A21, via Proquest, 6 March 1999.

113. Timothy Egan, "Oregon Freshman Goes to Court as Number of Deaths Rises to 4." A21.

114. Sandy Shore, Associated Press, "Gun Seller Admits Shooting with Teen Killers Three Times," *Boston Globe*, 5 May 1999, A24.

115. Wilgoren, "Society of Outcasts," A30.

116. Douglas T. Shapiro, "Misogynist Tendencies," *New York Times*, 27 March 1998, Editorial, via Proquest, 6 March 1999.

117. Kyle Velte, "The Whys? of the Jonesboro Shootings: Gender Bias, the Overlooked Answer," *American Jurist* (May 1998): 1.

118. Connell, *Masculinities*, 84.

119. Velte, "The Whys? of the Jonesboro Shootings."

120. Lori Leibovich, "Making Sense of Jonesboro," 6.

121. Michael S. Kimmel, "Rethinking 'Masculinity': New Directions in Research," in *Changing Men*, ed. Michael S. Kimmel (Thousand Oaks, Calif.: Sage Publications, 1987), 10.

122. Kimmel "Rethinking 'Masculinity,' " 16.

123. WNPR, Weekend Edition, Washington, D.C., Saturday, May 29, 1999, 9:30 A.M.

124. Natalie Angier, "Drugs, Sports, Body Image and G.I. Joe," *New York Times*, 22 Dec. 1998: New York Times.com <http://graphics.nytimes.com/images/> (accessed 16 June 1999).

125. Michael S. Kimmel and Michael Kaufman "Weekend Warriors: The New Men's Movement," 286.

126. Connell, *Masculinities*, 84.

127. Connell, *Masculinities*, 84.

128. In *The Science of Beauty* (Doubleday: New York, 1999), Nancy Etcoff espouses a comparable thesis encouraging women to capitalize on their appearance and give in to what she implies is a "natural hierarchy" that positions women who are considered most attractive to men in the most powerful female positions in society. Encouraging women to accept that making oneself as attractive as possible is a biological necessity, she even raises the ludicrous supposition that female children are abused by their parents *less* if they are more attractive; a perspective that

anyone who has worked with abused children knows is clearly inane. This classically "blames the victims" (i.e., women and children) espousing a disempowering female identity, as well as destructively dismissing the huge body of literature detailing complex familial dynamics and historically learned patterns implicated in such a pathology. (Tahra Zahra, "State of the Debate: The Anti-Feminist Seduction," The American Prospect [July-Aug. 1999], 85.)

129. George Gurley, "Women! Your Power Is in Sexual Restraint!" *New York Observer*, vol. 13, no. 7, 22 Feb. 1999, 1; 10.

130. Tahra Zahra, "State of the Debate," 85.

131. Karen Lehrman, *The Lipstick Proviso: Women Sex and Power in the Real World* (New York: Doubleday, 1997), 109.

132. Lehrman, *The Lipstick Proviso*, 135.

133. Lehrman, *The Lipstick Proviso*, 99.

134. Pollack, *Real Boys*, 150.

135. Pollack, *Real Boys*, 181.

136. Pollack, *Real Boys*, 160.

137. Pollack, *Real Boys*.

138. National Institute of Mental Health, "Women Hold Up Half the Sky," <www.nimh.nih.gov/publicat/womensoms.cfm> 18 July 1999.

139. Pollack "Angry Young Men Depression, Anger and Shame."

140. NIMH, "Women Hold Up Half the Sky."

141. Humanities Preparatory Academy, "Town Meeting: Quads and Triads: Reactions to Columbine." Advisor discussion, 29 April 1999.

142. *Time* Wire Reports, "Teen Pleads Guilty in School Shootings," A Nation in Brief/Kentucky, 6 Oct. 1998.

143. Humanities Preparatory Academy, "Writing Mentor Program with Nina Tietholz," 11 Nov. 1999.

144. James Brooke, "Little Was Done on Complaints in Littleton File," *New York Times*, 2 May 1999, A1, A12.

7

Scientism and the Ideological Construction of Violence, Poverty, and Racism

Paulo Freire and Donaldo Macedo

In the past few years, school violence has become central to the debate concerning educational reform. Although the focus has been largely on urban schools, national attention shifted quickly in 1998, when Andrew Cohen, eleven-years-old, and Mitchell Johnson, thirteen-years-old, effectively planned and carried out the execution of four classmates and a teacher and wounded ten other students in Jonesboro, Arkansas. Even though this mass killing of children by children could be treated as an isolated aberration, the facts point to an epidemic where young boys, mostly white, are indiscriminately killing numbers of people with shotguns, as was the case when Luke Woodham, age sixteen, went on a criminal rampage by first stabbing his mother to death and then going to Pearl High School in Mississippi where he opened fire with a .30-caliber rifle, killing two students and wounding seven others. He was finally subdued by the Assistant Principal, Joel Myrick, who asked Luke repeatedly why he killed the two students. Luke Woodham matter-of-factly answered: "Mr. Myrick, the world has wronged me."[1]

While the media, educators, and political pundits are calling for rigid and forceful measures to protect students in schools, the discourse that has emerged conspicuously fails to ask several fundamental questions: Is there a correlation between the culture of violence celebrated in our society and the violence in schools? Since the boys who tragically and cruelly killed their classmates in cold blood were all white, why doesn't the society hold the white ethnic and cultural groups responsible for the carnage? If these boys were African Americans, the entire black population would

163

be held responsible. Welfare and other remaining programs of the Great Society of the 1960s would be singled out as the culprits for creating, according to Patrick Buchanan, "a generation of children and youth with no fathers, no faith, and no dreams other than the lure of the streets."[2]

While we need to pay close attention to Luke Woodham's cry, "The world has wronged me," we need also to attend to the ways in which this democratic society has exacted both psychological and real violence against children, and particularly against children of color who, by virtue of their race, ethnicity, and class, are systematically devalued and dehumanized by schools that are charged to teach the values of democracy and social justice. How can schools teach us values of democracy and social justice when, for example, children in East St. Louis, who live in dilapidated and roach-and-rat infested houses, are locked in a life of hunger and malnutrition imposed by an average daily expenditure of $2.40 for food for each child? If schools were to truly teach values of democracy and social justice, teachers would have to expose the enormous gap between these values and the lives of children who endure the stark poverty and human misery that cities like East St. Louis exemplify. If schools were to engage in a true teaching of democracy and social justice, they would have to defossilize the Pledge of Allegiance so as to juxtapose the "hypocritical exhortation to patriotism"[3] inherent in the pledge's "liberty and justice for all" with the misery, hopelessness, and violence which characterize the lives of children in ghettos as described below:

> *Mr. Jones:* When I got home from our bus ride on Sunday afternoon, I found out that, in the morning, while we were eating breakfast, my cousin Tony got jumped by one of the gangs in the neighborhood. They beat him up so bad they put him in the hospital. He wouldn't let me interview him, but I recorded him while he told his friend on the phone what had happened.
> [Sounds of man talking on phone]
> Tony's saying they beat him up until they knocked him unconscious. Then they hit him a couple more times in the mouth. That woke him up and he got away. He says it's just a blessing that he made it back home.
> [Sounds of traffic]
> This is where the [unintelligible] took place last year, where the [unintelligible], exactly where we're walking now, it's a little—gangs and violence are just a way of life in this neighborhood. [unintelligible] A lot of kids we grew up with already joined gangs. When we were walking around the neighborhood, we spotted our friend, Gary, selling drugs.

> *Mr. Newman:* LeAlan asked him what he thought he would be doing in three years, since he already dropped out of school.

Gary: I ain't going to be alive in three years, [unintelligible] he going pop my ass.

Mr. Jones: He says he won't be alive in three years because with his selling dope, someone's going to shoot him before then. I don't know why some kids just give up hope and others like me and Lloyd hold on. Maybe it's just that both me and Lloyd have at least one strong person in our families to watch over us. But, no matter what the situation, every kid who live in this neighborhood has to grow up fast.

Mr. Newman: When I was nine, I knew where drugs came from. When I was ten, I seen my first automatic weapon, a Glock-9, two clips.

Mr. Jones: I seen all kinds of guns—.44s, .22s, tanks—

Mr. Newman: Mac-10s, Mac-11s, everything. Living around here, you hear shooting all the time.

Mr. Jones: Like Vietnam, sometimes, you might hear booga-looga-looga sound. I remember one time, I was over at my aunt's house, spending the night, and we were playing Super Nintendo. I hear this lady shout— "I heard you been looking for me, nigger." And then she goes: boom-boom-boom-boom-boom. She let off about eight shots. Then I heard the other girl fire off. And we just stood there playing, there, like nothing happened. And then, you—Vietnam, some people term that crazy. Hell, I live in Vietnam for what you think I'm going to be if I live [unintelligible].

Mr. Newman: Living around here, man, is depressing. It's depressing. [Sounds of rock music]

Mr. Jones: It's not a normal childhood, by any means. Now, we're walking toward the lake front. Sometimes when we're bored and got nothing else to do, we get on the bridge which goes over Lake Shore Drive, and we drop rocks on the cars below, try to crack their windshields, and then run.

Mr. Newman: Moving vans are one of our favorite targets. [Sounds of traffic]
Hit the white [unintelligible]. Right, right, right. Throw it now.

Mr. Jones: He's just driving the car, like—boom—I don't care about them people. Most of them are going to the suburbs.[4]

The radio transcript captures the symbolic and real violence[5] imposed on ghetto life and the ensuing hopelessness, human misery, and poverty endured by the children and adults who populate them. In this chapter, we will try to demonstrate that these conditions not only breed subhumanity, but that the social construction of dehumanization, even in the democratic societies, has often been rationalized through scientism. By scientism, we refer to the pseudoscientific endeavor in social sciences that embraces a narrow and "naive" empiricism parading under the rubric of "hard scientific objectivity." Thus, these pseudoscientists would argue that, in order to keep their research methodologies from contamination, it is important to keep ideological factors out. In other words, any form of knowledge that interrogates the ideological premises of their methodological structures are invalidated, by taking away the built-in critique mechanism inherent in any scientific inquiry.

Throughout history, oppressive dominant ideologies have resorted to science as a mechanism to rationalize horrendous crimes against humanity ranging from slavery to genocide by targeting race as a marker that licenses all forms of dehumanization. If we did not suffer from historical amnesia, we would easily understand the ideology that informed Hans Eysenck's psychological proposal suggesting that differences in IQ (i.e., intelligence) between black and white people might be accounted for, at least in part, by genetics.[6] It is this same amnesia that buries dangerous memories, keeping us disconnected from history like the Massachusetts law which provided monetary rewards for dead Indians: "For every scalp of a male Indian brought in . . . forty pounds. For every scalp of such female . . . twenty pounds."[7]

One could argue that the incidents cited above belong to the dusty archives of earlier history, but we do not believe we have learned a great deal from historically dangerous memories, considering our society's almost total embrace of scientism as characterized by the success of *The Bell Curve* by Charles Murray and the former Harvard professor Richard J. Hernstein.[8]

Our inability to see the obvious connections among historical events also anesthetizes our senses as we trample over human pain in a battered world where a huge population of people, by virtue of their race, culture, ethnicity, and gender, are violently condemned to poverty and human misery. It is the same social construction of not seeing that keeps us from connecting with the existence of ghettos which serve as public garbage and human dumps. The residents of these unofficial concentration camps are often forced to search through garbage piles in hopes of finding food and clothes—something to keep them alive. It was from one of these garbage piles that mark the ghetto borders in Brazil that a family took pieces of an amputated breast from hospital waste and used them to prepare their Sunday meal. The Brazilian media reported the case which temporarily horrified the population and may well have caused the usual pragmatic neoliberal fatalistic reaction: "It is sad, but what can be done? This is reality."[9]

Reality, however, is not inexorably so. It may become another reality through rejection by progressives of a deterministic view of the world which functions as an ideological mechanism to reproduce dominant values. In a deterministic worldview, we could hardly speak of options, decisions, freedom, and ethics. "What can be done? This is reality," would become a universal discourse—monotonous, hopeless, and repetitive as human existence itself would be. In such fatalistic history, rebellions and antagonistic positions could never find a way of becoming revolutionary. Hence, it behooves progressive educators to struggle for the exercise of our capacity and our right to decide. As progressive educators we must insist that history is possibility and not determinism. However, it is impossible to understand history as possibility if we do not recognize human beings as beings who make free decisions. We also cannot recognize humans as agents of history if we violently crush their spirit by reducing them to the dehumanizing conditions of poverty and misery.

One can argue that the example from Brazilian ghetto life we described above is a condition of the Third World. We would respond that the nomenclature "Third" versus "First" World represents a false dichotomy that often leads to a linguistic trap. It is just as easy to find First World opulence among the oligarchies of El Salvador, Brazil, and Guatemala as it is common to find islands of Third World human misery and poverty in First World cities like New York, Los Angeles, and Chicago. Let's take Jonathan Kozol's[10] description of the South Bronx as an example of Third World reality within the First World where "a waste incinerator was put in operation recently over objections of the parents in the neighborhood [and where] amputated limbs and fetal tissue, bedding, bandages, and syringes that are transported here from fourteen New York City hospitals" are burned, adding injury to a neighborhood where

crack-cocaine addiction and the intravenous use of heroin, which children I have met here call "the needle drug," are woven into the texture of existence. Nearly 4,000 heroin injectors, many of whom are HIV-infected, live here in Mott Haven. Virtually every child at St. Ann's knows someone, a relative or neighbor, who has died of AIDS, and most children here know many others who are dying now of the disease. One quarter of the women of Mott Haven who are tested in obstetric wards are positive for HIV. Rates of pediatric AIDS, therefore, are high. Depression is common among children in Mott Haven. Many cry a great deal but cannot explain exactly why. Fear and anxiety are common. Many cannot sleep. Asthma is the most common illness among children here. Many have to struggle to take in a good deep breath. Some mothers keep oxygen tanks, which children describe as "breathing machines," next to their children's beds.

The houses in which these children live, two-thirds of which are owned by the City of New York, are often as squalid as the houses of the poorest children I have visited in rural Mississippi, but there is none of the greenness and the healing sweetness of the Mississippi countryside outside their windows, which are often barred and bolted as protection against thieves.[11]

It is this violent poverty and debilitating human misery which are never factored into the construction of scientific "objectivity" as evidenced in *The Bell Curve*. "Objectivity" always produces a disarticulation between the interpretive discourse and the interests of the interpreter which often remains hidden in the positivistic denial of the dialectical relationship between subjectivity and objectivity. In effect, this has resulted in an epistemological stance in which scientism and its methodology are celebrated while "theory and knowledge are subordinated to the imperatives of efficiency and technical mastery, and history is reduced to a minor footnote in the priorities of 'empirical' scientific inquiry."[12] The blind celebration of empiricism has created a culture where pseudoscientists, particularly in schools of psychology and education, believe "that facts are not human statements about the world but aspects of the world itself."[13] According to Michael Schudson,

> this view is insensitive to the ways in which the "world" is something people construct by the active play of their minds and by their acceptance of conventional, not necessarily "true," ways of seeing and talking. Philosophy, the history of science, psychoanalysis, and the social sciences have taken great pains to demonstrate that human beings are cultural animals who know and see and hear the world through socially constructed filters.[14]

The celebration of research methodologies independent of theory and history denies the existence of ideological filters through which we come to know, see, and hear the world, giving rise to an anti-intellectual posture which is manifested either through censorship of certain bodies of knowledge or through the disarticulation between the theories of the discipline and its empirically driven and self-contained studies. What these pseudoscientists do not realize is that research based solely on the results of quantitative evaluation are "the product of a particular model of social structures that gear the theoretical concepts to the pragmatic of the society that devised the evaluation model to begin with."[15]

It is important to point out that these evaluation models can provide answers that are correct but nevertheless without truth. A study that concludes that African American students "perform" way below white mainstream students is correct, but such an answer tells us very little about the material conditions with which African American students work in the struggle against racism, educational tracking, and the systemic negation and devaluation of their histories. We would propose that the correct answer rests in a full understanding of the ideological elements that generate and sustain the cruel reality of racism and economic oppression. Thus, an empirical study will produce answers without truth if it is severed from the sociocultural reality of its subjects. For example, an empirical study designed to assess reading achievement of children who live in squalid conditions must factor in the reality faced by these children as accurately conveyed by the description of the Mott Haven housing project.

An empirical study that neglects to address the cruel reality faced by these and millions of other children in our supposedly classless society will never be able to explain the reasons behind their poor performance. Similarly, an empirical study that concludes that children who engage in dinner conversation with their parents and siblings achieve higher rates of success in reading is not only academically dishonest but also misleading to the degree that it ignores the class and economic assumptions that all children are guaranteed daily dinners in the company of their complete and nuclear families. What generalizations can such a study make about the 12 million children who go hungry every day in the United States? What can a study of this type say to thousands upon thousands of children who are homeless, who have neither a table nor the food to put on it? What about those who live in houses with no heat in freezing winter conditions, like the conditions that led a father of four to remark "you just cover up . . . and hope you wake up the next morning."[16] What dinner conversation could this man engage in with his children to improve their reading development when they may not be lucky enough to make it through the night alive? What dinner conversation would the Haitian immigrant, Abner Louima, have with his children after being brutally sodomized with a toilet plunger by two white policemen in a New York City police precinct? Would the reading teacher of Louima's children include the savage acts committed against their father as part of their literacy development?

These questions make it clear how distorted "research" can be when it is disconnected from the sociocultural reality that informs the study to begin with. In addition, such distortion feeds into stereotype development that, on one hand, blames the victims for their own social misery and, on the other hand, rationalizes the genetic inferiority hypothesis as advanced by pseudoscholars such as Murray and Hernstein. What these studies often neglect to point out is how easily statistics can be manipulated to take away the human face of their subjects, through a process that not only dehumanizes but also distorts and falsifies reality.

The inability to link research with larger critical and social issues often prevents educators not only from engaging in a general critique of the social mission of their own enterprise, but also from acknowledging their roles as gate-keepers in maintaining the values of the dominant social order. Unfortunately, in the present educational system, particularly in our schools of education, it is very difficult to acquire the critical tools necessary to unveil the ideology responsible for our inability to link different bodies of knowledge and thereby gain a better comprehension of reality. Courses that deal with the intricate interplay of social issues, ethics, and ideology are almost absent from teacher-preparation curricula. This serious omission is, by its very nature, part and parcel of the ideological foundation that promulgates a pedagogy of big lies.[17]

Because of our inability to deconstruct the interplay of race, ethics, and ideology it becomes more difficult to understand the present attacks on affirmative action, immigrants, and unwed mothers. This cruel onslaught perpetuates a historical context wherein blacks were "scientifically" relegated to a subhuman existence that, in turn, justified the irrationality of their alienating reality as slaves. After the abolition of slavery and the eradication of laws that protected its existence, the dominant white ideology resorted to still more "science" as a means to continue the dehumanization of blacks in the United States. These race-based mechanisms were very prominent during the Reconstruction. W. E. B. Du Bois, a black historian of the era, succinctly describes it this way:

> The South proved by appropriate propaganda that the Negro government was the worst ever seen and that it threatened civilization. They suited their propaganda to their audience. They had tried the accusation of laziness but that was refuted by a restoration of agriculture to the pre-war level and beyond it. They tried the accusation of ignorance, but this was answered by the Negro schools. It happened that the accusation of incompetence impressed the North . . . because the North had never been thoroughly converted to the idea of Negro equality . . . Did the nation want blacks with power sitting in the Senate and the House of Representatives, accumulating wealth and entering the learned professions? Would this not eventually and inevitably lead to social equality. . . . ? Was it possible to contemplate such eventualities?
>
> Under such circumstances, it was much easier to believe the accusations of the South and to listen to the proof which biology and social science hastened to adduce the inferiority of the Negro. The North seized upon the new Darwinism, "the survival of the fittest," to prove that what they had attempted in the South was an impossibility; and they did this in the face of the facts before them, the examples of Negro efficiency, of Negro brains, of phenomenal possibilities of advancement.[18]

Sadly, after more than a century, the United States continues to be embroiled in the debate centered on the false notion of the genetic inferiority of blacks and, by association, people of color. *The Bell Curve* by Murray and Hernstein once more presents "evidence" in support of genetic inferiority. This book has not only activated what had appeared to be the dormancy of racism in the United States after the enactment of the Civil Rights laws, but it also has resurrected an old form of intellectual lynching that, unfortunately, has been embraced by ever more powerful representatives of the far right and, with few exceptions, supported by liberals through their silence.

When we are confronted with the problem of racial discrimination, independently of the insidious explanations that racists proffer in order to negate the existence and equal rights of the other, our first reaction is one of anger mixed with pity. Our pity is not directed toward the victims of discrimination. We pity those who discriminate against them. We pity their lack of human sensibility. We pity their exaggerated arrogance toward the world and their ignoble lack of humility. For us, the use of science to prove the inferiority of blacks constitutes the epitome of an incompetent discourse. It is precisely because of the posturing of pseudoscientific discourse that we urge progressive educators to embrace humility and humanism.

We want to emphasize that when we oppose pseudoscientists and their scientism for their cruel, racist approach to scholarship, we remain unafraid of being criticized for not having a "scientific" basis upon which to make such a claim. We believe the only basis upon which to judge another is that of membership in the human race. We find the pseudoscientific effort to prove the inferiority of one group to another absurd. We believe that the innate human ability to learn provides ample support for our view. To disprove this, Murray, Hernstein, and others would have to demonstrate that blacks have less of this ability than whites. If their claim were to be "scientifically true," there would have to be no exceptions to the rule—we could not have a W. E. B. Du Bois, a Martin Luther King Jr., a Toni Morrison, a Nelson Mandela and a constellation of other great black leaders and intellectuals. If the claim of inferiority were true, all blacks in the world would have to be inferior in all domains and respects across time and space. If, in fact, blacks were genetically inferior, Amilcar Cabral, the leader of the movement for the independence of Guinea-Bissau and Cape Verde would not have created so many problems for the Portuguese government and, indirectly, its supporter, the United States. Amilcar Cabral and his black army, like so many other African leaders and their people, defeated their colonizers. It was their intelligence and ethical conscience that enabled the indigenous population to reacquire not only their land but also their human dignity by triumphing over the exploitation, dehumanization, cowardice, and deceit of the European colonizers.

It is important not only to underscore the intelligence evident in devising strategies that led to the defeat of colonialism, but also to emphasize the ethical and moral issues involved in the struggle for independence. This leads us to question how the Europeans who, according to pseudoscientists are superior and more civilized beings, justify the quasi genocide inherent in a process of colonialization designed to secure and help them consolidate European cultural and economic hegemony. How can they justify the worldwide human exploitation engineered by whites: the mass killings of elderly, women, and children by our Western-developed "smart bombs," the mass killing and raping of women, including children as young as five years old in Bosnia, as Western civilization watches from the sidelines? How can Charles Murray and his cultural commissars justify the superiority of the white race when the technology and military "intelligence" of whites leads American GIs to commit horrendous crimes against humanity as described by Vietnam veterans themselves:

> The girls were unconscious at that point [after repeated rapes]. When they finished raping them, three of the GIs took hand flares and shoved them in the girls' vaginas . . . .No one needed to hold them down any longer. The girls were bleeding from their mouths, noses, faces, and vaginas. Then they struck the exterior portion of the flares and they exploded inside the girls. Their stomachs started bloating and they exploded. The stomachs exploded and their intestines were just hanging out of their bodies.[19]

Murray, Hernstein, and their ilk do not consider these grotesque, barbaric, and horrendous crimes in their representation of intelligence. This is precisely why we need to keep dangerous historical memories alive as reminders of the consequences of all forms of dehumanization and particularly those sanctioned by science. It is for this reason that for each Museum of Fine Arts we build in a given city, we should also build a Museum of Slavery with graphic depictions of the dehumanization of African Americans when entire families were split and sold on the block to the highest bidder and where pictures of lynching would remind us of our racist fabric. For each Museum of Science built in a given city, we should also build a Museum of our treatment of Native Americans—their enslavement, the raping and killing of women and children, and the appropriation of their land. Although we built a Holocaust Museum in Washington, D.C., fifty years after the Nazis' horrendous crimes against Jews, Gypsies, and gays, we also need to build a Vietnam War Museum alongside the Vietnam Memorial, where explicit accounts of the atrocities committed by Western-heritage-trained soldiers would keep the dangerous memories of My Lai alive.

Although these museums would represent historical truths, we doubt very much that our society is willing to confront its demons as exemplified by the watering down and rewriting of history for the exhibition of the Enola Gay at the Smithsonian. After ferocious protests by veterans' groups, the exhibit not only brooked no historical analysis, it also suppressed historical facts, rendering the display a mere presentation of artifacts divorced from critical historical context.

For us, more important than "proving" the superior intelligence of whites is to study the interrelationship between white supremacy and dehumanization. It is only through our willingness to confront the demon in us that we become willing to stop demonizing the other. What is needed is not yet another study like *The Bell Curve* designed to rationalize the further abandonment and oppression of blacks. What is needed is the courage to transcend the ideology supporting and supported by a suspect and racist scholarship of scientism so we can move beyond the pipe dream of a democratic education to its reality. However, in order to democratize education, we must simultaneously democratize the society in which it exists.

Thus, the humanization and democratization of society implies the necessary transformation of the oppressive and unjust apparatus that guides and shapes society. When we are confronted with racist constructs like IQ tests and racist arguments like those put forth in *The Bell Curve*, we must take a stand against them both scientifically and humanistically. This is no easy task since the racist propositions of *The Bell Curve* have been embraced not only by right-wing ideologues who had been impatiently waiting for science to further legitimize their racism, but also by the media which facilitates wide dissemination of this racist agenda which, in turn, reinforces the racist fabric of our society and encourages its present assaults on affirmative action and immigrants. As David Duke, a presidential candidate in 1992, put it, "America is being invaded by hordes of dusty third-world peoples and with each passing hour our economic well-being, cultural heritage, freedom, and racial roots are being battered into oblivion."[20] One could argue that David Duke represents the fringe, but we find little substantive difference between his unveiled racism and the scientifically veiled racism of Murray and Hernstein. In fact, one could easily consider Charles Murray as a David Duke in academic regalia. Given that a major portion of the data used to provide the basis for the main arguments in *The Bell Curve* was funded by The Pioneer Fund, an organization with a long history of association with Nazi groups, and the fact that Murray, in his youth, flirted with the burning of the cross, should have been a wake-up call for those who profess to combat racism.

Instead, Charles Murray has appeared in all major media outlets from the conservative to the liberal, such as *Nightline, The MacNeil/Lehrer Report, All Things Considered*, and the *New York Times Book Review*, to mention just a few. The question remains as to whether or not the media would give an antiracist book that indicts our violently racist society equal time. Given our society's evasion of an open debate about our ethical posture concerning the Enola Gay exhibition and given the marginalization of major dissident scholars like Noam Chomsky, even though he is considered the most influential intellectual alive today, we can easily see why such questionable scholars as Murray and Hernstein are celebrated by a society complicit with their racist tirades. Although on the surface it may be hard to comprehend that our so-called democratic society is so racist, upon further analysis the racist structures that debilitate our ever more fragile democracy are easily unveiled. As John Sedgwick writes, "It shouldn't be hard to find [racist structures] in a country where blacks are far more likely than whites to grow up poor, fatherless, malnourished, badly educated, and victimized by crime and drugs . . . racism in America . . . like bloodstains on the hands of Lady MacBeth, cannot be washed away."[21] *The Bell Curve* represents the bloodstain of American racism. It cannot be washed away without the total transformation of the present oppressive racist structures that characterize our democracy in crisis. In fact, we would not want to wash away such bloodstains so as to make it part of our museum of inhumanity that may prevent cruel history from repeating itself.

NOTES

Some of the material in this chapter will appear in Paulo Freire and Donaldo Macedo, *Ideology Matters* (Boulder, Colo.: Rowman & Littlefield, in press).

1. Richard Lacayo, "School Massacres May Be an Aberration, But the Question Remains: Why Do Kids Kill?" *Time*, April 6, 1998, 38.

2. Adam Pertram, "Buchanan Announces Presidential Candidacy," *Boston Globe*, December 11, 1991, 1.

3. David Spritzler, cited in Donaldo Macedo, *Literacies of Power: What Americans Are Not Allowed to Know* (Boulder, Colo.: Westview, 1994), 10.

4. Cited in Macedo, *Literacies of Power*, 144–145.

5. See Peter McLaren, Zeus Leonardo, and Ricky Lee Allen, "Rated 'CV' for Cool Violence," this volume.

6. Hans Eyzenck, *The IQ Argument: Race, Intelligence, and Education* (New York: Library Press, 1971).

7. Howard Zinn, *A People's History of the United States* (New York: Harper-Perennial, 1990), 234–235.

8. Charles Murray and Richard J. Hernstein, *The Bell Curve: Intelligence and Class Structure in American Life* (New York: Free Press, 1994).

9. Paulo Freire and Donaldo Macedo, *Ideology Matters* (Boulder, Colo.: Rowman & Littlefield, in press).

10. Jonathan Kozol, *Amazing Grace: The Lives of Children and the Conscience of a Nation* (New York: HarperPerennial, 1996), 7.

11. Kozol, *Amazing Grace*, 4.

12. Henry A. Giroux, *Theory and Resistance* (South Hadley, Mass.: Bergin & Garvey, 1983), 87.

13. M. Schudson, *Discovering the News: A Social History of American Newspapers* (New York: Basic Books, 1978).

14. Schudson, *Discovering the News*, 6.

15. R. Fowler, B. Hodge, G. Kress, and T. Trew, *Language and Control* (London: Routledge and Kegan Paul, 1979), 192.

16. Kozol, *Amazing Grace*, 4.

17. Macedo, *Literacies of Power*.

18. W. E. B. Du Bois, quoted in D. Jackson, "Reconstruction Part Two." *Boston Globe*, July 5, 1995.

19. James William Gibson, *The Perfect War* (New York: Vintage, 1988), 202–203.

20. David Nyham, "David Duke Sent 'em a Scare but Now He Faces the Old Pro," *Boston Globe*, October 24, 1991, p. 13.

21. John Sedgwick, "Inside the Pioneer Fund," in *The Bell Curve Debate*, eds. R. Jacoby and N. Glauberman (New York: Random House, 1995).

8

The Psychology of Violence and the Violence of Psychology

Stephanie Urso Spina

WHY PSYCHOLOGY?

Professionals from many domains have been actively involved in trying to understand and deal with the violence that plagues our schools and society. Women and men from sociology, psychology, political science, social work, community organizations, education, health care, criminal justice, administration, and similar fields have worked earnestly and diligently, if not successfully, to address a variety of violence-related issues. So why has only psychology been singled out for chapter-length treatment? There are four interrelated reasons from popular, professional, empirical, and historical perspectives that justify this decision: (1) Psychology permeates popular discourse and culture; (2) Psychology's instrumental measures and diagnostic criteria that categorize, label, and separate set the standards for our models of "normal" behavior and frame the way we define violence, deviance, and pathology; (3) Of all the disciplines, psychology looks most directly at individual and group acts of violence; and (4) Despite an unregenerate history and because of its powerful presence in our lives, psychology in general and social psychology in particular hold the means and potential to serve as the nucleus and synthesizer of a move toward social justice.

Psychology has increasingly served as a dominant force in public and private sectors in America. It plays a pivotal role in debates ranging from family life to business and government. As evidenced by the celebrity status of psychologists, as well as by the preponderance of "pop" psychology self-help books promising easy formulas for everything from increasing self-esteem, improving intelligence, and loving your "inner child" to dying a "good" death, psychology permeates and shapes every sphere of American life.

Psychology's growing importance has paralleled the rise of corporate industry and the middle class. As early as 1890, with growing industrialization and large numbers of immigrants arriving, American psychologists began to serve as consultants to businesses, school administrators, and institutions for the "feebleminded."[1] In 1917, immediately after Congress declared war, the American Psychological Association held a meeting to develop a plan to involve psychologists in the military effort by devising standardized tests for recruits.[2] During World War I, the use of "intelligence" (IQ) tests to screen soldiers for military duty[3] legitimized psychology as a "science," despite the fact that the testing effort was a scientific and practical failure.[4] Psychology continued to court the government, industry, and institutions, reinforcing its position as part of the dominant culture. It is by identifying itself with "science" and power that psychology gained its cachet.

When two Colorado teens killed thirteen students and then themselves, once again leaving friends, relatives, and the rest of the country struggling to make sense out of seemingly senseless acts, psychologists were the "experts" called to impart meaning to the tragedy. They were interrogated by the media in an attempt to find causality (and thus some "other" thing or person to blame) "in much the same way that aviation investigators look for jammed rudders or ruptured fuel lines after an airplane crash."[5]

Many of the "experts" joined in the chorus blaming either one or more of the following: mental illness, neglectful parents, guns, television and movies, video games, or other elements of popular culture like the black trench coats worn by the Littleton murderers. They advised us to learn about the characteristics of potential killers so that they might be identified before another tragedy occurs. The National School Safety Center in California provided a list of warning signs which included mood swings, a preference for violent television, use of drugs or alcohol, frequent use of bad language and cursing, depression, antisocial behavior, and a fondness for guns and blowing things up (presumably a reference to the popularity of video games and "action" movies). How is this profile different from a description of most adolescents on a bad day? Although profiling based mainly on race is likely to be curtailed by public pressure and the dozens of lawsuits now pending across the country,[6] profiling for criminal tendencies among students is becoming increasingly common.

In an effort to maintain "comprehension,"[7] we look for familiar labels that isolate the events (and perpetrators) and minimize the threats to our belief systems. "Mental illness" often heads the list, allowing us to compartmentalize events like the Littleton massacre as "unusual" behavioral violence rather than symptomatic of the subterranean structural violence that forms the bedrock of our society. Although structural violence and behavioral violence are inextricably interwoven, it is important to note the ideological differences underlying the distinction. When violence is defined as criminal (behavioral), it is visible (observable) and identifiable. When it is a byproduct of our social and economic structure, it is largely invisible and so harder to recognize, although structural violence causes more deaths than behavioral violence.[8]

This chapter argues that psychology's focus on behavior as if it were independent of its sociohistorical context is, in large part, a result of its adoption of the scientific model and its partnership with hegemony. The purpose is not to reject psychology or science, but to argue for an alternative epistemology that places them in their social and historical context, including dissenting voices in a dialogic process of reciprocity, supporting generative inquiry, and fostering deeper insights into the complexities of "knowledge."

Psychology's insistence on using the rules of science to play the game of power has resulted in serious theoretical and methodological errors, grave personal and social injustices, and other forms of violence. After a look at how this is played out in the overt and covert practices of two well-known studies, we offer a necessarily brief, and by no means exhaustive, historical survey that aims to capture the philosophical and ideological presuppositions, content, and practices that demand we redefine and redirect psychology. This overview is followed by a look at the "violent" practices psychology has contributed to (its *history of questionable practices*) and, as counterpoint, the work of some psychologists to expose the assumptions underlying these practices (*questions of historical practice*). A look at the foundations of a critical psychology and a trip "back to the future" of a socially active psychology conclude the chapter.

VIOLENCE AND PSYCHOLOGY

Psychology, like other "sciences," has a *history of questionable practices* that most psychologists would decry and a *question of historical practice* that most psychologists would deny, even as they perpetuate it. The similarity of the terms is not meant to confuse or engage in sophomoric word play. It is meant to reflect the fact that the two notions are interrelated and not always separable. The *history of questionable practices* refers to morally and methodologically questionable practices used in the design and execution of a study or experiment. The process of identifying practices as questionable is extremely difficult because *historical practices* often render *questionable practices* invisible. (And I am painfully aware that this endeavor may also be subject to these pitfalls.) The *question of historical practices* refers to the normalized ideologies that become embedded both in and as scientific practices in and over time and surreptitiously contribute to what is *questionable* about these *practices*. Such ideologically laden practices have become so commonplace, so deeply embedded in our belief system, that we are often not even aware of them. We consider them neutral, normal, harmless. That is why they are so dangerous. The blindness created by embedded ideology also explains the paradoxes presented in the first sentence of this discussion. These concepts and the concerns they raise will be clarified in the following paragraphs.

There are many well-known examples of *questionable practices*, one of which is described below. All of these were logical extensions of the experimental paradigm of science. They were also, even if unintentionally, inhumane. Today, these practices would be considered unethical and there are regularly revised guidelines and procedures in place that attempt to safeguard and protect the rights of "human subjects" of psychological investigations. On the other hand, the *questions of historical practice* remain, for the most part, hidden. They are not readily observable and empirically verifiable, as a scientific experiment is by definition. They are implicit in science-as-practiced-in-our-culture and rigorous critical analysis of both scientific and cultural assumptions is required to raise them to consciousness.

The *history of questionable practices* in psychology has attracted strong ethical criticism. Many of these criticisms concern experiments that involve violence as either the subject of study and/or as caused by the study itself. Stanley Milgram's classic mid-1960s studies on "Obedience to Authority" are one of the most famous of these.[9] Milgram demonstrated that some people are willing to commit what they believe to be extremely violent acts. In this case, participants were led to believe that they were subjecting another "subject" (who, unknown to them, was actually an accomplice in the experiment) to a severe electrical shock when that person failed to complete a simple task correctly. The actual subject thought that the role of each man (as tester or testee) was determined by chance. Participants in the position of controlling the intensity of the shock tended to obey the "experimenter's" instructions to continue increasing the current even when they believed they were causing the "subject" severe, possibly even fatal, pain.

The infamous Tuskegee Syphilis Study was a medical, not psychological study, but it is included here because it exemplifies the *history of ques-*

tionable practices, is regularly used in graduate psychology ethics courses, and served as a catalyst for many human "sciences," including the American Psychological Association, to develop a stronger Code of Ethics.[10] The Tuskegee Study has become a symbol of the violence that takes place in the name of all sciences that treat human subjects as part of the experimental apparatus.[11]

In 1932, the U.S. government promised 400 poor, African American male residents of Macon County, Alabama, free treatment for "Bad Blood," a euphemism for syphilis, which was epidemic in the area. The "study" continued until 1972, when the press uncovered what was really going on.[12] During those forty years, the promised treatment was never given and 100 men died (even though penicillin was available and commonly being used against syphilis by the end of World War II). The government physicians conducting the study had never intended to treat the disease. Their deceptive research program was called "The Tuskegee Study of Untreated Syphilis in the Negro Male" and was actually meant to study the long-term effects of *untreated* syphilis. The poverty- and disease-stricken men were deceived into believing they would receive treatment and lured with incentives that included free physical examinations, free transportation to and from the clinics, hot meals on examination days, free treatment for minor ailments, and a guaranteed $50 burial stipend that would be paid to their survivors. When the story broke, the racism and immorality of the study became obvious to all but the doctors involved. They firmly believed and vigorously maintained that they were acting in good conscience according to sound scientific practices (if not the Hippocratic pledge to "first do no harm").

That brings us to the *question of historical practice* which is exemplified by the doctors' position. Normalized racism and classism are obvious today in the physicians' choice and (mis)treatment of subjects. But it was not even an issue to them. The scientific requisites of detachment and objectivity and the deification of the acquisition of "knowledge" blinded the researchers to the cruelty of their actions and provided additional means for rationalizing their barbaric study. Hiding behind their white coats of science, like the Nazi doctors they have been compared to, the Tuskegee physicians inflicted unspeakable horrors on their fellow human beings.

In the Milgram study, some *questions of historical practice* might also be seen as methodological issues today. The studies, as was usual in psychology, were conducted with white middle-class adult male subjects. Yet the findings were generalized to all "people." This was the common way of doing "science," and the hegemonic biases of this practice went unnoticed. Although Milgram does deserve credit for realizing and admitting, after the experiments, that his design did not adequately protect his subjects from psychological harm, there were other variables operating that he did not consider. For example, at the time the research was conducted, people were in awe of science and authority figures commanded more re-spect than they generally do today. The fact that harm was inflicted on an-other "in the name of science" under the direction of a revered "scientist" was not part of either side of the equation. The study focused on those who followed instructions and continued to administer the electric shocks. Those who resisted or refused, and thereby could have perhaps provided even more important insights into the processes as well as out-come of the experiment, were generally ignored. Ignoring the role of power in the design, execution, and outcome of a study is also a *question of historical practice*. This is not meant to detract from the contributions of Milgram and others like him nor to blame them. *Questions of historical practice* are so embedded in time and place that they are easier to see in hindsight or from the margins of a hegemonic paradigm. It is far more dif-ficult to see our own *questions of historical practice* than those of our pred-ecessors, but not impossible. Critical and feminist psychologists, for ex-ample, have demonstrated that power is implicit in the relationship between the researcher and the subject.

These are not the only examples, but they will suffice for our purposes. The point is that the core problems of the *question of historical practice* and the *history of questionable practices* are directly related to the discrepancy between psychology as the study of the human being in relation to others and the world, and the scientific framework it embraces and proclaims.

SOCIAL AMNESIA

In its race toward hegemonic recognition and success, psychology has, both consciously and unconsciously, tried to suppress memories of both its minority (including women) scholars[13] and its "nonscientific" past in an effort to maintain its cultural authority as a science. Yet even William Wundt (1832–1921), who is considered the founder of experimental psy-chology, saw the experimental method as having a very limited scope in psychology. Furthermore, Wundt's experimental model was not even modeled on that of the natural sciences. Wundt's experimentalism was the practice of a self-conscious community of investigators in which ex-perimenters and subjects were interchangeable.[14] He did not see the ex-perimental method as the only method or even as a better method. Wundt called for an ethnographic, social psychology—a *"Volkspsychologie"* con-cerned with higher cognitive functions which he believed existed in the "group mind."

Psychology, deliberately denying its philosophical roots, consciously chose to emulate the natural sciences in an attempt to gain legitimacy and boost its value. To justify the experimental "nature" of the "science" of psychology, Gordon Allport even constructed a "historical" positivist provenance for psychology by the selective interpretation of Auguste Comte's mid-nineteenth-century writings.[15] Allport conveniently ignored the philosophical and religious elements of Comte's work, which were more concerned with the nature of society and reforming it than collecting experimental data. Most psychologists continue to selectively ignore their less "scientific" ancestors. In the process, psychology has become ahistorical and atheoretical.[16]

Russell Jacoby called this phenomenon of suppressing the past *social amnesia*—memory driven out of mind by the social and economic dynamic of this society . . . a forgetting and repression of the human and social activity that makes and can remake society . . . a psychic commodity of the commodity society."[17]

Striving for positivistic purpose and prosperity, psychology became commodified,[18] turning from studying individuals as *subjects of experience* to studying them as *objects of intervention* so that behavior could be predicted and controlled, primarily by industry, the military, and the school system.[19] Psychology became teleological and, ironically to my way of thinking, illogical—presuming universal causality on the basis of preconceived precepts with validation provided by methods socially constructed to do just that. The individual, singly or in groups, became a useful entity from which to generalize "laws" of behavior. Performance, not action; product, not process; measurement, not understanding, became *de rigeur*. Psychology got lost because it chose the wrong path and forgot where it came from.

The popular belief that time (history) and science are steadily advancing in a continuum of *progress* contributes to our reluctance to recognize the road not taken, and our deliberate resolve to deny its existence. As a result of this commitment to "progress"—to the future—the impetus for scientific and, therefore, psychological efforts became not simply to understand the nature of a phenomenon, but to predict its behavior. History is replaced with futurity.

To claim our epistemological[20] heritage we must reclaim history. To reclaim history, we must first remember it—not as the selectively recorded exploits of the dominant forces, but as an excavation of the historical and critical content that has been buried by the dynamics of power.[21] It is only by taking a critical look at the deceptions of society and psychology that we can interactively join scholarship and advocacy to create new ways of knowing that generate change and interrupt power imbalances.[22]

ETYMOLOGY, EPISTEMOLOGY, AND HISTORIOGRAPHY

The word "psychology" originated in the fifteenth century to refer to the subdivision of philosophy concerned with the human soul (psyche). In

1732, Christian Wolf used the term "to denote the secular and philosophical analysis and *interpretation* of mental phenomena."[23] (emphasis added) The roots of psychology reach back to the beginnings of philosophy. In the West, that means Socrates, Plato, and Aristotle. The work of earlier Greek philosophers[24] is intentionally omitted from the canon because their work was profoundly influenced by the science and philosophy of India, China, North Africa, and the mid-East.[25] The existence of this rich Eastern heritage contradicted Western imperialistic notions of superiority, so any evidence of it was suppressed. By the time Descartes[26] (1596–1650) divorced the mind from the body and sensation from thought in the "Enlightenment," non-Western concepts had all but disappeared from Western thought.[27] Cartesian dualism is a thoroughly Western philosophy: individualistic, authoritarian, and reflecting patriarchal ideology in its privileging of detachment, control, manipulation, and disinterestedness.[28] Psychology remained wedded to philosophy until Kant's (1724-1804) attempt to synthesize empiricism and rationalism[29] shifted its meaning from a philosophic study of mental phenomena to a predominantly scientific one. A primary feature of science (and "scientific" psychology) is its assumption that it is possible to be free of perceptual or interpretive perspectives or biases. Centuries of different views were conveniently deemed moot and objectivity became the goal and practice of science.

The scientific paradigm, however, soon began attracting criticism from a few brave thinkers from outside of the discipline. Vico (1688–1744), in *The New Science*,[30] reacted to the determinism of the scientific model by refusing to create binary relationships between universals and particulars, "truth" and knowledge, the stable and the fluid. Instead, his epistemological stance highlights their interrelatedness. Nietzsche (1844–1900) insisted that no fact can stand by itself and every fact is interpretive, demanding that science "free itself of the moral judgments inherited from Christianity."[31] In the 1930s, critical theorists, including Adorno and Horkheimer,[32] again began to rigorously question social science's claims to value neutrality. Adorno (1903–1969) argued that "psychological analysis is insufficient without a theory that recognizes the psyche itself as the distillation of history."[33] But it was not until fifty years later that the implications of this statement became apparent. As Habermas said, ideology is transformed by scientists into technical questions which suppresses questions of value.[34]

Psychology has historically taken little initiative in questioning its own assumptions, including value neutrality, and how they are interwoven with culture and the dynamics that constitute and maintain it. However, a few psychologists have seen through the thick haze of normativity and addressed many of these issues with erudition and concern. These scholars have called for new configurations of knowledge,[35] for interdisciplinarity,[36] for multiple methodologies,[37] and for psychology's embracing of not only science but the humanities and arts as well.[38] Still, mainstream psychology has continued to ignore both internal and external challenges to the validity of its assumptions and methods by either total disregard,[39] selective attention,[40] or the categorical institutionalization or obliteration of more veracious challenges.[41]

Yet, even here, there have been a few glimmers of hope. These include isolated flashes of insight (usually from unexpected sources) whose implications were either not seen or fully understood, suppressed as a result of a variety of political and ideological biases (e.g., sexism, racism) or, more recently, celebrated by a minority of scholars as milestones on the way to a critical, socially just psychology.

In the 1950s, Gordon Allport (1897–1967), who intentionally constructed psychology's direct descendency from positivism and remained wedded to individualism, nonetheless also cautioned that "no experiment interprets itself."[42] In 1952, Solomon Asch (1907–1996) argued that psychology overemphasized the animal side of human nature.[43] The implications of their words, for the most part, were not engaged with and remained footnotes to the body of work they produced. During the same decade, Jane Loevinger strongly criticized the inadequacy of psychological validity, a complex epistemological and methodological typology that determines what counts as valid scientific knowledge or truth. Loevinger showed that knowledge claims made on the basis of validity procedures were dependent on conditions created by psychologists themselves, and so dependent on the very assumptions they were designed to eliminate. She was a woman ahead of her times and we would hear this critique from male "scientists" long before Loevinger's contribution was recognized.

Many of the milestones on the road to a socially just psychology were carved by feminist and other socially aware scholars. These psychologists continue to expand the critique of their field by exposing the androcentrism in scientific topics of study, choice of methodology, the methods themselves, the presentation of data, and even the conception of knowledge.[44] They argue, and rightfully so, that besides its role in defining and maintaining divisions between dominant social categories like sex, class, and generation, psychology normalizes oppressive standards,[45] perpetuates social inequities, and legitimates constructs as universal truths.[46] The purpose of these critiques is not to relativize knowledge claims but to treat them as social constructs. Only in this way can their normative function and inadequacies be exposed and viable alternatives proposed.

Valerie Walkerdine, for example, discusses how psychology presents misleading representations of power relationships, such as that created between experimenter and child "subject," when framing a psychological assessment as a task or game. Walkerdine illustrates how the structuring role of power inherent in the research relationship both produces and constrains meaning.[47] Cleo Cherryholmes, adding to Loevinger's earlier work, argues that validity, particularly construct validity, is a discursive production and should therefore be analyzed in terms of the power relations inherent in that discourse.[48] Rhoda Unger stresses the need for emphasizing critical reflexivity and social action in psychology.[49] Erica Burman and Ian Parker brilliantly deconstruct developmental and social psychology, respectively. They challenge the function, truth claims, and practices of psychology, arguing for interdisciplinarity, acknowledgment of the ahistorical and decontextualized treatment of psychological phenomena, and recognition of the subjectivities and paradoxes in the field.[50] Michelle Fine, Patti Lather, Lois Holzman, Jill Morawski, Kenneth Gergen, John Shotter, Martín-Baró, and many other "radical" psychologists[51] have also advanced the move toward a more critical psychology.[52]

Although each one approaches the issues differently, these radical psychologists share a belief in transformative research and socially just psychology—a psychology that would "sensitize" the public through theories having "the capacity to challenge the guiding assumptions of the culture, to raise fundamental questions regarding contemporary social life, to foster reconsideration of that which is 'taken for granted,' and thereby to generate fresh alternatives for social action."[53] We will return to the topic of social action toward the end of this chapter. For now, it is important to emphasize that, although it is promising that more and more psychologists are critiquing psychology's theoretical validity and methodological flaws and re-defining concepts like development, stress, risk, validity, and psychopathology, these are still rare exceptions.

BUSINESS AS USUAL

The majority of the research on violence, for example, drawing on Bowlby's[54] attachment theory, points to poor "attachment" as one important predictor of violent behavior.[55] Yet, a number of scholars have found serious problems with Bowlby's theory.[56] Their ignored critiques essentially argue that it contributes to and reflects dominant ideologies and myths about contemporary families and that these biases render the methodology used in typical attachment studies highly questionable.[57] As explained by Stanton-Salazar and Spina,

> one serious problem is that [attachment] theory does not take into consideration extended kinship formations, and that it claims that other care-taking arrangements, apparent across different cultural and socioeconomic groups, are detrimental to the healthy development of the child.[58]

No one would argue with the claim that children need warm, stable attachments, but the overly restrictive determinism of Bowlby's theory is biased toward the middle-class and assumes a traditional American nuclear family as universal. It does not recognize that the means taken to meet the need for security and attachment are socioculturally contextual. Attachment Theory reduces the social to the interpersonal and, as with many other psychological models, treats social problems as originating in the individual. Conventional assumptions that early attachment styles and other personality traits and coping patterns remain stable through childhood and adolescence and from one context (family) to another (the classroom) have become increasingly questionable.

Judith Harris, in her book *The Nurture Assumption*, questions the methodological assumptions and validity of a great deal of personality research in psychology.[59] She presents a wide range of empirical evidence showing that many personality characteristics and behavioral traits are context specific. Although an individual may exhibit a certain behavior in one context (e.g., in school), she may exhibit the opposite in another context (e.g., in the home). This implies that, for example, behaviors that have been identified with so-called proclivities toward violence may not necessarily have a basis in genetic predisposition or early childhood. They may have developed later as an adaptation to oppressive or alienating social structures within society.[60]

BORN TO BE WILD?

Despite evidence to the contrary, the belief that violence is innate persists in psychology and in the wider society. A combination of interrelated religious, scientific, historical, and social influences conspire to keep it so. As the story goes, Eve tempted Adam and humans have been born in sin ever since. Although there are variations in the details, a belief in the innately evil nature of humans is common to many religions. It is also common to psychology.

Sigmund Freud (1856–1939), considered the founder of psychoanalysis, saw civilization as the regulation of otherwise uncontrollable individual proclivities toward aggression. Bridging biology, psychology and anthropology, drive or instinct theory holds that aggression is innate—an outcome of evolutionary natural selection.[61] Following on Darwin's heels, Konrad Lorenz (1903-1989), in his well-known book *On Aggression*,[62] was among the first to suggest that the key to human violence lay in the behavior of animals.[63]

Drawing on Freudian theory and Behaviorism, an interdisciplinary group of researchers at Yale University in the 1930s hypothesized that aggressive behavior always presupposes frustration, and that frustration always leads to aggression.[64] Frustration was defined as an interrupted behavior sequence or the failure to achieve some goal because of an obstacle. This produces a desire to strike out and remove the obstacle. When frustration is too great, aggression is displaced toward a substitute or scapegoat who is usually powerless to respond. In individuals without aspirations, aggression is low because there is no desire to be thwarted. (See literacy and tracking discussions in chapter 10.) There is no distinction made between different types and levels of aggression. (For example, Aggression can be protective, as when it is directed toward countering a threat to survival. It is often considered a positive attribute in the business world, but never in the ghetto.)

A world totally devoid of aggression appears to be unreasonable. However, the fact remains that there is no conclusive evidence ("scientific" or otherwise) that an aggressive drive exists *apart* from social conditions or that it must take violent forms.[65] The belief that violence is biologically necessary may more accurately be seen as a way of sanctioning violent acts as natural. Biological explanations for violence are attractive to many because they provide "quick fix" solutions to problems and a rationale for ignoring societal and ideological issues. Yet, biological and physiological studies that have investigated relationships between violence and the brain, endocrine system, genetic make-up, and the like have, in fact, failed to demonstrate that these factors *alone* can cause violence.[66] It appears that even if a biological basis for violence were to be found, social processes are what determines what, if any, response is taken. The question is not so much whether or not there is a biological predisposition to violence, but how a society deals with violence. Psychology plays a critical role in the answer to that question.

PSYCHOLOGY AND VIOLENCE

Psychology generally holds that there is a relationship between aggression and violent behavior and (innate) child temperament,[67] even when it acknowledges evidence to the contrary. Psychological studies of gun-related victimization in and around schools are a case in point. These endeavors have found violence to be highly correlated with sociodemographic factors including low socioeconomic status (SES), high population density, and high unemployment.[68] Low SES has been related to high rates of hostility and frustration,[69] as well as to homicide.[70] These studies conclude that violence is not predicated by factors inherent in the school environment and can not be isolated from the problem of violence in the larger society, *yet they paradoxically continue to locate the determining factors in individual intra-psychic deficits* and *treat violent be-havior itself as the problem.*

The American Psychological Association Commission on Violence and Youth situates "aggression" and "antisocial behavior" in "the developmental crises of adolescence."[71] They have invented diagnoses like "oppositional defiant disorder" and used them with such abandon that, in effect, adolescence itself has been turned into a disease—a disease that begins in childhood. A child who is highly active, impulsive, easily distracted, frustrated, and more noncompliant—in short, a child who acts like a "child"—is considered "difficult" and "at risk" for "delinquency." These children are frequently labeled with psychological diagnoses such as Attention Deficit Hyperactivity Disorder (ADHD), or Oppositional Defiant Disorder (ODD).[72] "ADHD" and similar diagnostic labels are routinely used by schools to determine eligibility for the allocation of resources, to keep or add faculty, and for other, usually administrative, purposes.[73]

Remarkably, many behaviors now considered delinquent have a long history of being tolerated as a common aspect of children's behavior. Until as recently as 300 years ago, most children learned and used obscene language regularly, freely engaged in a variety of sexual activities, drank in taverns, and almost never went to school.[74] Children received no special consideration. The modern Western conceptions of "childhood" and "adolescence" are social constructions—a "discovery" the French historian, Philippe Ariès, connected to sociocultural changes that took place in Europe in the mid-1600s, which changed the idea of the nature of living and the family from public to private.[75]

Nevertheless, psychology presupposes that there is a "normal" progression of (cognitive, moral, social, etc.) development and ways to actually and accurately measure that development. These models of development (e.g., Piaget, Kohlberg) are based on white, male, middle- and upper-class samples, but are applied universally. This (mal)practice encourages labeling and other forms of stigmatization which can result in "blaming the victim" for their position and/or viewing what some now realize to be successful coping strategies as maladaptive.[76] Students are given labels like "delinquent" or "ADHD" and "emotionally disturbed" when they do not conform to the norm. The behaviors identified as indicative of these "disorders" are not easily distinguished from those manifested by "healthy" children (as constructed by our society). Theoretically, the typical ADD child will have difficulty concentrating or paying attention, sitting still, staying in his seat, or waiting his turn. He may be "overly" talkative, interrupt others, yell out "inappropriately," act distracted, and be forgetful. Initially, a diagnosis of hyperactivity was applied to overactive and impulsive children, especially boys. In the 1980s, the focus shifted to "short attention span" and the "problem" was reconceptualized so as to distinguish ADD from hyperactivity (ADD-HA or ADHD). The expansion of this diagnostic category made it more inclusive. With the additional ADD diagnosis, more teenagers, adults, and girls are covered by the umbrella of deviance.[77]

The variety of diagnoses that fall into this category "work in the predictable ways to deflect attention from the central place that context and convention play in the very creation of diagnostic categories."[78] Carrier argues that learning disability theory "misrecognizes and thus masks the effects of social practices and hierarchy"[79] and focuses narrowly on the troublesome or troubled individual. That is, the diagnoses of learning "deficits" blame the student without considering the effects of social ills and ideological biases. This is in no way meant as a blanket condemnation of all special education programs. They have helped many children—but they have also damaged many others.[80]

It is significant to note that, as one might expect from this psychologized and medicalized slight of hand, minority youth, especially African American and Latino males, are disproportionately represented in "deviant" groups.[81] Thus, it is also not surprising that young children who suffer from these "disorders" have been found to be at particularly high risk for criminal activity and imprisonment as adolescents and young adults.[82] Such practices, whether inadvertently or not, mark the poor as "other," as either a victim or menace to society. They depersonalize the other[83] while simultaneously normalizing this view,[84] making it easier to harm that person. Low income, darker skin, and language difference become synonymous not only with impaired social judgment,[85] and poor academic achievement[86] due to "limited intelligence,"[87] but also with pathology, deviance, and blame.

THAT'S NOT ALL

In what may be seen as an effort to reduce some of psychology's racial bias, the American Psychological Association (APA) has instead compounded the problem in two ways: (1) by once again missing the point and (2) by targeting phantom menaces. The following excerpt from the recent APA *Report on Violence and Youth*, is an example of the first type of error:

> Many social science disciplines, in addition to psychology, have firmly established that poverty and its contextual life circumstances are major determinants of violence . . . It is very likely that socioeconomic inequality—not race—facilitates higher rates of violence. . . . There is considerable evidence that the alarming rise in youth homicides is due to the availability of firearms.[88]

Although the APA is to be commended for at least recognizing the role of poverty, albeit at the expense of acknowledging the role of race, and for noting that the accessibility of guns contributes to violence, their position remains problematic and misleading. The report, for example, does not address the inconsistency of the above statement with the fact that the great majority of poor people of all colors do not commit crimes, whites are more likely to own guns, and although poor whites outnumber poor blacks three to one, African Americans, who comprise only 10 percent of the U.S. population, make up half of the prison population. (See section on normalized racism in the introduction to this volume.)

Yet, the APA *Report* has received strong official praise. Attorney General Janet Reno has enthusiastically recommended it, guaranteeing a wide audience of readers hungry for sacrificial lambs. In the report, mass media (a "phantom menace") comes in for far more than its fair share of blame. One conclusion the report draws is that for most individuals violence is learned behavior and media is a primary teacher. Yet, no one has asked where this predilection for violent media, on the part of both the creators and consumers, comes from. The report reads, "There is *absolutely no doubt* that higher levels of viewing violence on television are correlated with increased acceptance of aggressive attitudes and increased aggressive behavior."(emphasis added)[89] Correlation, remember, does not equal causality. The report also notes that "children from low-income families are the heaviest viewers of television." Following this "logic," aggressive attitudes and behavior should be present in both boys and girls from low-income families who watch television. Why, then, do girls have less than 10 percent the crime rate of boys? There is also no consideration given to other variables such as the environment poor children live in, or the effect of being subjected to numerous advertisements in television commercials, as well as programming geared to foster a consumer mentality and manipulating desires for products only available to the upper classes.

Psychological research on media violence has been going on for over seventy years. In the 1920s and 1930s, comic books, movies, and radio broadcasts were the answers to questions similar to those being asked today about television, video games, and the Internet. Where do children learn violent behavior? What is the cause of social violence? Who/what can we scapegoat so that we may be absolved? Then, as now, much of the research focused on children and adolescents. There have been more studies conducted on the effects of televised violence on young children than on the effects of actual violence.[90] Yet, although the media in Japan, for example, is more graphically brutal than that in America and video games are even more popular, a teenager in America is more than thirty-two times as likely to commit a homicide than his Japanese counterpart. In 1996, the murder conviction rate for Japanese teenage males (ages fourteen to seventeen) was 0.6 per 100,000; in the United States, it was 19.6 per 100,000.[91] Without an underlying national ethos that supports, if not promotes, various forms of violence, would our programming and viewing habits differ? Would our homicide rates be lower?

Some recent studies on the effects of "violent" music, video games, and other media have found that, for many adolescent boys, playing "blood and guts" video games and listening to rap, hip-hop, or heavy metal music actually dissipates aggression rather than encourages it. An important difference between this work and studies that reinforce the link between media violence and behavioral violence is their methodology. The latter are generally experiments conducted in laboratories and the former are ethnographic studies based on a combination of observation, interviews, discussions, and participation in actual "real-life" settings. Ethnographers have found outcomes that contradict those of the laboratory studies which usually show that media violence does have an effect on aggression. For example, in a 1980s study of low-income junior high school boys, Arnett, who is a self-avowed believer in the recklessness of teens, found that

> for many of these adolescents, heavy metal music served a purgative func-
> tion . . . they listened to it especially when they were angry, and it consis-
> tently had the effect of making them less angry, of calming them down. This
> result certainly does not lend itself to an argument that heavy metal music is
> dangerous and should be banned.[92]

Similarly, in a 1990s study of a lower- to middle-class multicultural group of thirteen year-old boys who were avid video game players, Spina found that playing the games provided a release of tension and anxiety, and served as a "safe" outlet for aggression. As some of the boys she interviewed emphasized:

> It's not real.
> It helps me unwind after a hard day at school.
> It gets the anger out.
> Nobody gets hurt and I feel better after I play.[93]

Perhaps more importantly, Spina learned that, although violence (and sex) are part of the video game experience, they remain ephemeral to a more significant element—power. The iconography and fantasy of the games usually center around power play of frequently mythic proportions. In these games, it is the deeply embedded mythic symbolism of life and death, good and evil, that "provide dramatic ground for the complex negotiations of meaning and the resolution of inter- and intra-personal conflicts."[94] As Spina explains:

While themselves part of the social fabric of our culture, video games can paradoxically provide a means of escape from the pressures of this culture. . . . Participation in such games may be seen as a ritual encounter with power and authority that turns the tables on hegemonic patriarchy. The strength and appeal of video games lie in their ability to symbolically broach boundaries and play with contradictions.[95]

In video games, the violence and risk-taking is only symbolic. Yet, although it does not involve real-world consequences, symbolic risk-taking serves many of the same functions as actual risk-taking.[96] That is, participation in symbolic risk and violence may reduce actual risk-taking and violent behaviors.

We must not forget that when it comes to technology, the playing field is very uneven. Access to computers and video games is either nonexistent or restricted for those with low incomes who live in poorer school districts. Because the interactivity of the games, whether video or computer, is an important part of the experience, it cannot be compared to watching television or listening to music, which, although more universally available, are more passive entertainments.

This is not to say that all individuals will not be negatively influenced by violence in the media, but to raise serious questions about anti-media-violence campaigns, as well as the APA's support, if not promotion, of media censorship. Yes, music and video games have been blamed for motivating the Littleton, Colorado, high school shooting. But what about the millions of teens who watch *NYPD Blue*, listen to Megadeth and Metallica, and play Mortal Kombat and Doom, and who, under the influence of the same violent media as Dylan Klebold and Eric Harris,[97] do not go on shooting sprees?

Should we also ban books, Beatles music, religion, and whatever else is known to inspire violence? Charles Manson said his horrifying killing spree was inspired by "Helter Skelter," a song on the Beatles' *White Album*. (The song is about an amusement park ride.) Albert DiSalvo, the "Boston Strangler," blamed Anglican church services for inciting him to kill. Shall we ban the Bible because it has inspired religious fanatics to kill gay men? Shall we ban the *Boy Scout Handbook* because Eagle Scout Charles Whitman killed sixteen people from a University of Texas tower with a high-powered rifle?

Although censorship is usually associated with right-wing religious and conservative groups, many of those blaming the media for inciting youth violence are liberals trying to reclaim the mantle of morality that conservatives have wrapped around themselves with similar speciousness. By now, most if not all of us "know" that the "average American child" sees 8,000 murders and 10,000 acts of violence on television by the time she or he completes grammar school. But what do we know about the millions of American grammar school children who are physically and sexually abused?[98] What do we know or not know about our role in creating and maintaining the "smokescreens and mirrors" that all but guarantee such discrepancies will continue? How do we know what we know and don't know?

BACK TO THE FUTURE

The preceding arguments all point to why now, more than ever, we need a critical psychology. A critical psychology would link the development of knowledge to the social, cultural, political, and economic environment and critically analyze the meaning of such relations—from how they frame what questions we begin with to the methods we use and the conclusions we reach. Being a critical psychologist "does not entail giving up the technical role the psychologist now performs, but it does involve scrapping the theoretical assumptions about adaptation and interventions made from a position of power."[99] The challenge is to move psychology beyond its medicalized focus on symptomotology. Interventions, predictions, and cures can become "simply a palliative that contributes to prolonging a situation which generates and multiplies the very ills it strives to remedy."[100] The challenge is to generate critically informed knowledge based in action and action based in that knowledge.

So how do we do this? I have argued that we must begin by reclaiming our suppressed historical and epistemological heritage. I will continue that argument here, focusing on more recent developments in social psychology.

Although the Depression of the 1930s focused concerns on social issues, the psychological study of social problems in this country can be traced back to the pre–World War I Progressive movement. Progressivism describes an organic relationship between self and society. John Dewey[101] attacked American individualism and liberal capitalism, calling for new attempts to reconcile private aspirations with the public good. He argued for a more holistic social philosophy with cooperative and collectivist values. He supported his call for radical social change by actively attempting to organize a third political party.[102] Those attempts failed, but Dewey went on to publicly criticize New Deal programs because they compromised with capitalism.

In 1936, the Society for the Psychological Study of Social Issues (SPSSI) was founded. The purpose of the original organizers of SPSSI was to combine research *and* social action. Unfortunately, the group decided to focus on research alone in order to attract a larger membership. The rationale was that socially relevant research would lead to social improvements. SPSSI did, in the beginning, support work on social issues but then took the politically safer position of scientific objectivity during World War II. The relationships developed with grassroots political organizations and the labor movements of the working class dissolved as the role of *compañero* was replaced with that of intermediary and interpreter.

By the 1960s, when the civil rights movement was growing stronger and other socially just causes such as women's liberation and antiwar protests gained momentum, social psychology had retreated to the laboratory and away from applied research.[103] By the early 1970s, American social psychology had drifted so far from its earlier model that it had split into separate fields of experimental (scientific) and applied (humanistic) social psychology. European psychologists separated themselves from American social psychology, complaining it was "too American," too individualistic.

Hope was not lost. Out of this fissure grew alternative social psychology(ies), both here and abroad, that critiqued the status quo and sought a return to social relevance and, to varying degrees, concern. The movement for reconstructing psychology, as Gergen has argued, begins by replacing the modernist assumptions of a psychology grounded in the Enlightenment tradition[104] with a social epistemology grounded in the alternative tradition.[105] These alternatives include "social constructionism," "social representations," and other movements which attempt to address the dialectical nature of knowledge, its social construction, and its consequences. The underlying assumptions are change instead of progression, relativity instead of universality, subjectivity rather than objectivity, and a dynamic rather than static world. These are valuable contributions in line with a critical psychology. They draw our attention to what has been lacking in mainstream psychology, but (with the exception of the feminists and a few others) rarely address the how and why of these lacunae, questions that are critical to a critical social psychology.

WHY CRITICAL? WHY SOCIAL?

Martín-Baró has said:

> Given what psychology deals with, we must ask ourselves whether, with the tools at our disposal today, we can say, or more important, do something that will make a significant contribution to solving the crucial problems of our communities. In our case more than anyone else's, the principle holds that the concern of the social scientist should not be so much to explain the world as to transform it.[106]

Social psychology, perhaps more than any other branch of psychology and the other social sciences, has a history of commitment to and action

for social change. Even though a commitment to the active pursuit of social justice has not been consistently present throughout the annals of social psychology, there have always been at least a few "outliers" calling it
to task. Social psychology also has a history of being relegated to the low-
est rung in the hierarchy of psychologies. It does not have as much power
as mainstream psychology or ready access to the eager ear of the public.
Yet, because of its early history and marginalization, as well as the fact
that its purview includes the operation of power and the manipulation of
public opinion, both of which are concerns of critical theory, social psychology has great potential for transformation (and insurgency).

Critical theory has been a guiding perspective for studying the ideological biases in all branches of psychology and other social sciences.[107]
Concern about freedom, social justice, and collective well-being are common threads that weave through critical theory and all human "sciences."
If one believes, as critical theorists do, that the individual cannot be separated from social context, social psychology can, at least theoretically, encompass and unite other subdivisions of psychology (and the other social
sciences), even though it is idealistic and naive to think that this would
happen. (The best outcome would probably be either détente or a complete separation between the transformative and traditional camps.) Nevertheless, because critical psychology provides a framework that allows
for contradiction and conundrum and does not simply rationalize (i.e., explain away) or obscure conflict and paradox, that possibility exists. In
keeping with a Freirean approach, it would not condemn different approaches or damn their values, but dialogically examine how they are historically and socially constructed.

TOWARD A MORE CRITICAL PSYCHOLOGY

From a critical standpoint, psychology, like science, is a social construction, and as such is dialogically the result of and reason for our perceptions of the world. Thus, it is both a component and a consequence of the
U.S. market-economy focus on the all-important individual consumer. Although the European psychologists distanced themselves from this virtually antisocial stance, American psychology, like almost everything else
"American," shares the philosophical, colonial, and religious heritage of
the Europeans. As we have seen earlier in this book, this has been historically and ideologically problematic. For these and other reasons which
will become obvious as we proceed, we should not restrict our journey
only to roads constructed within our borders.

During the early years of the twentieth century, a Russian psychologist,
Lev Semenovich Vygotsky (1896–1934) argued for a psychology which

could be used as a means of change rather than just a method of description and prediction; a psychology for social purposes, what he called a "General Psychology"—a theoretical framework that would unify (i.e., integrate, not just assimilate) psychology's divided factions. It is an aesthetic social psychology,[108] if you will—the difference between *living with* and *living in* a paradigm.

A general psychology must be *built* on sound philosophical foundations. It is a "ground up" proposition. Vygotsky's is a psychology born of cultural and political struggle. Writing on the heels of the Russian Revolution, Vygotsky noted: "Our science could not have developed in the old society. We cannot master the truth about personality and personality itself as long as mankind has not mastered the truth about society and society itself."[109] The same is true today.

Many of Vygotsky's ideas are compatible with and can contribute to a critical psychology,[110] For example, in *The Development of Higher Mental Functions*, Vygotsky argued at length that psychology, isolated from history, becomes "a self-satisfying process governed by internal, self-contained forces, subject to its own immanent logic."[111] He rejected artificial divisions and abstractions and argued for studying psychological phenomena in all their complexity, not in isolation.

As James Wertsch said,

> Vygotsky managed to tie various strands of inquiry together into a unique approach that does not separate individuals from the sociocultural setting in which they function. This integrative approach to social, semiotic, and psychological phenomena has substantial relevance today, [more than] a half-century after his death.[112]

Wertsch was the first to turn to the work of another Russian, the linguist M. M. Bakhtin (1885–1975), to provide a framework to account for the mediational processes inherent in Vygotsky's integration of the individual and the social. Bakhtin's *dialogism* addresses the ways in which individual "voices" connect and interanimate each other to create meaning that is simultaneously social and unique to each individual. Dialogism gives us a way to deal with conflict and different points of view that is not binary or oppositional because additional factors add other dimensions to these poles. That is, dialogism goes beyond situation and relation to time and space.

In *The Dialogic Imagination*, Bakhtin argues that our image of what is human is always concrete, i.e., temporally and spatially positioned in the universe.[113] *Chronotope* is Bakhtin's term (borrowed from the Einsteinian mathematics' term for the inseparability of time and space) for this dimension. Ideology operates through chronotope, making certain perspectives seem natural because they are seen to reside in chronotopic "reality."

In Bakhtinian terms, psychology, religion, and science, for example, can be seen as *genres*, or particular ways of looking at the world. Meaning is *polyphonic* (a word Bakhtin borrowed from music to mean multivoicedness). The aspect of the situation that you see, but I do not (because although we share an external space and time and are physically simultaneous, inside our head we each see what the other cannot) is what Bakhtin calls "surplus of seeing." By adding your surplus to mine, a whole can be conceived or constructed out of the situation. Since Bakhtin places so much emphasis on otherness, and on otherness defined precisely as other "values," community plays an enormous role in his thought.

As community and culture become increasingly global, American psychology must take advantage of the opportunity to move beyond its parochial paradigm. For example, Chang and Holt argue that, in the East, causation is multidirectional, not unidirectional as in the West.[114] A Buddhist view of the world sees it as a shifting, interdependent set of forces, "the slightest change in any of which leads to far-reaching alterations in all the others."[115] Causality, in the East, focuses on social context and relationships, not cause and effect.

Even the "hard" sciences of the West are discovering that order is a result of interacting independent variables—those usually subsumed in statistical analysis under the "error" term, the "noise" in the system, the "outliers" in the model. The very model psychology persists in emulating is becoming part of a larger paradigm shift,[116] a (r)evolution in our image, conception, and understanding of the world. Perhaps psychology has been looking for answers in the wrong way, in the wrong place. Perhaps we need to become more comfortable with understanding that there are some things we may not be able to explain. We must be open not just to non-Western "culture" and ways of knowing and thinking, but to alternative forms (e.g., artistic, spiritual) of thought (from both hemispheres of the world and brain) that are not defined in terms of their relationship with or irreducibility to the logic of scientific rationalism. We need to raise the questions of psychology in new and perhaps disconcerting ways.

CONCLUSION

This effort is not an attempt to denounce psychology, but to reveal its material and ideological bases and biases so that we may create something better through the reintegration of a theory and practice that is aware that science is both productive and oppressive, a partner in and product of politics and power. It is an effort to move psychology away from the idea(l)s of advancement, refinement, and replacement toward a new way of understanding, beyond the commodification of history, of psychology, of ideas made rapidly obsolete by technological advances. To move toward this goal, we need to reconsider our theoretical foundations and return to a basic understanding of psychology as the study of fundamental human processes in all their complexity, to resist the temptation to fall back into the binary divisiveness that separates and subordinates difference. Most importantly, we need to approach this work with humility and not the arrogance born from assuming a higher moral ground. We need to be critically reflective and aware. Only then can we stay the course. Only then, with a cautious stride tempered by reality and seasoned by hope, can we embark on the road that will make all the difference—the road toward social justice.

POSTSCRIPT: THE ULTIMATE VIOLENCE

It seems appropriate, if we are to truly expand the dialogue on violence, to conclude this chapter about psychology with a look at the often ignored but (for)ever-present threat of annihilation that hovers over our individual and collective subconscious. Since 1945, the awareness that a nuclear apocalypse could occur at any time has been inescapable. Now, more than half a century later, the vast majority of the world's population has never lived without the image, effects, and fear of the mushroom cloud.

Robert Jay Lifton, who has long colored outside of rigid disciplinary lines, has written extensively and critically on atomic weapons and our ways of coping with cataclysmic violence such as that suffered on Hiroshima. The connections between that catastrophic event and violence in our schools, streets, and homes may be stronger than we think and should not be overlooked. These connections can be traced to what Lifton calls "psychic numbing," or "a diminished capacity or inclination to feel," that began with Hiroshima.[117]

It is not unusual for victims of trauma to adopt some type of dissociation as a way of coping. But when Lifton studied psychic numbing in survivors of the atomic bombing of Hiroshima, he also found psychic numbing on the part of the perpetrators of these horrors—from those who created the weapon to those who decided to use it and those who carried out the bombing, as well as in the general American population, where it served to ward off potential feelings of guilt.

This suggests several possibilities and raises some important issues. It is possible, and more than likely, that our fifty-five-year-old official sanctioning of national numbing has expanded to include other "threatening diseases" like poverty, domestic violence, homelessness, and racism. As numbing spreads, we all risk becoming increasingly insensitive to the violence and suffering around us. This may be a contributing factor to *normalization*, or the legitimization of biased views as neutral norms. The danger is that an increased insensitivity to the violence and suffering around us both excuses and encourages it. Because it also implies absolution of those who should be held accountable for such conditions, it leaves them, and their indifferent abettors, blameless. Who are these accomplices? We, the American people, are—whenever we, unwittingly or not, assume the motives and values of the state as our own.

We can also develop psychic numbing in response to other traumatic events, many of which have been described in this volume. The habit of numbing can be a useful way of coping, as it was for many survivors of Hitler's death camps, but it can, and often does, extend into life beyond the traumatic situation. Lifton uses the words of a character in one of Alice Walker's novels to illustrate this: "The trouble with numbness . . . is that it spreads to all your organs, mainly the heart. Pretty soon after I don't hear the white folks crying for help, I don't hear the black."[118]

As one way to cope with trauma and violence, Lifton explains, we construct a psychological and sometimes physical barrier around it to contain it and keep it from our consciousness so we can avoid any feeling about the event or situation. Thus, for example, we have developed a national "habit" of numbing about the bombing of Hiroshima and its lingering effects, we build walls and fences around our memories and around poor areas of our cities, we banish the homeless from the landscapes of our minds by averting our eyes and from our consciences by sweeping them from our streets whenever some important dignitary visits.

These desperate attempts at avoidance are symptomatic of a growing sense of communal loss, a loss of continuity and connectedness. Our continuing attempts to ward off the emptiness with denial and to fill it with the frantic acquisition of material goods are futile. Our disease is contagious. But it does not have to be fatal. Even under the most horrendous conditions, Lifton found that the yearning to keep hope alive remains constant.[119] He talks about a principal of *commonality* underlying this hope; a commonality "of the characteristics we share as a species, and, even more, the life experiences we share as well."[120] This does not imply sameness or similarity, but a common humanity amidst our diversity. It is "individual people reaching toward global belonging . . . a path of hope."[121] As Lifton explains, "One may experience that hope, and even a modest personal liberation, in consciously embracing that direction. The embrace is an act of imagination and, as such, a profound beginning."[122] They are words that speak of and to our very essence as human beings. They are words fitting of psychology as the study of our "souls." They are not "scientific." They are not "objective." But they resonate with the ring of truth.

NOTES

1. Fred Newman and Lois Holzman, *The End of Knowing: A New Developmental Way of Learning* (New York: Routledge, 1997).

2. Newman and Holzman, *The End of Knowing.*

3. Kurt Danziger, *Constructing the Subject: Historical Origins of Psychological Research* (New York: Cambridge University Press, 1994).

4. Lois Holzman, *Schools for Growth: Radical Alternatives to Current Educational Models* (Hillsdale, N.J.: Lawrence Erlbaum, 1997), 36.

5. Sheryl Gay Stolberg, "Science Looks at Littleton, and Shrugs Its Shoulders," *New York Times,* 9 May 1999, Sec. 4, 1, 4.

6. This topic is discussed in the introductory chapter.

7. I use quotations because it is actually a blind equilibrium that is sought, an avoidance of actual understanding.

8. This sad fact is not limited to the United States. Globally, 18 million deaths a year are caused by structural violence, compared with about 100,000 deaths per year from armed conflict. That is, approximately every fifteen years, as many people die because of relative poverty as would be killed in a nuclear war that caused 232 million deaths, and every single year, two to three times as many people die from poverty throughout the world as were killed by the Nazi genocide of the Jews over a six-year period. This is, in effect, the equivalent of an ongoing, unending, in fact accelerating, thermonuclear war or genocide, perpetrated on the weak and poor every year of every decade, throughout the world. (See James Gilligan, *Violence: Reflections on a National Epidemic,* New York: Vintage Books, 1997, 196.)

9. Stanley Milgram, "Behavioral Study of Obedience," *Journal of Abnormal and Social Psychology* 67 (1963): 371–378. See also: Stanley Milgram, *Obedience to Authority: An Experimental View* (New York: Harper and Row, 1974). For an additional example from psychology, Philip Zimbardo's *Stanford Prison Experiment,* see <http://www. stanford.edu/dept/news/relaged/970108prisonexp.html>. For a slide show of the controversial experiment, see <http://www.napier.ac.uk/depts/pas/psycho/prison/index.html>.

10. The APA Code of Ethics is available online at <www.apa.org/ethics/code.html>.

11. Unfortunately, despite attempts to protect research participants, controversy around the *history of questionable practices* exemplified by Tuskegee study continue. For example, a psychiatric study completed in 1999 at Bellevue Hospital Center in New York City was criticized by state investigators for not keeping accurate medical records (including failure to document prior medical and psychological history that would require exclusion from the study) and for not obtaining proper informed consent from emergency room patients, half of whom were homeless, when admitting them into a clinical trial for a new anti-psychotic drug. (Kathleen Kerr, "State Raps Bellevue Drug-Trial Procedures," *Newsday,* 14 Mar. 2000, A42.)

In June, 1999, the federal Office of Protection From Research Risks (OPRR) exonerated the New York State Psychiatric Institute of any ethical wrongdoing for experiments on black and Latino boys (using a drug now banned by the Federal

Drug Administration (FDA). The subjects were thirty-four healthy boys between the ages of six and ten. All were the younger brothers of juvenile delinquents. (Another issue not raised by the OPRR investigation was why the Department of Probation provided the boys' names to strangers.)

John Oldham, the executive director of the institute, issued a press release defending the experiments: "With the disasters in Littleton and elsewhere, it has become abundantly clear that studies of aggressive behavior in children are imperative." The OPRR held that despite risks posed to the children, the research would provide valuable "generalizable knowledge about the subjects' condition."

Calling the experiments "unethical," "racist," and "dangerously close to eugenics," a coalition of activists demanded the federal investigation and pressured lawmakers for legislation to "warn families about possible side effects of future experiments and to notify the New York State health commissioner about the justification for research based on ethnicity or sex." In March, 2000, Surgeon General David Satcher announced the formation of a National Advisory Council on Human Research Protections composed of independent experts. Satcher described the purpose of the Council as setting standards that address the protection of human subjects. As this book goes to press, the bill, signed by forty-six democratic legislators, is being introduced (for the second time) by New York State Assemblyman Albert Vann. The institute continues to do studies on children, but not with fenfluramine, the drug involved in the investigated experiment.

Dr. Peter Breggin, director of the International Center for Psychiatry and Psychology in Bethesda, Maryland, is among those challenging the OPRR decision. Breggin and his colleagues have fought against inhumane experiments since 1972, when they discovered that a Southern University was implanting electrodes in the brains of black children as young as five-years-old. The electrodes were heated to melt areas of the brain that regulate emotion and intellect in order to control "hyperactive and aggressive behavior." Haider Rizvi reports that

> At this critical juncture, health advocates are not letting up pressure. "It is a disaster that the OPRR exonerated the Psychiatric Institute," says Breggin. "It's a blank check to do experiments on any inner city child; if you are poor and black, you are at risk," he says. "Experiments like those should never be carried out again."

(Haider Rizvi, "An Unscientific Method? Activists and Legislators Urge Safeguards for Human Subjects in Experiments," the New York *Village Voice* (5–11 Apr. 2000) accessed 20 Apr. 2000 <http://www.villagevoice.com/issues/0014/rizvi.shtml>)

12. See James H. Jones, *Bad Blood: The Tuskegee Syphilis Experiment* (New York: The Free Press, 1981).

13. See Jill G. Morawski, *Practicing Feminisms, Reconstructing Psychology: Notes on a Liminal Science* (Ann Arbor, Mich.: The University of Michigan Press, 1994/97).

14. Danziger, *Constructing the Subject*.

15. Gordon W. Allport, *The Historical Background of Modern Social Psychology, vol. 1.* (Reading, Mass.: Addison-Wesley, 1954) and F. Samelson, "History, Origin Myth, and Ideology: Comte's 'Discovery' of Social Psychology." *Journal for Theory of Social Behavior* 4 (1974): 217–231.

16. A look at recent articles in leading psychological journals will confirm that few, if any, references are more than twenty years old.

17. Russell Jacoby, *Social Amnesia* (Boston: Beacon Press, 1975) 4–5.

18. Commodification is the process by which culture becomes increasingly materialistic under the influence of the logic of capitalism in which every thing/person is reduced to a commodity (object) and thus to its market value.

19. Danziger, *Constructing the Subject*, 66.

20. Epistemology deals with the origin, nature, and limits of knowledge. It concerns how we understand the nature of "reality." An epistemological framework specifies what is (i.e., counts as) knowledge, how to recognize it, and who the gatekeepers of that knowledge are.

21. This critique of "science" is not just a recent development. Others have provided thorough and critical reviews of the sociohistorical development of psychology. The necessarily truncated overview presented in this chapter aims only to provide some idea of the scope and tenor of that work. The reader is urged to see references listed in notes 27, 42, and 50.

22. Patti Lather, *Getting Smart, Feminist Research and Pedagogy with/in the Postmodern* (New York, Routledge, 1991).

23. W. M. O'Neil, *The Beginnings of Modern Psychology* (Sussex, U.K.: The Harvester Press, 1968/82), 1.

24. Heraclitus (circa 500 B.C.E.) argued, for example, that everything is constantly changing and that makes knowing impossible.

25. Stanley Aronowitz, on page 179 in his recent book, *The Knowledge Factory: Dismantling the Corporate University and Creating True Higher Learning* (Boston: Beacon Press, 2000), provides a valuable list of resources for those interested in learning more about Eastern philosophy and social sciences:

G. W. F. Hegel's *Philosophy of History* begins with a treatment of the "Oriental World" which comprises the one hundred thirty three pages of Part One. His *Lectures in the History of Philosophy* begins with Eastern philosophy, not the Greeks. And two of Max Weber's earlier writings *The Agrarian Sociology of Ancient Civilizations* and *The Religion of India* remain of contemporary interest, especially the latter work's sensitive study of Hinduism and its relation to the caste system. Louis Dumont's *Homo Hierarchicus* and the fine essay by Barrington Moore at the beginning of *Injustice The Social Bases of Obedience and Revolt*, on discontent among India's untouchable caste might provide a counterpoint to Weber's treatment. . . . The "near eastern" forerunners of Greek science and philosophy are explored in J. B. Pritchard's edited volume *Ancient Near Eastern Texts and their relation to the Old Testament*.

26. René Descartes (1596–1650) was a French mathematician and philosopher. Descartes's position was dualistic, mind and body were separate and distinct. The body was considered mechanical and to be understood through physical and mathematical study; the mind through rational means. His work is popularly, if reductively, summed up in his words, *"Cogito, ergo sum."*

27. Aronowitz, *The Knowledge Factory*, chapter 7.

28. L. L. Lopes, "The Rhetoric of Irrationality," *Theory and Psychology* 1, 65–82, 1991; Susan Bordo, *The Flight to Objectivity: Essays on Cartesianism and Culture* (Albany, New York: SUNY Press, 1987); Evelyn Fox Keller, *Reflections on Gender and Science* (New Haven: Yale University Press, 1985) and "Gender and Science: Ori-

gin, History, and Politics," *Osiris* 10 (1995): 27–58; Jill Morawski, "The Science Behind Feminist Research Methods" *Journal of Social Issues* 53, 4, (1997) 667–681; Liz Stanley and Sue Wise, *Breaking Out Again: Feminist Ontology and Epistemology* rev. ed. (New York and London: Routledge, 1993).

29. Danziger, *Constructing the Subject*.

30. Giambattista Vico, *The New Science of Giambattista Vico*, trans. Thomas G. Bergin (Ithaca, N.Y.: Cornell University Press, 1984).

31. Stanley Aronowitz, *Science as Power: Discourse and Ideology in Modern Society* (Minneapolis: University of Minnesota Press, 1988), 256.

32. Max Horkheimer and Theodor Adorno, *Dialectic of Enlightenment* (New York: Continuum, 1976).

33. Theodor W. Adorno, "Scientific Experiences of a European Scholar in America," in *The Intellectual Migration*, eds. Donald Fleming and Bernard Bailyn (Cambridge, Mass.: Harvard University Press, 1969), cited in Christopher Lash, introduction to Jacoby's *Social Amnesia*, i–xv.

34. Jürgen Habermas, "Modernity vs. Postmodernity" *New German Critique* 22 (1988).

35. See J. F. Lyotard, *The Postmodern Condition: A Report on Knowledge*, trans. G. Bennington and B. Massumi (Minneapolis: University of Minnesota Press, 1984).

36. See Lev S. Vygotsky, "The Historical Meaning of the Crisis in Psychology," (1926) in *The Collected Works of L. S. Vygotsky, Vol. 3: Problems of the Theory and History of Psychology*, eds. R. W. Rieber & J. Wollock, trans. R. Van der Veer (New York: Plenum Press, 1997), 233–370; L. S. Vygotsky "The Methods of Reflexological and Psychological Investigation," in *The Collected Works of L. S. Vygotsky, Vol. 3, 35–49.

37. See Vygotsky, "The Historical Meaning of the Crisis in Psychology."

38. See Lev S. Vygotsky, *The Psychology of Art* (Cambridge: MIT Press, [1915–25] 1965/68/71); Lev S. Vygotsky, "The Problem of the Environment," in *The Vygotsky Reader*, eds. R. van der Veer and J. Valsiner (Oxford: Blackwell, [1935] 1994), 338–354; Seymour B. Sarason, *The Challenge of Art to Psychology* (New Haven, Yale University Press, 1990).

39. See Newman and Holzman, *The End of Knowing*.

40. See Wilhelm M. Wundt, *Elements of Folk Psychology* (New York: Macmillan, 1916).

41. See Stephanie Urso Spina, "Demythifying Multicultural Education: Social Semiotics as a Tool for Critical Pedagogy." *Teaching Education* 9 (1997): 27–36.

42. Gordon W. Allport, *The Historical Background of Modern Social Psychology*, vol. 1, 50.

43. Solomon Asch, *Social Psychology* (New York: Prentice-Hall, 1952).

44. See S. Harding, *The Science Question in Feminism* (Ithaca, N.Y.: Cornell University Press, 1986); E. F. Keller, *Reflections on Gender and Science* (New Haven: Yale University Press, 1984); S. Bordo, *The Flight to Objectivity, Essays on Cartesianism and Culture* (Albany: SUNY Press, 1987); Linda Alcoff and Elizabeth Potter, *Feminist Epistemologies* (New York: Routledge, 1993).

45. See Freire and Macedo, this volume.

46. See Aronowitz, *Science as Power* for a thorough treatment of these and related issues.

47. Valerie Walkerdine, *The Mastery of Reason* (London: Routledge, 1988).

48. Cleo H. Cherryholmes, "Construct Validity and the Discourses of Research," *American Journal of Education* 96 (1988): 421–57.

49. Rhoda Unger, "Through the Looking Glass: No Wonderland Yet!" *Psychology of Women Quarterly* 8 (1983): 9–32.

50. Erica Burman, *Deconstructing Developmental Psychology* (London: Routledge, 1994); Ian Parker, *The Crisis in Modern Social Psychology*. (London: Routledge, 1989).

51. I put quotation marks around the word "radical" because, at least without explication, it is not a term all of these scholars would necessarily apply to themselves. However, in addition to the common use of radical to mean "extreme," radical also means "fundamental; going to the root," and since all of the psychologists listed do address root (implicit, hidden, basic) issues, it seemed an appropriate descriptor.

52. See, for example, Jill Morawski, *Practicing Feminisms*; Kenneth Gergen, *Toward Transformation in Social Knowledge* (New York: Springer-Verlag, 1982). John Shotter, *Social Accountability and Self-Hood* (Oxford: Basil Blackwell, 1984); Ignacio Martín-Baró, *Writings for a Liberation Psychology*, eds. Adreanne Aron and Shawn Corne (Cambridge, Mass.: Harvard University Press, 1994); Patti Lather, *Getting Smart*; Newman and Holzman, *The End of Knowing*; Steiner Kvale, *Psychology and Postmodernism* (Thousand Oaks, Calif.: Sage, 1992); John Morss, *Growing Critical: Alternatives to Developmental Psychology*. (London: Routledge, 1995).

53. Gergen, *Toward Transformation*, 109.

54. L. Bowlby, *Attachment and Loss* (New York: Basic Books, 1969).

55. M. D. Ainsworth, S. M. Blehar, and S. Wall, *Patterns of Attachment* (Hillsdale, N.J.: Lawrence Erlbaum, 1978).

56. See Burman, *Deconstructing*; K. A. Clarke-Stewart, "The 'Effects' of Infant Day Care Reconsidered," *Early Childhood Research Quarterly*, 3 (1988): 293–318; D. White and A. Woollett, *Families: A Context for Development* (New York: Falmer Press, 1992); Ricardo Stanton-Salazar and Stephanie Urso Spina, "Network Orientations of Highly Resilient Minority Youth: A Network-Analytic Account of Minority Socialization and Its Educational Implications" *The Urban Review: Issues and Ideas in Public Education* (in press).

57. The Strange Situation Test was developed by Ainsworth as a test of Bowlby's theory (See Ainsworth, Blehar, and Wall, 1978). Attachment style was determined on the basis of observations of children's reactions to maternal separation under three conditions: (1) when they are brought into an unfamiliar setting with their mothers, (2) when a strange adult enters the setting where the child and mother are, and (3) when the mother then leaves. Children from about two and one-half years of age are expected to adapt to the mother's absence. If the child in the first situation does not play at some distance from the mother or exhibit the "confidence" to explore her surroundings while the mother is present, the attachment is considered insecure. The same conclusion is drawn if the child fails to protest when the mother leaves. The child who exhibits distress at separation from the mother is labeled "insecure."

58. Stanton-Salazar and Spina, "Network Orientations."

59. Judith Harris, *The Nurture Assumption* (New York: The Free Press, 1998).

60. Stanton-Salazar and Spina, "Network Orientations."

61. See Sigmund Freud, "Instincts and Their Vicissitudes," in *The Standard Edition of the Complete Psychological Work of Sigmund Freud, Vol. 14.*, ed. J. Strachey (London: Hogarth Press, 1957); Konrad Lorenz, *On Aggression* (New York: Bantam Books, 1963/1971); Irenaus Eibll-Eibesfeldt, *The Biology of War and Peace: Men, Animals and Aggression* (New York: Viking, 1979).

62. Konrad Lorenz, *On Aggression*.

63. Aside from problems with applying conclusions drawn from animal observations and experiments to humans, Lorenz does not differentiate between male and female. As in society, most psychological studies treat male behavior as the universal norm. Women are either not considered or, if they are, it is through this same normative lens which distorts perception.

64. J. Dollard, N. Miller, O. H. Mowrer, and R. R. Sears, *Frustration and Aggression* (New Haven: Yale University Press, 1939).

65. Eric Fromm, *The Anatomy of Human Destructiveness* (New York: Holt, Rinehart and Winston, 1973); David Adams et al., "The Seville Statement on Violence," *Peace Review*, 4, no. 3 (1992): 20–22.

66. K. E. Moyer, *The Psychobiology of Aggression* (New York: Harper and Row, 1976).; George A Gellert, M.D., *Confronting Violence: Answers to Questions About the Epidemic Destroying America's Homes and Communities.* (Boulder, Colo.: Westview Press: 1997); Debra Niehoff, *The Biology of Violence* (New York: Free Press, 1999).

67. N. Brier, "Predicting Antisocial Behavior in Youngsters Displaying Poor Academic Achievement: A Review of Risk Factors," *Developmental and Behavioral Pediatrics* 16 (1995): 271–276.

68. See, for example, J. F. Sheley, Z. T. McGee, and J. D. Wright, "Gun-related Violence In and Around Inner City Schools." *American Journal of Disabled Child* 146 (1992): 677–682.

69. See S. Kadel and J. Follman, *Reducing Violence in Florida: A Southeastern Regional Vision for Education.* (Greensboro, N.C.: University of North Carolina, 1993).; R. J. Gelles, and D. R. Loseke, *Current Controversies on Family Violence* (Newbury Park, Calif.: Sage, 1993).

70. P. J. Meehan and P. W. O'Carroll, "Gangs, Drugs, and Homicide in Los Angeles." *American Journal of Diseases of Children* 146 (1992): 683–687.

71. American Psychological Association, *Summary Report of the American Psychological Association Commission on Violence and Youth*, Vol. 1 (Washington, D.C.: American Psychological Association, 1993): 54–55.

72. T. E. Moffitt, "The Neuropsychology of Juvenile Delinquency: A Critical Review," in *Crime and Justice: A Review of the Literature*, eds. M. Tonry and N. Morris (Chicago: University of Chicago Press, 1990).

73. For example, in New York City Public Schools, 13 percent of all students are classified as special education students. This is more than twice the national average. See L. Richardson, "Special Education Loses Money but not Students," *New York Times*, 17 October 1995, A1, B8.

74. L. T. Empey, *American Delinquency: Its Meaning and Construction* (Homewood, Ill.: Dorsey Press, 1978).

75. Philippe Ariès, *Centuries of Childhood: A Social History of Family Life* (New York: Vintage Books, 1962).

76. See, for example, Michelle Fine, "Contextualizing the Study of Social Injustice." In *Advances in Applied Social Psychology*, vol. 3., ed. Len Saxe (Hillsdale, N.J.:

Lawrence Erlbaum, 1986); Michelle Fine, *Disruptive Voices: The Possibilities of Feminist Research*. (Ann Arbor, Mich.: University of Michigan Press, 1992); Lenore Terr, *Unchained Memories: True Stories of Traumatic Memories, Lost and Found*. (New York: Basic Books, 1994). Stephanie Urso Spina, "A Review of *Stress, Risk, and Resilience in Children and Adolescents: Processes, Mechanisms, and Interventions*, R. J. Haggerty, L. R. Sherrod, N. Garmezy, and M. Rutter (Eds.)," *Mind, Culture, and Activity* 5 (1998): 235–239; Niobe Way, "Using Feminist Research Methods to Understand the Friendships of Adolescent Boys," *Journal of Social Issues* 53, (1997): 703–723.

77. It should be noted that the drugs used to treat hyperkinesis and other behavioral "diseases" were available as long as twenty years before the disorder was "discovered." In addition, beginning in the mid-1960s, pharmaceutical companies ran massive campaigns to promote medications (Ritalin or Dexedrine) for these new disorders. See Peter Conrad and Joseph Schneider, *Deviance and Medicalization: From Badness to Sickness* (Philadelphia: Temple University Press, 1992).

78. Conrad and Schneider, *Deviance and Medicalization*, 285.

79. Quoted in Conrad and Schneider, *Deviance and Medicalization*, 285.

80. See Donna Gaines, *Teenage Wasteland*, (New York: Harper Perennial, 1990).

81. Executive Committee of Council for Children with Behavioral Disorders, "Best Assessment Practices for Students with Behavioral Disorders: Accommodation to Cultural Diversity and Individual Differences," *Behavioral Disorders* 14 (1989): 263–278.

82. D. P. Farrington, "Childhood Aggression and Adult Violence: Early Precursors and Later Life Outcomes," in *The Development and Treatment of Childhood Aggression*, eds. D. J. Peplar and K. Rubin (Hillsdale, N.J.: Lawrence Erlbaum, 1991), 5–29; R. Loeber, "The Stability of Antisocial and Delinquent Child Behavior: A Review," *Child Development* 53 (Dec. 1982) 1431–1446.

83. See McLaren, Leonardo, and Allen, "Rated 'CV' for Cool Violence", this volume; see also: L. Alcoff, "The Problem of Speaking for Others," *Cultural Critique* 23 (1991-92): 5–32; Leslie Roman, "Spectacle in the Dark: Youth as Transgression, Display, and Repression." *Educational Theory* 46 (1996): 1–22.

84. See Stephanie Spina and Robert H. Tai, "The Politics of Racial Identity: A Pedagogy of Invisibility," *Educational Researcher* 27 (1998): 36–40.

85. See K. A. Dodge, J. M. Price, J. A. Bachorowski, and J. P. Newman, "Hostile Attributional Biases in Severely Aggressive Adolescents," *Journal of Abnormal Psychology* 99 (1990): 385–392; S. Graham, and C. Hudley, (1992). "An Attributional Approach to Aggression in African-American Children," in *Student Perceptions in the Classroom*, eds. D. Schunk and J. Meece (Hillsdale, N.J.: Lawrence Erlbaum), 75–94; P. H. Tolan, N. G. Guerra, and P. C. Kendall, "A Developmental Perspective on Antisocial Behavior in Children and Adolescents: Toward a Unified Risk and Intervention Framework," *Journal of Consulting and Clinical Psychology* 63 (1995): 579–584.

86. Macedo and Freire, "Scientism and the Ideological Construction of Violence, Poverty, and Racism," this volume.

87. T. Hirsch, and M. J. Hindelang, "Intelligence and Delinquency: A Revisionist Review." *American Sociological Review* 42 (1977): 571–587.

88. *Summary Report of the American Psychological Association Commission on Violence and Youth*, Vol. 1. (Washington, D.C.: American Psychological Association, 1993).

89. American Psychological Association, *Summary report.*

90. Jo Ann M. Farver and Dominick Frosch, "L. A. Stories: Aggression in Preschoolers' Spontaneous Narratives After the Riots of 1992," *Child Development* 67 (1996): 19–32.

91. United Nations, 1996 Demographic Yearbook (1998).

92. J. Arnett, "Adolescents and Heavy Metal Music: From the Mouths of Metalheads," *Youth and Society* 23 (September, 1991): 76–97.

93. Stephanie Urso Spina, *Carnival and Carnage: A Semiotic Look at Video Game Culture,* Multimedia presentation at the annual meeting of the Semiotic Society of America. Toronto, Canada, October, 1998.

94. Spina, *Carnival and Carnage.*

95. Spina, *Carnival and Carnage,* 4.

96. Although there is not room for an in-depth explanation of this phenomenon here, the reader is referred to C. Lightfoot, *The Culture of Adolescent Risk-taking.* (New York: Guilford Press, 1997).

97. Klebold and Harris are the two boys who killed eight boys, four girls, one male teacher, and wounded twenty-three students before committing suicide in Littleton, Colorado, on April 20, 1999. See Klein and Chancer, this volume.

98. See reports issued by the U. S. Advisory Board on Child Abuse and Neglect.

99. Martín-Baró, *Writings,* 44.

100. Martín-Baró, *Writings,* 122.

101. John Dewey, *Individualism Old and New* (New York: Minton Balch, 1930); John Dewey, *Liberalism and Social Action* (New York: Putnam, 1935).

102. E. J. Bordeau, "John Dewey's Ideas About the Great Depression," *Journal of the History of Ideas* 32 (1971): 67–68.

103. See R. L. Rosnow, *Paradigms in Transition: The Methodology of Social Inquiry* (New York: Oxford University Press, 1981); Kenneth Ring, "Experimental Social Psychology: Some Sober Questions About Some Frivolous Values," *Journal of Experimental Social Psychology* 3 (1967): 113–123.

104. The Enlightenment refers to most of the seventeenth and eighteenth centuries when European thought focused on the foundations of knowledge, as evidenced in the philosophy of Descartes, Locke, and Kant building on Aristotelian and Platonic thought.

105. The foundations of social epistemology go back to the pre-Socratic philosophers who were influenced by Asian and African thought. (See note 24.) This "school" includes work of Giambattista Vico, Friedrich Hegel, and Karl Marx, among others.

106. Martín-Baró *Writings,* 19.

107. See, for example, Erica Burman, *Deconstructing Developmental Psychology;* Ian Parker, *The Crisis in Modern Social Psychology;* Isaac Prilleltensky, *The Morals and Politics of Psychology : Psychological Discourse and the Status Quo* (New York: SUNY Press, 1994); Richard A. Shweder, James W. Stigler, and Gilbert Herdt, eds., *Cultural Psychology: Essays on Comparative Human Development* (Cambridge University Press, 1990); Dennis Fox and Isaac Prilleltensky, eds., *Critical Psychology: An Introduction* (Newbury Park, Calif.: Sage, 1997); Jane M. Ussher, ed., *Body Talk: The Material and Discursive Regulation of Sexuality, Madness and Reproduction* (New York: Routledge, 1998).

108. Stephanie Urso Spina, "The Concept of Culture in the Work of L. S. Vygotsky," unpublished manuscript, City University of New York, 1997.

109. Vygotsky, "The Historical Meaning of the Crisis in Psychology," 342.

110. It should be noted that not all of Vygotsky's ideas are consonant with a critical psychology. For example, his developmental theory was hierarchical and some of his assumptions remained particular to the biases of his time and place. See, for example, Barbara Rogoff, *Apprenticeship in Thinking: Cognitive Development in Social Context* (New York: Oxford University Press, 1990). Spina, *The Concept of Culture.*

111. Lev S. Vygotsky, "The Development of Higher Mental Functions. (1931), in *The Collected Works of L. S. Vygotsky.* Vol. 4: *The History of the Development of Higher Mental Functions,* ed. R. W. Rieber, trans. M. J. Hall (New York: Plenum Press, 1997), 9.

112. James V. Wertsch, ed., *Culture, Communication, and Cognition: Vygotskian Perspectives* (New York: Cambridge University Press, 1985), 16.

113. M. M. Bakhtin, *The Dialogic Imagination: Four Essays by M. M. Bakhtin,* ed. M. Holquist (Austin: University of Texas Press, 1981). See also Stanley Aronowitz, "Literature as Social Knowledge: Mikhail Bakhtin and the Emergence of the Human Sciences," in *Bakhtin in Contexts: Across the Disciplines.* ed. A. Mandelker (Evanston, Ill.: Northwestern University Press, 1995), 119–135; M. Holquist, *Dialogism: Bakhtin and his World* (New York: Routledge, 1990).

114. H. Chang, and G. R. Holt, "The Concept of Yuan and Chinese Interpersonal Relationships," in *Cross-cultural Interpersonal Communication,* eds. S. Ting-Toomey & F. Korzenny (Newbury Park, Calif.: Sage, 1991), 29–57.

115. Chang and Holt, "The Concept of Yuan," 33.

116. Thomas S. Kuhn, The Structure of Scientific Revolution (Chicago: University of Chicago Press, 1996).

117. See, for example, Robert Jay Lifton, *Death in Life: Survivors of Hiroshima* (University of North Carolina Press, Reprint edition, 1991); Robert Jay Lifton and Greg Mitchell, *Hiroshima in America : A Half Century of Denial* (New York: Avon Books, 1996). See also Robert Jay Lifton, *The Nazi Doctors: Medical Killing and the Psychology of Genocide* (New York: Basic Books, 1988).

118. Quoted in Lifton, *Hiroshima in America,* 339–340.

119. That "yearning to keep hope alive" and a sense of our common Species Self has inspired Lifton to become a key figure in Physicians for Social Responsibility and the antinuclear and peace movements. See Charles B. Strozier, introduction to *Trauma and Self,* eds. Charles B. Strozier and Michael Flynn (Boulder, Colo.: Rowman & Littlefield, 1996), xiv.

120. Lifton, *The Protean Self: Human Resilience in an Age of Fragmentation* (New York, Basic Books, 1993), 213.

121. Lifton, *Protean Self,* 232.

122. Lifton, *Protean Self,* 232.

9

Essay on Violence

Stanley Aronowitz

In this essay I adopt the commonsense conception of violence in which someone has been physically assaulted by another or, in international relations, armies and whole populations are subject to weapons of destruction. Now, I do not deny the limited utility of ideas such as "symbolic violence" when applied to education, for instance,[1] or the idea that communication may be fraught with linguistic violence that hurts feelings, bears on self-esteem, and so forth. I am aware that, in the course of describing relations between men and women, violence has become a descriptive and an explanatory tool for feminists and many writers do not employ the word metaphorically.

But I am not inclined to accept the tendency, all too pervasive in the academy, to broaden the use of the term "violence" so widely that it loses its specificity. To equate invective, linguistic manipulation and the like with physical acts aimed at intimidation and which may threaten life itself misses the point of the rise of violence in this century and loses the grave consequences of its deployment. Moreover, when applied to communicative action its use conceals more than it reveals. For example, it is perfectly true that the power of schooling on kids occurs on more than the level of discipline. The curriculum is an unwanted imposition but this insight hardly amounts to "violence." At some point the student who sticks with the curriculum must buy in and succeed in its terms. How else could it be? And there is no question that many of the routines associated with

211

marriage and other gender and sexual relations hide the coercion visited by the structure on women. But how to distinguish acts of physical force from those that function at the institutional and psychological levels? There is, of course, such a thing as psychological warfare, economic warfare and so forth. The stronger surely holds the advantage over the weaker combatant. But, even though the subtext of many instances of these forms of struggle is the possibility that the loser may be subject to force, the moments of involuntary detention, torture, and the prospect of death are qualitatively different from "symbolic" violence and its consequences. Let us grant at the outset that there is a continuum rather than a categorical break between language and force. But it is important to maintain the difference. So, although I shall have occasion below to refer to the more nuanced usages of violence, it is by way of illustration of the process by which insult may become physically imposed terror.

Spring 1999 was a bloody one in Kosovo, Yugoslavia, and Littleton, Colorado, among other sites where violence was the decisive method to solve political and social conflicts. Violence is not all that unites these incidents. Like most events in modern war they shared a tendency to rope in noncombatants who happened to be in the way of guns and bombs. Senseless? Maybe so. But there might good reasons for these bad outcomes which, however unjustified on moral grounds, often make good strategy. Having set up Yugoslav President Slobodon Milosevic as a reliable supplicant of the U.S.-dominated International Monetary Fund (IMF), and unconscionably dawdled during his ethnic cleansing program in Bosnia, the Clinton administration and its European allies, belatedly found reasons to turn on him. When, responding to mounting protests and guerrilla activity, Yugoslav troops entered Kosovo and drove nearly a million people from their homes, the Clinton administration wasted little time bombing military and civilian targets in Belgrade and other Yugoslav cities as well as in Kosovo. The relatively swift military response to the Kosovan crisis contrasted sharply with Allied hesitation during the earlier conflict when NATO remained paralyzed for months as Yugoslav bombs rained on Sarajevo and Serbian militia allied to the Yugoslav government killed and maimed thousands and forced many more to flee their homes.

For the purposes of this essay I want to reserve discussion of whether the wars against Yugoslavia and Iraq were "justified" on human rights criteria. I do not accept the idea advanced by many critics that since the U.S. actions were selective they should inevitably be shunned. "What about Rwanda and other African cases of genocide? After promising to support the Kurds why didn't the United States stop Turkey's victimization of its Kurdish minority." Although I take the point that United States policy is more concerned with conflicts in Europe than those in the South or the East, the logic of such thinking is that unless one is an equal opportunity human rights intervenor, no intervention that might save some lives is legitimate. Nor is the view promulgated by some nurtured in the Vietnam War era that *any* United States military action is to be condemned before the fact as evidence that as an imperialist power any American intervention must necessarily be an extension of a policy of aggrandizement. While it can be shown that U.S. intervention in Kosovo was surely not free of political motivations, only naïve moralists could plausibly demand as a condition of support that war aims be pure. On such criteria U.S. participation in the war against fascism could be, and was, condemned by those who were not pacifists. For the moment it is enough to note that unless one renounces the use of force to resolve conflicts between sovereign states under any conditions, the criteria for determining the difference between just and unjust war stand between approbation and condemnation.

Let us acknowledge that the issues are complicated. In the Yugoslav case, was the U.S. claim to have defended human rights undermined by the scope and the effects of the bombings? Or can it be argued that when the majority of the Serbian population knowingly supports acts such as ethnic cleansing the concept of "civilian" loses its traditional meaning? Note well the uneven parallel between arguments about murderous American raids on German cities such as Dresden during World War II, the nuclear bombing of Hiroshima and Nagasaki, and the recent Belgrade bombings. Although by no means equivalent in their destructive outcomes, they are held together by the common thread: punishing civilian populations as if they were complicit in the war aims of their leaders.

Should the whole people have been held responsible for the calumnies of its leaders? Fifty-five years after the fact, the debate about the degree of responsibility of the German people for the Holocaust still rages. And, even if this distinction is untenable, can it be shown that the consequences of these apparently brutal bombings shortened their respective wars, as Paul Fussell has recently claimed, and ultimately saved more lives than were lost?[2] The U.S. government's program of beating the enemy into submission by uprooting and terrorizing the civilian population, as well as disabling its military capability, is continuous from Dresden to the two Japanese cities, from the wanton bombing and arson committed by U.S. forces in Southeast Asia to Baghdad and Belgrade.

The policy may be viewed as an instance of a *de facto* rule of modern technological war: Once the major war aim is the enemy's unconditional surrender, it is strategically criminal not to deploy every conventional weapon of mass destruction at "our" disposal where, after Hiroshima, "conventional" means any instrument of mass destruction but chemical and nuclear weapons. For it does appear that, Fussell's and Harry Truman's argument notwithstanding, the political costs of using these weapons has become prohibitive. As a result modern warfare has trod a very thin line. Many conventional weapons have become so powerful that their use over a relatively short period of time can all but destroy in a matter of weeks the economic and military infrastructure of a country the size of Pennsylvania and, according to some experts, cause as much destruction as medium-sized nuclear weapons. In this regard, the willingness of some nuclear powers such as the United States to ban nuclear weapons may not be viewed with as much relief as might be the case if technologically sophisticated conventional arms were not nearly as deadly.

The saliency of my discourse on war to local acts of violence becomes apparent when we inquire into the question of the use of violence to resolve apparently local conflicts between groups. It may be objected that relations between nations are different from those between political groups such as Kosovan and Serbian nationalists within the scope of single nation-state. Yet, as we have seen, the concept of national sovereignty has come under substantial revision since the Vietnam war when perhaps a majority of the American people questioned the justice of American engagement in what was perceived as a civil war. Under the newly established rules of engagement it is possible for an external power to intervene in the internal affairs of a nation-state if it can persuasively claim egregious human rights violations by one or both sides. What seems remarkable is that the notion of a "civil war" about which the rest of the world may remain indifferent has, since the collapse of the Soviet Union, lost its traditional sway. Until the 1990s the Great Powers confined their support for one or another side to military material, money, and political power on the international stage.

But many would argue that personal relations are of a different logical type from political relations in both their international and intranational contexts. Indeed the distinction underlies the bourgeois–liberal insistence on the separation of the private and public. Theorists like Hannah Arendt have warned about the threat to freedom posed by the increasing tendency of liberal-democratic states, let alone those of the totalitarian variety, to intrude into the private sphere.[3] Of course she does not deny that private life is increasingly subject to public scrutiny and state regulation, and she reminds us that in advanced industrial societies the space for freedom is ever narrower. Even if it is true that, despite the rightward turn in American politics after 1968, on questions of political speech American courts have made at least a ninety-degree turn to protect the First Amendment since the 1950s, no national administration except for the Nixon presidency has done more to set the clock back on civil liberties than that of Bill Clinton's.

Since there is no serious political opposition in the United States, political repression has been displaced to wider police surveillance and control of the poor, numerous incidents of brutality and criminal frameups against members of racial minorities, and to the war against crime. The sweeping deployment of electronic devices by private and police authorities to monitor individuals and groups deemed dangerous, not only to public safety and occasionally to national security but also to the industrial secrets of corporations, is notorious and quite public. In the name of fighting the drug wars, it has undertaken semisecret military action in Latin America, pouring billions into the military capability of reactionary governments if they agree to fight the communist guerrillas as well as the drug lords. At home the Clinton administration has sought wider powers to restrict personal freedom in the name of fighting crime and violence. In the course of a critique of Hillary Clinton's liberalism, Wendy Kaminer argues:

> Consider Clinton's tacit support for the repressive juvenile justice bill proposed by the Senate. . . . It was the vehicle for a few modest restrictions on guns and ammunition sales, passed with enthusiastic Administration support by Al Gore's dramatic tie-breaking vote. When Clinton joined her husband (and most Senate Democrats) in celebrating new initiatives to protect kids from guns, she was in effect urging passage of a law that encourages states to persecute 14 year olds as adults, loosens restrictions on housing juveniles with adult offenders, relieves states of the obligation to address racial disparities in juvenile justice systems, federalizes more juvenile crime and imposes harsh mandatory sentences on children.[4]

Add to these the Clinton administration's antidrug policies: federalizing and enforcing longer mandatory sentences for growers and dealers; authorizing the Firearms and Tobacco Agency to burn marijuana crops in California and arrest growers (a step now emulated by state authorities in Florida), and supporting legislation to add 100,000 police to the cities to fight crime, much of it drug-related, the result of which is a booming prison-industrial complex, itself aided by federal funds.

From wife beating to child abuse, in ambiguous as well as precise understandings of these terms, state institutions have assumed broad jurisdiction over family life. For example children may be taken from parents if the police and investigating social service agencies suspect wrong–doing even before hearings before a judge are held. Often in collaboration with private religious and social service organizations which assume the mantle of sex police, many state authorities have seized on archaic state laws and local ordinances to regulate sexual behavior among adults as much as children. Although contested by civil libertarians and gay activists, severe antisodomy laws are still employed in some states to justify arrest and imprisonment of adults engaged in consensual sex. And consensual sex between an adult and a minor subjects its adult participant in all states to stiff legal penalties.

With respect to inheritance, health benefits, and child adoption, in most states unmarried partners typically do not enjoy the same rights as those who are married, and gay partners, when not subject to criminal sanctions, are not recognized for the purposes any civil action. Needless to say, neither the Clinton administration nor the Democratic minority in Congress has proposed legislation to remedy discriminatory local laws against unmarried partners of whatever sexual preference. Moreover, the clear prejudice of the courts is to restrict custody rights of single women parents if their former husband remarries or claims custody on the ground that he earns more money than the mother and can provide the child with more opportunities.

The war at home in 1999 was exemplified by the shootings at Columbine High School in Littleton, Colorado, Atlanta, Georgia, and elsewhere which, alongside the Kosovan conflagration were catapulted to the front pages and the top of TV screens. These events, which involved mass shootings by middle-class white kids of other middle-class white kids, shocked the media and the public because of the challenge they posed to the conventional wisdom about who uses violence. In this narrative, violence as a method of resolving differences is reserved for the most part, if not exclusively, to those who are economically and culturally deprived or, in its more anthropological expression, to those caught in the "culture of poverty."[5]

Some social scientists acknowledge that, in precincts of the economically and culturally impoverished, lawlessness is a product, even an entailment, of powerlessness and social disorganization. The poor simply have little purchase on the game of peaceful conflict resolution and for this reason have little motive to observe its rules. Looking a little deeper, it turns out since, as Jay McLeod reports for black male youth, "there ain't no makin' it" [in white middle-class society], some stuck at the bottom make up their own rules.[6] In this game violence is an acceptable tool of conflict resolution as it is for warriors of the nation-state. Moreover, to refuse to play the game on these terms may subject the individual to the group's ethic of retributive justice—once viewed as an anomaly in a caring society, but now elevated to a state policy principle. So it does not matter whether an individual agrees with the rule of force or not. As long as she stays in the discursive or geographic community, she is as obliged to observe its rules as a driver is to stop at a red light. Since for most members who are subject to the power group that rules the streets or the school, there is no option of voice or participation, the only recourse to consent or, in the vernacular, "loyalty," is to exit.

Our common understanding is that the regime of the rule of violence does not apply to middle-class communities except in extreme individual cases of severe mental imbalance such as serial killers, wanton pedophiles, angry lovers, and unusual family disputes. The main narrative of how the middle class deals with conflicts is by means of rules and procedures and the presuppositions upon which they are based. The basis is a contract: In exchange for renouncing force as a means of resolving differences individuals and groups submit to the rule of "law" which assures justice and restricts the arbitrary exercise of authority. Individuals and groups are assumed to have different interests, but not so different that they cannot find common ground upon which to resolve differences. The tacit agreement is to achieve compromise if possible and justice if necessary, which must be voluntarily observed by the disputants. When the power to impose justice is vested in administrative authorities it works if, and only if, the disputants recognize this authority as legitimate. Following Hobbes's advice they have renounced their power to take direct action or even negotiate directly with their adversary because they have faith in the state and its institutions to administer justice.[7]

Albert O. Hirschman argues that people in social, political, or economic organizations have three options to express their consent or dissent: They confer *loyalty* upon those in power and, on this choice, suspend disbelief in the leadership's decisions either on conviction or on a system of rewards of which they are beneficiaries; they may exercise *voice* in criticism of, and propose alternatives to, the existing leadership but, even when defeated, elect to remain within the system; or they may *exit*, in which case they have determined that they have no place in the system and renounce their right to participate. Plainly the selection of the exit option is by far the riskiest choice. In the absence of alternatives that allow for what Arendt calls "irregular" behavior, opting out of the system may result in isolation and even greater powerlessness than would eventuate if the individual or group exercised their voice(s). Yet, without the ability to exit, the consequent structural limits on individual freedom may result in the stagnation and decline of a community or society.[8]

For even when rarely used, under some circumstances, exit may be the only way to retain opposition. If individuals are deprived of the exit option, those in power can and do force people out of the community under terms that benefit the system, not the individual. Such was the case in Nazi Germany: Communists, gays, Gypsies, and Jews were denied the choice to leave, except when escorted by the Nazis to the camps. No less genocidal, the Rwanda example differs insofar as the method of extermination lacked subterfuge. The victims were shot on the spot. In the light of what seems to be an unlimited effort by established powers to indiscriminately bring ever-widening types of conduct within the purview of the definition of "crime" thereby erasing the necessary distinction between crime and irregularity, it is no wonder that, absent the possibility of being heard within the system, many in all walks of life, not only those at the bottom, opt out or suffer the closure of options.

The unstated feature of liberal (middle-class) justice and the basis of consent is that the aggrieved possesses "rights" or voice. Those who participate are assured that some form of institutional justice exists to air or to mediate their individual complaints. In its ideal form the participant enjoys democratic rights, at least to choose representatives and at most to participate directly in decision making. However, even as in most workplaces and in schools where these institutional forms are not routinely available to the person as a matter of right, she is more likely confer loyalty when some procedures are available to adjudicate her grievances. The manager or the school authority may hear the dispute and make a decision, but based on her personal sense of justice because no explicit rules have been disseminated against which to evaluate her decision. Whether the individual wins or loses in this game, he must come away feeling that he has had his day in court and that he understands the rationale underlying the resolution.

Thus, for example, if a child misbehaves in class by talking to his friend while the teacher is talking and is sent to the assistant principal's office, he may wax resentful about the punishment but knows the reason for it. Presumably, if he disagrees with the punishment he may complain to the assistant principal who, ideally, will carefully consider his argument(s). Even if the teacher is upheld in her action, as is likely to be the case, the student is secure in the knowledge that he has, at least, been heard. From the point of view of authority the ultimate solution is, of course, that even if he does not internalize restraint when others, especially the teacher, is speaking the child is able to exercise self-control. This is a sign he respects the rule that he must raise his hand to gain the right to participate in class. The student knows that under no circumstance may the student disrupt its proceedings. Since the middle-class student recognizes the authority of the teacher he will obey the rules that govern classroom decorum.

Extend this simple and well-known example to relations among peers. Suppose a schoolmate hurls an epithet in the halls of the school such as "hey, faggot," which is not interpreted as a playful jibe uttered by a friend but as a verbal assault with malicious intent of sometime in the future committing violence against the "irregular." The rules of nonviolent response prescribe that the person who is the object of the insult confront the offender with his wrongful outburst, expressing his own feelings of hurt and degradation that the remark has provoked. The possibility of a nonviolent resolution presupposes that both share the same set of values that whatever one's evaluation, sexual preference is a private matter. Therefore accusing another of a deviant, that is, nonsanctioned sexual orientation is wrong or the orientation is not deviant and should be treated as "normal." In which case, although accurate, the accusation is unwarranted in its pejorative connotation, and there is reason to expect that the person whose utterance was intended as the verbal equivalent of a "slap in the face" will relent in the wake of the confrontation with the victim. If the liberal–democratic assumption that everyone in the discursive community has "voice" holds, the victim may ask for an apology or at least the opportunity to engage in fruitful discussion. He should expect his taunter to express remorse. Failing productive dialogue, under the rules the offended has no right to strike back either verbally or physically but is obliged either to "turn the other cheek," in the expectation that his interlocutor will eventually see the light, or if sufficiently distraught (it might be the latest in a long series of similar incidents) to report the incident to proper authorities in the hope of gaining redress.

What's wrong with this scenario? In film and television, as much as "real life," traditional liberal models of justice and of mediation are experiencing a major crisis, not only among the poor where, it can be argued, the models are never really applied, but respect for the contract has also eroded substantially in the working class and professional and technical fractions of the middle classes. While a "few" scattered instances of unexpected violence may not describe the activity of a whole generation of middle-class youth, there is reason to insist that coherent models of nonviolent social conduct are losing their moral suasion; rather, they are increasingly projected by school and other societal authorities as a cultural ideal rather than as a practical model. In the criminal justice system's growing disregard for human rights, such as those manifested in the police abuse of Abner Louima and Amadou Diallo, as much as the new penchant of the nation to engage in "total" war, organs of established power are providing models that cannot be reconciled with the prescribed rules of middle-class justice. Consequently, why shouldn't we expect kids to invent rules of combat that correspond more to what they observe in the theater of history than to models of liberal rationality?

After being ignored by the school and vilified by their peers for being "weird" and "faggots" the kids who committed the heinous crime at Littleton had, in fact, chosen the exit option; they separated themselves from the mainstream but remained caught in the system's tentacles. The school still had legal authority over them. As academically ambitious students they were obliged to attend classes where they interacted with fellow students who had, in effect, forced their exit but maintained psychological pressure, reminding them that as "weirdos" they were rank outsiders and were held in utter contempt. As Jessie Klein and Lynn Chancer argue in this volume,[9] they may be victims of the masculinist prejudices of their classmates. The mass shootings were not the actions of badly socialized individuals. On the contrary, some were academically successful. Their fatal aggression against fellow students may be interpreted as both a rebellion against ostracism perpetrated by homophobic male teenagers and as an attempt to offer proof of their own masculinity. Exemplified by war, crime, and horror movies where with few exceptions women are victims, the prevailing images of masculinity are inextricably linked to violence. But Littleton may be read as an instance of how difficult is the life of marginality in a society that demands loyalty even in the wake of its refusal to provide space for irregular voices but, simultaneously, denies the option of exit, except in suicide.

We may seek a clue to the agony of the contemporary teen condition by briefly examining one of the more ubiquitous of current film genres, the teen film. Once consigned to a fairly restricted niche whose narratives were chiefly romantic and often combined with the musical and romantic-comedy genres, the teen romantic film has taken a back seat to horror and crime genres. The last decade of teen films which, in the 1990s commands a huge audience and market share in the industry, may be grouped under three distinct variants: the black, male gang movies, coded in terms of the "hood," a double entendre of neighborhood and hoodlum; the middle-class horror film; and comedies, but no longer of the conventional romantic type. The new teen comedy persists in exploring relationships between the sexes, but often exhibits graphic sexual exploration ingeniously packaged to avoid the "R" rating.

The gang film is a narrative of hopelessness and almost invariably depicts the inexorable devolution of black youth towards crime and mayhem. This genre rarely concerns the so-called underclass or the culture of poverty. In these films we can see a powerful metacommentary on the inapplicability of middle-class rules of the game to "ghetto" youth. But their neighborhoods are inhabited, not by welfare cheats or lowlifes, but by people who work, live in families, and are homeowners. The older generation of black parents stand in for the conventional morality of the working middle class, but young people almost invariably refuse to imbibe their parents' ethics of hard work, church going, and other family values. There are different rules on the streets. The kids simply do not believe they can achieve their parents' level of middle-class comfort through hard work and frugality. The upward mobility that might be available through attending to the school curriculum is ignored except by rejection. The prevailing rule here is group loyalty; voice within the community is always contested and the option of exit extremely improbable. In this genre violence rules as the ultimate arbiter of all relations between people, between the individual and society and its institutions.

In its ideal/typical form exemplified by the late 1970s and 1980s *Halloween* series, violence is portrayed in psychoanalytic strokes as the work of the death wish in comfortable suburban middle-class surroundings. *Scream* is representative of films about middle-class teen life in the 1990s. Kids of relatively homogeneous social class families attend the same (suburban) high school and hold a huge party in the large luxurious home of one of the crowd. Two boys, both of them well integrated into the society of the kids, plan and execute veritable serial killings of their friends. They have confused motives: jealousy, fascination with violence, and sheer hubris. At the bottom they exhibit an appalling nihilism that seems to be the main caution of these films. Lacking a respect for the sanctity of human life, base instincts are bound to take over. Born and raised in the same comfortable suburban environment as the boys who murdered their classmates in Littleton and Georgia or raped a retarded girl in Glen Ridge, New Jersey, earlier in the 1990s, we are left at the end without genuine understanding of why the rules no longer apply save the invocation to remain loyal to conventional morality in all of its connotations.

At first glance the third genre seems far more innocent. The rush of these films into theaters may be viewed as a repudiation of recent attempts by the sex police to block and reverse the growing acceptance among wide layers of society of that teen sexuality may be expressed openly. In *American Pie* the only male adult character of consequence, a boy's father, is guilty of only one sin: trying to counsel his son on the ABCs of sex. His glaring ineptitude provides one of the more humorous moments in the film. Needless to say, the father recognizes it is too late to advocate teen abstinence but perhaps not to offer a cautionary tale of restraint. We may understand the middle-class teen romance film as perhaps the most serious attempt in the wake of the reconciliation of most middle-class parents to the prospect that their children are fated to be sexually active before marriage—or even not to get married—to redeem the convention that sex is meaningless without love or similar feelings of empathy.

In contrast to the teen horror and the black 'hood genres, in the current teen comedy genre things fall apart only temporarily but in concert with the comedy genre they have happy endings. Recall that the earlier teen musicals of the 1950s and 1960s were content to suggest the latency of sexuality but their characters, played by Sandra Dee and Frankie Avalon, remained chaste. On the surface the new variant of teen comedies may be seen as more sexually explicit versions of "coming of age" narratives that, despite their apparent amorality, are heavily laden with anti-nihilistic moral lessons. In many of these films, the boys are obsessed with their own overripe virginity and seem to spend most of their time and energy in the pursuit of getting laid. Much of the plot is devoted to the process by which, in their own confusion and gross fumbling, it is left to the girls to seduce them. But not all of the young women are concerned to convince them there is more to relationships than the physical acts of sex.

In *American Pie* (1999), since the woman is taken as instrumental object, not as a partner lacking a concept of sex as a reciprocal act, nihilistic sex is a stand-in for male violence and social insensitivity. In *American Pie*, violence is systematically displaced to sports, innocuous verbal abuse, fairly brutal scenes of male sexual anxiety coded as slapstick, and by what may be described as "grossed-out" humor. Violence appears in the guise of embarrassment rather than inducing us to recoil in horror. It has to do with the graphic display of various bodily functions discharged under bizarre circumstances such as defecation (an extreme case of dysentery caused by a friend's surreptitious administration of a laxative), masturbation (with an apple pie), and premature ejaculation in the midst of foreplay with an eager female partner. Another crucial difference from the early forms of this genre is the decisive break with the stereotype that while men respond to their gonads all women are driven by love and caring. In a tacit acknowledgment of the sexual revolution among women in this film two of the women, one the parent of the boy's friend, are interested in sex, period.

Films like *American Pie* break ostentatiously with the rule of concealment that marks the older teen comedies, just as the tendency of many American films to leave less to the sexual imagination have violated the old invocation to leave sex to viewer inference. But I do not interpret these shifts as signs that films are encouraging violence or even explicit sexual behavior among teens. Instead the new modalities may be read as signs that, despite the best efforts of the sex police in and out of government to censor films, sexuality itself can scarcely be denied. But there is reason to see these films in relation to the spiritual and physical violence that surrounds us. And they may also be comprehended in terms of the growing despair, shared by many teens, that our key institutions of loyalty and of voice are decrepit but see no alternative in trying to make them work. As Donna Gaines showed in her study of North Jersey suburban youth, *Teenage Wasteland*, for many there is no exit except self-destruction.

Recognizing the danger inherent in the rash of teen and preteen violence that seems to be sweeping suburban as well as urban schools and neighborhoods, there is today a national movement known as *mediation*. The adult leaders of this movement understand that the exercise of the arbitrary authority of adults in and out of state institutions, such as schools and the criminal justice system, cannot hope to stem the epidemic of guns and other lethal weapons that now are in the hands of many young men and boys. Consequently they have embarked on a preventive program that begins in elementary school to teach kids how to resolve conflicts without the use of force. Instead of relying on adult authority, the program, usually led by a teacher, "trains" a select group of kids to become peer mediators. The training is tacitly oriented toward establishing unconventional institutional mechanisms for justice—in effect, trying to provide space for the voice option rather than relying on established adult power, abstract loyalty to the school and its promise of success, or risking the social costs of exit.

Mediators do not enjoy sovereignty in resolving differences between kids and between kids and the school; they work on a track parallel to institutional power and for this reason their efforts are frequently undermined by the authority of the principal and his administration. In rare instances where the authorities are fairly benign and willing to surrender some their prerogatives, the procedures of mediation may work to resolve some disputes. But the program is frequently disarmed by politicians, more comfortable with supply-side repression than with education, imposing policies that restrict access to guns and, by placing restrictive labels about violent and explicit sexual content on films, television, and records, and by sermonizing among parents to inculcate guilt.[10]

School officials, religious leaders, and the media have targeted parents to act as a home guard. They recruit parents to assist their children in homework assignments and are admonished to participate in censoring what their children watch on television and what records they listen to. But since the school as the main site of socialization has, in the wake of the turmoil, remained embedded in the traditions of bureaucratic authority, these interventions are largely ineffective in convincing kids to confer loyalty upon the system. Needless to say, the main effect is to keep parents anxious and busy. Most kids know these censorious programs are a sham; teens often outmaneuver "R" rated movies and record store restrictions by buying forged ID documents. When they perform well in class, they are often driven by fear, not learning. And what they do in their free time is mostly hidden from adults. The society of kids is often cruel and unyielding to outsiders and intolerant of otherness, whatever its forms, but it is not a place where adults can easily enter. And it has ever been thus. Emotional separation from parental and school authority is the condition for the formation of the adult self and secrecy is a powerful weapon of youth. What is different today is the near-hysterical environment that drives authorities to try to intrude and, failing moral suasion, to put in place practices of legal retribution ranging from wholesale school expulsions to imprisonment.

The symbols of violence appear in urban high schools in the personae of armed and unarmed guards at the entrances and exits, assistant principals and assigned teachers patrolling the hallways, and a regime of school discipline which increasingly imitates the criminal justice system. The of-

ficial story is that these shackles have been placed upon the schools to re-
strain a significant minority of kids who are disruptive of teachers and
those students who wish to learn, and may even be dangerous to the
safety of members of the school "community." Certainly schools have always contained (in the double sense) a significant number of students
who see little or no sense in being there. State laws forbid school-leaving
before students are sixteen because child-labor legislation bars minors
from holding industrial and many service jobs. So some students who
might respond to good occupational and alternative academic programs
are offered neither, choose to cut most of their classes and when they attend express their displeasure with acts of disruption, as defined by
school authorities. Failing to engage them in mastering the curriculum,
and resisting developing an alternative to it, the schools blame the students for their disaffection, and many students are marginalized and
blamed again for their school failure. Equipped with psychological categories to label marginal kids "hyperkinetic," "disruptive," intellectually
challenged—or worse, psychotic—school authorities see little alternative
to meting out punishments that fit the crime of what may, for many students, be a case of undisguised boredom.

We know that many children, including teenagers, get bored easily.
Even "high achievers" light matches, take drugs, or become unruly when
they have "nothing to do." Since school pedagogy is often stilted and, in
any case, is oriented to the student who, highly motivated to succeed in
conventional academic terms, will tolerate whatever the teacher dishes
out, marginalization and punishment may result in a more angry and ultimately violent response from the intolerant.

Why did the governments of the United States and of Europe remain
silent when, after the breakup of Yugoslavia, Milosevic, in 1989, canceled
Kosovan political autonomy, annexed the region directly into the new
Serb-dominated Republic, and gave no support to the internal Serbian
opposition? Recall the snail-like reaction of the United States and European powers to Milosevic's attempt to create a greater Yugoslavia by col-
onizing Bosnia, mercilessly bombing Sarejevo, and undertaking a systematic program of ethnic cleansing. The NATO powers were not concerned
about Kosovan political autonomy; from their point of view this had been
an internal affair. It was only when Milosevic attempted to loosen his
regime's ties to the International Monetary Fund, which held a virtual
mortgage in the Yugoslav economy, and took steps to solidify Serbian
control over a rebellious Kosovo, that the U.S. government was prompted
to intervene and European planes joined the campaign. But Milosevic's
attempt to break from his debt obligations and NATO's embarrassment of
allowing his government to occupy Kosovo with troops and militia,

which promptly began a continuation of the program of ethnic cleansing, had, after the Bosnian scandal, become unacceptable. Within weeks after suffering losses estimated at 60 percent of the country's industrial and commercial resources, thousands of civilian as well as military casualties, and growing popular unrest, the Yugoslav government agreed to withdraw its troops and submit to allied occupation of the province.

From the perspective of the fabled "Vietnam Syndrome"—that American public opinion will not tolerate significant losses and injuries to its servicemen and women, at least for the conduct of "little" wars—it was a felicitous illustration of U.S. military strategy first unleashed during World War II but perfected in the Gulf War. Without sustaining appreciable American casualties, the United States has adopted the doctrine of victory through the brutal use of overwhelming airpower to clobber the enemy into submission. The operative word here is "brutal" for the U.S. government justified bombing nonmilitary industrial plants and inflicting heavy civilian casualties on the grounds of the veritable genocidal policy of the Yugoslav government in Kosovo.

Taking the high ground to legitimate military and economic warfare, the U.S. government has, in the post-Communist era, routinely insisted that human rights trumps national sovereignty. On the other hand, the scope of the bombings to include civilian and nonmilitary industrial targets, for example to destroy a cigarette factory as a strategic target aimed at the civilian population which depends as much on cigarettes as it does on food, was among the few instances of the more or less overt tie between our increasingly "eye for an eye" domestic criminal justice policies and international military policy. The Gulf and Kosovan wars provide convincing evidence that visiting terror against civilian populations in order to invert public indignation against their own governments, rather than the putative aggressor, is becoming an acceptable aspect of warfare.

Ours is an era when loyalty is the value that overrides the other options. We know that Saddam Hussein had made Iraq a reliable outpost of the West before the Kuwait invasion. And had Milosevic, who managed to win the confidence of the IMF long enough to considerably amplify the huge $22 billion loan inherited from the Tito era, maintained some kind of payment schedule instead of trying to get out from under its thrall, it is conceivable that he could have weathered criticism of his internal policies and made permanent the American government's hesitation to disturb the status quo. The problem is that the price of IMF support is that recipients fully embrace austerity policies which entail dismantling the elaborate social welfare systems that sustained Communist and Socialist power, privatizing state enterprises, and opening wide the door to foreign investment on terms that many would not expect from more stable capitalist countries. The leaders were willing, but it turned out that these demands were politically risky. In Yugoslavia, a population that was long cynical of bureau-cratic, authoritarian socialism had nonetheless become accustomed to one of its entailments, a measure of economic security. In consequence, the IMF philosophy of detaching citizens from their economic rights, even as it was indifferent to their civil rights, became controversial, especially after the Russian debacle of relentless privatization and free-market economic sui-cide. Fearful that submission might bring social disorder, the Iraqi and Ser-bian leaderships quelled the emerging opposition by means of aggressive nationalism, a step that temporarily consolidated their power but earned both regimes severe military reprisals and exclusion from the international economic and political system.

Loyalty broke down in Yugoslavia and Littleton; lacking the means with which to express difference, whether by speaking out within the sys-tem without severe reprisals or by exit from it, the likely outcome is re-bellion against established power and authority, or implosion. Even when they cannot express themselves, those who choose to rebel usually have a program of creative destruction and rebuilding the system on a different foundation. We may hope for explosions to topple the regimes in Bagh-dad and in Belgrade. But the kids cannot hope to inherit the system they oppose. Their best chance lies with the remnant of progressive reformers who have enough vision to see that the educational system cannot expect to win the loyalty of youth unless it concedes some power. Lacking this improbable outcome we may expect more instances where youth turn on the system and attempt to blow it, and themselves, up. Those who act to implode the system have lost hope; redemption is sought in bringing down themselves as well as the edifice that has oppressed them. And in recent years we have witnessed what kids will do when avenues of escape or reform are closed. If the school system wishes to save its own ability to command the loyalty of its teenage members, it could try to initiate re-forms that amplify the opportunities for participation—even for dissent—without penalty of expulsion or worse, forms of detention. But there is less than a glimmer of expectation that either the Yugoslav authorities or those who run our high schools possess the imagination and generosity needed to save their institutional orders.

NOTES

1. Pierre Bourdieu and Jean-Claud Passeron, *Reproduction in Education, Society and Culture* (Thousand Oaks, Calif.: Sage Publications, 1977).

2. Paul Fussell, *Great War and Modern Memory* (New York: Oxford University Press, 1989).

3. Hannah Arendt, *The Human Condition* (New York: Harcourt, Brace and Jovanovich, 1968).

4. Wendy Kaminer, "Clinton for Senate?" *The Nation* August 9–16, 1999, p. 4.

5. For the classic statement of this position see Oscar Lewis, *La Vida: A Puerto Rican Family in the Culture of Poverty—San Juan and New York* (New York: Random House, 1966).

6. Jay McLeod, *"There Ain't No Makin' It,"* 2nd ed. (Boulder, Colo.: Rowman & Littlefield, 1997).

7. Thomas Hobbes, *The Leviathan* (London: Penguin Classics, 1990).

8. Albert O. Hirschman, *Exit, Voice, and Responses to Decline in Firms, Organizations, and States* (Cambridge, Mass.: Harvard University Press, 1970).

9. Jessie Klein and Lynn S. Chancer, "Masculinity Matters: The Omission of Gender from High-Profile School Violence Cases," this volume.

10. See Stephanie Spina, "When the Smoke Clears: Revisualizing Responses to Violence in Schools," this volume.

10

When the Smoke Clears

REVISUALIZING RESPONSES TO
VIOLENCE IN SCHOOLS

Stephanie Urso Spina

The hidden context of violence unearthed in this volume is deeply rooted
in our collective and individual consciousness. Once we confront our own
entanglement in these matted, choking roots we may be profoundly over-
whelmed and even immobilized by their pervasiveness. However, although the situation is depressing, complicated, and seemingly insur-
mountable, it is *not* irreversible, repressive, or hopelessly deterministic.
There are still significant opportunities for resistance and agency within
the contradictions and tensions of the hegemonic order. Why else would
those at the top of the hierarchy expend so much energy and engage in
such extreme measures of subterfuge to maintain the status quo? It is their
hope that public will believe they are indeed powerless in the face of the
illusions and obstacles constructed by the elite and so will not attempt to
doubt, to question, to learn, to act.

In order to effect change, one must believe change is possible. One must
also know that it is not an easy task. It takes a long-term commitment,
hard work, and the determination to weather setbacks that sometimes
seem far greater than the successes. Idealism must be tempered with
skepticism; rhetoric must be backed by commitment; commitment must
be realized as social action.

Violence is about power. The United States is unrivaled in institutional-
izing violence to the point where it is acceptable behavior. We have seen
in earlier chapters how research tends to ignore institutionalized or struc-

tural violence and treat behavioral violence as homogeneous, without consideration to potentially important differences both between individuals and within individuals over time and in different contexts. The same can be said of schooling.

Current methods of addressing school violence often consist of adding some new rule, piece of technology, or curriculum on to existing structures. They ignore the weak foundations they are building on as if their house of cards could withstand a stronger tremor or gust of wind if it only were taller. These methods include, but are not limited to, increasing security in schools,[1] using punishment and threats of punishment as a deterrent of and consequence for violent behavior, introducing conflict resolution programs into middle and high schools, and restricting by mandate the basic rights of students (e.g., requiring uniforms, participation in patriotic ceremonies, and allegiance to Judeo-Christian religious beliefs). Since security in schools is discussed at length in the introduction, these other issues are addressed here in turn. Following that, I look at approaches that take a more systemic view of school reform: tuition vouchers, charter and magnet schools, "high standards," and "back-to-basics" curriculum. School reform is not specifically or exclusively designed to prevent or intervene in violence, but is of great importance because of the prominent position of schools in society and their recent role as designated scapegoats of violence. Public health policy initiatives are then discussed, as well as alternative models of school reform and violence prevention, the role of teachers, pedagogy and literacy issues, and efforts that go beyond the school system in their attempts to decrease violence. Following a survey of national financial follies, I conclude with a look at some new ideas and initiatives that hold promise for a more equitable and peaceful future. My purpose in taking this broad approach is to provide context—a road map if you will—to lead the reader to more indepth exploration and serious consideration of the issues raised here.

DISCIPLINE AND PUNISHMENT

Corporal punishment is forbidden in Europe, England, Japan, Puerto Rico, the nations of the former USSR, Canada, and other countries. It is still legal in almost half of the United States. (Most corporal punishment in U.S. schools occurs in Southern and Southwestern states, the least in the Northeast.[2]) Corporal punishment, whether in school or in the home, is most staunchly defended by Anglo-American Protestants proffering theological and moral justifications for inflicting pain on children.[3] However, minority and poor white children receive "lickings" four to five times more frequently than middle- and upper-class white children.[4]

This "get tough" attitude is perhaps best exemplified by Joe Clark, the controversial former principal of New Jersey's Eastside High School. The author of *Laying Down the Law* and inspiration for the film *Lean on Me*, Clark is rewarded for his much-publicized and admired bat-wielding, bullhorn-toting disciplinary efforts with appearances on *60 Minutes* and the cover of *Time Magazine*. He is praised for "turning around" a failing, violent school through strict disciplinary measures. On a single day during his first week at Eastside, Clark became famous by expelling 300 "leeches and parasites" (a.k.a. students) for profanity, fighting, vandalism, and drug possession. By way of analogy, if you remove all students with less than passing grades from a school, can you claim credit when subsequent tests show academic improvement? Doesn't it seem that punishment by suspension or expulsion from school, although popular and common, is an absurdly ironic, not to mention ineffective, way to deal with violence in school? What happens to those former students? Like many other "interventions," "getting tough" treats the problem in isolation and perpetuates a reliance on failed methods.

RESTRICTING BASIC RIGHTS

In the name of violence prevention, students have been required to wear uniforms, attend flag-raising ceremonies, or participate in a daily "meditation" (often a euphemism for prayer) time. In the aftermath of the school shooting in Littleton, Colorado,[5] some schools banned the wearing of black trench coats because that was what the perpetrators of that crime wore. Wearing gang colors, tattoos, and certain hair styles has also been banned. Although these strategies appear harmless, they can easily be counterproductive and of questionable constitutionality.

In another irrelevant effort to stem school violence, Congress ridiculed morality and ignored a 1980s Supreme Court ruling declaring a similar effort unconstitutional by passing a youth crime bill including measures allowing the Ten Commandments to be posted in public schools. Never mind that, despite the wisdom contained in the commandments, the Judeo-Christian tradition has never been known to prevent violence. When Moses first brought the Commandments to the Jews, he was so angered by their worship of a golden calf that he smashed the stone tablets they were inscribed on. Ever since their violent introduction, the selective application of the Commandments have bred brutality as well as morality. Despite injunctions against adultery, stealing, and killing, for example, many of these crimes have been committed in the name of God throughout history in wars instigated by "religious" fervor and greed. This underscores the hypocrisy in other troubling provisions of the "Commandments" bill passed by Congress, such as mandating minimum prison terms for youth involved in gun-related crime and giving prosecutors the discretion to try juveniles aged thirteen years and up as adults.[6] The U.S. House of Representatives went on to overwhelmingly agree to recruit the surgeon general to study "how to combat the sickness of violence and to rebuild our national spirit," and to fund anonymous "school safety hot lines" for reporting troubled students.[7] Shortly after approving this travesty by a vote of 428 to 180, the House passed a watered-down version of an already weak gun-control bill that had been passed by the Senate. This bill, designed to address a "loophole" in a federal law, prohibits anyone under twenty-one years of age from buying a handgun at a gun shop, but *not* at gun shows. The Senate version provided as much as three days for background checks on gun show purchases. The House reduced it to a one-day waiting period, knowing that, according to the Justice Department, twenty-four hours was too brief to conduct an adequate investigation of the purchaser. Needless to say, the National Rifle Association (NRA) was delighted.[8]

The two bills discussed above are directly related because together they shift the blame for violent behavior from the use of guns to a lack of religious involvement. The Reverend Barry Lynn of the United Church of Christ called the measure "frighteningly silly," adding in an interview: "Congress always seems to turn to religion as a political football when they can't solve the problem they are working on." This is not a serious attempt to change the culture of violence in America.[9]

CONFLICT RESOLUTION

Conflict resolution programs are one of the most popular "prevention" and intervention methods used to address violence in schools. Their major focus is to teach students the communication and social skills needed to resolve disputes nonviolently. Because they are inexpensive to implement and, as Webster argues, "an intuitively appealing and politically expedient response,"[10] conflict resolution programs have been eagerly adopted by thousands of middle and high schools and some states are made them mandatory.

Yet, evaluations of intervention programs of this type have not been encouraging.[11] Researchers have found, for example, that improvements in social skills do not lead to behavioral changes outside of the controlled setting.[12] The finding should not be surprising. The strategies of such violence-prevention programs are doomed to fail when they merely impose beliefs and behaviors belied by the experiences of those they are supposed to "help."

Conflict resolution programs are based on a behavioral (behavior is learned and so can be unlearned) deficit (youth who engage in violent behavior lack the skills or ability to resolve conflicts nonviolently) model that assumes a homogeneity of needs and determinants of violence that do not exist. Different people turn to violent behavior for different reasons.[13] Furthermore, such programs are grounded in a decidedly middle-class culture where "conflict" generally means a disagreement between two or more parties that can potentially be solved through negotiation. The taunts, put-downs, shake-downs, retaliation, competition, and contests of dominance related to status and respect do not easily lend themselves to the resolve-conflict-by-negotiation model. As Nancy Guerra points out, "A sixteen-year-old who sticks up a McDonald's does not have a conflict with the person behind the cash register."[14] Have you ever tried to reason with someone pointing a gun at you? Even more importantly, promoting conflict resolution programs may actually cause more damage by diverting attention from the social, political, and economic conditions that engender violence. "Cures" targeting "youth violence" don't work because youth violence does not exist as a singular, separate issue from adult violence and societal violence. The only purpose they serve is the exoneration of adults and the diversion of attention from the real issues. This is not to say that conflict resolution programs never work, but that success is rare and highly dependent on the fit between the program, its resources, and its implementation and the needs of the group the effort is presuming to "help."

SCHOOL REFORM

While the above are focused on violent behaviors, other initiatives address schools themselves. Evidence reported by The National Research Council[15] suggests the level of violence in schools increases with the percentages of students who do not view schooling as relevant. A majority of older Americans also see public education as a failure academically, competitively, and morally.[16]

There are currently vigorous debates around four popular strategies for addressing these issues. On an organizational level, school reform (sometimes called "restructuring"), tuition vouchers, charter schools, and magnet schools are hot topics. Related to these are arguments for raising academic "standards" and what is known as a "back-to-basics" curriculum.

Reformers believe the school system can be changed from within. While long needed, systemic reform seems overwhelming, if not impossible, if only because of the size and structure of the U.S. education system. In addition, as reform from the top down, it does not address the basic failures of the present model and so is destined to fail. School reforms are often based on models designed to improve quality control and increase productivity in complex business organizations. When transferred to a school environment where the emphasis *should* be on the *processes* of learning and not just outcomes, the corporate model can suffer from many of the same inadequacies that characterize other attempts to increase "standards." When reform-as-restructuring has decentralization as a goal, local governance of schools is more likely but is highly dependent on the relinquishing or sharing of power by the administration, the willing participation of teachers, family, and community, and district bureaucracy and rigidity. Even if these conditions were favorably resolved, societal impediments of political isolation and economic devastation, especially in urban areas, would not be conducive to lasting changes in schools. If reformers do not transform the environment schools are situated in, their reforms will remain placebos.

Another way of deregulating schools involves vouchers where public funding is used to pay private school tuition. A variety of private school organizations have formed a coalition that is a strong political advocate for vouchers. Most members of the coalition are from religious organizations. Because sectarian schools are included in this scenario, there is a question of constitutionality on the basis of separation of church and state, as well as the possibility for religious conflict and the establishment of fringe schools.[17] In part, because vouchers invite privatization, conservatives, who as a group have the most to gain, are the strongest advocates of vouchers. Teachers' unions and public service organizations, with the most to lose, are its loudest critics.

Charter schools offer a less controversial political alternative to tuition vouchers but they, too, are not an effective solution. Charter schools differ from sectarian and for-profit schools in that they are minimally subject to the curricular and staffing supervision of the public school system. First introduced in 1991, charter schools began as an effort to free schools and teachers from bureaucratic constraints, which was supposed to improve the quality of the teaching and learning in those schools. But because many charter schools do not honor salary agreements with teachers' unions, pay is low and staff turnover is high.[18] In some districts, charter schools are expected to be innovative or progressive. They are supposed to increase diversity and be more responsive to the community they serve. However, they are still accountable for student performance. Curricular innovations are limited by required outcomes and standardized assessment. As a result, the shift is more one of emphasis than substance, much like in sectarian schools.

Magnet schools are another alternative. They are similar to charter schools in that they also have more freedom from district control. Magnet schools also share many of the problems of charter schools. Exclusivity, separatism, and other forms of inequality are possible negative outcomes.

Magnets are public schools that offer specialized programs in areas such as science, the arts, and music. They are usually created by urban districts to promote racial balance and/or to attract students to schools or neighborhoods considered "undesirable." Admission is on the basis of different criteria including application, lottery, grades, student interests, and/or teacher recommendations. Magnet schools of this type are usually able to attract middle-class white students and provide better opportunities for some minority students. But the students who apply for admission to magnet schools are almost exclusively the most academically successful. The situation in an urban Pennsylvania district is typical. A science magnet program at one school attracted all of the high academic achievers in the city, creating district-wide imbalances and inequities.[19] Magnet schools tend to have better academic records than neighborhood schools, but they generally start out with students who are high achievers and would likely be successful in any school. When compared to neighborhood students who applied to magnet schools and did not get in, the academic records are comparable.

All of the above, to varying degrees, come under the rubric of school choice—an umbrella term covering a variety of models, the complexity of which the brief summary above does not begin to capture. Regardless of the forms it takes, the school choice movement is directly related to fundamental American ideology issues. It is important to understand that the school choice movement grew out of the particular social, economic, and educational context of the 1980s, which Peter Cookson, Jr., describes as a time when

[a] patina of wealth masked serious economic problems [and] the rootlessness of much American life became transformed into lifestyles based on consumption and status, and social commitment to public institutions, with the exception of the military, virtually disappeared.[20]

Perhaps the strongest argument for "choice" comes from political scientists Chubb and Moe,[21] who call it a "panacea."[22] Chubb and Moe believe that competitive free-market forces will drive out bad schools and reward good ones. This consumerist-based argument does not address the choice and consumer restrictions placed on people by poverty. It also does not acknowledge that for capitalism to flourish, a lower class is virtually essential. This dishonesty distorts the situation and, through sleight of hand, draws a following from among those who have the most to lose.

Support for school choice is strong among many minority groups who have been convinced that choice will give them the same educational opportunities that the privileged have. In reality, however, choice offers advantages to the wealthy who would still have disproportionate access to the most desirable schools. Private alternatives to public education are frequently a "pseudosolution." That is, it "seems convincing on paper but, in reality, is no solution at all."[23] As Cookson argues, the private school advantage does not come from choice, but from the motivations and cultural capital resources of parents and students who choose private schools.[24] It appears likely that all choice would change is the way school systems presently track students. Poor students would still have limited access to "better" schools. Students from a higher income bracket would be subsidized for attending the private schools many are already enrolled in. As Aronowitz points out, "The tendency to privatization has become stronger [as] a corollary of consumer society and the widespread perception . . . that all social problems are subject to purely technical solutions."[25] For-profit schools exhibit all of the inequity, biases, and bottom-line morality of our market-driven society. They operate on a principal of maximizing profits and are driven by test results. As a result, class and race divisions in American society grow larger and present problems are exacerbated.

BACK TO BASICS AND HIGHER "STANDARDS"

Conservative educational reformers call for a "back-to-basics" model and "higher standards" which they claim is the solution not only for the problems of schools but for those of society as well. The problem is, standards are not neutral. The "back-to-basics" model is designed to reproduce existing stratification. Despite their verbal support for critical literacy skills, the agenda of "back-to-basics" reform guarantees that the curriculum includes only the traditional canon of literature (i.e., white, male, European) and perpetuates official versions of history. (They also ignore the fact that most schools never stopped using the pedagogical model they want to go "back" to.) Alice Miller calls this "poisonous pedagogy" and writes about the extensive damage caused by rigid and coercive pedagogy which uses a highly moralistic tone to justify its use.[26]

The "basics" camp is fond of quoting statistics comparing performance of U.S. schools with those in other countries. What they do not report is that U.S. schools are actually less elitist and less homogeneous than most foreign school systems. The heterogeneity of the U.S. population today is unprecedented. Students in the United States come from a greater variety of backgrounds and speak many more languages than in any other country. A recent study found 276 different ethnic groups[27] in the United States speaking more than 153 languages.[28] In the New York City school system alone there are now over 114 languages.[29] Many of the foreign schools that receive higher rankings selectively winnow their student body as it progresses through grade levels until only the highest academic achievers remain. The result is an unfair and misleading comparison of part (a sample of foreign students heavily weighted toward high academic achievers) to whole (a sample of all U.S. students that is representative of the variation in the total population).

In this climate of national standards, national curricula, and national testing (for teachers and students), bureaucracies become even more oppressive and less democratic. As power at the highest administrative levels increases, diversity decreases and it becomes easier for the private sector to promote their commodified interests in the public schools. Corporations, like the Princeton Review and ETS (Educational Testing Services), with a financial stake in assessment based largely on the tests they produce, obviously support of standards, eagerly increasing their pretentious and profitable business. As a result, a model based on the education of upper-class European men and designed for the industrial age of the early 1900s is perpetuated even though it fails to prepare children for the global, technological world we live in today, let alone for their future.

The incompatibility of skills learned through schooling and the requirements of the current job market tempt many to support vocational education (read, *training*) for those "less academically successful." Vocational education supposedly gives predominantly poor students and students of color employment opportunities. Aside from problems associated with the blatant tracking inherent in vocational models, the greater injustice is that this is a short-term solution at best. As Stanley Aronowitz argues:

> Vocationalization is the wrong way to go. Notwithstanding their anxiety about the future, students are ill-served by educational regimes that tailor their learning to a rapidly changing workplace whose technological shifts belie the assumptions driving many specialist curricula. *Ironically, the best preparation for the work of the future might be to cultivate knowledge of the broadest possible kind, to make learning a way of life that in the first place is pleasurable and then rigorously critical.* For it is only when the learner loves literature, enjoys puzzling out the meaning of art works and those of philosophy, is intrigued by social and cultural theory, or becomes an indefatigable researcher that she acquires intellectual habits that are the precondition for further learning.[30] (emphasis added)

REFORMING SCHOOL REFORM

Waves of school reform have ebbed and flowed, but we have yet to turn the tide. As long as school reform remains wedded to a bureaucratic, scientized market model it will not succeed. Education is not a commodity whose value is measured by profitability. Education should be measured by ethical social standards, not crass commercialism. This is not as far-fetched or impossible as many would think. There is promise in an innovative and comprehensive reform program suggested by Peter Cookson, for example, that begins to address social justice as well as educational issues. Cookson explains that

> in a society that is highly stratified and where the financing of education is also highly stratified, it is necessary in a redesign plan that the monetary worth of an educational share be in inverse relation to the family's income.[31]

A major part of Cookson's proposal is a plan to support public-service inner-city private schools with public funds while avoiding the pitfalls of vouchers. His model would provide long-term, low-interest loans from banks and other lending institutions, guaranteed by state and federal governments. These loans would be available to both religious and non-religious schools which have 60 percent or more of its students with family income at or below the poverty line. Private schools that did not serve the disadvantaged would not be entitled.[32] Cookson's "Educational Trust" also provides strong economic incentives for a "managed choice" public school system to recruit *at least* 20 percent of students from those with family incomes at or below the poverty line. This method would, Cookson argues, reward schools with social commitment. Although the brief outline sketched here oversimplifies the "Trust Fund" plan, it illustrates that public education can be responsive to social needs.

PUBLIC HEALTH MODELS

Public health models of violence prevention are another, even broader response to social needs. The public health movement arose from the realization that violence is a major contributor to health-care costs,[33] as well as mortality. Although not without serious problems, the public health approach also has considerable strengths. It is one of the few approaches that at least looks at schools-in-context and moves beyond isolated school-based programs which it correctly views as ineffective and insufficient. It is based on an alliance between health care professionals, educators, and the community and focuses on health care and education with an emphasis on preventing violence. The public health model has the potential to strengthen care, continuity, and integration in children's lives, although it does not guarantee it.

Still, we must be careful of three dangers inherent in this model. One is the possibility that this approach can easily place already overburdened and underpaid teachers in the position of having to take on additional responsibilities and even more bureaucratic paper work. The reorganization of curriculum and scheduling would require careful consideration. It would have to provide teachers with time for cooperative work with each other as well as with health care professionals and community members. Secondly, it is important to recognize that the communities that most need support for health care and other services are those that have the least resources and therefore are least able to support them. The current downward trend in U.S. social support does not encourage the view that funding would be made available to subsidize programs in the poorest neighborhoods. Lastly, although it is clear that any future school reforms require collaboration, and the public health model is a step in the right direction, it's presuppositions raise serious concerns. The public health approach is overly dependent on a medical model with "risk factors" and "labels," "interventions," and "cures" (the dangers of which are spelled out in chapter 8), and it does not address economic, social, and political problems.

PUBLIC POLICY

Public policy initiatives addressing educational problems are recommended by many professional, research, and advocacy groups including the American Psychological Association,[34] the U.S. Department of Justice, The Carnegie Corporation,[35] the National Research Council,[36] and the U.S. Department of Justice Office of Juvenile Justice and Delinquency Prevention.[37] Most have not been implemented and those that have fall woefully short. As Furhman contends, "Policy typically has [little] effect on practice. . . . While policy can set the conditions for effective administration and practice, it cannot prescribe solutions to problems that need to be addressed at those levels."[38]

In addition to ignoring the interplay of policy, administration, practice, and sociocultural context, educational policy making has been fragmented and, at times, contradictory. For example, many states raised standards for teacher education and certification while creating or allowing loopholes to avert a shortage of teachers.[39] These include options such as alternate certification for those with nontraditional backgrounds, emergency certification, or assigning teachers to positions not in their fields.[40] More than 25 percent of those newly hired as teachers are not fully prepared and licensed for their jobs,[41] and these are the people assigned to teach the most vulnerable children.[42] In other cases, due to special interests, turf battles, lack of research, or other manifestations of incompetence, parallel policies have been known to cancel each other out by their ambiguities and contradictions. This is what happened when some states instituted new teacher evaluation programs at the same time they were mandating curricular content for students with few or no attempts to explore the match between what the teachers were required to learn and what they were required to teach their students.[43] Discrepancies between state and local policies, unrealistic time frames for implementation, lack of support such as funding, training, and hiring additional personnel as necessitated by policy changes, and a lack of attention to local requisites compound the problems. As a result, compliance is often superficial or virtually impossible.

Policy making is often just another search for a quick-fix that doesn't exist but provides legislators and governors with political currency at the expense of our children and their teachers. At best it is benign or ineffective; at worst, it compounds the problems it is supposed to solve. A national effort on a level that goes beyond policy making, vote garnering, and pandering to corporate interests, is needed.

ALTERNATIVE APPROACHES TO SCHOOLING AND SAFETY

The previous section discussed school reform on a basically structural level. However, the amelioration of violence in society cannot be accomplished without also producing schools that provide rich, creative learning environments that are meaningful and relevant to children's lives. Successful schools are also safe schools. When one looks beyond "the system," the existence of such schools become possibilities. From instruction in the home to a variety of alternative independent and public school movements, alternative schooling models, although frequently ignored, have been shown to be consistently superior to public schools on a wide variety of measures.[44] The reason for these two rather incompatible facts might best be explained by what is perhaps the only characteristic alternative schools share—their range of philosophies and methodologies are very different from traditional models. They are also very different from each other, but all generally share certain features which contribute to their success. These include a focus on students' interests, open-mindedness and trust, participatory democratic structure, a coherence between theory and practice, an emphasis on process not product, the importance of the arts, and the power of play. The physical environment is welcoming and respectful. Notably absent are symbols of authority and control, and physical and psychical intimidation. The schools are small and personal and involve and are involved with parents and community in a variety of mutually trusting, supportive, and beneficial relationships. These schools foster resiliency, critical thinking, problem-solving skills, responsibility, and creativity. They are supportive and challenging, not coercive. They call into question our commitment to the acquisition of knowledge as the accumulation of facts and the bifurcation of mind and body, affect and intellect, subject and object.

Those of you familiar with John Dewey's "progressive" model of education may have noticed some similarities between his model and the aforementioned qualities of successful alternative schools. Dewey, for example, advocated a restructuring of schools as "embryonic communities."[45] He argued that these communities would foster growth, development, and democracy. Dewey also emphasized the child's feelings and interests and an interdisciplinary, integrated curriculum that emphasized experience and active learning. Although Dewey would likely consider the more radical alternative models too permissive and possibly unstructured, attending to their commonalities of history, theory, and practice has much to teach us.

PEDAGOGY AND LITERACY

A major focus of so-called educational reform, and particularly of the national standards and back-to-basics movements, is what is commonly referred to as the "literacy crisis." Ironically, this "dilemma" is one created by the very mechanisms being proposed to alleviate it. The ruling classes have historically privileged literacy as a means of "knowledge," status, communication, and control. In the early years of the United States, teaching a slave to read and write was considered a crime punishable by imprisonment or death.[46] Today, this tradition of depriving the underclass of access to literacy continues in the name of schooling. As Cummins and Sayers explain:

> [T]he "literacy crisis" is a direct consequence of a power structure that has systematically denied educational or social advancement to marginalized groups. This is clearly not a recent development, and it assumes the proportions of a "crisis" only because at this historical juncture, advantaged groups perceive their vested interests threatened by the "fact" that the literacy levels of coworkers, an increasing proportion of whom are of minority background, are inadequate to cope with the expanding literacy demands of the workplace.[47]

At the same time, hegemony fears that literacy in the hands of the lower classes could become critical literacy, in which case the dominant position of the elite would be threatened. Access to literacy is access to power.

According to Freire, literacy is "a reading of the world *and* reading of the word. Literacy is not a reading of the word alone, nor a reading only of the world, but both together, in dialectical solidarity."[48] It is a dialectical, active, transformative process that makes possible new forms of consciousness that recover historical memory. It is a literacy of the symbolic, a "critical engagement [that] enables one to deconstruct and thereby resist both explicit and implicit manipulation."[49] That is, it is not just learning to read and write. It is learning to read the surrounding reality. It is a tool for promoting social justice.

Freire's approach to literacy and pedagogy starts with the sociohistorical context that constitutes the culture of subordinate groups. By locating pedagogy within the experience of the learner, the process opens a space for debate and affirmation. It provides the conditions for students to give voice to their knowledge, hopes, problems, fears, despair, and dreams. It leads to what Maxine Greene calls "wide awakeness," an awareness of what it is to be in the world; an awakening of imagination— "An imagination that brings an ethical concern to the fore, a concern that, again, has to do with the community that ought to be in the making and the values that give it color and significance."[50] It encourages students to question, to seek their own meaning, and to recognize their right and responsibility to take action. To adapt an analogy from Paulo Freire's *Pedagogy of Hope*, the content of curriculum is the salt and "salt ain't but part of the seasonin'."[51] What one needs is an understanding of the relationships between ingredients in the seasoning, their flavors individually and as a totality.

For example, contrary to popular practice, having a class celebration day in "honor" of Puerto Ricans being "granted" U.S. citizenship in 1917 is not critical pedagogy. Similarly, substituting "politically correct" information for what students may already "know" by telling students that Puerto Ricans do not consider citizenship to have been "granted" to them but rather "imposed" on them involuntarily, is still not critical pedagogy.[52] It only becomes critical pedagogy through a dialogic analysis and interpretation of different perspectives, embedded in their time and place, which provides a basis for understanding and action. As I have argued elsewhere:

> A discussion that honestly places the relationship between Puerto Rico and the United States in past and present historical (Puerto Ricans were made U.S. citizens in 1917. Some say this was purposely to provide increased manpower for World War I.), economic (After taking over Puerto Rico in 1898, U.S. absentee landlords, soon followed by large corporations, displaced the local economy and created dependence on the United States.), and political contexts (Puerto Ricans today are divided over the issue of statehood.), and grapples with the implications of this for both the two countries and their people, would contribute toward that goal.[53]

Underlying a critical approach to education is the assumption that the purpose of learning is to be able to understand the meaning of something. American schools emphasize received knowledge, which is not the same as understanding. The current positivist paradigm of education (which makes claims to objectivity and therefore sees knowledge as neutral and universal) equates knowing the "truth" with understanding its meaning. This is wrong. The nature of understanding, as Shank explains, "is different than the nature of knowing, because understanding deals with meaning and knowing deals with [empirical] truth."[54] *Knowledge* must be *understood* in the context of its social/political/economic milieu.

A second characteristic of critical pedagogy is that it goes beyond the bifurcations and fragmentation inherent in artificially created oppositional categorizations of race, sex, ethnicity, and so on. It provides a more integrative framework that directs our attention to the complexity and interrelations among categorizations of race, ethnicity, language, sex, sexual orientation, physical ability, and class. It explores the dynamics of these interactions and exposes the subtleties of their exclusionary reductionism. One way this is done is by foregrounding discussions of the sociocultural construction of these categories. For example, societal norms that equate masculinity with toughness and dominance over women must be challenged, as must the related ideologies of racism and the homophobia inherent in the construct of heterosexuality.

The point is to awaken a critical consciousness—what Freire called *concientización*. *Concientización* merges the personal with the social and political to foster *empowerment*. Power is a crucial issue. It is neither positive nor negative but dialectical with both a positive and negative force. This is but one reason why we must be careful that our efforts toward social justice do not lead to a different form of violence or new types of domination. Toward this end, it is important to emphasize that "empowerment" is not a verb. It is not something one does to or for others. Empowerment is a process one undertakes for oneself.

Critical pedagogy is an empowering, transformative pedagogy for all involved. It is not a methodology. It is a collaboration that recognizes education as a dynamic and critical process grounded in lived experiences—not the static entity that canned curriculum and dogmatic management techniques promote. Thus, critical pedagogy is liberating for teachers as well as students. Teachers have been de-intellectualized by teacher education programs and devalued by society. This has eroded their ability for critical engagement and independent authority. Institutional practices which discourage, if not prevent, peer contact and opportunities for reflection and dialogue, as well as contact with the larger community, further disempower teachers. Yet, the success of education in schools is directly related to the quality of their teachers and their involvement with the community.

THE ROLE OF TEACHERS

As one might expect, more successfully nonviolent schools are the ones where teachers are facilitative and supportive, not directive; autonomous and creative; reflective and honest. Yet the historic legacy of the role of teachers does not support such confidence in their abilities.

In 1890 Horace Willard, a New England teacher, argued that teachers, in comparison to other professionals,

> lived lives of mechanical routine, and were subjected to a machine of supervision, organization, classification, grading, percentages, uniformity, promotion, tests, examination . . . [with no room for] individuality, ideas, independence, originality, study, investigation."[55]

These sentiments were echoed forty years later by Henry Holmes, the dean of the newly formed Graduate School of Education at Harvard University, in his critique of the 1930 *National Survey of the Education of Teachers*. He bemoaned the survey's view of teachers as "routine worker[s] under the expert direction of principals, supervisors, and superintendents . . . that virtually undermined the development of teachers as critically-minded intellectuals."[56]

The current propagation of specific instructional methods continues to reinforce the notion of teaching as technical—as "scientific." But teachers' adherence to "instructions for instruction" yields preconceived results. To go beyond prescription, mechanistic views of instruction need to shift to a critical view that considers the sociopolitical dimensions of education[57]—to a pedagogy that is responsive to the needs of students instead of prescribed teaching methods and materials which are restrictive to students and exploitive of teachers by their lack of trust in teachers' judgments and debasing of their professionalism.[58]

John Dewey's distinction between "knowledge" and "habit" can illuminate the differences between these pedagogies. Habit is skill acquisition and knowledge is the ability to apply that skill in new situations.[59] Mechanistic practices like recitation, drill and practice, and memorization instruction result in learning-as-habit. Critical pedagogy results in learning-as-understanding. Dewey gives the example of a mechanic whose habituated skill will not help him in a unexpected situation. Unless a mechanic understands the machine and why the habits are usually effective, he will not be able to respond appropriately to the novel condition.

Critical pedagogy is not easy. It requires more than well-intentioned, committed teachers. It requires talking to students and *listening* to what they are telling us. It requires that teachers have a broad knowledge base and that schools (and school systems) be structured to encourage strong relationships. It requires hard work.

The logic of bureaucratic education is not congruent with critical pedagogy. The typical hierarchical school district is a pyramid staffed predominantly by women at the bottom and headed by male administrators who make decisions about everything from curriculum and schedules to assessment, discipline, and teacher accountability from offices usually isolated from district schools. A critical approach would include shared decision making, including student as well as teacher and parent participation. It would include community involvement on local and global levels. It would be interdisciplinary. It would not driven by the clock. It might include classes with mixed age groups, team teaching, having the same teachers stay with a class for longer than one year, and any number of other arrangements more conducive to teaching and learning than "schooling."[60]

We can only change teaching by changing the environment in which learning to teach and teaching take place.[61] Universities must recognize the importance of schools of education and stop relegating them to the bottom of the university status and funding hierarchy.[62] Teacher-education programs need to emphasize teaching as meaning-making, not mastering a set of techniques. In traditional schooling, teaching frequently means slavishly enforcing lesson plans developed by curriculum writers with no relationship to the social contexts—to the lives—of the students. The origins of the "knowledge" and its underlying ideology are not questioned. The role of social forces in the reproduction and privileging of the dominant culture remain invisible. Public schools must develop collaborative, inquiring environments for teachers at the same time they are being developed for students.

Teachers need time to think and plan and to work with each other, with parents, with the school administration, and with the community as well as students. Teaching is a demanding profession which requires continual learning, reflection, and concern with the multiple effects of one's actions upon others. Society must see teaching as the important, respectable activity it is and both trust and compensate teachers accordingly.

Individual teachers have enormous potential to affect children's lives. Even the poorest schools and those considered among the most violent often have at least one classroom where meaningful learning is taking place. One question this raises is why are there so few of such teachers. Having taught New York City teachers in a university graduate school of education for several years, I can tell you that it is not because those attracted to teaching are not competent, concerned, committed educators. Neither are they, as anyone familiar with the New York City Board of Education pay scale can tell you, in it for the money, hours, or benefits. The evidence points to something about the structure and culture of our society that propagates the destructive dynamics so prevalent in our schools.

Individual schools or teachers cannot change a society that increasingly either ignores or vilifies a majority of its citizens. They can be a significant source of support to their students, but, as Hernandez argues in chapter 1, teachers (and schools) cannot (and should not have to) do it alone. They have neither the resources nor the sole responsibility to stop violence. They may, as Geoffrey Canada[63] claims, play a part in protecting students from risks encountered outside the classroom, but it is simplistic to believe that schools can counteract explicit and implicit societal messages or that behavioral, curricular, cognitive, or disciplinarian interventions in schools can change the continuing effects of poverty, guns, substance abuse, and the cultural-economic system that drives them. To be successful, as Anyon has cogently argued, educational reforms must be seen as part of the larger effort to address the problems of poverty and racial isolation in our inner cities.[64]

BEYOND SCHOOLS

Even critically-minded experts on violence do not agree on the best role of schools. Canada, for example, sees schools as safe havens from the surrounding world, arguing for stability and consistency in a caring environment.[65] Jean Anyon sees schools as more porous with the environment outside their walls.[66] Others, like Shirley Brice-Heath and Milbrey McLaughlin, acknowledge that "there is no fixed formula"[67] but the multiple roots of the problems of inner-city youth require inclusive responses.[68] One thing they all do agree on is that, whether on a global or local scale, community is essential.

Community, as used here, is not defined by homogeneity of some demographic or geographic variable. Often, for example, school districts, neighborhoods, and religious and ethnic communities do not coincide. In addition, as Aronowitz has argued

> the *community* (emphasis in original) as an autonomous cultural as much as a geographical site of social action is increasingly weakened by the various strands of massification, especially the centralized state and the equally centralized institutions of mass communications.[69]

Community cannot exist if there are power struggles. This does not mean there cannot be disagreement, but that the contributions and experience of all participants must be equally valued.

Policy makers, schools, and other public institutions have typically resisted any attempts to develop strong community-based social networks of support.[70] School environments are often organized to maintain control and dispense academic content via authoritarian, mechanistic methods which lead to distrust and detachment. Although a few schools may successfully implement programs that foster community involvement, conventional practices of ignoring students' subjectivity, lived experiences, and internalized oppression ultimately undermine even the most well-funded, well-intentioned initiatives. We maintain that neglecting to nurture students' critical ability to "read the world," to decipher the hidden codes of our society and its institutions, as well as the tools to cope with the complexities and conflicts they will encounter, is a major contributor to the failure of these efforts.

At this point, it might be helpful to look at a community as a complex network of opportunities and constraints which can provide positive institutional and social support and as well as restrict access to it, especially for youth.[71] Stanton-Salazar and Spina[72] have proposed a network model with three overlapping and interrelated parts, all of which are grounded in critical theory and which integrate Freirean pedagogy, families, community, and agency. A critical model that fosters coping strategies that are self-empowering and intellectually enlightening, instead of models that replicate mainstream ideology and practices, has much to offer.

What would such a model look like? According to Stanton-Salazar and Spina:

> The first element entails mentoring or incorporating committed agents in the school and community into every student's personal social support network. This is not an easy task, given that dominant ideology and entrenched thinking define the various roles assumed by personnel (i.e., teachers, social workers) in terms of a narrow range of professional duties.[73]

It would also involve educating professionals for assuming a more expanded set of duties and compensating them accordingly, as well as engaging unions to share in this new vision. Training must include critical understanding of minority socialization and appropriate ways of responding to the compounded distress of students. Mentors must also be willing to confront conventional ways of thinking that obscure rather than enlighten. They must be willing to address their own assumptions, complicity, and distress, "wrought by years of working in an institutional environment that systematically blinded them to the hidden and multiplicative ways they were forced to play host to class and racial forces of exclusion."[74] Stanton-Salazar and Spina explain that,

> enhancing the social capital of low-status youth, entails working with mentors and youth to co-create an institutional culture which not only fosters authentically supportive relationships and collaborative learning, but also addresses the persistence of racism, sexism, homophobia, ageism, capitalist imperialism, and colonialism, and its manifestations in society and its institutions centered on the appropriation and distribution of social and economic wealth.[75]

The second part involves the development of critical consciousness (*concientización*) or, in other words, the empowerment of youth (and their mentors) to decode and critique the hidden codes of our culture (e.g., racism, sexism, individualism, meritocracy). A critical consciousness implies being able to understand, analyze, question, seek one's own meaning, and recognize one's right and responsibility to take actions that have an impact on the explicit and implicit sociopolitical and economic realities of our lives.[76] It is most important to realize that critical consciousness requires more than good intentions. It requires action. *Concientización* not only transforms consciousness, it changes lives. It mobilizes schools, families, communities, and institutions in a collaborative effort toward social justice.

The third part borrows from innovative group-counseling programs currently being formulated and organized by many Latina/o and African American mental health providers around the country. These efforts arise from their collective assessment that the mainstream psychological community has failed to directly and adequately address the realities of oppression among people of color.[77] These group counseling programs have much in common with Freirean principles of cultural literacy, problem-posing, and political activism.[78]

Following the lead of this therapeutic community, group "counseling" would incorporate the development of critical consciousness with a focus on existing coping strategies within the community. Adolescents, for example, might share with the group some of the principal stressors encountered in their daily lives (e.g., witnessing a violent event in the neighborhood). This experience would then be linked to participants' past experiences with violence. Discussion might then focus on how adolescents in the group and members of the community have coped with violence, as well as on the personal and social costs or consequences of different coping strategies (e.g., dissociation, desensitization, resignation). Youth would subsequently move toward exploring how these stresses and traumas are rooted in the ways society and its institutions are socially organized. Creative exploration of alternative ways of coping would provide a wider repertoire of skills to draw on in dealing with stressors. Ultimately, the group would examine how social structures could be transformed in ways that would no longer victimize or dehumanize people, particularly the young.

Stanton-Salazar and Spina, like the authors in this volume, rightly situate school reform as *part* of a broader strategy for social change. Such change has to come from the bottom up. It has to come from the people (of all ages). It has to come from commitment. It has to come from a sense of justice. If we do not redistribute wealth and opportunity, we will continue to be an oligarchic capitalist state and not the democracy we claim to be and never were. Other countries provide working and workable models that contradict predictions of impossibility and dire consequences. Denmark, for example, has long made social welfare a top priority, providing *no-expense* health care and social services for *every* Dane. Every Dane over sixty-seven years of age, or younger but unable to work, receives a pension from the state. The work week was recently reduced to thirty-seven hours and five weeks of paid vacation is guaranteed. Unemployment and sick benefits are 90 percent of most workers' salaries. (There is a cap on benefits for higher salaried employees.) Daycare is provided and education through the master's degree is free. Lest you think this destroys the Danish economy, note that tiny Denmark currently ranks thirteenth in world per capita income and is also a leader in providing aid to other countries.

In contrast, U.S. national health care efforts have been repeatedly squashed, welfare programs cut, and the unemployed removed from eligibility for a small, taxable, weekly check (and the unemployment "rate") after thirteen weeks. Employed Americans have longer workweeks and less vacation than most other postindustrial countries. Reducing work time and increasing wages in lower-rung jobs would employ more people more equitably. National conscience and corporate responsibility should not be oxymorons.

Not surprisingly, there are no signs of sufficient resources being provided to support change of this magnitude in either or both school systems and the wider context. This does not mean that the resources are not available—only that our national priorities must be changed.

FINANCIAL CONSIDERATIONS

In addition to changes in the national consciousness and political processes, we must support social justice through the reallocation of resources and, if necessary, through raising additional funds. Discrepancies between rhetoric and social practice, between social benefits and their price, between participatory government and hegemonic politics cannot be tolerated.

Decreasing violence requires reallocating funds to inner cities and poor rural areas—not by building more prisons, but by investing in the nation's social infrastructure. Yet, between 1980 and 1995, the U.S. federal education budget dropped from $27 to $16 billion (while the federal corrections budget increased from $8 to $20 billion).[79] (See the discussion on prisons in the introductory chapter to this volume.) California "now spends more for prisons than for public higher education,"[80] though the state once spent several times as much on universities as prisons.[81] During the 1990s,

New York State added more than $750 million to its prison budget while cutting the budgets for the City and State Universities of New York by almost the same amount.[82] By 1995, under Governor George Pataki, New York's funding for prisons surpassed that for higher education for the first time in state history. The difference totaled $300 million.[83] The United States ranks first in world-wide per capita income among eighteen industrialized countries,[84] but fifteen of those countries spend a greater percentage of per capita income on public education than the United States.[85]

Our legislators continue to ignore facts that show that the economic cost of maintaining the status quo and its concentration of power is self-defeating. The cost of high school dropouts alone is conservatively estimated as

> $50 billion in foregone lifetime earnings alone. Also associated with this cost are foregone government tax revenues, greater welfare expenditures, poorer physical and mental health of our nation's citizens, and greater costs of crime, as well as a variety of social costs to which it is difficult to attach dollar figures.[86]

The economic costs of medical care necessitated by acts of violence have topped $13.5 million[87] annually. This does not include the costs of intentional injuries, lost lives, or psychological trauma in the lives of victims as well as their parents, children, friends, classmates, and neighbors.

Defense spending is another source of funding disparities and well-documented enormous waste.[88] Seymour Melman offers a provocative comparison of our military costs in dollars as well as in social terms.[89] As Melman reports, the $114 billion spent on 650 F-22 fighter planes could have modernized and expanded all U.S. mass-transit systems, creating cleaner, more efficient, more economical transportation. The $100 billion budgeted for Trident II submarines and F-18 jet fighters could clean up 3,000 of the worst hazardous waste dumps in the country. The additional $25 billion that paid for a fleet of C-17 jet cargo planes could have created more than 1 million public housing units. The almost $5 billion we spend on the Atcam and Hellfire missile programs would allow all eligible children to enter a Head Start program. The $3.7 billion TOW-2 missile program would pay for Medicare for an additional 4 million adults and 2 million children. The $2 billion price tag of a single B-2 bomber would build 400 new elementary schools. The $479 million spent for 28 F-16 fighter aircraft would pay the salaries of 40,000 new teachers. And this does not include the costs of Trident submarines, at $1.4 billion each, the $6.7 billion for stealth bombers and similar weapons, and the billions that numerous "smaller" defense expenditures add up to.

Besides the inflated military expenses that benefit defense industries and special interest groups, corporate subsidies and tax breaks are at least as staggering. These include more than $1 billion in special deductions for oil companies, $700 million ethanol subsidies, $1.4 billion sugar subsidies, $3.5 billion in tax breaks for companies in U.S. territories, $3 billion cash payments overseas to buy American weapons, and so on ad nauseam if not ad infinitum.[90]

In addition, in early summer, 1999, President Clinton announced that there could be tax surpluses of almost $3 trillion over the next decade. Politicians are already bickering over what to do with the windfall. Suggestions include reducing taxes like those on capital gains and large inheritances which benefit the wealthy, despite the fact that working Americans' taxes rose from 4.5 percent of their income in 1993 to almost 27 percent in 1998. Others argue that the money should be used to reduce the $4 trillion national debt (the value of which is also debatable), or funding social programs (which, given Washington's mentality and recent track record, are unlikely to do much if any good).[91]

Other areas of gross inequity (to mention just a few) include the ability of the wealthy to avoid estate taxes, the growing disparity of salaries for heads of corporations and their employees, and loopholes in income tax laws that favor the rich. Tax reform under the Reagan administration, for example, resulted in a 53 percent tax cut for millionaires. In 1986, a millionaire paid an average alternative minimum tax of $116,395, or about 11.6 percent of his income. By 1989, the same millionaire would pay only $54,758, or 5.4 percent.

By way of remedying some of this blatant budgetary bias, Jean Anyon has called for large corporations to "pay their share" and take on the responsibility they have historically shirked by polluting the environment, relocating, and leaving society to pick up related costs such as retraining and unemployment.[92] One suggestion she makes is a national urban tax on American-based corporations and those based in other countries who profit from American business, payable regardless of where they are located. This money would be used to resuscitate the cities, which, as Anyon argues, would enhance urban governments' access to state and federal political power. She calls for renewed federal and state initiatives against poverty, housing, job discrimination, and racial resegregation.

Comer echoes Anyon's the call for a socially responsible, nationally coordinated approach that includes better health care, economic opportunities, policy adjustments, and community support.[93] Perhaps schools must be reconceptualized as multipurpose community service institutions, similar to those suggested by public health models of violence prevention, but addressing the problems raised in the previous discussion of their shortcomings, perhaps by implementing the suggestions made by Stanton-Salazar and Spina.

Whatever changes are adopted, we must be wary of continuing the assumption that it is the schools' role to be responsible for everything wrong in society and the teachers' role to "fix" it. Changing our social, economic, political, and legal institutions to a socially just model can perhaps do more to prevent violence than all the scare tactics, threats, rhetoric, and punishment in the world. The task is to reform those institutions in such a way that they do not replace one form of hegemonic power with another. To accomplish this, a critical understanding of the bases of violence and a concerted effort of political action informed by that understanding is needed across sectors.

MAKING THE ROAD BY WALKING THE TALK

Communication is crucial to critical understanding and a movement toward social justice. There are many inner-city, suburban, and rural community groups across the country whose members have built homes, playgrounds, and soup kitchens; promoted unionization for better working conditions and pay; organized neighborhoods against the violence of police brutality, toxic waste, and changes in zoning laws; and fought for better street lighting, handicapped access to public buildings, and improved social services. Typically, however, these groups act in isolation from each other and few interact with schools. Communication among these community groups would improve their effectiveness, increase their access and ability to funding and other resources, and provide connection, social support, moral(e) reinforcement, and strategic information. Pockets of local resistance and agency would lead to coalitions of activists, and then to coalitions of coalitions of activists. As Arlo Guthrie might say, before you know it, we'd have a movement.[94]

The recently formed Paulo Freire Institute for Popular Education, in New York City, is one attempt to address these possibilities. Founded to honor the memory and carry on the legacy of Paulo Freire, the Institute is an independent center grounded in Freire's work and guided by his example.[95] Recognizing the need to move beyond the fragmented organization and short-term campaigns that have characterized reform efforts over the past twenty-five years,[96] the Freire Institute strives "to assist and prepare individuals and movements for a deeper, more grassroots and participatory forms of social action that go beyond resistance,"[97] because, as Freire knew, when popular education assists educators to be better organizers and organizers to be better educators true grassroots collective self-organization grows stronger. The Institute brings together educators and organizers from labor, community-based organizations, and public schools to share problems and approaches, knowledge, and strategies in a variety of ways from on-line dialogues and informal meetings to workshops and international conferences.

Computerized communication has been an important vehicle for disseminating information, discussing issues, and collaborating on projects. Although we must remember that access to computers and other forms of technology is still very uneven, technological grassroots mobilization, such as that realized through the use of the Internet by the Zapatistas in Chiapas, offers tremendous potential.[98] It is a powerful medium that allows the few to reach many and provides a venue for the dissemination of suppressed information, for the exchange of ideas and strategies, for support and mobilization, assuming that the technology is made available to everyone. That is not only a very large assumption in terms of economics and cultural capital. It may also be seen in political terms, as evidenced by recent efforts to regulate and control the Internet (i.e., restrict who has access to computers and the technological network). The reasons for the restriction of technology by hegemonic gatekeepers are also the very reasons the rest of us should fight against it: The access to information and communications provided by computer technology holds possibilities for radical change, for truly global community and participatory democracy, for social justice.

The beginning of the twentieth century, when Dewey wrote his early treatises on the philosophy of education, was a time of great social, economic, and demographic change due to the growth of industry and the large numbers of immigrants it attracted. Today, one hundred years later, we face comparable challenges as we move from an industrial to technological society and immigrants from an even greater number of countries arrive daily.

We need deep social, political, and economic change—and that takes time and effort. The archaic system we have now does not work because it does not fit the needs of life on the cusp of the twenty-first century. Without new questions, new ideas, and significant change in our culture, we cannot solve our problems. But that does not mean there is nothing we can do now. We do not have to reject change in our education system until a radical change in society is brought about. We do not have to reject social change until we can revolutionize the entire political system.

The fact that there is no single, perfect solution does not mean we are powerless. Even one person can make a difference by becoming involved, by taking action. You have undoubtedly heard of MADD (Mothers Against Drunk Driving). What you may not know is that it was founded in 1980 by one woman, Candy Lightner, with the help of a few volunteers, after her thirteen-year-old daughter was killed by a repeat-offender drunk driver. (Drunk driving is one of the nation's most frequently committed violent crimes.) By the late 1990s, the nonprofit organization had grown to nearly 3 million members and supporters. Their national headquarters has a staff of sixty people who direct training, education and awareness programs, fundraising, media campaigns, and state and federal legislative activities. Funding is primarily by individual contributors (with the average contribution being $13.00), augmented in more recent years by corporate sponsorship (e.g., the donation of large quantities of red ribbon) and federal funding by the U.S. Department of Transportation. From its small grassroots beginning, MADD has grown to have a significant impact on societal attitudes and behavior related to drinking and driving. It did not happen overnight and the effort is still not totally effective, but, since 1982, annual alcohol-related traffic deaths have been reduced 36 percent. The National Highway Traffic Safety Administration estimates that approximately 125,000 lives have been saved between 1983 and 1996 due to the decrease of alcohol-impaired drivers.[99] All because one person decided to *do* something meaningful, to replace despair with hope, despondency with agency, and inertia with action. Like Candy Lightner and the many others like her, we need to be outraged, to join together, to have purpose, to find possibilities, to seek justice.

Recognizing and accepting the need for change are the first critical steps toward achieving it, but a difficult journey lies ahead. To borrow from Magritte, *Ce n'est pas une conclusion.* It is but the beginning.

NOTES

1. See discussion in introductory chapter to this volume.

2. T. Rose, "Current Uses of Corporal Punishment in American Public Schools." *Journal of Educational Psychology* 76 (1984): 427–441.

3. See Philip Greven, *Spare the Child* (New York: Knopf, 1991). For the views of supporters of corporal punishment, see Proverbs, King James Version; Roy Lessen, *Spanking: Why, When, and How?* (Minneapolis: Bethany House, 1979), and Larry Christenson, "God's Order for Parents," in *Christian Family*, L. Christenson, ed. (Minneapolis: Bethany House, 1983), all of which are still being printed.

4. L. Jones, "Why Are We Beating Our Children?" *Ebony* (March 1993): 80–81; R. Richardson and E. Evans, "Empowering Teachers to Halt Corporal Punishment," *Kappa Delta Pi Record* 29 (1993): 39–42.

5. See Spina, "Violence in Schools: Expanding the Dialogue" and Klein and Chancer, "Masculinity Matters: The Omission of Gender from High-Profile Violence Cases," both in this volume.

6. See section on prisons in Spina, "Violence in Schools."

7. See "surveillance" section in Spina, "Violence in Schools."

8. Michael Grunwald, "Culture Wars Erupt in Debate on Hill" *Washington Post*, 18 June 1999, A1; Michael Kranish and Eun Lee Koh, "House Passes a Gun Measure Backed by NRA. Vote Follows Move to Let Schools Post 10 Commandments," *Boston Globe*, 18 June 1999, A1. See also Spina, "Violence in Schools," for a discussion about guns and youth versus adult crime.

9. Kranish and Koh, *House Passes Gun Measure*, Al.

10. Daniel W. Webster, "The Unconvincing Case for School-Based Conflict Resolution Programs for Adolescents," *Health Affairs* 12 (Winter, 1993).

11. See M. Posner, "Research Raises Troubling Questions about Violence Prevention Programs," *The Harvard Education Newsletter*, 10 (1994): 1–4.

12. Webster, "The Unconvincing Case."

13. Posner, "Research Raises Troubling Questions."

14. Quoted in Posner, "Research Raises Troubling Questions," 2.

15. The National Research Council, *Understanding and Preventing Violence* (Washington, D.C.: National Academy Press, 1993)

16. Peter W. Cookson, Jr., *School Choice: The Struggle for the Soul of American Education*, (New Haven: Yale University Press, 1994).

17. Cookson, *School Choice*.

18. Harlow G. Unger, *School Choice: How to Select the Best Schools for Your Children* (New York: Checkmark Books, 1999).

19. Andrew C. Porter, John Smithson, and Eric Osthoff, "Standard Setting as a Strategy for Upgrading High School Mathematics and Science," in *The Governance of Curriculum: 1994 Yearbook of the Association for Supervision and Curriculum Development* (ASCD), eds. Richard F. Elmore and Susan H. Fuhrman (Alexandria, Va.: ASCD, 1994): 138–166.

20. Cookson, *School Choice*, 13.

21. John E. Chubb and Terry M. Moe, *Politics, Markets, and American Schools* (Washington, D.C.: Brookings Institute, 1990).

22. Chubb and Moe, *Politics*, 167.

23. Cookson, *School Choice*, 49.

24. Cookson, *School Choice*.

25. Stanley Aronowitz, *Science as Power: Discourse and Ideology in Modern Society* (Minneapolis: University of Minnesota Press, 1988), 137.

26. Alice Miller, *For Your Own Good* (New York: Noonday, 1983/1990).

27. The study was by Gollnick and Chin and is reported in R. F. Wasson, P. L. Stuhr, and L. Petrovich-Mwaniki, "Teaching Art in the Multicultural Classroom," *Studies in Art Education* 31 (1990): 226–233.

28. L. Brenner, "The New New York," *New York Woman* (April, 1991): 68–81.

29. Brenner, "The New New York."

30. Stanley Aronowitz, *The Knowledge Factory: Dismantling the Corporate University and Creating True Higher Learning* (Boston: Beacon Press, 2000), 161.

31. Cookson, *School Choice*, 130.

32. Cookson recognizes that his proposal may cross the boundaries between church and state and cogently argues the issue on the grounds of equity issues presented here. See Peter W. Cookson, Jr., *School Choice*.

33. See Spina, "Violence in Schools" and section below on financing.

34. American Psychological Association, 1993.

35. The Carnegie Corporation, 1994.

36. National Research Council 1993, 1996.

37. See publications by the U. S. Department of Justice, Office of Juvenile Justice and Delinquency Prevention, e.g., F. E. Zimring and G. Hawkins, *Incapacitation: Penal Confinement and the Restraint of Crime* (N.Y.: Oxford, 1995)

38. Susan H. Fuhrman, "Legislatures and Education Policy," 36.

39. Fuhrman, "Legislatures and Education Policy."

40. Linda Darling-Hammond and Barnett Berry, *The Evolution of Teacher Policy*, document prepared for the Center for Policy Research in Education (Santa Monica, Calif.: RAND Corporation, 1988).

41. National Commission on Teaching and America's Future, *What Matters Most: Teaching and America's Future*, (New York: Author, 1996).

42. Linda Darling-Hammond, "Teacher Quality and Educational Equality." *The College Board Review* (Summer 1988): 16–23, 39–41; Jeannie Oakes, *Multiplying Inequalities: The Effects of Race, Social Class, and Tracking on Opportunities to Learn Mathematics and Science.* (Santa Monica, Calif.: RAND, 1990).

43. Fuhrman, "Legislatures and Education Policy."

44. See Lois Holzman, *Schools for Growth* (Hillsdale, N.J.: Lawrence Erlbaum, 1997); R. Miller, *What are Schools for: Holistic Education in American Culture* (Brandon, Vt.: Holistic Education Press, 1992); J. Mintz, ed., *The Almanac of Education Choices: Private and Public Learning Alternatives and Home Schooling* (New York: Macmillan, 1995).

45. John Dewey, "The School and Society" and "The Child and the Curriculum," both in *Dewey on Education*, ed. Martin S. Dworkin (New York: Teachers College Press): 33–90 & 91–111.

46. Frederick Douglass, *Narrative of the Life of Frederick Douglass, an American Slave, Written by Himself* (Bedford Books, 1993).

47. Jim Cummins and Dennis Sayers, *Brave New Schools: Challenging Cultural Illiteracy through Global Learning Networks* (New York: St. Martin's Press, 1995), 87.

48. Paulo Freire, *Pedagogy of Hope: Reliving "Pedagogy of the Oppressed"* (New York: Continuum, 1994). 105.

49. Stephanie Urso Spina, "Representation, Education, and Transformation: Social Semiotics as a Tool for Critical (Multicultural) Education," *Teaching Education*, 9 (1997): 27–36.

50. Maxine Greene, *Releasing the Imagination: Essays on Education, the Arts, and Social Change.* (San Francisco: Jossey-Bass, 1995).

51. Freire, *Pedagogy of Hope*, 71.

52. Sonia Nieto, *Affirming Diversity: The Sociopolitical Context of Multicultural Education* (New York, Longman, 1996).

53. Spina, "Representation, Education, and Transformation," 28-29.

54. Gary Shank, "Educational Semiotic: Threat or Menace?" *Educational Psychology Review* 42 (1992): 201.

55. Powell, quoted in Henry A. Giroux and Peter McLaren, "Teacher Education and the Politics of Engagement: The Case for Democratic Schooling," in *Breaking Free: The Transformative Power of Critical Pedagogy*, eds. P. Leistyna, A. Woodrum, and S. A. Sherblom (Cambridge, MA: Harvard Educational Review Reprint Series 27, 1996), 301.

56. Quoted in Giroux and McLaren, "Teacher Education and the Politics of Engagement," 302. It should be noted that the devaluation and control of teachers and teaching is directly related to the historical "feminization" of the teaching profession at the lower levels. Today, about 85 percent of elementary school teachers are women. At the high school level, which is more prestigious to many, about half

of the teachers are women and half are men. Nine out of ten teachers are white. Those choosing to become teachers are most often below average academically, five years older than the typical U.S. worker, married, and not politically active. See "Schools and Organizations and Teacher Professionalization," in *Exploring Education*, eds. Alan Sadovnik, Peter Cookson, Jr., and Susan Semel (Boston: Allyn and Bacon, 1994), 243–261

57. Lilia Bartolomé, "Beyond the Methods Fetish: Toward a Humanizing Pedagogy," in *Breaking Free: The Transformative Power of Critical Pedagogy*, 229–252.

58. D. Carlson, "Teachers as Political Actors: From Reproductive Theory to the Crisis of Schooling," in *Breaking Free: The Transformative Power of Critical Pedagogy*, 273–300.

59. John Dewey, *Democracy and Education: An Introduction to the Philosophy of Education* (New York, The Macmillan Company, 1916).

60. I am referring here to Miles Horton's distinction between schooling and education. We all know what schooling is. Horton differentiated it from Education, which he defined as "cradle-to-grave learning."

61. See Deborah Meier, "Reinventing Teaching," *Teachers College Record* 93 no. 4 (Summer 1992), for an analysis of changes that would promote better teaching.

62. John Goodlad, *Teachers for Our Nation's Schools* (San Francisco: Jossey-Bass, 1990).

63. Geoffrey Canada, *Fist, Stick, Knife, Gun: A Personal History of Violence in America* (Boston: Beacon Press, 1995).

64. Jean Anyon, *Ghetto Schooling: A Political Economy of Urban Educational Reform* (New York: Teachers College Press, 1997).

65. Canada, *Fist, Stick, Knife, Gun*.

66. Anyon, *Ghetto Schools*.

67. Milbrey W. McLaughlin, "Embedded Identities: Enabling Balance in Urban Contexts," in *Identity and Inner-city Youth: Beyond Ethnicity and Gender*, eds. Shirley Brice Heath and M. W. McLaughlin (New York: Teachers College Press, 1993), 59.

68. McLaughlin, "Embedded Identities."

69. Aronowitz, *Science as Power*, 137.

70. Michelle Fine, *Framing Dropouts: Notes on the Politics of an Urban Public High School* (Albany: SUNY Press, 1991), 183; Ruth Sidel, *Women and Children Last: The Plight of Poor Women in Affluent America* (New York: Penguin, 1986/1992).

71. Barry Wellman, "Network Analysis: Some Basic Principles," in Randall Collins, ed., *Sociological Theory* (San Francisco: Jossey-Bass, 1983) 155–200.

72. Ricardo D. Stanton-Salazar and Stephanie Urso Spina, "The Network Orientations of Highly Resilient Urban Minority Youth: A Network-Analytic Account of Minority Socialization and Its Educational Implications," *The Urban Review* (in press).

73. Stanton-Salazar and Spina, "The Network Orientations of Highly Resilient Urban Minority Youth."

74. Stanton-Salazar and Spina, "The Network Orientations of Highly Resilient Urban Minority Youth."

75. Stanton-Salazar and Spina, "The Network Orientations of Highly Resilient Urban Minority Youth."

76. Paulo Freire, *The Politics of Education, Culture, Power, and Liberation* (South Hadley, Mass.: Bergin & Garvey, 1985).

77. Eduardo Aguilar, *Re-evaluation Counseling: A "Culturally Competent" Model for Social Liberation* (Seattle: Rational Island Publishers, 1995); Harvey Jackins, *The Human Situation* (Seattle: Rational Island Publishers, 1991).

78. Paulo Freire, *Pedagogy of the Oppressed* (New York: Herder and Herder, 1970); *Education for Critical Consciousness* (New York: Continuum, 1974); *Learning to Question: A Pedagogy of Liberation* (New York: Continuum, 1989).

79. Robert Slavin, "How Can We Target Programs That Work? Making Money a Difference" *Rethinking Schools* 9 (1995): 10ff.

80. Miller in Lawrence M. Friedman and George Fisher, *The Crime Conundrum: Essays on Criminal Justice*, (Boulder, Colo.: Westview, 1997), 3.

81. *The Consequences of Mandatory Minimums* (Federal Judicial Center Report, 1994).

82. Ellen Yan, "Report Slams Prison Funds," *Newsday* 1 Dec. 1998, A16.

83. Yan, "Report Slams Prison Funds."

84. According to the Luxembourg Income Study reported in "Children: Progress Elsewhere," *U.S. News & World Report* (28 Aug. 1995): 24.

85. Among industrialized nations, only Ireland and non-secular Israel spend less on public education.

86. Gary Natriello, Edward McDill, and Aaron M. Pallas, *Schooling Disadvantaged Children Against Catastrophe* (New York: Teachers College Press, 1990), 43.

87. Jocelyn Elders, "American Violence Is Home Grown," *Focus* 22 (April 1994):7.

88. See Dina Rasor, *The Pentagon Underground* (New York: Times Books, 1985); Richard A. Stubbing and Richard A. Mendel, *The Defense Game: An Insider Explores the Astonishing Realities of America's Defense Establishment* (New York: Harper and Row, 1986); Richard Halloran, *To Arm a Nation* (New York: Macmillan, 1986).

89. Seymour Melman, *Rebuilding America: A New Economic Plan for the 1990s*, (Westfield, N.J.: Open Magazine Pamphlet series, 1992).

90. Daniel Franklin, "Ten Not So Little Piggies," *The Nation* (27 Nov., 1995).

91 Stephen Moore, "New Rules for the Federal Surplus," *Newsday*, 18 July 1999, B5.

92. Anyon, *Ghetto Schooling*, 167.

93. James P. Comer, *Waiting for a Miracle: Why Schools Can't Solve Our Problems — and How We Can* (New York: Dutton, 1997).

94. This is a reference to the lyrics of Arlo Guthrie's song, "Alice's Restaurant," © 1967 Appleseed Music Inc.

95. Freire did not just write about critical pedagogy and activism. From his literacy campaigns in Guinea-Bissau, forming five Centers for Popular Education with Lula and the Workers Party in Brazil to serving as Secretary of Education there, Freire lived it.

96. For example, as stated in the *Paulo Freire Institute Concept Paper*, "Community activists rarely focus on the ways in which their constituents struggle to make a living and trade unionists almost never address issues such as housing, education and community empowerment. This conception of education and organizing

in which work space and living space are separated by an unbridged gulf is no longer adequate to the task."

97. Gregory Tewksbury and Stanley Aronowitz, *Paulo Freire Institute Concept Paper*, unpublished manuscript, 1998.

98. Peter McLaren, Introduction to *Critical Education in the New Information Age*. eds. Manuel Castells, Ramon Flecha, Paulo Freire, Henry A. Giroux, and Paul Willis (Boulder, Colo.: Rowman & Littlefield, 1999). See also Cummins and Sayers, *Brave New Schools*.

99. This information was gathered from a variety of MADD publications.

Subject Index

Author Index

About the Contributors

Ricky Lee Allen is a Ph.D. student at the UCLA Graduate School of Education and Information Studies and visiting instructor of education at Whittier College. He teaches courses in multiculturalism, social foundations of education, and qualitative research methods. He has worked as a public school teacher in inner-city Los Angeles, suburban Kentucky, and rural Indiana. His publications emphasize critical studies of spatial theory, identity politics, and whiteness.

Stanley Aronowitz is distinguished professor of sociology at the Graduate Center of the City University of New York. He is author or editor of seventeen books, the latest of which are *The Knowledge Factory* (Beacon Press, 2000) and the paperback edition of *Ashes of the Old American Labor and America's Future* (Basic, 2000).

Lynn S. Chancer is visiting associate professor in sociology at Fordham University. She is the author of *Sadomasochism in Everyday Life* (Rutgers, 1992), *Reconcilable Differences* (University of California Press, 1998), and the forthcoming *Provoking Assaults: Gender, Race and Class in High Profile Crime Cases* (University of California Press). She has written numerous articles on gender, social theory, and crime.

Paulo Freire, renowned scholar, is considered the most globally influential educator of the last fifty years. His contribution to this volume is one of the last pieces he wrote before his death in 1997. Freire's prolific books, articles, and essays have inspired educators, scholars, and activists from Africa, Asia, Europe, Australia, and North and South America. Paulo Freire believed that education should lead first and foremost to liberation while rejecting all forms of oppression. His classic book, *The Pedagogy of the Oppressed*, has been translated into more than twenty languages worldwide and has sold close to one million copies. His work continues to influence a wide range of disciplines from the political and social sciences to education and theology.

Donna Gaines is a journalist and sociologist. She holds a master's degree in social work and a Ph.D. in sociology. She is a New York State certified social worker, and has worked on a suicide hotline, as a parent advocate, with teenagers on the streets of suburbia, and as a consultant on contemporary youth issues. In addition to writing for publications such as *Rolling Stone, SPIN,* and *The Village Voice,* Gaines contributes to scholarly collections, conferences, and underground 'zines. She teaches sociology at Barnard College of Columbia University.

Henry A. Giroux holds the Waterbury Chair Professorship at Penn State University. His most recent books include: *Channel Surfing: Racism, the Media, the Destruction of American Youth* (St. Martin's Press), *Pedagogy and the Politics of Hope* (Westview), *Stealing Innocence: Youth, Corporate Power, and the Politics of Culture* (St. Martin's Press), *The Mouse That Roared: Disney and the End of Innocence* (Rowman & Littlefield), *Impure Acts: The Practical Politics of Cultural Studies* (Routledge).

Charles "Paco" Hernandez is completing his master's degree in education at Boricua College. He is the building personnel coordinator at the Horizon Juvenile Center for the New York City Department of Juvenile Justice and recently re-enlisted with the New York Army National Guard, where he is a specialist pursuing a position as chief warrant officer. The featured subject of the 1991 documentary, *Drugs, Guns, Kids: America's Wake Up Call,* Charles is currently working on a follow-up film, *America's Wake Up Call, Ten Years Later.*

Jessie Klein is a Ph.D. candidate in sociology at the CUNY Graduate Center. She is also a guidance supervisor at a NYC public high school, Humanities Preparatory Academy. Her dissertation on masculinity and school violence is titled *Being a Boy in America Shouldn't Have to Mean Becoming a Killer*. She lives in New York City and is training for a triathlon.

Zeus Leonardo earned his doctorate at UCLA's Graduate School of Education and Information Studies. He has published several articles and book chapters on critical educational theory. Leonardo is co-editor (with Tejeda and Martinez) of *Charting New Terrains in Chicano[a]/Latina[o] Education* (Hampton Press, in press). His work can best be described as the intersection between ideology, discourse, and school reform. Formerly an assistant professor at the University of St. Thomas, Minnesota, Dr. Leonardo is an assistant professor of education at California State University, Long Beach.

Donaldo Macedo is distinguished professor of liberal arts and education and director of graduate studies in applied linguistics at the University of Massachusetts, Boston. He is a leading authority on language and critical pedagogy and has published extensively in the areas of critical literacy, Creole studies, and linguistics. He is a long-time collaborator of Paulo Freire and has co-authored several books with him including *Literacy: Reading the Word and the World* and *Ideology Matters*, which has just been completed. Donaldo Macedo is also the author of *Literacies of Power: What Americans Are Not Allowed to Know*.

Peter McLaren is a professor in the division of urban schooling at the Graduate School of Education and Information Studies, University of California, Los Angeles. He is the author and editor of more than thirty books and numerous articles on critical pedagogy, the sociology of education, critical ethnography, and Marxist social theory. His most recent books include *Revolutionary Multiculturalism* and *Ché Guevara, Paulo Freire, and the Pedagogy of Revolution*. His works have been translated into twelve languages.

Jennifer Obidah is an assistant professor in the division of educational studies at Emory University. Her research focuses on the social and cultural context of urban schooling, particularly on issues related to violence in schools, multicultural education, racial and cultural differences between teachers and students, teachers as critical pedagogues, and teacher preparation. She is co-author, with Karen Teel, of *Crossing Racial and Cultural Boundaries as Teacher Researchers* (Teachers College Press, 2000). A graduate of the University of California, Berkeley, she was the recipient of a 1995 National Institute of Mental Health (NIMH) postdoctoral fellowship at UCLA.

Stephanie Urso Spina is in the Ph.D. program in psychology at The Graduate Center of The City University of New York. She holds advanced degrees in education from Adelphi and in human development and psychology from Harvard. Stephanie is a certified teacher in elementary, art, and social studies education with practical experience teaching at all levels from pre-kindergarten through graduate school. An interdisciplinary scholar, she is an internationally published author, a professional artist, and a consultant on issues related to education and the arts. Her current research focuses on how inner-city students use the arts to mediate the violence in their lives.